Telling Sexual Stories

The world has become cluttered with sexual stories. From child abuse scandals to lesbians and gays coming out; from Anita Hill and Clarence Thomas to the troubles of Michael Jackson; from sexual surveys to therapy groups – sexual talk has become more and more evident.

This book explores the rites of a sexual story telling culture. Taking three major examples – rape stories, coming out stories, recovery stories – it examines the nature of these newly emerging narratives and the socio-historical conditions which have given rise to them. It looks at the rise of the women's movement, the lesbian and gay movement and the 'recovery' movement as harbingers of significant social change that encourage the telling of new stories. In a powerful concluding section, the book turns to the wider concern of how story telling may be changing in a postmodern culture and how central it may be in the creation of a participatory democratic political culture.

Ken Plummer illustrates how 'the narrative turn' of cultural studies may be taken up within sociology and suggests that a sociology of stories asks different questions about stories from those posed within cultural studies. The fascination with texts – with narrative structure, genre and metaphor – is now supplemented with questions around the social and political role that stories play, with the social processes through which they are constructed and consumed, with the political changes that stories may encourage. *Telling Sexual Stories* is a major contribution to our understanding of sexuality and the cultures of intimacy.

Ken Plummer is Reader in Sociology and Head of the Sociology Department at Essex University.

Telling Sexual Stories

Power, Change and Social Worlds

Ken Plummer

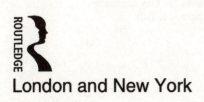

London and New York

First published 1995
by Routledge
11 New Fetter Lane, London EC4P 4EE

Simultaneously published in the USA and Canada
by Routledge
29 West 35th Street, New York, NY 10001

Typeset in Times by
NWL Editorial Services, Langport, Somerset
Printed in Great Britain by
Mackays of Chatham PLC, Chatham, Kent

British Library Cataloguing in Publication Data
A catalogue record for this book is available from the British Library

ISBN 0–415–10295–2 (hbk)
ISBN 0–415–10296–0 (pbk)

Library of Congress Cataloging in Publication Data
Plummer, Kenneth.
    Telling sexual stories: power, change, and social worlds / Ken Plummer.
        p. cm.
    Includes bibliographical references and index.
    ISBN 0–415–10295–2: $65.00. – ISBN 0–415–10296–0 (pbk.): $15.95
    1. Sex. 2. Intimacy (Psychology) 3. Sexuality in popular culture.
  4. Storytelling. 5. Coming out (Sexual orientation) 6. Gay liberation
  movement. 7. Sexual abuse victims. 8. Feminism. I. Title.
  HQ23.P58   1995   94–12150
                                                          CIP

For Everard Longland

Contents

Preface

This book has had a long gestation, and has finally become something quite different from what was originally intended. Indeed, the book has been drafted in at least three different forms with varying problems over a number of years. It started as long ago as 1978 as an empirical study of sexual diversity sponsored by the then Social Science Research Council in which the life histories of 'paedophiles', 'transvestites' and 'sadomasochists' were to be analysed sociologically. Some remnants of that study remain, but the main contribution of that research to this book was to suggest the problem of how and why people are willing to provide such interview material of their sexual life stories (or indeed why I should want to know, and a reader want to read them). A second version was informed much more by feminist debates during the 1980s and was concerned with the rise of new social movements around sexuality.

Neither of these books saw the light of day, but they clearly led me to this one. The first full draft of this particular version emerged in roughly four months of 'free space' given to me by a combination of leave from my home university of Essex, England and hospitality from the Sociology Department at the University of California at Santa Barbara. The beach, the ocean, the mountains, the sun, the restaurants and the wine suddenly seemed to make the content of this book become much clearer to me, though whether this is so for others remains to be seen. It also made it much more 'American'.

This book, however, has always lived in two cultures – England and North America. Problems and 'solutions' found in one have often been transferred to the other. The stories I analyse have counterparts in each culture and indeed are often the same. In an increasingly global world where media and social movements play prominent roles, it becomes more possible to write of several cultures as one. Yet there are also very important differences.

On balance, I suspect that the culture of story telling is more in evidence in the USA – it is the strong case for my arguments. In part, this is due to it being a more 'therapeutic culture': as I shall explain, the USA is characterised by an intense individualism which has long been linked to self-reliance and self-actualisation. Many sexual stories now link directly to this. Further, I experience the USA as a much more 'media' society. The stories in the US seem more pervasive, certainly in such media as TV chat shows or 'recovery paperbacks'. *Donahue*, for instance, is relayed on over 200 networks twice daily in the USA – whereas in the UK it gets a very late slot at 2.00 a.m. once a week!

The 'public domain', however, may be richer and more developed in the UK. If the media is regarded as the new 'public forum' where ideas may be articulated and debated, then British television – at least until some of the recent 'privatising' changes – has been much more aware of this role, and has generally served the country well through its documentaries, its discussion programmes, its 'alternative television' (initially on BBC2, latterly on Channel 4). Its only real rivals in the USA are public television and CNN – and a myriad of small networks: but there is no real 'national' audience for good public debate. The Presidential Forums on TV generally reveal the very low standard of public debate – with Clinton playing his saxophone! This is not America-bashing: the standard of debate in other spheres such as American universities is every bit as high in the USA as the UK, if not generally higher.

Social movements also differ between the two countries. In general, the UK has taken class to be the central organising social movement whereas the USA has not – a much wider array of special interest groups are at work and have to be taken more seriously by politicians. Two of the most prominent examples discussed in this book are the gay and the women's movements. In the UK, both had strong connections in the socialist/class-based movement; this was much less striking in the USA. And their relatively greater successes in the USA seems to me to be geared to their focus on single issues. It is hard to make comparisons between the gay movement in the USA and the UK. A professional organisational talent exists which is much rarer in the UK. And in the gay communities there is little comparison: in the UK there are no gay choirs, no gay Olympics, no gay bands and not really many magazines or publishing houses. The communities of support simply seem so much stronger in the USA. In the UK, there is London and Manchester and a few other spots. But it is hard to see anything like the scale of lesbian and gay culture in the USA.

All of this is to highlight differences that are concealed in much of the book. Generally, I think the USA is the strong case for my arguments; but they are certainly also applicable to the UK – maybe with less force.

A preface is perhaps the place to voice some obvious misgivings about this book and indeed the whole enterprise of adding yet further to the deluge of writing about sex that now awaits anyone who cares to look. Anyone who writes about sex these days stands at the intersection of a vast literature speaking about sex from every conceivable persuasion. It is indeed one argument of this book that we have become the talking, babbling sex. It is now quite impossible to read even a scratching of the writing on sex: huge computer-based bibliographies on every aspect of sex from every discipline and angle can be found or created: but nobody can actually read all the stuff! Thus any book ignores vast fields of writing and whole disciplines. Those traditions one elects to ignore or exclude – and in this book there are many – will almost certainly ignore or exclude this book in return, so that little stocks of books grow up speaking to little stocks of other books with vast libraries lying outside. For someone trained as a sociologist, I have certainly had to jump frequently into fields of inquiry that I feel much less competent within – most notably literary and political theory; and others which these days simply cannot be avoided by sociologists – feminism and cultural studies being the obvious areas. But the vast world of 'sexology' in all its myriad forms is almost wholly ignored, as is the incredibly obscure world of what I call the 'philosophers of discourse', whose arguments grow wilder and wilder by the day.

My position remains that of a pragmatic symbolic interactionist ethnographer! This position went out of fashion for much of the 1970s and 1980s, but some of its arguments have recently been taken seriously again. I do not spend much time detailing this position but it is the background to the whole study. It entails a reflective and reflexive hearing of voices – that goes much against the grain of conventional social science, with which I have grown increasingly weary. A huge debt is incurred by all those myriad little studies of social life which rarely get funding on a grand scale – if indeed on any scale. But cumulatively they often add up to a more sensitive and politically engaged understanding of the world than many of the multi-million surveys that standardise, and get lost.

And finally: a little book like this accumulates a great many debts, some which are less to do with this book than some of its predecessors. My first home is the Sociology Department at the University of Essex – a department remarkable for its friendliness, diversity and talent. The Fuller Bequest Fund also provided financial support. My second 'home' has been the Sociology Department at the University of California at Santa Barbara, where I have been a frequent visitor since 1985. Amongst people who have been especially supportive at various times and whom I would like to thank here are: Chris Allen, Kum Kum Bhavani, Henning Bech, Brenda Corti, Pam Dan, Peter Davies, Norman Denzin, Jean Duncombe, Annabel Faraday, Dwight Fee, Dick Gadd, John Gagnon, Mary Girling, Cathy Greenblatt, Cassandra Heiland, Mary McIntosh, Dennis Marsden, Joan Murdoch, Harvey Molotch, the late Linda Molotch, Martha McCaughy, Wayne Mellinger, Peter Nardi, Janet Parkin, Lynn Randolph, Chris Rojek, Beth Schneider, Bill Simon, Diane Streeting, Andrea Tyree, Jeffrey Weeks, Theo Sandfort, Judith Schuyf, Nigel South, Arlene Stein and Glenn Wharton. I also owe a great deal to many students on my Santa Barbara summer school course Soc 176 who always had a lot to say.

During the spring of 1992, as the first draft neared completion, I presented a summary version of the book at Rice University, the University of Houston, and the University of California at Los Angeles, San Francisco and Santa Barbara, as well as at a meeting of symbolic interactionists at the Stone Symposium in Las Vegas. I always received stimulating and encouraging comments from students and faculty and was very grateful for these opportunities for feedback. Helpful comments on the entire first draft came from Stan Cohen, who reminded me that not all stories are gay, and Peter Nardi, who suggested most are!

Finally, this book is dependent upon a legion of people who have told their story. The book is indeed centrally about this: my own story, the stories of those kind enough to be interviewed but whose voices are not heavily drawn upon here, those interviewed by others and discussed by me, and those who have simply told their own story. To them all, I am very grateful.

Ken Plummer
Wivenhoe and Santa Barbara

Part I

Entering the story zone

If we would have new knowledge, we must get a whole world of new questions.
(Suzanne Langer)

Stories are necessary to weave a web of meaning within which we can live. We all live in story worlds.

(Miller Mair)

We tell ourselves stories in order to live.

(Joan Didion)

Chapter 1

Prologue
The culture of sexual story telling

Who could have supposed that this childish punishment, received at the age of eight at the hands of a woman of thirty, would determine my tastes and desires, my passions, my very self for the rest of my life, and that in a sense diametrically opposed to the one in which they should normally have developed? . . . I have spent my days in silent longing in the presence of those I most loved. I never dared to reveal my strange tastes, but at least I got some pleasure from situations that pandered to the thought of it. To fall on my knees before a masterful mistress, to obey her commands, to have to beg for her forgiveness, have been for me the most delicate of pleasures; and the more my vivid imagination heated my blood the more like a spellbound lover I looked . . .

Now I have made the first and most painful step in the dark and miry maze of my confessions. It is the ridiculous and the shameful, not one's criminal actions, that it is hardest to confess. But henceforth I am certain of myself; after what I have just had the courage to say, nothing else will defeat me.

(Jean-Jacques Rousseau, *Confessions*, 1782)

Four years after Rousseau's death, the world was to learn his 'sexual story' through a celebrated posthumous autobiography. For many, it is the first 'modern' story of its kind. It tells of the 'loving' childhood punishments he had received from one Mlle Lambercier; of the beatings becoming a secret preoccupation of his adulthood; of a silence about his passion and desire which he almost took to his grave. But not quite. For his *Confessions* took the first painful step of *telling*, not just the story of his life but the story of his 'sadomasochistic' desire. It was a bold personal narrative of sex that broke a silence.[1]

One hundred years later, at the end of the 'Victorian' era, all manner of sexual desires were being made to speak. From the latinate prose of the 'anxiety makers' who made people tell of their damned desires and the emerging clinical case studies of Krafft-Ebing 'freaks' and Freudian 'neurotics', through the sensational narratives of 'sex crimes' printed in the penny press and early tabloids, and on to the confessional tales of a Walter's Secret Life, personal sexual stories were given a voice.[2]

Today, yet a hundred years further on, the modern western world has become cluttered with sexual stories. We have moved from the limited, oral and face to face tales told throughout much of history in epic poems, songs, and narratives; through the development of a public print inscribing sexual stories in limited texts, first for the few and then for the 'masses'; and on to a contemporary late modern world where it seems that 'sexual stories' know no boundaries. Indeed, every invention – mass print, the camera, the film, the video, the record, the telephone, the computer, the 'virtual reality' machine – has helped, bit by bit, to provide a veritable *erotopian* landscape to millions of lives. The media has become sexualised.

Sex, then, has become the Big Story. From Donahue and Oprah getting folk to tell of their child sexual abuse to Dr Ruth's televised advice programmes listening to the stories of 'rape survivors'; from the letters of men and women to a Nancy Friday telling of their changing sexual fantasies to the collected writings of lesbians and gay men 'coming out'; from the research studies of Shere Hite, encouraging the telling of 'sex lives', to the therapeutic declarations of 'sex addicts'; from the inner musings of Freudian patients to the masturbatory raunch of the Dial-A-Sex lines; from Clarence Thomas and Anita Hill telling the whole of America about sexual harassment to women speaking out at a 'Reclaim the Night' rally; from the paperbacking of sexual confessions to the hyper-selling of Madonna's *Sex*, a grand message keeps being shouted: *tell about your sex.*

Tell about your sexual behaviour, your sexual identity, your dreams, your desires, your pains and your fantasies. Tell about your desire for a silk hanky, your desire for a person of the same sex, your desire for young children, your desire to masturbate, your desire to cross dress, your desire to be beaten, your desire to have too much sex, your desire to have no sex at all, and even your desire to stop the desires of others. Tell about your sexual dsyfunction, your sexual diseases, your orgasm problems, your abortions, your sexual addictions. Let us know what you get up to in bed – or what you don't get up to! Tell about your partner who loves too little or too much, who is gay or transexual, who is older or younger.

Different moments have highlighted different stories: puberty stories, marriage-bed stories, perversion stories, coming out stories, abuse survivor stories, women's fantasy stories, men's tribal fairy stories, stories of living – and dying – with Aids. And more. Once outside the world of formal story telling, we are all being enjoined to do it daily to each other. Somehow the truth of our lives lies in better communication: in telling all. There should be no 'sexual secrets'. Tell your partner exactly what you desire. Tell your children every nook and cranny of the erotic world. Come out to your parents if you are gay, tell your teacher if you've been sexually abused, tell your therapist if your husband is a sex addict. Stand in the public square and shout through a microphone the story of your rape, or your abortion or your gayness. Go on television to announce your impotency, to demonstrate your sadomasochism, to reveal the innermost secrets of your heart, to get a 'Blind Date' or find a 'Hunk'. Tell, tell, tell. An intimate experience, once hardly noticed, now has to be slotted into the ceaseless narrating of life. If once, and not so long ago, our sexualities were shrouded in silence, for some they have now crescendoed into a cacophonous din. We have become the sexual story tellers in a sexual story telling society.

Most of these stories have been taken as signs of a truth: they have been presented to us as 'fact' and presumed to tell us something about our sexual natures. I suppose I started both this book and my research with this view in mind. We could and can find out 'the truth about sex' and the flood of sexual story writing will enable us to progress in our understanding of our myriad sexual problems. And of course in part this is the case. Thus, research will tell us what we do through orgasmic bookkeeping; tell us who we are through accounts of our identity struggles; tease us back through our sexual histories to a sense of our sexual nature. All the medical tales, the historical narratives, the psychodynamic case studies, the agony columns, the oral histories, and twelve-step recovery stories will, indeed, reveal things. But it is much more than this. They do not in fact take us towards the Sexual Truth: towards a full, absolute, real grasping of our essential, inner sexual natures. If I once thought, naively, that all these sexual stories may be seen as signs of the truth, this has long since ceased being my view and is not the argument of this book. For instead of taking all these dazzling stories mentioned above as givens – as providing rays of real truth on sexual lives – *sexual stories can be seen as issues to be investigated in their own right*. They become topics to investigate, not merely resources to draw upon.

That we live in a world of sexual stories should come as no surprise. The ceaseless nature of story telling in all its forms in all societies has come to be increasingly recognised. We are, it seems, *homo narrans*: humankind the narrators and story tellers.[3] Society itself may be seen as a textured but seamless web of stories emerging everywhere through interaction: holding people together, pulling people apart, making societies work. Recently, from all kinds of different theoretical perspectives in the human studies – the folklorist, the oral historian, the semiotician, the anthropologist, the political scientist, the psychoanalyst – there has been a convergence on the power of the metaphor of the story.[4] It has become recognised as one of the central roots we have into the continuing quest for understanding human meaning. Indeed, culture itself has been defined as 'an ensemble of stories we tell about ourselves'.[5] Barbara Hardy has expressed this so well that she is worth quoting at length:

> We cannot take a step in life or literature without using an image. It is hard to take more than a step without narrating. Before we sleep each night we tell over to ourselves what we may also have told to others, the story of the past day. We mingle truths and falsehoods, not always quite knowing where one blends into the other. As we sleep we dream dreams from which we wake to remember, half-remember and almost remember, in forms that may be dislocated, dilapidated or deviant but are recognizably narrative. We begin the day by narrating to ourselves and probably to others our expectations, plans, desires, fantasies and intentions. The action in which the day is passed coexists with a reverie composed of the narrative revision and rehearsals of past and future, and

in this narrative too it is usually hard to make the distinction between realism and fantasy which we make confidently in our judgements of literary narratives. We meet our colleagues, family, friends, intimates, acquaintances, strangers, and exchange stories, overtly and covertly. We may try to tell all, in true confession, or tell half-truths or lies, or refuse to do more than tell the story of the weather, the car, or the food. We may exchange speaking silences or marvelous jokes. And all the time the environment beckons and assaults with its narratives. Walls, papers, mass-media, vehicles, entertainments, libraries, talks, slogans, politicians, prophets and Job's comforters persuade, encourage, depress, solicit, comfort and commiserate in narrative forms. Even when we try to escape narrative, as when we listen to music or do mathematics, we tend to lapse. Even logicians tell stories. Humankind cannot bear very much abstraction or discursive reasoning. The stories of our days and the stories in our days are joined in that autobiography we are all engaged in making and remaking, as long as we live, which we never complete, though we all know how it is going to end.[6]

Sexual stories are part of this and are also probably as old as human time. But in this late modern world – at century's end, at the *fin-de-siècle*, at the turn of the millennium[7] – they seem to have gained an unusual power and prominence. It is curious, perhaps, that they should have become so celebrated. When I grew up as a child in the late 1940s and 1950s such stories resonated a deafening silence.[8] But now the time has certainly come for personal sexual stories to be told – at least for some groups. In this book I ponder what this is all about: what the stories are, why people are telling them, where they are heading. *I focus on the personal sexual narratives in which folk recount some aspect of their most 'intimate' life, seeing how they come to be told, the role they play in contemporary lives, and where they be may be heading at century's end. The book moves from a general analysis of the 'sociology of stories' to an examination of some specific 'tales of sexual suffering and surviving' such as those of 'rape victims', lesbians and gays 'coming out' and 'recoverers'; and on to an analysis of the political role of such stories and their potential future in creating a new form of intimate citizenship – one in which 'intimate relations' become a key focus.* Although the focus throughout is on the specific instance of personal sexual story telling at century's end, the ultimate aim of this study is broader: *to help build a more general, formal sociology of stories.*

SIGHTING SOME SEXUAL STORIES: REPORTS FROM THE FIELD

What is a 'sexual story' and just what kinds of 'sexual stories' will this book specifically examine? They are simply the narratives of the intimate life, focused especially around the erotic, the gendered and the relational. They are part of the wider discourses and ideologies abroad in society, and they have much in common with all manner of other stories with differing foci – detective stories, travel stories, life stories, near-death stories. They come in many forms. There are scientific sex stories which narrate sex in a scientific rhetoric, historical sex stories which place sex in the historical narrative, fictional sex stories which provide imagined worlds. While many kinds of stories will be mentioned in this book, *personal experience narratives around the intimate* will be my prime concern. To set the scene this introduction will provide glimpses of these stories and the kinds of questions I plan to address.

THE STORY OF AN EVERYDAY LIFE

First, it will help to begin with one fleeting autobiographical tale, from a multitude. And we could all tell our own.

> It is the mid 1960s and I am a young man, going through many of the little pains of adolescence. Only, like many others although I didn't know it then, my pains went a little further. One evening I recall the pains becoming too much: I am sitting with my parents watching television, I hurl a book at them, burst into tears saying 'that's about me', and leave the room. The book was by the English criminologist Donald West, and was called 'Homosexuality'. It must have been influential for several generations of young would-be-gays in the UK at that time. Gay Liberation was still five or so years away, and this 'scientific' book was at least not outrightly hostile and in places indeed was decidedly liberal.
>
> My loving parents were confused and upset: like most parents of that time, it was not only a 'bad thing' but also beyond their comprehension. My father went to the family doctor, who arranged for me to see a psychiatrist. The psychiatrist asked me a few perfunctory questions. I told her bits of my story and she arranged for me to have a brain scan; luck had it that my brain waves were normal! She asked me if I could accept being gay, and I said that I could. In which case she said, it was no problem. I think I was lucky . . .

This truncated little tale is one bit of my 'coming out story'. I could, as many others have,[9] make it much longer, and indeed such 'coming out stories' will become a central focus of the second part of this book. There are many other kinds of personal tales that people tell of their sexual lives: of marital breakdown through lack of sex – or too much sex; of sexual disinterest, dysfunction or delight. But 'the coming out tale' will suffice for here and now. Many questions arise from the brief vignette above. What, for instance, brought me to the story of my own gayness, and was it a 'true story'? What made me tell my parents – I recall it being a huge emotional struggle, so what made it matter? Why did I tell them this way – by literally throwing a 'text' at them, and what does this say about the way I view the world? What would have happened if my psychiatrist had received my story differently, even hostilely? And what would have happened if I had *not* told my story – to myself, to my parents or to my psychiatrist: as so many people haven't both before and since? What role did this personal experience narrative of my intimate life perform both in my life and the wider social world?

THE MEDIA IS THE MESSAGE

To move quickly from the very private personal story to the much more public personal tale, the late modern world has become increasingly saturated by the mass media – in ways that simply weren't possible for earlier generations. As I shall argue later, it may well be that the changing media is the key to the growth of sexual story telling. For the moment, consider a few more vignettes, this time of media stories (and add your own):

I am in the USA, and switch on my television at 9.00 a.m. and *Donahue*, the talk show, is showing.[10] The topic for the next hour is Teen Sex and Teen Pregnancy. The amiable but aggressive Donahue introduces us to an audience of mainly 12, 13, 14-year-olds from various New York schools, an expert from California and her 15-year-old daughter who – together it turns out – have written several books on sex for teenagers. Provocatively, Donahue announces that 40 per cent of teenage girls will become pregnant before they are 20 and that 25 per cent of New York teens are sexually active before the age of 15 (though where these figures come from he does not say). For the next hour, interspersed by a host of domestic advertisements for cookies, cleaning fluids and dentists, the children clamor to have their stories of sex heard, while a few adults and a few phone callers get squeezed in too. Later that day, at 2.00 p.m., I switch my set on to *Jenny Jones*, a much more downscale chat show. She has three middle-aged women sitting in front of her audience, and one by one they each describe how they have reached multiple orgasms; the whole audience – largely composed of women – are then invited to give their comments and match their experiences. A male 'expert' is finally brought on for his views on the Female Orgasm. This spectacle of sexual story telling flows through the morning and afternoon of every weekday in North America, with one talk-show host after another clamouring to bring yet another new sexual story to the nation's attention. On one day alone I discovered stories being told about 'marrying transexuals', 'spurned men', 'male infertility and relationships', 'affairs and marriage', 'religious leaders and sex', 'transvestite couples', 'Transexual Tula', 'Washington sex scandals' and 'selfish husbands'.[11] The same is not quite as true of the UK. *Donahue*, for example is relegated to one night in the week and screened in the middle of the night. *Oprah* has a more regular slot around tea time – but the sexual stories are largely banished from it and relegated to a late night season of *Adult Oprah*. But the UK has its own brand of media stories: series of oh so serious documentaries in which sadomasochists, the abused, the impotent are interviewed (always after 9.00 at night). And a stream of regular programmes invite viewers to speak of their sex: *Talking Sex, Sex Now, The Good Sex Guide*.[12]

In 1988, Nancy Ziegenmeyer, an Iowa wife and mother of three, was raped in a deserted parking lot at 7.00 a.m. A year or so later the rapist was brought to trial, found guilty and sentenced to life imprisonment. Ziegenmeyer told her story to the *Des Moines Register* in a series of articles that went on to win the Pulitzer Prize in 1991. They were internationally reported. She became a prominent guest on chat shows like *Donahue* and *Oprah*. Subsequently, her story became a television docudrama (with the actress Patricia Wettig playing the Ziegenmeyer role) and a book (co-written by Larkin Warren): both were called *Taking Back My Life*.[13] After this she appeared on a number of chat shows again. Ziegenmeyer says that the book and film are not just about rape, but 'about a young woman finding her voice and accomplishing something from finding that voice'.[14]

I go to my local bookshop in California, where I have been regularly browsing and shopping for a decade. It is not an unusual day. I move from a section on men's studies to a section on women's studies to a section on gay and lesbian studies. I browse through a section on Sexuality bristling with books on every aspect of sex. I go to a therapy and recovery section where problems of sexual addiction, sexual dsyfunction and orgasm are discussed in a myriad of personal case studies. Stories of every kind of sex now seem to flood the book market. The UK is similar – maybe not so many therapy stories, but a large number of sexual stories nevertheless.[15]

Here then are situations where the most personal and private narratives have become the most public property. The domains of public and private have crumbled. Whilst the contents of these few media samples is surely of interest, so too is the form. For the mass media has become a key story teller of our personal sexual lives in ways that even thirty years ago would have been inconceivable. Imagine the apocryphal sociological martian visiting Planet Earth for the first time and wanting to understand its character. It gathers up a set of videotapes of TV programmes, books and other media products and takes these home to analyse social life. What, one wonders, would this martian make of such 'sightings' as the ones described in the vignettes above? What would be made of the parade of people talking about the most intimate features of their lives on the television and the thousands of books written on every aspect of sex? The martian would probably muse that sex for humans lies more in the talking than the doing, that we are indeed the 'speaking sex',[16] and ponder what brought these curious folk to say all this. What was the social role of all this, and how was it being produced? Like the martian, these are my concerns.[17]

TALES FROM THE RESEARCH FIELD

Over a decade ago I had the good fortune to receive a small grant to gather life histories of a number of people who perceived themselves as sexually different.[18] Employing a research worker and a transcriber of tapes, we set forth enthusi- astically interviewing and studying men and women who faced an array of sexually different experiences. We found ourselves in the midst of so-called (usually self-identified) 'paedophiles', 'sadomasochists', 'women of strong desires', 'transvestites', 'transexuals', the 'sexually dysfunctional', 'prostitutes' and so on. We were indeed part of that vast research project that has grown since the famous studies by Alfred Kinsey into the 'Sexual behaviour of the human male and female' during the 1940s in the USA. 'Sex Research' in this age of Aids is now taken for granted.

At first our study seemed to go well. The aim was to gather life histories and to examine experiences previously always considered individual, medical and clinical, and to examine their social aspects. But step by step the whole project became more and more troublesome in every way: practically, personally and politically. In the end, the data never saw the light of day; they were filed and left. But they have remained a haunting presence, and at several points in this book they will be drawn upon. They were the starting point of this book, however, in so far as they helped focus on the problematic nature of people's own stories about sex. Just what was this sex research business all about – and, indeed, all the other kinds of story telling about sex?

To give you an idea of what the research was all about, here again are a few of the briefest vignettes. These stories have never been published, except in the slightest of brief extracts. But their very voices became more and more worrying to me – raising too the problematic nature of all such similar research, of which now there is a great deal. What do the following mean?

I travel to the North of England where I meet a young man in his early twenties in a hotel lobby. We go to my hotel room, and he tells me in enormous detail of his desire to be trodden upon by women in high heels. As this happens, he fantasises a dagger being plunged into his stomach. It is a long story, which takes me through his childhood memories of this and the 'driven' nature of his 'single' adult life. I record the conversation, and respond very sympathetically to him: he seems a nice enough man. Back at my university, the tape is transcribed and makes fascinating reading. The secretary names him Jack (a pseudonym: but interestingly her husband is called Jack!). This transcript is sent to Jack, who comments profusely on it. A short correspondence is set up, and I send him a copy of a key book in this field: *The Sex Life of the Foot and Shoe*. For the past ten years, the transcript and its commentary sits in my filing cabinet. I have lost contact with him.

Mr Quick, a Belgian physician in his late sixties, comes to see me in my office and we spend the day together in discussion and interview. He tells me his tale: a tale of surgical sadomasochism. He shows me illustrated books he has produced on this – some with diagrams and some with photos. He is a very educated man, and has developed a quite complex theory of the masochistic experience which he tells me in detail. His accent is thick, and so the tape is hard to transcribe and a lot of the material gets lost. But I still have his 'theory' and some of the books. We got on quite well for the day, but he wanted a lot more contact. I found him a little disturbing, and decided not to go to Belgium to follow his story further.

I meet 64-year-old Ed at my university where he also works. He has heard of my research and thinks that he might be of interest to me. We meet, and he tells me of his life long interest in boys. It is a rich and interesting story, and I ask him if I can do a 'life history' on him. He seems pleased and even flattered; and for the next two years he becomes a part of my life, my friendship network, and my work. Transcripts pile up as he goes over his life with me. He tells others of his involvement, though he swears me to confidentiality. An interesting tale emerges in lots and lots of different interviews. But how should all this data be synthesised into a coherent tale? And in any event, did the story not have a rehearsed artificial ring to it which somehow did not quite seem to match the life as it was lived in my presence?

I visit James in London and spend the day with him in his flat. After chatting generally over a light lunch, we get down to serious talk. He is a producer of straitjackets for a market of the sexually interested. He describes his own interest in this field of escapology, citing his hero Houdini. There is, it appears, quite an extensive market for straitjackets, and he describes in some detail the different styles and meanings associated with them. It is an exercise in phenomenology: straitjackets clearly vary in their meaning to a whole array of different people, I discover. After much discussion, he takes me to his workshop where he suggests I try on a straitjacket. With much temerity, I do.

I visit Mr and Mrs Brown in their middle-class suburban home, and sit in their living room drinking cups of tea with them and their 19-year-old daughter. I conduct my interview with Mr Brown, and daughter and wife leave the room for a while. Afterwards, they invite me to stay for supper. The whole event is shrouded in middle-class conventions and pleasantries. But there is really only one major topic of conversation: bondage. For Mr Brown runs a nationwide organisation for sadomasochists. He holds meetings, runs a magazine, writes articles and even conducts social surveys on sadomasochism. He is a masochist himself; his wife plays the role of a dominatrix; his daughter thinks it's all fun.

These little vignettes could be multiplied many times: each interview had its own character, from being pursued sexually and running out of the house; to interviewing a number of men who liked to be encased in rubber, dress up in uniforms, urinate in their clothing, wear women's underwear, hold parties for 'heavy leather' in their garages and their cellars; to meeting one who traveled the world to be with eunuchs; to pleasant encounters with many people talking of their endless frustrations. Many a tale was told. But this is no longer my point. What they all said is important; but as important now – over a decade later – is to question the nature of this whole enterprise, and similar ones. Just what are these stories told to curious sex researchers all about?

Taking Jack above as one example, what are the issues? What brought me to seek out a man who wanted to talk about his 'unusual' sexual life? Why should I, or anyone else, want to coax anyone to tell about their sexual lives in the name of

Holy Social Science? What brought him to the hotel room to tell me all about it? How could he produce such stories, and how did my 'tolerant' responses to him actively encourage him to tell a certain sort of story – he could sense very early on that I was not going to be shocked or censorious in any way. But didn't that make him say certain things rather than others? And to leave endless undetected absences? How much of his story was a performance of a dress rehearsal he had practised many times in solitude before? What, then, was the relationship of my transcribed interview to his actual life? And how was I to write this? In his voice, or in my voice, or in his voice through my voice, or even in my voice through his voice? And then, once read by others – including me and him – what multiple interpretations would it be open to? Would there perhaps be a correct reading which would finally get us all to the truth of such foot fetishists? Or would it be used as an occasion for condemnation, or curiosity, or simple titillation or as a guide for someone else to locate their sexual nature? What would it do to Jack once published? And indeed, what has it done to him since it has *not* been published, but sits unread in a filing cabinet? And so it goes on. The questions proliferate. I became more and more aware of these questions at the time of doing the research, and they slowly incapacitated me. Just what *are* these sexual stories gathered for research?

But I was not alone in my plight. The above can be seen very easily and correctly as me standing right on the edge of what has been called the 'fourth wave of ethnography'.[19] When anthropologists first went into the field to study their 'tribes' they brought back descriptions that were relatively unselfconscious: these were simple stories of what the natives were like. Although there remains a legion of unreflective, uncritical social scientists, increasingly, throughout the twentieth century, such unreflective knowledges have become harder and harder to justify: research is saturated with problems of ethics, ethnocentrism, interpretation, politics. Research accounts cannot simply be understood as direct copies of an assumed reality. So, once again, the sexual stories gathered from research are not mere resources, but become topics of investigation in their own right. They can no longer be taken as transparent and unproblematic in their search for truth. Instead, the social scientist is part of the very process being observed, analysed and ultimately written about: I am part of this process and it is deeply social. It can be seen as one more manifestation of the increasing self-awareness some social scientists are facing. So: just what was I – indeed any social science researcher at all – doing? The research stories of hundreds of sexological studies conducted over the past few decades are not mere reflections of our sexual lives, but play an active role in their construction.

TELLING STORIES OUT OF SCHOOL

I have been teaching courses 'about sexuality' in both North America and England for over fifteen years. Although I often try to stop it being so, most of this teaching proceeds pretty uneventfully. Out of thousands of students, there are clearly lots and lots of sexual stories that I have told and been told: sometimes in an easy-going class, sometimes in the haze of a student bar, sometimes in the coldness of my office, sometimes from a desperate phone call. Again, a few vignettes – chosen at random from a scanning memory – may help set the scene to some stories that will appear later in the book. What do the following mean?

Beth, a Californian student, stands by the lecture theatre door at the end of my Soc 176 class (Sexism and Sexual Liberation) in the mid 1980s. She wants to talk with me; and tells me she can no longer continue with the class as it is too painful. She is in therapy, has been persistently sexually abused by father and boyfriends, and sees herself as a victim. We meet in private over a number of occasions and talk about it. She writes a journal exploring her feelings on all this.

A male student, Steve, comes to the class and is an eager participant. He discusses the course materials and gets good grades. Lesbian and gay topics are a focus one week, but at no point in the discussions does he indicate that he is gay to me or the other students. When the course is over, I see him at a gay disco and he tells me he's gay but he could not, dare not, would not, say it in class. It was just too difficult.

Students write essays and journals for various courses and during the process they tell me all sorts of things: they have been raped and abused; they have had abortions; they have been single mothers from an early age; their brothers, sisters, mothers and fathers are gay. Even on the day I am writing this, two students visit me in my office hours. One, an Hispanic woman, tells me her father is gay, her mother is very upset about it and she doesn't know what to do. Another, an Anglo man, tells me he doesn't feel or want to be like other men: he prefers the company of women to men. But he doesn't want sex at all. He feels confused.

Many of the above are pleas for help. The story is not easily said – indeed it appears with a struggle, often tearfully, and it is told to me because in some way I am sensed to be a teacher and maybe an 'expert'.[20] Again, questions galore appear: why do people tell these sexual stories – or not tell them? Indeed, why do they turn what was not so long ago a private, secret world into a public one? How do they choose their language to articulate their concerns – where do the words come from? What sort of situations enable people to find a voice, and what happens to people once they give voice to their sexual story? What gets left out of the story? How do I 'hear' the story, and what do I do when I hear it? Again, it is not simply *what* people say that is my concern, *but the complex social processes involved in the tellings*.

Here, to conclude these sightings, is one voice speaking to me in a journal for a course. It is a painful voice generated in part through the very teaching experience. A voice leading the speaker to therapy. A voice leading the speaker to tearfulness in my office. A voice located in a wide spectrum of abuse stories, upon which she so clearly draws. In the early 1990s, having read, heard and indeed lectured on this story in many ways before, this Californian student of mine, Jane, wrote in her journal, and with permission for me to use, the following:

As a child I was sexually abused by an alcoholic father.... For years I denied what happened to me between the ages of 7–13 years. I denied it because the guilt and shame was too much; I felt responsible for what happened – I wrecked everything – I was the whore. Having read so much on incest and child abuse I know that all the guilt and responsibility should lie with my father – but for some reason it is much easier to blame myself and feel anger and hatred for myself than it is to hate him, especially since he did it when he was so drunk and felt nobody loved him. I tried to tell my mother, but our relationship has always been strained so she never believed me, and when she finally did believe me, her hatred of me multiplied because I was the other woman, he had wanted me more than her; she just couldn't see that if she had been around or listened to me more it might never have gotten so bad. But that doesn't excuse what he did in the least. Last Christmas I tried to confront him, but he's living in a world of denial and a world where everything revolves around drink – so I was the liar, it was all my fault. I'm evil and nasty and I destroy and wreck everything – just like I destroyed my parents' marriage.

I no longer can live a lie. I can't deny something that affects me daily – so many of my views about everything are warped, especially where sex and guys are concerned. Being a Roman Catholic has also added to the guilt in so many ways – but that's another story. Even a year ago nobody knew: it was my secret that I carried although I always felt everyone could tell just by looking at me what I'd done, and how disgusting I was. Friends and counselling are helping me to face myself and to confront the sexual, physical (because my father and brother also beat me) and emotional abuse. It's not easy trying to relive a past I tried so hard to forget, and knowing that it will affect me still for many years since it is a pattern of behaviour I learned and lived for twenty-one years – in some ways – abuse is all I know, is all I feel comfortable with.

Listening to some of the lectures and classes was so hard – sometimes I wanted to scream and others I felt so much I just sat there and listened as if it wasn't really me there, but my defence mechanism of pretending to be someone else always got me through until I felt calm and strong enough to deal with it, and then would come the tears, the questioning, the guilt and shame. But I needed to go through this. I consciously chose to do this course, just as I chose to do this journal, so that I could learn and try to understand. It's hard knowing so many children have been and are going through what I went through, even if I know that I'm not alone anymore. It's just so unfair, so unjust, no one should have to suffer like that and yet the really sad thing is that both my parents, like other abusers, have been through hell in their childhood too. For me, I just want to get on with my life, to break the cycle, to feel free of the guilt and shame and constant pain I carry around. I don't want to be just another victim, I'm a survivor.

Jane's story is a painful story of a painful experience, and there is much that can be learnt from it. It contains many elements heard in many stories of 'abuse survivors', and it is a voice that moves centre stage in Chapter 5. It was a story which could hardly be heard in the 1970s, but which by the late 1980s I confronted very regularly in classes, discussions, reading. My concern in this book is not with child sexual abuse *per se* (and some may think this in itself an abuse!). Rather my concern is with the tellings, the voices, the stories that have emerged around it. How are we to analyse and understand such 'intimate stories'?

ON WITH THE TALE: THE BOOK IN OUTLINE

These four little 'reports' capture the kinds of sexual stories this book will discuss, and I will return to some of these examples. But there are many other kinds of 'sexual stories' which have been told throughout history: they are the stuff of great drama, comedy and tragedy. And these days such stories invade all the media: there are sex thrillers (*Basic Instinct*, *Fatal Attraction*), sex musicals (much of MTV), sex soaps (*Dallas*, *Brookside*), sex comedies (Woody Allen), sex science fiction (*Barbarella*). Some genres of sex writing are indeed specifically geared to the erotic alone: pornography is the prime example.[21] Sex fiction of many kinds, then, is everywhere. But these many forms are not the direct concern of this book, important as they are. Rather, I plan to look at one form of everyday social experience in which people put their own sex lives into a story. A personal experience narrative is constructed around their most intimate experiences. It overlaps with, but is not quite the same as, a life story, a biography, a self story.[22] The sexual stories for discussion here are the personal narratives that are socially embedded in the daily practices and strategies of everyday life.[23] They thus differ from the purely fictional stories of much writing and film, and from the confessions of a more formal medical, legal or religious situation.[24] Such personal narratives also take many forms, and my prime focus will be on one sub-genre: stories of suffering, surviving and surpassing.[25] These are the stories told to me in my research, my teaching, my readings of the media and in my own life. This is a narrower focus, but a necessary one.

These personal narratives do not always give a prime focus to the 'sexual' itself, though they are always connected. I see, for instance, the personal narratives of Aids as providing stories of illness, politics and grief as much as tales of sex; the stories of abortion activists as providing tales that link to motherhood, reproduction, feminism and politics; and tales of rape being as much about power and violence as sex. Sexual stories cannot be sealed off hermetically from allied story telling.

Such personal narratives come in many forms. Consider one compelling personal story that grew widely in the 1980s and which has developed into a genre of its own: the Aids narrative. Here are full-length autobiographies (Paul Monette's *Borrowed Time*, Barbara Peabody's *The Screaming Room*, Ryan White's *Ryan White: My Own Story*), chat show interviews, testimonies in therapy and support groups, academic interviews (as in Lonnie Nungesser's *Epidemic of Courage*), public speak-outs (Larry Kramer's *Reports from the Holocaust*) and documentary first-person film accounts (*Common Threads: Stories from the Quilt*).[26] What does not fit are stories told firmly in the third person: the film-makers, biographers and journalists of 'the other' (although even here there are boundary problems, such as the journalist case study like Randy Shilts's *And the Band Played On*). My concern is with *the voices of people who aim to capture their own intimate life through their stories about it.*

Such stories are not simply 'languages' or 'texts' or even 'discourses'. I want to move right away from the current, almost obsessive, concern of much analysis which reduces dense, empirical *human* life to *texts*. Social reality may be appro-ached metaphorically as a text, but it is not in actuality a text. More: this is not a work of literary theory but of sociology, and as such *the sexual stories I will be discussing must be seen to be socially produced in social contexts by embodied concrete people experiencing the thoughts and feelings of everyday life.* I will stress frequently how these stories are found in a stream of power – of opening and closing choices, constraints and controls. Some of these stories are screamed aloud in intense rage; some are clouded in bitterly tearful silence; others are quietly told to a researcher with a tape recorder. If they are 'texts', then they are texts embodied by breathing passionate people in the full stream of social life. I will argue that personal sexual stories are everywhere, and they make a difference: a difference to our lives, our communities, our cultures, our politics. This book seeks to explore some of these differences.

Part I aims to sketch a sociological framework (derived from the renaissance of interest in symbolic interactionist theory)[27] for the analysis of story telling in general and sexual stories in particular. I see story telling as a stream of social actions and suggest an array of problems for analysis. Crucial to this analysis is a concern with power – with capacities to tell stories or to remain silent – and with the gendering of such stories: how the stories men and women come to tell may have different qualities.

In Part II, I turn more specifically to three key case studies: rape survival stories, lesbian and gay 'coming out' stories and 'recovery' stories. Whilst these are very different stories, they do all provide a basic narrative structure for many sexual stories that have to deal with 'suffering, surviving and surpassing'. They are 'modernist tales' with a clear structure of story telling. But the concern here is not with the narrative structure of the stories *per se* (which would be of greater interest to the literary theorist) but with the grounded social conditions of their emergence. I will examine the ways in which for such stories to be 'successful' (and I will claim they have been), there needs to be *social worlds* embodying a strong community of support waiting to receive them. The gay movement, the women's movement and the therapy movement have provided such social worlds whilst other stories – especially the more banal tales of everyday upset from impotency to unrequited love – generally lack such communities of support and hence are less developed as stories. They may be waiting in the wings for their time, their voice, their audience.

Thus, in Part III of the book my interest turns – perhaps polemically – to the ways in which stories perform political tasks, and I examine some of the stories currently emerging which may play a role in the future. If we are moving into a new world order – an order I choose to call 'late modern' rather than postmodern – then we may well expect a change in our sexual story telling, both in what we say and how we say it. New personal sexual stories may well be in the making. Looking at some of these, I suggest the importance of such stories in creating change in our intimate lives and our communities. Coining the term *intimate citizenship* to suggest a cluster of emerging concerns over the rights to choose what we do with our bodies, our feelings, our identities, our relationships, our genders, our eroticisms and our representations, I sketch a fragmented agenda of new sexual stories that are in the making and may indeed help construct a future intimate citizenship.[28]

A final caveat may be in order. Although this book is ostensibly about 'sex', it will soon become very clear that the book has a wider project. It is as much interested in helping shape a sociology of stories as it is the topic of sexuality. Taking the substantive concern of sex, the book seeks to provide many of the elements for building *a formal sociology of stories*. It aims to push away from the dominant interest in stories simply as texts awaiting analysis and instead to see stories as *social actions embedded in social worlds*. It is the task of the next chapter to make this social nature of stories clearer.

Chapter 2

An invitation to a sociology of stories

I recount the facts, just as they happened, insofar as I am able to recollect them; this is all that I can do . . . a secret life must not leave out anything; there is nothing to be ashamed of . . . one can never know too much concerning human nature.

(Walter, *My Secret Life*)

So here we are. Who am I? Why am I what I am? At the beginning of this book I told you how I feel about people trying to find reasons for me. I am what I am, and I fully embrace that. I'm just riding with the punches. I am human – much to the amazement of some people. Because people still place themselves on a pedestal and think they have the right to judge the inner feelings of another, that's why I have had some rough times. People told me I was sick because I was not like them, and then proceeded to convince me of it and cure me at the same time. To tell you the truth, I was convinced for a while. Our system is set up to make the unusual like the usual. I fight against this. I am me, and the only person who carries the thoughts and actions the way that I do. Not that there are not other transexuals – there are. But I am the only one exactly like me, and I'm damn proud of it. But why does the world rebel against the fact that some people are different than they are? Why must I be punished for the failings of society?

(The closing paragraph of the sociological life history
of a transexual edited by Robert Bogdan:
Being Different: The Autobiography of Jane Fry (1974))

'Stories' have recently moved centre stage in social thought. In anthropology, they are seen as the pathways to understanding culture. In psychology, they are the bases of identity. In history, they provide the tropes for making sense of the past. In psychoanalysis, they provide 'narrative truths' for analysis. In philosophy they are the bases for new forms of 'world-making' and the key to creating communities. Even economics has recognised its 'storied character'.[1] Everywhere, it seems, there is an interest in stories, and social scientists have now finally grasped this point. Sociologists may be the last to enter this field explicitly, although much of their work over the past century has in one way or the other implicitly been concerned both with the gathering of other people's stories (through interviews and the like) as well as telling their own stories (of modernity, of class, of the degradation of work). But a clear 'narrative moment' has now been sensed. Sociology is bound up both with obtaining stories and telling stories. At the extreme, Patricia Ticineto Clough has argued that 'all factual representations of empirical reality, even statistical representations, are narratively constructed',[2] whilst David Maines has presented an agenda for narrative research, arguing that 'nearly anything a sociologist might want to investigate can be done so from the narrative approach'.[3]

In this book I am concerned with helping develop a sociology of stories, but I do it at an angle. I take as my topic *the personal experience narratives of the intimate* – a story that haunts us everywhere today in ways it did not in the recent past. I have in mind the stories told by men and women of coming out as gay and lesbian; of women who discover they 'love too much'; of the tales told by the survivors of abortion, rape and incest; of the 'new men' who are rediscovering their newly masculine roots through mythical stories. And many others. This book is about the proliferation of personal narratives of the intimate in the late twentieth century. *But the ideas in this book could be applied to any story telling process: the focus on sexuality is merely one instance.* This chapter is hence concerned with laying out some of the contours of a sociology of stories with wider applicability than just the intimate.

Maines and others in their proposal for a 'narrative turn' in sociology have focused primarily upon narrative structures. Thus key elements of narrative have a concern with the way 'events are selected from the past'; with the 'story elements' of 'plot, setting and characterization'; and with the creation of a 'temporal ordering'.[4] But for me, a sociology of stories should be less concerned with analysing the formal structures of stories or narratives (as literary theory might), and more interested in inspecting the social role of stories: the ways they are produced, the ways they are read, the work they perform in the wider social order, how they change, and their role in the political process. Whilst I have taken as my 'case' the distinctly modern quest to provide personal narratives around the sexual life, much of what will be said could be applied to other genres of story work. Although recent developments in literary theory and cultural studies will prove useful, and there is indeed a need for analysing the formal properties of stories, I will constantly return to the social work they perform in cultures. *It is time to go beyond the text.* This chapter may be seen as a digression for those who want to hear more about sexual stories. But the task here is to provide a fuller backdrop that will ultimately help to develop a sociology of stories. It aims to provide a series of problems, many of which will be taken up later. For, as Suzanne K. Langer once remarked, 'if we would have new knowledge, we must get a whole world of new questions'.[5] Here the task is to see stories in two linked and critical ways: as symbolic interactions and as political processes. This chapter sets forth some images and questions, to be explored more fully in subsequent chapters.[6]

STORIES AS SYMBOLIC INTERACTIONS[7]

Whilst sociology may provide many roots into the study of stories,[8] this study takes a symbolic interactionist view. Briefly, this century-old and now revitalising position takes as its baseline the view that the social world for human beings can be helpfully viewed as a vast flow of ever-changing symbolic interactions in which we are set actively adrift in a never-ending stream of practical activities. Isolated individuals and abstracted societies are there none. We human beings are social world-makers,[9] though we do not make our social worlds in conditions of our own choosing.[10] Through symbols and languages, we are able to reflect upon ourselves and others, and we cannot but help acting in, on and through the world. We work and worry, pray and play, love and hate; and *all the time we are telling stories* about our pasts, our presents and our futures. We are constantly doing things together[11] – no person is an island: even when alone, especially when alone, there is an awareness of others. We are constantly writing the story of the world around us: its periods and places, its purposes and programmes, its people and plots. We invent identities for ourselves and others and locate ourselves in these imagined maps. We create communities of concern and arenas of activity where we can make our religions, tend to our 'families', practise our politics, get on with our work. We experience our bodies and our feelings, as well as our behaviours and talk. And everywhere we go, we are charged with telling stories and making meaning – giving sense to ourselves and the world around us. And the meanings we invoke and the worlds we craft mesh and flow, but remain emergent: never fixed, always indeterminate, ceaselessly contested. Change is ubiquitous: we are always becoming, never arriving; and the social order heaves as a vast negotiated web of dialogue and conversation. So-called social science is not cut off from this activity but is itself very much part of it: it is simply an occasion of more systematic reflection and story telling upon the world. It too is a stream of practical activities – doing things together, immersing ourselves in the world, facing problems, creating working solutions, making meanings to make a difference. It too is a flow requiring constant change, more adjustment, equivocation and contest. Truth which emerges as helpful for one time may not be so at another. Active problem-solving is required anew of each group. And all the time it is itself a vast symbolic enterprise, feeding on the world as much as shaping it.[12]

Story telling can be placed at the heart of our symbolic interactions. The focus here is neither on the solitary individual life (which is in principle unknown and unknowable), nor on the text (which means nothing standing on its own), but on *the interactions which emerge around story telling*. Stories can be seen as *joint actions*. 'Everywhere we look in a human society we see people engaging in forms of joint action.'[13] People may be seen as engaged in fitting together lines of activity around stories; they are engaged in *story actions*.

Some of the folk engaging in joint actions may be seen as *producers* of sexual stories: these are the sexual *story tellers* who write lengthy autobiographies exploring their inner sexual natures. They are the sexual story tellers who produce voluminous correspondence or diaries which display the minutiae of their erotic lives. These are the people who provide life histories for sociologists, oral histories for oral historians and case studies for psychologists and clinicians. They even, and more complexly, can *perform* their stories – not just in words and scripts but as emotionally charged bodies in action.[14]

Closely allied to these tellers are a second kind of producer: *the coaxers, coachers and coercers*. These folk possess the power, at least momentarily, to provoke stories from people. Their line of activity is to seduce stories: coaxers become listeners and questioners. They probe, interview, and interrogate. They send out questionnaires and solicit 'problem letters'. Sometimes they gather in groups to make others tell their stories and sometimes as individuals they just simply clasp their hands, smile and listen. They are the Sigmund Freuds, the Oprah Winfreys, the Shere Hites who poke and probe for the personal narrative. They are even the parents demanding to know what their child has been up to. They are the courtroom interrogators, the doctors, the therapists, the tabloid journalists. They coax, coach and coerce people to tell their stories. My own role as a sociologist conducting research into the lives of the sexually different in the 1970s turned me into a coaxer: bringing people to the edge of telling a story they might never have told before, and coaching them to tell it in a certain way. My questions, my style, my theory meant that the story they told me did not emerge as it did a century before in the hands of a Krafft-Ebing. Whereas he looked for – and found – pathological tales, I looked for – and found – tales of normalcy. Coaxers can play a crucial role in shifting the nature of the stories that are told.

Another major group are the *consumers*, *readers*, *audiences* of sexual stories: their line of activity is to consume, to interpret and make sense of all these stories. These are the viewers who watch the documentary of a transvestite life on prime-time TV; the bookworms who consume the biographies of Rock Hudson, Jan Morris, Magic Johnson, Woody Allen, Madonna or the latest 'sexual scandals'; the control agents who scour a person's tale for the sexual signs; the student who is compelled for her course to read the biography of Herculine Barbine, Jane Fry or Dora.[15] Just how these 'readers' interpret the story is a crucial process in understanding stories. Sometimes they are brought to outrage and sometimes to better understanding. Sometimes such consumption becomes a passionate hobby and sometimes it is all a matter of great indifference. Sometimes it is a tool-kit and manual for guidance and sometimes it is a source where a person can literally find themselves in the text. Sometimes a text is read in relative isolation and sometimes it is read through a social world or an imagined community – of class, of race, of gender, of experience, of taste. Sometimes people hear so lightly what others say so intensely, and sometimes people hear so intensely what others say so lightly.

All these people – producers, coaxers, consumers – are engaged in assembling life story actions *around* lives, events and happenings – although they cannot grasp the *actual* life.[16] At the centre of much of this action emerge the story *products*: the objects which harbour the meanings that have to be handled through interaction. These congeal or freeze already preconstituted moments of a life from the *story teller* and the *coaxer* and await the handling of a *reader* or *consumer*. The meanings of stories are never fixed but emerge out of a ceaselessly changing stream of interaction between producers and readers in shifting *contexts*. They may, of course, become habitualised and stable; but always and everywhere the meaning of stories shift and sway in the contexts to which they are linked.

Stories get told and read in different ways in different contexts. The consuming of a tale centres upon the different *social worlds* and *interpretive communities* who can hear the story in certain ways and hence not others[17] and who may come to produce their own shared 'memories'.[18] As I shall show, a woman claiming she has been raped is a story that was interpreted very differently by communities half a century ago, and most of the sexual stories that now regularly appear on TV chat shows would not have been possible even twenty years ago. But even today, stories feed into different communities, evoking contrasting responses. The stories of people with HIV infection feed into some communities where support, love and care is offered; but into others where exclusion, stigma and fear is the interpretive frame. Hence these communities are more than just cognitive or symbolic units (though they are that), they are also emotional worlds. More, such communities are not permanent and fixed: when, for instance, the US basketball player Magic Johnson announced his HIV status in 1991, his story became accepted in the same youthful communities (where he was an established hero) that had previously shown enmity to Aids stories.[19] Prior rage and hostility amongst the young turned to tears and bafflement. Youthful communities may lend support to the telling of some tales but not others. Adult stories may not easily be heard in youthful worlds, and youthful stories may not be heard easily in adult worlds. Stories of young mums with no husbands may be heard very differently in black ghettoes and white suburbia. Further, these communities themselves are part of wider *habitual or recurring networks of collective activity*.[20] Stories do not float around abstractly but are grounded in historically evolving communities of memory, structured through age, class, race, gender and sexual preference. There is often an organised pattern behind many of the tales that are heard: audience studies of television for instance suggest that the reception of television programmes may be strongly gendered – with men exerting more control over what is watched, focusing more upon 'newsworthy' and public stories and being more silent in their watchings than women – who talk more, and watch in a less focused manner (often because they are so distracted by family matters such as the children or the ironing!).[21] Likewise with age: teenage girls, for example, look for their stories in teenage girl magazines – in the UK magazines like *Jackie* and *Just Seventeen*. The magazines bring together a community of girls bonded through the common reading process. But, again, they are not consumed in any straightforward fashion – reading is a complex but highly social process. As Angela McRobbie says of *Jackie* readers:

Reading routines vary enormously according to time, place and other available activities. [Girls] flick through *Jackie*, they read it in segments, they read it voraciously to cut off from the family noise around them, and they read the same issue again when they have nothing else to do. *Jackie* makes sense to them as a weekly ritual. It punctuates the end of the week and thus creates a feeling of security. This is reinforced by its repetition and its continuity. The stories that seem to go on forever and the features which are the same over the years also fulfill this function of reassuring sameness.[22]

Finally, the *mechanisms* through which the story is told will matter: 'the media is the message.' Telling a story face to face around a log fire is very different from telling a story through a pulp-paperback book, telling a story to a therapy group that engulfs you in its twelve-step programme, or to telling your story in full frontal glare on *Kilroy* or *Oprah*![23] These are the differences between oral, print and electronic cultures – creating very different modes of story telling.[24] Whereas sexual stories were most surely told in the oral narratives modes of folklore and myth, increasingly sexual stories have become a part of the 'mediasation' of society. They have been engulfed as most of modern life has – in the permeation of symbolic forms through media technologies. It is not true to suggest, as Walter Benjamin and others have, that story telling is in decline:[25] rather the channels for telling stories have changed. For many, film has become the narrative medium of the twentieth century. And the solitary verbal tale has now become the public media tale.

Figure 1 below puts all this simply in schematic form. It suggests there is much in common with recent developments in linguistic, literary and media theory,[26] but goes beyond this to sense the fully social nature of story telling as joint actions.

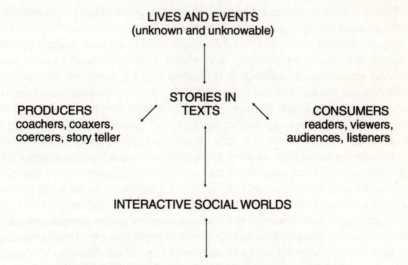

Figure 1 Stories as joint actions

From this it is possible to see that the telling of a story has no simple, unitary or fixed character. For setting it out like this deconstructs, decentres and destabilises the story. Stories depend upon a constant flow of joint actions circulating between tellers, coaxers, texts, readers and the contexts in which the stories are told: tellers can only select, coaxers can only sift, texts can only sieve and readers can only interpret. Each of these processes compounds the others till the link between reality and the story become very fragile.[27] There is much in common here with what is often called postmodern social theory except that this sociological approach offers distinctive advantages because it does not stay at the level of textual analysis: it insists that story production and consumption is an empirical social process involving a stream of joint actions in local contexts themselves bound into wider negotiated social worlds. Texts are connected to lives, actions, contexts and society. It is not a question of 'hyperrealities' and 'simulacra' but of practical activities, daily doings and contested truths.

QUESTIONS FOR A SOCIOLOGY OF STORIES

With all this in mind, several questions can now be asked of sexual stories. The first concerns *the nature of stories*. This is the classic question of literary theory, asking about the genres and tropes of stories. What common forms do stories take? How are they organised – through plot and time? What are the metaphors embedded within them? Much of such analysis aims to detect underlying structural forms, the formal properties for instance of tragedy, comedy or romance. As such it has a root in some sociology which seeks the underlying structures of social order. The morphology of story telling meets structural sociology.

Thus, for instance, in this book I have chosen one genre of story to analyse: that of the personal experience narrative – the tale told by a person about the self. This is only one kind of sexual story – others might include the pornographic tale, the fictional tale, the scientific tale. And within these sub-classifications, more classical genres may be examined: in looking at Aids narratives, for instance, Judith Williamson has detected their affinity to gothic and melodramatic forms of story telling, whilst Linda Williams's analysis of pornographic movies over the past century keeps detecting shifting links to other genres – most intriguingly to the musical![28] The task here is to unpack the types, the languages, the tropes at work inside the text of a sexual story. But for the sociologist it must go further. The genres and structures of story telling may also link to the generic social processes and structures at work in social life. In Part II, I attempt to make some of these connections around the stories of 'rape', 'coming out' and 'recovery'.

A second question concerns *the social processes of producing and consuming stories*. These are the questions that have been of prime concern to media theorists, but they are centrally sociology of knowledge questions. How do stories get produced: what brings people to the brink of tellings? How do people come to construct their particular stories (and possess them as their own)? Further, what might silence them, and what might bring people to the *emotional* brink of revealing all? Some of the stories told trip lightly off the tongue: but for others there is immense emotional work involved. And why do they tell this particular kind of story rather than another – where does the story they tell come from?

But tellings cannot be in isolation from hearings, readings, consumings. When can a story be heard, and most especially how is it heard? A voice with no listener is a silence. How might a reader interpret a text and what role might the story play in the consumer's life? How do some readers find themselves emotionally in a text, whilst others may readily dismiss it? And how might such readings connect to the social worlds – real, imagined, interpretive, symbolic – in which they are read?[29] Further, producing and reading should not be seen as separate events. There is a flow of action and producers become consumers whilst consumers become producers. What, then, are the links between the story and the flow of production and consumption? How does one feed into and upon the other such that the making and consuming of stories are closely bound together?

A clear example of this is to be found in the work of Constance Penley. Her feminist research interests led her, curiously, to focus upon the TV stories of *Star Trek* and a large group of women who, since the early 1970s, have been avid fans. Starting off their lives as consumers of this popular product, these women turned increasingly to a rewriting of the stories so that the lead male characters became sexualised and gay. Rereading the original texts (and turning them into something almost resembling 'gay porn'), they moved from consuming to producing in a highly active writing spiral – making their own fanzines, magazines, books and holding major conventions. Here, production and consumption became part of a continuous active spiral.[30] Chapter 3 takes some of these concerns further.

A third question concerns *the social role that stories play*. Once told, what functions might such stories serve in the lives of people and societies? How might stories work to perform conservative functions maintaining dominant orders, and how might they be used to resist or transform lives and cultures? Stories seem a prominent feature of all societies, though their shape and content shift. Sexual stories are also common as a type, as any review of legend and mythology through history would show – highlighting universal themes of passion and desire. But in the modern world, the workings of personal confessions – in the press, in biography, on chat shows, in paperbacks, in therapy groups, in social science – seem to have taken on an especially important role in highlighting a key aspect of culture. The epilogue addresses some of these concerns directly, but they are a theme of the book.

Finally, a fourth question should address issues of *change, history and culture*. What are the links between stories and the wider social world – the contextual conditions for stories to be told and for stories to be received? What brings people to give voice to a story at a particular historical moment? What are the different social worlds' interpretive communities that enable stories to be told and heard in different ways? And as the historical moment shifts, perhaps into a late modern world, what stories may lose their significance, and what stories may gain in tellability? These issues become my concern in the closing chapters of the book where the focus turns to potentially new stories in the making.

I do not deal with all these wide-ranging questions in detail in this book, but I do consider a number. Chapter 3 deals with some aspects of the making, consuming and flow of sexual stories. Chapter 4 looks at a few contours of narrative pattern. In Part II my main concern turns to the contexts and social worlds of rape, recovery and gay and lesbian stories, and the conditions for their emergence. The final chapters glimpse some of the issues raised both by social change and politics. Throughout, this book remains an introductory inquiry and I can make no pretence at completeness.

STORY TELLING FLOWS IN THE STREAM OF POWER

Stories are not just practical and symbolic actions: they are also part of the political process. Sexual stories ooze through the political stream. Power[31] is not so much an all or nothing phenomenon, which people either have or don't have, and which resides either here or there. Rather, it is best viewed as a flow, a process, a pulsate – oscillating and undulating throughout the social world and working to pattern the degree of control people experience and have over their lives. Power is the process which shifts outcomes and distributes control and regulation. It affects hierarchy, patterns of domination and the distribution of resources. It connects processes which make a difference to the conduct of life. Power is not a simple attribute or a capacity, but a flow of negotiations and shifting outcomes. As electricity is to the physical world, so power may be to the social world: it is the conduit through which much life gets enacted. But its shapes and forms are immensely varied. Like the air we breathe, or the blood that flows through our veins, it is omnipresent. It is not a property of people *per se*, nor is it zero-sum: we do not either have it or not have it. Instead it flows through all interaction, though in starkly different ways. It is both *negative* – repressing, oppressing, depressing – and *positive* – constructive, creative, constitutive.[32] It flows into *lives* making some abundant in capacity (empowered, actualised) and others diminished (inferiorised, marginalised, weak, victims). It flows into *situations*, making some open, flexible and participatory and others closed, rigid and limiting. It flows through the *habitual networks of social activity*, making some alive with possibilities (democratic, participatory) and others infused with oppression and dominance (hierarchic, authoritarian). And ultimately it flows through the whole *negotiated social order* – controlling and empowering, closing and opening, making some things possible and others things impossible.[33] Power is a process that weaves its way through embodied, passionate social life and everything in its wake. *Sexual stories live in this flow of power. The power to tell a story, or indeed to not tell a story, under the conditions of one's own choosing, is part of the political process.*

To put this more concretely: what allows a 'rape story' to be told, to be felt, to be heard, to be legitimated? When can a traumatised raped woman tell herself this story? When can she give public voice to it, and indeed to which public will she voice it: her partner, her child, her parent, the police, the media, the court, a rape hot line, the defendant? When will it be a credible voice, and when will it be an incredible one? This entire process of opening up and closing down the spaces for her talk and the acceptance of her talk can be seen as a political flow. A quarter of a century ago few women could speak of rape, and even fewer would believe such stories once said: the political flow stopped even self-recognition. Today, at least for some women under some circumstances, in many parts of the western world, talk is more possible and belief a little more likely. It may be easiest for wealthy, white women with access to resources and hardest for poor, black women: matters such as literacy, economic security and resources shape the capacity to tell the story. But, for reasons explored later, rape stories have become politically both more feasible and more plausible. *Lives* have become empowered as (some) women have come to tell their story and, with increased emotional strength, see themselves as active survivors. *Situations* have become transformed as a new set of spaces have been created for women to come together and talk, for police and courts to shift their practices from the past, for a greater possibility to see how rape impacts on women's lives. And at the broadest level of *social order*, a new set of challenging understandings about rape have started shifting a little of the patriarchal hierarchies, the dominant stories of sexuality which have silently terrorised many women's lives in the past.[34]

The same is true of 'gay and lesbian stories'. To speak of being gay or lesbian in the early part of the twentieth century in the western world was to invite dramatic social exclusion in all its forms: incarceration in concentration camps, criminal sanctions and imprisonment, medicalisation – treatments and therapies of all sorts, religious banishment, community ostracism and mockery. Not only did the person not tell the 'other', frequently they could not even tell the self. With feelings denied and personal control reduced, a politics of emotion was at work.[35] An organising feature of gay and lesbian life may be seen as the 'Closet'. Here secrecy keeps any story of lesbian and gay life from public view.[36]

But what makes people empowered enough to tell their coming out stories? What enables people first to tell themselves the gay story of their lives; then to tell another – a friend, a lover, a member of the family; then to tell more and more people; and then – for many throughout the 1980s – to shout it passionately from the street corner or the gay parade? And finally, to anticipate a future that may not even be possible, to exhaust the story: to feel it no longer needs to be said. All this is about the flow of power. Here are hierarchy and patterns of domination which facilitate the ability to tell the story of 'being gay': both personal power that allows stories to be told or withheld; and social power which creates spaces or closes down space for stories to be voiced. Here, then, is a flow of negotiations and shifting outcomes, enabling gay life stories to be told at one moment and not another. As gay life story telling has increased, so has the power some gays and lesbians feel over their lives: in the recent past, most lacked this power and even today, in the early 1990s, many may feel powerless to tell their story to self or other. Likewise, some social orders refuse any space at all for such stories to be told – most schools for example, and until very recently, the military. The ability to tell the story of being gay shifts in different 'arenas' of interaction: economic, religious, work, home, media, government. To tell the story of being gay may well be linked to the ability to take the role of others (local, specific and 'significant' as well as wider, abstract and 'generalised'); to the kinds of reference groups and social world perspectives assumed. Likewise, gay story telling is never fixed or final: there will be moments it can be told, moments it is precarious, and moments when it is best kept quiet! The outcome of telling a story is never clear in advance but always under different degrees of contestation and conflict. Emerging everywhere, telling a gay story will open up some possibilities and close down others. It is positive and negative, both releasing capacities in a life whilst also closing down others. Telling gay and lesbian stories does not float around in some heavenly void: it is an everyday and grounded matter. It works its way through practical everyday experience: the child at school who hears peers mock gays will soon realise that this is a story of danger that cannot be safely told to (m)any; the woman in her office may hear jokes about lesbians that make her segregate her worlds to those where she can tell her lesbian story and those where she remains silent. And now there is 'outing': where relatively empowered 'out' gays and lesbians elect to tell the story of privileged (powerful) others without their consent.[37] Power is everywhere in sexual stories.

This power is strongly connected to emotion: shame may prevent a story being told, pride may lead to it being shouted.[38] The telling (and not telling) of stories is usually accompanied by strong feelings – many of the tales underlying this book have been told with tears, with anger, with passion. Power cannot easily be grasped without sensing its links to feeling – or not feeling. Many writers on Aids, for instance, speak simultaneously of emotional pains which lead to blocking any ability to tell their Aids stories, but also of the emotional empowerment that flows from telling.[39] John Preston, in the introduction to a series of personal testaments and stories around Aids, reveals both how emotion can work to bring a story together and how it can work to keep a story silent. On learning of his own HIV status, he writes:

> In 1987 . . . I learned that I was infected with the disease myself. It was then that I truly understood the difficulties that many other writers had with their stories, and I became all the more admiring of those who would tell their truths. Because I couldn't do it. Not for well over a year. The manuscript sat on a shelf in my study, something too raw for me to read, too difficult. The epidemic became more immediate, became suffocating, became the way I learned of my lover's and friends' deaths. Now the book seemed, in its own strange way, to become the harbinger of my own infection. Faced with pressing medical decisions and a sense of dread about the repercussions of having Aids in today's society, it seemed there was not time to create a book, there was no relief from the oppression of the illness. How could one reflect on what was happening *when it was happening now*?
>
> But, in fact, this collection (of stories) was one of the means I had at my disposal to come back to life. These articles had helped me fight the feeling that Aids was overwhelming me.[40]

Stories, then, can often not be easily told, and they are always embedded in the political flow. Every part of the interactionist story telling model presented above needs to be placed in this political flow. And so another series of questions arises:

1 The nature of stories   Which kinds of narratives work to empower people and which degrade, control and dominate? Some stories may work to pathologise voices, or turn them into victims with little control over their lives; other stories may sense human agency and survival, giving the voice a power to transform and empower. Stories may also be told in different ways by different groups – giving some kinds of stories much more credibility than others? Talk from 'below' may be marginalised and excluded, whilst 'expert' talk from above may be given priority and more credibility.[41]

2 The making of stories   What strategies enable stories to be told, how are spaces created for them, and how are voices silenced? How do stories feed into the wider networks of routine power? Does a coaxer, for example, facilitate stories (enabling new voices to be heard) or entrap stories, into a wider story of his or her own? In a famous instance, Arthur Munby, the Victorian gentleman of letters with a sexual turn-on by the 'dirty work' of housemaids – amongst other things he got his servant to go up the chimney naked! – coaxed his servant Hannah Cullwick to write her diary and reveal her sexual life – 'he told me not to forget to put them things down what I'd been telling him'. When stories are told under such circumstances how might it shape them? Are they really the authentic voices of women, or do men speak through these women's voices?[42] Likewise, in the great parade of sexual survey research, how far does the coaxing role of the interviewer have a part to play, even to the extent that many are more like the researchers' stories than the subjects'?[43]

3 The consuming of stories   Who has access to stories? Where is the reader located in the political spectrum? How far can one gain access to a story on television, hear it on a radio, buy it in a book, read it in a newspaper, find it in a library? Can one afford to buy it? Does one know where to look? What cultural and economic resources – literacy, knowledge, money, time, space – are needed to consume a story? And how interconnected are these consumers? Although some stories may be told, they may not have the space to be told widely, and they may be told in ways which restrict them to narrow groups. It is quite likely, for instance, that the black feminist lesbian biography which now has a voice is only really read by black lesbian feminists, to whom it makes a big difference.[44] But it has no wider audience than that. How might the consumption of stories be extended?

4 The strategies of story telling   How might various strategies of talk be implicated in this story telling? Issues of role-taking, turn-taking, impression management, pausing, body gesture, spatial arrangements, shame spirals and the like help 'open' stories or 'close' them down?[45] For instance, some have suggested that some women may speak 'in a different voice' – one that is much less formally rational, linear and abstract than 'male voices', more prone to particularities, interconnections and 'care'. In this view, women's stories may actually be told in a different way – and have a different outcome.[46] They may 'stumble' more, be told with less assuredness and boldness, be more qualified and hesitant, and hence (initially) sound less convincing. Women may generally find it harder to consider their stories as possessing 'authority', harder to express themselves in public, harder to believe that others will respect their story. There is almost certainly a massive gender skew to sexual story telling.[47]

5 Stories in the wider world   How do stories sit with the wider frameworks of power? The story telling process flows through social acts of domination, hierarchy, marginalisation and inequality. Some voices – who claim to dominate, who top the hierarchy, who claim the centre, who possess resources – are not only heard much more readily than others, but also are capable of framing the questions, setting the agendas, establishing the rhetorics much more readily than the others. These social acts become habitual networks of domination congealing around gender, race, age, economic opportunity and sexuality: certain stories hence are silenced from a saying. Children, for instance, are usually denied access to sexual stories; the elderly who speak of their desires may be looked at suspiciously; 'black voices' around single motherhood and alternative voices may be co-opted into white voices talking of pathology; 'underclass' sexualities are silenced. The importance of 'finding a voice' and 'telling one's story' has been well recognised in the politics of the new social movements over the last decade, and it is an important backdrop to this study. As bell hooks so tellingly has remarked: 'Oppressed people resist by identifying themselves as subjects, by defining their reality, shaping their new identity, naming their history, *telling their story*.'[48] There are many political processes involved in story telling in general, but in looking at 'sexual stories' a sexual hierarchy needs to be made clear. Gayle Rubin, in a much celebrated and discussed article, has outlined what this means and it is worth quoting her in full:

> Modern Western societies appraise sex acts according to a hierarchical system of sex value. Marital, reproductive, heterosexuals are alone at the top of the pyramid. [i.e. their stories are heard loud and clear]. Clamouring below are unmarried monogamous heterosexuals in couples, followed by most other heterosexuals. Solitary sex floats ambiguously. The powerful nineteenth-century stigma on masturbation lingers in less potent, modified forms as an inferior substitute for partnered encounters. Stable, long-term lesbian and gay male couples are verging on respectability, but bar dykes and promiscuous gay men are hovering just above the groups at the very bottom of the pyramid. The most despised sexual castes currently include transexuals, transvestites, fetishists, sadomasochists, sex workers such as prostitutes and porn models, and the lowliest of all, those whose eroticism transgresses generational boundaries.[49]

Those at the bottom of the hierarchy have stories that cannot easily be told, and this book will in part be investigating how some of these voices are slowly being heard. But many stories, whose nature at present we can only guess at, are not being told. Such a hierarchy needs to be criss-crossed with gender (which is probably why rape is not on Rubin's list of those low on this hierarchy!), class and race (which would make the black, working-class drag queens and sex workers a pretty low-down, marginalised story![50]).

An image of a 'gendered heterosexism' may also help reveal the hierarchy of sexual stories. This notion refers to a set of acts which are organised around the divisions of men and women, and through which heterosexual relations – usually leading to some kind of heterosexual coitus, potential reproduction and coupling/ marriage – are given priority. Gendered heterosexism takes on many historically varying forms, but here it will mean that those stories that will be most readily said and heard will be those which facilitate standard gender divisions and the paramountcy of heterosexual relations. Again, they will be criss-crossed with class, race and age. Stories which fall outside of this, or worse, challenge this, will have a much harder time being said and heard.[51] But it is precisely these stories which will most interest me in this book.

IN CONCLUSION

This chapter has been much less concerned with sexual stories *per se* than it has been with providing a wider agenda of questions for the newly emerging sociology of story telling. It should be clear that for sociology, the world of stories is much larger than a mere focus on narrative – overflowing to the social and political conditions that generate some stories and not others, enabling some to be heard and not others. A sociology of stories seeks to understand the role of stories in social life. The remainder of the book returns to a fuller focus on sexual stories.

Chapter 3

Making sexual stories

I came to the conclusion that the inner dilemma was the one that had to be sorted out. I only came to that conclusion a couple of years ago, so that when I say I have sincerely tried, I mean it. I've tried for not less than fifteen years. For the most part I feel the time has been wasted, as I would have been better employed coming to terms with myself. But I couldn't dress all the time. I thought that I was the only man who wanted to dress as a woman and that therefore I must be some kind of nut. Not being the sort of thing that people could talk about, and even less understand, there was nobody to tell me what I was all about. All I could do was grasp words that came up in Sunday newspapers – like homosexual, pervert, people in the twilight world and so on. But with my limited knowledge all these words seemed to me – seemed to be – synonymous. I assumed that everyone else would think they were too, and although I felt the *News of the World* descriptions didn't apply to me exactly I still felt that I must belong to that category because nobody wrote to say that there was another group of people. Reading of the distaste shown by people, and of convictions brought about, etc. I felt that I must be wrong. Yet there wasn't a wrong thought in my head. How is it that I should feel that I would be misinterpreted if I was to say what I felt? One paragraph read that 'Maurice was standing in the dock wearing a flowered blouse, a pleated skirt and white heels'. All I could feel was envy that he had the guts to dress the way he did. Although later I came to realise that his motives were different from mine. I used to gather piles of old newspapers, a habit which has not yet dried, for any article that might throw some light on the subject. But all I found was a series of articles of varying types and lengths, about all sorts of odd situations in which men were dressed as women, and the only thing they had in common was the fact that they were objects of ridicule and social rejection. This led me to believe that I too would be an object of ridicule and rejection. So my secret had to be a closely guarded secret. Another set of articles that had a touch of sympathy, only a touch mind, were those sensational articles on people who had actually changed their sex. To me this was incredible. Men had actually become women. Now how I had absolutely no idea. So much for my knowledge. It was all found out from the public university of lavatory walls. And I didn't believe half of it.

In the late 1970s, I interviewed (with a colleague) a number of people about their sexual lives – a process that I now see as the collection of an array of 'sexual stories'.[1] In this chapter I will ponder some of the elements that help people tell and read such stories. The above opening quotation is a brief extract which comes from a man, Richard, who was then in his early thirties and had a strong desire to cross dress. This was an account he actually wrote as part of a much longer 'autobiography', a practice that is not at all uncommon amongst both 'transexuals' and 'transvestites'. Indeed, at times it seems that for transexuals it is almost compulsory to write a biography (and indeed it often is, since much of the required surgery is dependent on telling the right story!).[2] Richard wrote his story, I suspect, partly for catharsis, partly for clarification and partly with a dim sense of possible publication. It will serve as a helpful starting point for examining the making of sexual stories. To continue a little more with his voice:

> A number of passages made an impact on me, which have not left me even yet, although some of them I read more than twenty years ago. To me the classic case was April Ashley and I've never had anything but an admiration and envy for her. Roberta Cowell and Christine Jorgensen, and the name William Calhoun haunted me for years. I slept with my penis in my hand lest it should disappear in the night. I wished it would. But on the other hand, what would I say? I couldn't keep that a secret could I? It was some time later that I connected the loss of the penis with the operation they talked about, so that I knew I would have to be rather more possessive if it was going to happen to me. I knew at the time that there was no chance of my having the operation, not because I thought I was not transexual, and therefore that my problem was not so acute, but for the simple reason that I wouldn't know where to begin, at least not at that early age. Anyway who would believe a young boy when he said he wanted to be a girl? Who in fact would perform an operation like that on a person so young? My parents would not believe or even begin to comprehend my inner feelings, but apart from the feeling of wanting to shout that I was really more of a girl than a boy, I had no knowledge of what causes a person to believe such a thing. So I thought an operation was out of the question. I wonder whether my feelings were just fantasies and I would grow out of them. They weren't and I haven't.

Here are the beginnings of a story of The Story. It can be taken as emblematic of many. It hints at many themes found in many sexual stories. There is a self-consciousness at work here which scans the past life for clues to one's sexual being. There is a sense of an identity – here that of a transvestite or a transexual – hidden from the surface awaiting clearer recognition, labelling, categorising. There is a searching through the public world – of newspapers, books and 'experts' – for a language and a means to make sense of the story. There are the significant others and role models who became momentary heroes for a story. There is the harking back to a motivational story to be found in childhood. And there is a solitude, a secrecy and a silence, alongside a longing to shout. Richard's story anticipates the stories of many.

Not everyone writes their 'sexual autobiography' like this (never mind that it goes on for another hundred pages). But for many like Richard who feel their sexual lives have become a source of suffering and anguish, the telling of a story is literally a 'coming to terms'.[3] It is sensed as a necessary way of dealing with a sexual and gendered life. Commonly, such stories are taken to be signs of The Truth. When we read the results of modern sexological surveys – and the Big Books that entrap them – we take the producer of the sexual tale to be someone pursuing the truth. Less seriously, but seriously enough, when we read the agony aunts, watch the chat shows, or buy the recovery guides to sexual problems we still take them as some kind of sign of a truth. Here are the quasi-scientific stories told by men as responses to the Shere Hite questionnaire on male sexuality; here is the autobiography of a person with Aids or the Nancy Friday letter with its authentic statements of real fantasy and thwarted desire; here is the Phil Donahue 'guest' revealing the latest 'sexual suffering' about which something ought to be done – the 'women who love too much' and the men who suffer from the 'Casanova Complex'.[4] And in each case, the sexual stories are assumed to be an approximation to the truth of the sexual. Richard's story above is one more instance.

But there is a very different way of stating all this. No longer do people simply 'tell' their sexual stories to reveal the 'truth' of their sexual lives; instead, they turn themselves into *socially organised biographical objects* They construct – even invent, though that may be too crass a term – tales of the intimate self, which may or may not bear a relationship to a truth. Are their stories really to be seen as the simple unfolding of some inner truth? *Or are their very stories something they are brought to say in a particular way through a particular time and place?* And if so, where do they get their 'stories' from? Once posed this way, the sexual stories can no longer be seen simply as the harbingers of a relatively unproblematic truth.

In this chapter, I turn to such questions, beginning a discussion of how it is that people assemble their sexual stories. The key questions for this chapter thus become: *how are sexual stories produced? How are stories, once produced, consumed? What is the relation between the ongoing process of producing stories and consuming them?* All this can be seen as evolving over four levels: *the personal, the situational, the organisational and the cultural/historical.*

The Personal level is straightforward enough: it concerns the motives people have for telling their tale. Allport, for instance, suggests many reasons why people might tell a life story – and they apply as well to sexual stories. Thus people may tell their sexual stories as a relief from tension, for monetary gain, as part of a therapeutic encounter, for 'redemption and social reincorporation', through a desire to help science, further service or even as a course-work assignment. They may tell their tales though a desire for immortality, a desire for order, as special pleading or simple exhibitionism![5] For many the telling of a tale comes as a major way of 'discovering who one really is'. It is a voyage to explore the self. I will return to this theme at many points.

The Situational level examines the processes through which people turn themselves into self-indicated social objects. This is my prime focus in this chapter, as I ask how people come to find their stories. They become myth-makers, story tellers, dreamers, definers of situations, scriptwriters, world-makers, producers of 'programmes' about their own sexual lives.[6] How do people come to 'find themselves' in their stories? The root image here is that of folk turning themselves into social objects.[7] Just *how* do they do it?

The Organisational level focuses on the organisational elements in shaping a story. Stories are not, in the end, random elements simply sucked from the culture: they are patterned, sequenced, formalised, given shape through the organisational frame of the settings in which they are generated: the structure of the writing act, the formal properties of the research interview, the organisation of television talk, the procedures of a courtroom, the turn-taking of conversation, the social rules of a therapy group, the logic and formats of the media. All of this gives sexual story telling a definite pattern and shape, allowing some things to be said and others to remain in silence.

The Cultural/historical level will become a major focus of this book in later chapters. It concerns the historical moment at which a story enters public discourse – the moment of public reception. One of the driving questions of this book concerns 'the tale and its time': how certain stories can only be told when key social worlds await the telling, when an audience is ripened up and ready to hear. Many stories are in silence – dormant, awaiting their historical moment.

All four levels are important elements in understanding the social construction of sexual stories. To return briefly to Richard's story above we can see all four levels at work. First, there is his personal motivation: a combination of self-exploration, catharsis, personal clarification. Second, there are the situational elements that help him assemble his story: the *News of the World*, 'piles of old newspapers', the earlier stories of April Ashley, Roberta Cowell and Christine Jorgensen. Third, there is the organisational frame of writing a personal autobiography: the rules of narrative that govern such matters as sequence, plot, voice, metaphor are all at work in this 'writing act'. And finally, there is the cultural/historical moment: a tale told in the late 1970s – but one made possible through the slow accumulation of 'transvestite' case records through the 1950s and 1960s. This was not a new voice, but a voice mirroring many others.

In this chapter, my prime focus will be with the second of these levels. Much is said about the cultural/historical level in later chapters.

BUILDING A PERSONAL NARRATIVE OF INTIMACY

bit by bit, putting it together

(Stephen Sondheim)

Richard, above, tells his story in relative isolation – although it is not really isolated as it draws from the wider culture: he reads all those newspapers to get a sense of who he is. Maybe the most solitary of sexual tales is the masturbatory fantasy –

told in private to the self and heard in private by the self. But even here, the fantasy is normally sucked out of elements available in the culture. The fetishistic tale of gas masks, or rubber or PVC raincoats – all popular fetishistic 'turn-ons' – depends upon a culture that has used gas masks and developed new materials! Story elements are built out of cultural bricolage.

So from just where do we get our stories? The most apparent answer is to suggest that they simply emerge from within: through thought, through reflection, through creativity. In part this has to be true. But it is also the case that all stories emerge as a practical activity: as we go about our daily rounds we piece together fragments from the tool-kit of culture that ultimately (but maybe only momentarily) cohere into 'our stories'. Stories may be established from the disparate elements sucked out of the wider narrative bricolage found in the culture. Culture, in this sense, is a *tool-kit of resources*.[8] Richard's 'transvestite story' above shows this process at work: bits from the *News of the World*, fragments of the heard stories of Cowell, Jorgensen and Calhoun, incredible scribblings from the 'public university of lavatory walls'. Here, bit by bit, 'traces' are assembled into the story of a life.

There are many such traces that can be drawn upon in assembling the story. The notoriety of Madonna's fake but best-selling account of *Sex* reveals the bricolage of cultural events available to the young and fashionable in 1992: sadomasochistic props, lesbian and gay signifiers, paedophilic allusion. Her book sucks out of the culture fashionable elements and recycles them into her new and somewhat sensational story. But she is extreme.[9] All stories do this to differing degrees: utilising an array of devices to tell their stories. Amongst the most significant 'traces' to be drawn upon are personal props and the clues provided by generalised and significant others. Amongst the major story telling *strategies* to be evolved are those of 'motivating' and 'memorising' – strung together through 'creative moments'. In what follows I will isolate a few of these elements.

Picking over the 'traces'

Personal props   Some years ago, a masochistic man well into his thirties recalled to me the power of armour:

> somewhere around the age of 9 or 10 I went to the Tower of London and saw all those fabulous suits of armour. And my reaction was, I'd love to try one of them on. It'd be marvelous to be inside that lot. I think anything like that from that sort of age – the idea of being totally encased – appealed to me.[10]

This may be seen as an unusual 'prop' to draw upon – not everyone recalls armour so vividly! But we all possess a litany of props, in actuality and in word, which helps us construct our stories. Actual 'props' are deposited in a trail behind one as a life is lived. These objects need interpreting in order to recall a sexual story. Documents galore can help one come to see the sexual life one has lived: diaries which highlight dates, people known, passions done and over; address books which list friends and lovers long since forgotten; letters which freeze suspected intimate feelings; photographs albums which display family rituals, holidays with former partners or brief encounters; and most recently videos which may recall a marriage ceremony, but can equally recall past sexual acts. None of this can be *the* life but they can all be taken as *signs* of it. Only the most ardent biographer would search these sources in detail but many a life can raid them intermittently to establish a truth. An array of possessions may also help accumulate a sense of who one is sexually: a record or piece of music which can elicit a story of passion lost; a pile of pornographic magazines or romantic novels which solidify a well-known fantasy into a sexual story; the clothes worn on a celebrated sexual occasion may even bring back the smells, the touches, the feelings so closely identified with a sexual moment; and, for some, boxes of favourite fetishes which signpost people and feelings for a hitherto untold story or one that can only be told in darkest silence.[11]

Generalised community   Borrowing from George Herbert Mead,[12] these are the most abstract expressions and images around a life. They are all kinds of community narratives, the 'grammars of the self',[13] and even the 'fictional worlds'. Community meanings – including fiction – may provide ways for imagining the tales of the erotic life, as indeed may all 'artistic objects' from film to video and from opera to pop music – all stuffed full of romance, m desire and danger.[14] For many – more so in the past than today – theological tales weave their webs through a whole biography: the madonnas and the whores, the pure and the sinners. Likewise the philosophers, and even the social scientists, may hurl into the world metaphors, images and rhetoric through which lives can subsequently be organised: the damaging 'sex drive' metaphor; the cliché that sex is 'really natural'; the convictions that 'all men are like this and all women are like that'; the massive sexual characterologies – transvestites, transexuals, sadomasochists and the rest – that have been invented in the modern period. Anthony Giddens has highlighted this 'recursive' nature of contemporary 'institutional reflexivity', suggesting how social science now plays a critical role in feeding back into the cultures from which it originally sprung, providing key context for changes in lives and societies. He writes of the Kinsey Reports:

> Like others following on, [the Kinsey Reports] aimed to analyse what was going on in a particular region of social activity, as all social research seeks to do. Yet as they disclosed, they also influenced, initiating cycles of debate, reinvestigation and further debate. These debates became part of a wide public domain, but also served to alter lay views of sexual actions and involvements themselves. No doubt the 'scientific' cast of such investigations helps neutralise moral uneasiness about the proprietary of particular sexual practices. Far more importantly, however, the rise of such researches signals, and contributes to, an accelerating reflexivity on the level of ordinary, everyday sexual practices.[15]

Perhaps the most neglected area for understanding story construction is the most obvious: stories can breed stories and fictional worlds can help fashion personal narratives. Nelson Goodman, in his *Ways of Worldmaking* has written how 'Fictional worlds are metaphors for real worlds, metaphors that may themselves become literal descriptions. Fictional worlds make, unmake, and remake real worlds in ... ways that may be recognised as real'.[16] Consider the lesbian community and its fiction. Since the 1970s the lesbian novel has changed: the secret and somewhat morbid world of *The Well of Loneliness* has become transformed into *Ruby Fruit Jungle*, which in turn changed into the more sleazy world of *Macho Sluts*.[17] Bonnie Zimmerman, in a marvelous study of this fiction and its changing shape, shows how lesbian communities, selves and relationships have shifted side by side with shifts in the fiction about them. At one point sad; at another clear and political; most recently, more complex and contradictory. She argues:

> fiction has provided a way for writers to shape the fantasies, politics and everyday experiences of the lesbian community. We write (and read) to reflect our realities, but also to create new realities. .... Our fiction continually sets up a version of reality and then pulls it down again. We write, and rewrite, and rewrite once more the stories and myths of the dominant culture and our own alternative lesbian culture. The result is a complex and contradictory literary genre.[18]

It is in these texts that many women have found their lives: text, life, story and culture are deeply intermingled. The same is true for many other experiences: black feminists have created and discovered their voice through fiction[19] while the new mythopaeic men's movement has turned to archetypes as a source for understanding.[20] Here there is often a direct turning to myths, fairy stories and folklore from the past in order to assemble the modern story: suggesting the strength and continuity of much story telling. In the early 1990s, and primarily in North America, the new men's movement plundered a series of fairy stories in order to help assemble texts about the real nature of an essential masculinity that was being lost and destroyed in a modern (feminist world), where boys were no longer gaining access to the stories of their inner strength. Robert Bly's celebrated *Iron John*, for instance, draws explicitly on the 'Iron Hans' fairy tale – 'first set down by the Grimm brothers around 1820, this story could be ten or twenty thousand years old':[21] it has become the basis for the 'wild man' movement. Likewise, Robert Moore and Douglas Gillette's *King, Warrior, Magician, Lover* taps into four major 'archetypal' stories which will help men to discover their 'mature masculine' powers. The title says it all.

Most intimate experiences now have their fictions, which may be cherished and appropriated into the daily stories of life. Some of these can be controversial and assume an almost subterranean existence, having to be dug out by those on the sexual fringe.[22] Even the more marginalised erotic groupings – the paedophiles and the sadomasochists for instance – have their own fictions from which the story of a love or a life may be partially built. A small but salient 'paedophile' literature can provide a core of comprehension for would-be and actual paedophiles. Bryan Taylor has described the work of the 'Uranian poets' – including F.E. Murray, W.B. Nesbitt and Ralph Chubb – as the basis for constructing 'guilt-free pederastic sex'.[23] In the collections of many paedophiles are found books on the themes – some surely for erotic titillation, but many also because they enable the reader to 'find himself' in the text. A sense of community of belonging. The popularity of Thomas Mann's *Death in Venice* – book, film, opera – in part links to a wide community of association: Tadzio is many a pederast's dream, just as Lolita is the tale of many a heterosexual male's story. Books, films, opera – all can be drawn upon in assembling the sense of a story and a life.[24]

Significant others[25]   These are the key folk – the most influential ones – whose stories can be drawn upon in building your own. Parents tell you what you were like as a 'baby', peers rehearse significant events of your school-days, a spouse reminds you what you were really like before marriage, a lover assembles your erotic nature in a sweaty post-coital talk. Again, none of this is *the life*, but it is the very stuff for assembling the sexual biography. The tales that significant others give may be amongst the most fundamental shapers of a life story.

Consider another man interviewed in the late 1970s, Gavin. He was a man who specialised in making straitjackets for the 'bondage' market. A new significant other to emerge in his story was the long-since dead escapologist Houdini:

> since being a child I've been interested in Houdini, the exploits of Houdini and the like. I've always grabbed any opportunity that crossed my path to experiment with that sort of thing if I found anybody else who was interested. Since being a kid I've always had tying up sessions and things like that. I was always interested but could never find books on Houdini in the library – if there were any they were always out. So I did some research on Houdini whilst I was in America and wrote a little on it . . . and I went to see a couple of escape artists, and said I want to see you get out of a straitjacket, I want to talk about the rope tie challenges and how Houdini got away with them for 26 years.

Here it is the dead that haunts a life and helps write its story. But the living can do it just as well.

Strategies of tellings

'Motivations'   Stories need plots, sequences of time and characters. But the thread that typically holds them all together is an underlying sense of motivation – what 'pushes' people to do this or that. A key element in building modern personal stories around sexuality is the location of a motivational well – a source point for explaining what is going on, who one is, why one is the way one is. For many societies, this motivational well has been a religious and spiritual one – the sexual life is explained through priests and religious texts, and stories are carved out of this.[26] This is still true for many modern stories, but in the increasingly secular world there are many other sources of explaining a life: therapists and therapy text provides a storehouse of motivational explanations, as do 'experts' of all kinds.

One of the key motifs in understanding sexual story telling is to grasp the underlying motivational plots. 'Recovery tales' for instance are held together by a model of 'dysfunctional families';[27] many lesbian and gay tales are organised through an implicit biological determinism;[28] and the stories of rapists are organised through motivational stories of powerful sex drives, drink, compulsion and emotional problems.[29]

'History', 'memory' and 'nostalgia'   A crucial strategy of story telling is the creation of a sense of a past which helps to provide continuity and order over the flux of the present. At the community level, this may be a sense of history and the mythologies this may bring; at the more personal level it raises issues of 'recollection', 'reminiscence', 'memories' and 'nostalgia' – all of which help to organise such a past.[30]

At the personal level, 'memories' may be seen as our *best stories*. They are the people, events, feelings, ideas that we have 'indicated' to ourselves so often before that they ring very true. They are the repetitive and ritualised tales that we 'indicate' to ourselves about ourselves. As Bruner has remarked in a wider context:

> I believe that the ways of telling stories and the ways of conceptualising that go with them become so habitual that they finally become recipes for structuring experience itself, *for laying down routes into memory*, for not only guiding the life narrative up to the present but directing it into the future.[31]

We all have our good stories that we like to tell often. But they can come to assume an autonomous life of their own – the story takes on a certain style, an embellishment, which may be much removed from what actually happened. A 65–year-old paedophile recalled this childhood fairy story often: it was a major 'memory', frequently rehearsed before me:

> the earliest I can trace in my mind – a tender age I cannot determine – an age when I would be reading such stories as Hansel and Gretel . . . I had a picture book in which there was a picture of a very beautiful boy, and a girl for that matter. Now you know the old story: the old woman took these children and locked them up in their separate cages. I think she intended to eat them. And so she used to fatten them up and kept going and looking at them through the bars. And I was fascinated by this picture of the boy, and I remember thinking, well now I wish I was the old witch. . . . I'm not a bit interested in the girl, but I'd like to have the boy. I wasn't thinking I'd like to eat him; I was just thinking how nice it would be to possess him. It's something that would belong to me. . . . I don't think I was even old enough to think about sex, but I had this possessive

feeling and I think this feeling has been with me all my life. This desire to possess.

This story occurred in several interviews, repeated more or less verbatim. Yet it speaks of a time sixty years in the past. What brings someone to recall an event like this, out of a myriad of childhood experiences? It may be, simply, that it was powerful, shaping, formative and hence memorable. But it may be that stories once told become more tellable, more likely to assume an autonomy of their own, irrespective of their original significance. They may come to 'keep the wolf of insignificance from the door'.[32] There is a 'functional autonomy of stories' by which the story comes to assume an organising life of its own, independently of its initial source or rationale.[33] The significance may lie in the repeated telling of the story of the past.

But memories may be more than just the properties of individuals. There is also *social memory*. As one commentator remarks: 'the important issue . . . is why historical actors constructed their memories in a particular way at a particular time.'[34] This is a memory which is attached to social groups – the common stories talked about and heard within particular groups that often come to have a life of their own. Oral testaments, books, ceremonies all come to help in the construction of this 'memory'. This is often recognised and seen as centrally a feature of tribal/primitive societies dependent upon an oral culture, but it is clearly also true of many contemporary groups, communities and social movements. The gay and women's movements, for instance, come to develop their own folklore of stories which get transmitted in part from generation to generation, complete with ritualistic days and marches – Stonewall, Gay Pride, Aids Awareness, etc. – which help to provide a sense of shared history.[35] Many sexual stories of the current day build out of these 'social memories'.

Creative moments   All of the above certainly help fashion the stories that are told – they provide antecedents and causal constituents in the making of stories. But to focus simply on these is too mechanical and misses something important: the creative moment, the 'magic in motivation', the 'genuine experiential creativity' in telling stories.[36] Many stories are indeed mechanically rehearsed and repeated, and become clichéd very quickly. But others have a spontaneity, an emotional freshness that makes a story *new*. Many of the sexual stories that I have witnessed or read in preparing this book have had a rehearsed quality about them, a sense of having been there before. But others are born out of struggle and creativity.

READING AND CONSUMING SEXUAL STORIES

During my own research, I became increasingly aware of how my subjects had assembled aspects of their stories from a sprinkling of sources: psychiatric accounts, newspapers, films and plays, as well as the classic text of 'psychopathia sexualis'.[37] Richard's story given at the start of this chapter is full of such references. Given the intense secrecy that has surrounded the lives of the sexually different, this searching for narratives is hardly surprising. Here are two illustrations:

> I must have been 23 or 24 when I bought Hirschfield in Praed Street. I took it off the shelves and – very embarrassing – bought it. Two or three pounds – a lot of money in those days. And then I began to realise that there were all sorts of activities that were deviations [showing me the book!]. This was the one I mentioned to you. I was just looking at the paragraph there about transvestites and their various aspirations, how some of them want to be maids or governesses or ladies of high society. . . . But until then I didn't put a name to it, I just knew I'd like to dress.

Cedric gathered his information from the sex magazine *Forum*:

> Until the magazine began to publish letters like that [on urolangia], I had no idea at all that kind of thing interested anybody at all. The letters quite undoubtedly show that people are interested, but whether they're fact or fantasy, or how much of each, it's quite impossible to say.

Going further, many self-defined transexuals and transvestites sounded as if they could run literary courses on their experiences – being fully aware of the relevant autobiographies and more famous case studies. Indeed, in the case of transexuals, this is carried to extremes, for it is often only by incorporating the 'textbook accounts' into their life that they can become eligible for transexual surgery. At its most extreme, it is a 'con game' – learning the best story to fit the part. As one transexual patient has remarked to his therapist: 'When I assumed the feminine role, I really researched and studied for the part, and in essence I have conned you and otherwise charmed you into believing me.'[38] More generally,

> Unlike the old medical saw that claims the last time you see a textbook case of anything is when you close the textbook, we began to see patients that appear to be nearly identical – both from a subjective and a historical point of view. . . . Soon it became conspicuously and disturbingly apparent that far too many patients presented a pat, almost rehearsed history, and seemingly were well versed in precisely what they should or should not say or reveal. Only later did we learn that there did and does exist a very effective grapevine.[39]

One of many intriguing accounts of the textual reconstruction of a sexually different life comes from the book-length reflection of a Danish feminist, Maria Marcus, who places herself into the difficult (especially for feminists!) category of masochist. Her entire book – *A Taste for Pain* – can be read as voyage of self-reflection on the texts she has read around sadomasochism. Starting early with Fabricus-Moller's book on perversion – 'the description etched itself on my memory. It was the first description of its kind I had read in a serious book'[40] – it continues through Freud, Kinsey and the rest, a path well trodden by twentieth-century pursuers of the sexual truth of their lives. As Marcus says of these earliest readings:

> the most important thing I had gained was the simple matter of having acquired a name. So I was *something definite*. I was included in a definite category. I had my own place. The drawer I belonged in didn't smell quite so nice as the others, but it was a regular drawer with a label on it. In some way or other, this seemed comforting, a kind of acknowledgment. Being given a name seemed to be the first act of consciousness-raising, as if a whole disorganised mess of granules had gathered themselves into a solid picture, not only something definite, but also something *special*, something not really as it should be. Not quite like a crime, but something close to it.
>
>   I consulted many more books, wanting to know much more.[41]

Marcus takes her readers step by step through the literature that she, like so many of the sexually different, explored. Finding those authors who saw it as normal; looking out for the statistics on incidence; scanning pictures to find herself; looking at the way in which 'childhood experiences bound up with humiliating sadistic forms of punishment have been the cause'; and finding new terms for herself – 'algolagnia – for a moment I felt homeless, but then I saw I was surrounded by all my usual friends'.[42] It is through this long cultural searching of texts that she slowly comes to assemble her masochism, and her story of it – now available for others to consume. What Marcus's tale – and those of many others – also signposts is the deep interconnection between the production of stories and the consumption of them. Marcus keenly consumes the production of others – of Krafft-Ebing and de Sade – in order to produce her own text. There is a circle of text production and consumption at work.

SEXUAL STORY TELLING AS COMMUNITY BUILDING

The proliferation of sexual stories, then, is connected to a proliferation of sexual consumption: stories are not just told, but consumed – read, heard, watched, bought.[43] 'Sex sells' records, books, films, videos, magazines, newspapers and paperbacks; and the production of stories I have outlined above is connected to their consumption. Often this very consumption is closely and directly linked to production: we consume stories in order to produce our own; we produce stories in order to consume them. Stories can be appropriated in a multiplicity of ways.[44]

So far, through the words of Osbert, Cedric, some transexuals and Maria Marcus, we have heard a little from the readers of sexual stories and how they can craft the tales of others to be in part the tales of their lives. But such reading/consuming is rarely an isolated or wholly capricious act. 'Readings' are socially patterned: even when done alone, we 'read' media from pre-established experiences of sex, of marriage, of violence, and from pre-established positions of gender, of class, of race, of sexual interest; and often we 'read' our stories in the company of others. Women who have experienced violence in their lives may read violent sexual stories in a more subtle, complex, demanding and concerned way – with a much greater degree of sophistication in interpretation than those who have not experienced such violence.[45]

The media is increasingly generating its own fictive communities, interpretive communities, communities of memory.[46] Here, people consuming media come to identify with a social world or community without any direct face to face relating. Media 'audiences' hence become sources for sensing new communities and new social worlds – sharing common stories, icons, memories. One paedophile, for instance, writing to a house journal for paedophiles in the late 1970s sensed this community very strongly:

> Being paedophile is a lonely business, but I don't need to tell most of my readers that. However it was with a rare sense of communion with our members that I settled down to watch Mark Lester in 'Eyewitness' one Sunday evening last month, and the feeling was repeated the following evening with the screening of 'Walkabout' starring Lucien John.
>
> Why communion? Well, it's not often that you can say with a fair degree of certainty that you know exactly where ninety per cent of our members are at a particular time, and moreover you know exactly what they are doing! ... somehow I think we were all hooked there. Oh, if only we could have got a thirty second advert for PIE on the telly that evening, our membership would have multiplied one hundred fold.[47]

This takes a sexual interest as the basis of a sensed community. It is still a solitary tale but one linked to shared community.[48] Increasingly, however, the stories themselves are not such isolated tellings but are mass-produced and mass-consumed stories. Indeed, much sexual story telling in the modern period has moved out of the local and private zones into a more public world of mass consumption. They have been 'mediasised' – infused into the symbolic work of public communications.[49] The 'self help' writing industry has made this process almost a commonplace. Thus, self help manuals – *Men Who Can't Love, The Peter Pan Syndrome, The Wendy Syndrome, Women Who Love Too Much, What Every Woman Should Know About Men* – are written to tap a new secret problem, but in turn generate more and more 'lookalike' readers and writers. Colette Dowling, author of the best-selling *The Cinderella Complex* saw her book as a way of overcoming loneliness: 'Maybe if I described the experience I would find there were others out there like me. The idea that I might be an anomaly, some kind of helpless, dependent misfit, alone in the world, was horrifying'.[50] The book went on to be a bestseller, and from what we know of consumer studies of such books became important in many (women's) lives as a source for their story. The story simply couldn't survive without a market. Likewise, Robin Norwood's *Women Who Love Too Much* was written initially as a result of her own experience, but it ultimately went on to spawn a second volume composed of letters from readers who had subsequently identified with her book.[51] A private experience is turned into a snowballing public event with stories of 'women who love too much' proliferating at every turn.

Nancy Ziegenmeyer's biographical account of her rape went on to produce a flood of responses from friends, strangers and 'victims'. As she wrote:

Women who'd been raped last year, two years ago, five years ago, ten years ago, forty years ago. Women who had been raped when they were children, or raped by their boyfriends in college, or raped by men who climbed into windows and held guns to their heads, or raped by estranged husbands who 'had their rights'. Women who had never told anyone, not even their husbands, or their doctors, or their mothers, or their ministers. Women who'd lived in silence with their secret, and had believed they were alone and somehow to blame. Every day, more phone calls, more letters, from farther and farther away. They were all out there someplace, and they were all talking to me.

It was simply the most amazing thing I had ever seen.[52]

Here is the making of a new kind of community of support – one that is not based on locale, or any kind of direct face to face contact, but based on media. Sharing a common experience through books, or television or computers, is one of the most distinctive features of telling sexual stories in the modern world. Stories are told; stories are read; communities are born. But it can all be done at a distance.

On an even grander scale, consider the media event of late 1991: the Anita Hill/Clarence Thomas hearings which were broadcast to a massively engrossed American television audience. Here was the overnight creation of a community of viewers who took sides over an issue which brought the sexual story of harassment into every living room – criss-crossed at every turn with issues of race and racism, gender and feminism. The whole country was galvanised, polarised and turned into a massive speech community where people had to take sides and then told their stories of harassing and being harassed. Through one major symbolic media event, a new community of shared 'harassment stories' could be heard and told, and then retold in new ways. Further, it was not just an American experience; this new audience of reception became global. And it spawned its own industry of publications – telling yet more harassment stories for some people to locate themselves within.[53]

SEXUAL TALES AND SOCIAL WORLDS

This chapter has examined some of the processes involved in telling and hearing sexual stories; but there is a lot more to say. A major theme to have emerged in the discussion concerns the ways in which sexual stories feed into real or imagined social worlds. The examination of narrative on its own lacks depth. What is required, sociologically, is a full return to the social and historical conditions that facilitate the making and hearing of stories. It is this task which the second part of the book hopes to illustrate through case studies of the emergent tales of sexual suffering and sexual survival.

Part II

Coming out everywhere: modernist stories of desire, danger and recovery

I am what I am,
I am my own special creation

(*La Cage Aux Folles*)

In silence secrets turn to lies,
Secrets shared become sacred truth. . .

(Terry Wolveton)

Chapter 4

Coming out, breaking the silence and recovering

Introducing some modernist tales

When did you come out?

The question is inescapable. Every gay man has his story, and his friends and lovers will, sooner or later, ask him to tell it. It is our common bond with one another, uniting the different races, classes, educational backgrounds and other groups that make up the gay community. Whether or not our lives have shared the same experiences, a coming out story stirs a powerful empathy in each of us, and brings to mind our own years of fear and pain. .... Coming Out is not only a personal statement of worth and self-respect, it is a statement of dissent – a voice raised in defense of diversity and genuine democracy.

(Wayne Curtis)[1]

A truly radical feature of feminism has been the permission we have given each other to speak. We understand that through speech we could discover what women were and how we had been constructed; talk and the analysis that followed were the first steps towards change. And so we spoke. We shared our doubts and disappointments, rages and fears; we nurtured the strengths we discovered and the insights that had been unappreciated for so long. We talked about our mothers, our fathers, our lovers or the ones we wanted to have. We sought through the comfort of words to articulate in a collective effort at clarity, what had been vague, confusing, debilitating, and painful. We spoke the unspeakable: we broke the taboo on silence.

(Paula Webster)[2]

The modern world is cluttered with all kinds of sexual stories. Yet one major pattern has proliferated and developed most rapidly in the latter part of the twentieth century. These are the stories of sexual suffering, surviving and surpassing.[3] They have grown from being insignificant to being widespread; they have prefigured major social changes as a result of being told; and – like all good stories – they have been replayed, copied and borrowed over and over again. They are a story of our time. They may by now – at century's end – have started to become somewhat 'tired' or 'clichéd' and new story ways may well be in the making. We shall examine how far this is true in Part III. But in the late twentieth century these pervasive stories were most surely tales whose time had come.

Stories of suffering, surviving and surpassing are personal experience stories[4] which speak initially of a deep pain, a frustration, an anguish sensed as being linked to the sexual. They speak of a silence and a secrecy which may need to be broken. They are stories which tell of a need for action – something must be done, a pain must be transcended. There is a move from suffering, secrecy, and an often felt sense of victimisation towards a major change: therapy, survival, recovery or politics. Often haboured within is an epiphany,[5] a crucial turning point marked by a radical consciousness raising.[6] The narrative plot is driven by an acute suffering, the need to break a silence, a 'coming out' and a 'coming to terms'. These are always stories of significant transformations.

At their boldest, most developed and most 'heroic', these stories are clearly exemplified in the 'coming out' narratives of both lesbians and gay men, in the accounts given of rape and sexual abuse by victims and survivors and in the anguished tales of sexual co-dependents, dysfunctional families and love and sex-addicted personalities on their therapeutic voyages of recovery. There are major and important differences between these experiences, but there are also striking parallels between these stories – and indeed many others that have followed in their wake. They constitute a recognisable pattern, form or genre in the modern world, but – as we shall see – have their roots in classical stories of redemption and transformation. Nevertheless, in their current manifestations, these are stories that were largely unheard before the mid-twentieth century. Now they are everywhere. Ultimately my concern is to ask: how did this happen?

The narrative tells of a form of suffering that previously had to be endured in silence or may indeed not even have been recognised at all. The stories always tap initially into a secret world of suffering. They proceed to show the speaker moving out of this world of shadows, secrecy and silence – where feelings and pains had to be kept to self and where tremendous guilt, shame and hidden pathology was omnipresent – into a world which is more positive, public and supportive. There is a coming out, a shift in consciousness, a recovery through which a negative experience is turned into a positive identity and a private pain becomes part of a political or a therapeutic language. There are often less 'heroic', more banal stories that are told in this mode, but here I wish to get clear what I see as the strong cases: those of rape stories, coming out stories and recovery stories.

Rape stories   Many, many women and quite a few men have experienced forced sex against their will throughout history. But it has quite commonly passed 'unclaimed' and 'unnamed'. Sometimes it has simply been *unrecognised* – much marital rape until very recently was simply not recognised as such by law, and only very recently has acquaintance or date rape come to be recognised as forced sex.[7] Very often, the experience has been *denied* by the victim – much rape is so painful that the victim may repress all knowledge of it. But even when it has been recognised for what it is, the stigma of being raped or abused may be sensed as so great that it has been kept *silent*. Husbands and partners could not be told for fear that it reflected in some way on the woman's behaviour. Police and courts could not be told for fear, notoriously, that the woman might be put through a second rape – probing physically and emotionally the woman's very being to see if her claim was 'really true'. Rape stories, then, were once hard to tell. They still are. But over the past twenty years a new story has become more and more heard, more and more visible. This takes the initial suffering, breaks the silence around it (usually with the help of other women) and then uses the traumatic experience as a mode of radical change – to become a survivor. A leading feminist writer on rape, Susan Griffin, captured the changing story at the end of the 1970s, and it is worth quoting her at length, as it captures this whole process at work:[8]

> To believe something about oneself (or of others that one has power over) is to help to make it true. . . . Hence this movement of disbelief, in which women formed a kind of mental energy wave and began to unburden ourselves of any notion that we liked suffering or oppression, was a radical act, a transforming act. Even the act of naming our suffering as oppression transformed us. The more we believed we did not like suffering, the less we found suffering, of the sort that is inflicted on one being by another, tolerable. We allowed our anger over the infliction of pain to be expressed and in that expression found more of the truth of our feelings. . . .
>
> In our actions we went right to the sorest wounds. The stories we heard of women who, after being raped, were hounded by the police in a kind of inquisition as if the woman has provoked the rape, created a terrible pain in us. We moved to act there, to stop the bleeding there. After numerous speak-outs were held, in which women stood up and told of having been raped, and then abused by the police and the judicial system, after giving ourselves the so desperately needed time to speak about a long-hidden injury, we worked to change these more outrageous injustices inflicted on us by the very system which claimed to protect us.
>
> Hence a body of listeners and seers became, as part of our movement, an institution. We created rape protection centers. Women sat and listened as another woman who had just been raped told her story. *She was heard.* And this was healing of a festering wound, even to those of us who had never been raped, because such is the nature of a community or a movement. We all suffer what the others do in our minds.
>
> And so we have centers for the care of rape victims and in many places police procedures have been changed. In other places, they are changing. (And in many places the old wrongs are repeated.) And then we moved also to change the courtroom procedures and the laws. That old practice whereby the woman who was raped was scrutinized in the courtroom, the history of her personal relationships brought in as evidence that she was not in essence rapeable, was changed because of the feminist movement in many states.[9]

Susan Griffin wrote this in 1978, and it captures the link between telling stories, a cultural moment and a politics that helps structure a new form of rape survival. Despite the changes she recognises as being so powerfully produced by woman's experience, rape still goes on and it still remains a physical and emotional pain. But these new stories do seem to have played a positive role in the life of many women. The silence has been, however partially, broken. The women's movement has hurled into the world new stories – in books and docudramas, in chat shows and newspaper articles, in pamphlets and films, in marches and 'Take Back the Night Demos' – that have at least started the process of turning rape suffering into rape surviving, and maybe, eventually, rape surpassing. But it is a new story – scarcely twenty years old. It is now heard everywhere and it has transformed the late twentieth century approach to rape. It is these stories and their reception that will concern me in Chapter 5, where a main focus must be why and how this new story emerged.

'Coming out' – lesbian and gay stories   A second major example of stories of sexual suffering concerns lesbian and gay 'coming out' stories. Although same-sex experience probably exists universally across time and space, the notion of 'the homosexual' is a very modern thing. The term seems to have been invented around 1867 by a Belgian doctor, Benkert; and even though there were clearly secretive homosexual networks and cultures throughout much of the twentieth century, it is not really until the advent of a host of political activities in mid-century – symbolically linked to Stonewall and the Gay Liberation Front – that the full-blown, public 'gay' and 'lesbian' comes into being.[10] And herein lies the story – similar, but different, to the rape one.

This story is widely recognised as the coming out story. Many anthologies can be found in the lesbian and gay world which document this oh so common experience. For hundreds of thousands of lesbian and gay men during the 1970s and 1980s – it may be changing for the 1990s – this has been the pivotal 'rebirthing experience'. It is a tale told by a few at the start of the century and by millions at its end. It tells initially of a frustrated, thwarted and stigmatised desire for someone of one's own sex – of a love that dares not speak its name; it stumbles around childhood longings and youthful secrets; it interrogates itself, seeking 'causes' and 'histories' that might bring 'motives' and 'memories' into focus; it finds a crisis, a turning point, an epiphany; and then it enters a new world – a new identity, born again, metamorphosis, coming out. It is a story that has been told in fiction, in film, in research, and of course in the daily lives of many.[11]

One of the earliest 'modern' accounts of coming out comes from the pseudonymous Donald Webster Cory, written in 1951:

Since my early adolescence, I have been aware of the homosexual problem. My first awakening was the bewildering attraction that I felt for a young man a few years my senior. I had never been taught that there are men who are attracted to other men; no one had attempted to seduce me or to tempt me. I knew that I felt a drive, of a vague and troublesome character, toward gratification with one other person. I wanted to be near him, to embrace him. . . .

In the years of later adolescence and early manhood, I studied myself and those like me, delved into every volume of literature which might shed light, sought to understand why I could not be like others. I was deeply ashamed of being abnormal and was aware of the heavy price that must be paid if anyone were to discover my secret.

I traveled through many stages in the years that followed. I struggled against my homosexuality, sought to discipline myself and to overcome it, punished myself for failures to resist sinful temptations. . . . Then, revolting against the struggle, I developed many friends in homosexual circles and alternately felt myself trapped by a human tragedy to which I could never adjust, or blessed as one of the elite of the world. . . .

Today . . . I sit down to relate what it means to be a homosexual.[12]

Thirty years later, an American teenager, Aaron Fricke, tells his story in a book-length account. From being the darkest of secrets, his story moves to the situation where he is 'out' and takes his lover to a much-publicised high school prom. Of his earliest experiences, he writes:

When I entered high school I was completely isolated from the world. I had lost all concept of humanity; I had given up all hopes of ever finding love, warmth, or tenderness in the world. I did not lie to myself, but I did keep other people from thinking I was a homosexual . . .

I retreated into my own world . . . the only goal left to me in life was to hide anything that could identify me as gay . . . self-doubt set in. I thought that anything I did might somehow reveal my homosexuality, and my morale sank even deeper. . . . I withdrew from everyone and slowly formed a shell around myself. Everyone could be a potential threat to me. I resembled a crustacean with no claws. . . . This shell helped me protect my secret, but it could not protect my feelings from the prejudice I constantly encountered . . .

I knew no openly gay people. There was no one to tell me about gay literature. . . . But early in the summer after tenth grade, at the height of my weight problem, my parents and I took a day trip to Provincetown . . . in the distance, I heard a faint cry of voices calling in unison . . . a group of clean-cut people were moving towards us. At first I could not read their enormous banner, but soon the words came into view: PROUD TO BE GAY. And they were chanting PROUD TO BE GAY. PROUD TO BE GAY. I was astonished by the force with which they screamed their claim. Could these people really be 'proud to be gay'? I wanted so badly to rush up to the group and chant with them.

And at the end of his book, after coming out, he concludes:

I will be reminded *daily* of the torments gay people face. My writing will hopefully serve as a vehicle to make others more actively aware. I will remind heterosexuals that we are human. And I will remind gay people struggling for a positive identity that, in the words, of André Gide: 'It is better to be hated for what one is than loved for what one is not.'[13]

Recovery tales　A third version of the sexual suffering story has also proliferated in recent years. Here all manner of new sufferings have been discovered in a personal experience narrative: the women who love too much, the men who cannot love, the sex compulsives, the dominant women and the submissive men, the women with G spots and the men with sexual dysfunctions. These new stories have been in silence until recently: millions of women presumably have long been suffering with dysfunctional men. But now through the media of paperback bestseller, television chat show and therapy groups, these stories have 'come out'. And again, the suffering – once identified – can be transformed, through reading, through talk, through therapy, into a new awareness, a new identity, a positive story. Again, this story differs from both the rape story and the coming out story, but it also has features in common. I turn to a fuller consideration of recovery tales in Chapter 7. But the remainder of this chapter aims to look at both the similarities and differences in these stories.

THE GENERIC ELEMENTS OF MODERNIST STORIES[14]

In listening to stories, one very common concern has been to extract the generic elements found in the tale. Attention is focused upon the underlying patterns of narrative, their functions and structures. Most famously, Vladimir Propp did this for the Russian fairy story, and it has led to a whole tradition of formal literary analysis – reducing stories to their underlying structural elements. At a very simple level, all the stories I have located above can be shown to have three common elements: there is always a *suffering* which gives the tension to the plot; this is followed through a crisis or turning point or *epiphany* where something has to be done – a silence broken; and this leads to a *transformation* – a surviving and maybe a surpassing. Rape stories, recovery stories and coming out stories all minimally have this in common.

It can be taken further. Recently, in the tradition of Propp,[15] Elsbree has suggested that there are really only a very limited number of generic plots to be found in modern stories. Indeed, he suggests a mere five basic plots: *taking a journey, engaging in a contest, enduring suffering, pursuing consummation, establishing a home*. In their classic, condensed and archetypal forms, they look like this:

1　The Journey, as in *The Odyssey*, *Tom Jones*, Rousseau's *Confessions*, White's *A Boy's Own Story*. There is a progression through stages – most frequently starting in earliest childhood memories, working through various crises on the way to something. 'The initial momentum is the need to break away, or to find a new home, identity or commitment, or to return to a remembered place.[16]

2   Enduring suffering, as in *King Lear*, *Waiting for Godot*, *One Flew Over the Cuckoo's Nest*. There is a struggle: life has not been easy; all sorts of difficulties have been strewn along the journey; agonising, soul-searching moments of great intensity are retold. 'What was done to merit such agony or hardship? Could it have been prevented? What meaning can the suffering have? What can or must be done to escape it? At what cost?'[17]

3   Engaging in a contest, as in *Taming of the Shrew*, *Women in Love*, *The Prime of Miss Jean Brodie*. This suffering is overwhelmingly accounted for in terms of 'enemies': somebody out there does not like me or has done me wrong. This enemy becomes the target of attack. A struggle ensues. 'Here the action is the winning of the contest, or, the coming to terms with the opponent. . . . Its object is to clear the ground for, assert, or protect the integrity of the self.'[18]

4   Pursuing consummation as in *The Iliad*, *Candide*, *War and Peace*. A goal has to be established, and sometimes it is only dimly sensed at the outset. Once established, however, it will be strongly pursued; one cannot be fulfilled until this goal is met. 'Here the basic action is the seeking of transcendence, the obliteration or the abolition of the self.'[19]

5   Establishing a home, as in *To the Lighthouse*, *Robinson Crusoe*. The more optimistic stories finally 'arrive' somewhere – usually in a new identity, a new community, a new politics. All may not be that well; but at least a home has been found at last. 'It is the creation of order out of chaos so that the self becomes possible.'[20]

These more general narrative patterns resonate through the stories of sexual suffering that I have introduced above. Indeed, one reason for their 'success' in the late twentieth century – their widespread appearance – may well be that they speak to much wider human stories that are part of our heritage and which are emotionally identifiable by listeners and tellers. They tell 'grand stories'. Certainly, over the years, from fieldwork, interviews and reading I have heard the elements of these narratives over and over again in the substance of the lesbian and gay coming out stories. Here are men and women engaged on a voyage of discovery to be true to their inner self. The titles of anthologies reveal this: *The Lesbian Path*, *Lesbian Crossroads*, *The Coming Out Stories*.[21] So frequently this journey starts with some early recollection that 'I was different', even a 'freak or a monster'[22] and then proceeds, often for years and years, to explore why this is so. Terrible sufferings are recounted: of sexual desire, of secrecy, of solitariness, of shame. An enemy is created: parents, friends and ultimately the whole homophobic, heterosexist, patriarchal, racist, classist and unbearable 'straight' world! In some stories, it is powerfully contested; in others it forms a silent backdrop for the suffering. Slowly the 'true' nature of one's being is revealed: 'I *am* gay', 'I *am* lesbian'. And from this the task is on to make this inner being more and more the outer being. 'Closets are not for living in.' There is, to quote several titles from an anthology of gay coming out stories, 'the end of a long silence', 'my discovery of me', a 'coming to terms', an 'ending [of] the charade'; one is 'out of the cocoon'.[23] And, despite further difficulties along the way, if one is lucky one will arrive home: coming out, taking on a strong identity, becoming part of a community.[24]

But more. The stories of many rape victims also connect to the same formal elements. Here, most commonly, a woman – or girl, or sometimes a man or boy – is forced into an extraordinarily painful sexual experience which traumatises them and causes great *suffering*. The enemy is clear: the rapist, the abuser, the patriarchal order. The *contest* is on to establish how foul this abuser is. There is a *journey* to get out of this traumatised state – one that may start years after the event, but which cannot be completed till one recognises that 'I *was* a victim' and now 'I *am* a survivor'. A new life may be rebuilt, sex may become possible again, the enemy is dealt with, *consummation* is achieved. A new *home* is established – often with other survivors, or other women. Once again, this says nothing of the enormously complex personal stories behind such narratives; nor can it reveal that in many individual instances the stories will not fit each sub-plot, but only some. But again there is a striking commonality of the tales I have read and heard to the generic one above.

I am pushing my luck to suggest this pattern also fits the recovery story, but it clearly does! Here is a *journey* at work – and usually it follows the famous twelve steps first enunciated through the Alcoholics Anonymous movement which emerged in the 1930s. There is a definite sequence to the journey. There is clearly a *suffering* – that is the core of the plot: to reveal the addiction, the dysfunction at work. The *contest* provides the dynamic to the story: the enemy of the family, or the husband or the partner has to be challenged and changed. From this, through therapy most frequently, *consummation* can be achieved and a new *home* established![25]

Whilst such condensed narratives do no justice at all to complexity, they have a remarkably common ring. Yet gay and lesbian stories and rape stories are not alone in this. As we shall see in a later chapter, the tales of transvestites, transexuals, sado-masochists, paedophiles, child sex abuse victims, the sexually harassed, sex addicts, and many others have all been recounted in a strikingly similar language in the western world over the past two decades.[26] Indeed, whilst coming out, rape and recovery stories may be the *paradigm stories*, they have served as a model for many others to follow suit. Coming out stories are coming out everywhere.[27]

SECRETS, BOUNDARIES AND COMING OUT

As well as having a suffering at the base of these stories, there is also the harbouring of a secret and a silence which may eventually be given a voice, disclosed, brought out of the private world into a public one. Many important issues appear here: of privacy, of lying, of passing, of defences, of exposure, of deceptions, of transparency.[28] Sometimes there is a suggestion that all secrecy is negative and that all secrets should indeed eventually be brought out into the open; but this is far from my point. Personally and socially, secrets can perform vital functions: secrecy may create necessary social boundaries and personal autonomy. They may help build identities, protect us from dangers and regulate intimacies by creating a distance that is sometimes necessary.[29] They may indeed be vital to a sense of our own powerfulness: to tell all, for all to be known, can render people extremely vulnerable. As Sissela Bok has remarked in her important book on *Secrets*:

> To be able to hold back some information about oneself or to channel it and thus influence how one is seen by others gives power; so does the capacity to penetrate similar defences and strategies when used by others. . . . To have no capacity for secrecy is to be out of control over how others see one; it leaves one open to coercion. To have no insight into what others conceal is to lack power as well. . . . Control over secrecy provides a safety valve for individuals in the midst of communal life. . . . With no control over such exchanges, human beings would be unable to exercise choice about their lives. To retain some secrets and to allow others free play; to keep some hidden and to let others be known; to offer knowledge to some but not all comers; to give and receive confidences and to guess at far more: these efforts at control permeate human contact.[30]

Sometimes, then, there are good reasons not to speak which can indeed lead to empowerment. But in the stories that I am considering here, harbouring a secret is more usually seen to be damaging, and it signposts a relative powerlessness. Keeping secrets can 'isolate us from those we love', 'lower our self-esteem', 'contribute to sexual problems' and 'prevent the healing of emotional wounds'.[31] Much sexuality is still engulfed in secrecy, despite the seemingly endless spiral of babble that does now exist through books, talk shows, press columns and the like. *Still a lot is not said.* But in the next few chapters I am particularly concerned with how some sexual stories – once wholly silenced – have started to be said by many. This is the process of 'consciousness raising' and of coming out.

Consciousness raising became a central concern of the early women's movement, whilst 'coming out' – as a phrase – became popular in the days around the creation of the early Gay Liberation Front, during the late 1960s and early 1970s. Indeed, the terms seem not to have been widely used before that.[32]

Consciousness raising started with the student and black movement of the late 1960s, but it 'eventually achieved spectacular success in the women's movement'.[33] Here, women would gather to explore the personal experiences of oppression, telling their stories to each other and in the process gaining insight into their sufferings. Here talking about personal experiences was seen to 'clear out your head; uncork and redirect your anger; learn to understand other women; and discover your personal problem is not only yours'.[34] Coming out was the critical life experience of lesbians and gays during the 1970s and 1980s (there are signs it is becoming less central in the 1990s)[35] and it can be seen to capture four critical processes (which are *not* in a fixed sequence): *coming out personally*, in which a self-conversation emerges which clarifies who one is; *coming out privately*, in which the first steps are made to tell specific others – family, friends, work peers – in delimited spheres; *coming out publicly*, in which many others are now told the story, and indeed it may become public knowledge out of the self's own control; and finally *coming out politically*, in which the story is used very widely as a means of social change.[36]

On a personal level, a dim sense of the story must be told to the self. How easy this will be depends on the cultural resources available to support the story and enable it to be assembled. For many, stories are clouded in defences and repressions which simply do not allow any articulation: environment and support are needed for it to be brought out. During the 1980s the number of sexually abused women (and men) suddenly became phenomenal. There were reports of abuse that had happened decades earlier. But it was hitherto unspoken and often unknown, or in the case of marital rape and 'date rape', the actual experiences were simply not open for recognition.

On a private level, coming out involves problems of disclosure. Here the story is told to a specific other, usually in 'strictest confidence'. In many gay stories, a close friend is often confided in before coming out occurs. Or in the case of recovery stories, a therapist may be told. On a public level, the story comes right out: known to all who would hear. When Aaron Fricke chooses to go to the High School Prom with his lover, the story is available to all. And finally, there is political coming out. For many indeed the very phrase 'coming out' is meant to be exclusively a political one – many of the anthologies of gay politics bring this title to the fore, and it becomes a central issue in the 'Outing' controversy. Rob Eichberg, who established a national workshop on coming out asks all gays to come out:

> If you are homosexual, and 'pass' as heterosexual, I am asking that you disclose your homosexuality and realise that by hiding your sexual orientation you have contributed to the prevailing stereotypes of what it is to be gay and can make a major contribution in changing these stereotypes. If you are heterosexual and know and love someone who is gay, I am asking that you come out as well. You too have supported oppression by not stating that you have a son, daughter, mother, father, cousin, friend or acquaintance who you care about and who is gay.[37]

These four issues of coming out are not in any particular order. It is perfectly possible to come out politically without any of the other processes being at work: much 'political lesbianism' is like this. The story is shouted about male supremacy, women's subordination, and women-identified women long before it is told personally to the self or to close friends.[38] Further, experiencing any one form of coming out does not imply experiencing all the others: a rape victim may tell the police a story but not previously have told it to the self and will not tell the story publicly ('I can't go to court'), or politically ('I was to blame').

DIVERGENCE AND DIVERSITY IN SEXUAL STORIES

Stories breed stories. Twenty years ago the tale of coming out as a gay man or lesbian belonged to gay men and lesbians. Now it has rippled into the coming out stories of all those involved in their lives: as we shall see, parents tell the stories of gay children, children tell the stories of gay parents, gay men tell their story to their old schools or old churches.[39] These were stories hardly heard even in the early 1980s.

That the late twentieth century has witnessed the growth, proliferation and consolidation of new sexual stories around suffering and survival seems unmistakable. But so far the emphasis has been on similarity: tales of suffering that are common to both gays, rape victims and co-dependents. Yet whilst there is a commonality in the stories, there are also crucial differences.

For a start there is a difference in the *sources of suffering.* A simple distinction may be drawn between the *sufferings of danger* and the *sufferings of desire.* In the former, the content of the story is about fear, violence, defilements, degradation: a 'sexuality' is imposed upon a person that they do not want, and the story brings this painful, coercive sex to the forefront. In the latter, the content of the story is about frustration, about thwarting, about damned desires: a story is told which recognises a desire (often from a fairly early age) for some kind of satisfaction in a personal (emotional, erotic, intimate?) life which is persistently thwarted. Whilst there may be similarities in *form* between danger stories and desire stories – as tales of suffering – there is also clearly a significant difference in *content.* At its bluntest, stories of transforming desire may often be distinctly at odds with stories of transforming danger: a politics of 'sexual liberation' straining against a politics of sexism. Indeed, this conflict became the basis of significant splits between gay men, lesbians, women and factions within feminism, from the early 1970s on, and gave rise to the 'sex war debates' (notably around pornography) which polarised 'purity, revolutionary feminists' telling tales of sexual danger, and 'pro-sex, socialist feminists' telling tales of sexual pleasure. This is not the place to rehearse this debate, which has often been extraordinarily heated, except to note that it has helped to push along the diversification of sexual stories available.[40]

There is also a significant difference in the *path of change* in the stories. Although they all seek survival/surpassing/transcendence in one way or the other, some do so in ways that stress an *individual route* – it is individual change, personal growth, or self-actualisation that matters. Others seek a more *collectivist change* – where the route is more overtly political, bringing about change in the wider community. Recovery tales clearly connect more to the former, where some kind of therapy is usually the royal road to salvation. But lesbian and gay stories are much more likely to connect to the latter: for this story, the solution to problems comes out of a strong lesbian and community. The path is much more one of political change. Rape stories often fall between both poles: they certainly require personal growth and change, but the story itself usually sees this as best happening with a wider awareness of the need for social and political change in the workings of patriarchy.

A final key difference centres upon *who is telling the story.* For both the coming out stories and the rape stories, the narrator is the person experiencing the suffering – and their story is not usually co-opted into an expert's story. It is true that some lesbians and gays travel the country with coming out workshops, and some rape crisis centres do employ professionals. But in the main these stories are *participant stories*, untrammelled by the worlds of experts, professionals, elites. This is less true of 'recovery tales': although these also start out life as participants' stories, they much more frequently get caught up in 'expert systems'.[41] There are institutes, courses, video-tapes, manuals of guidance and all sorts of 'experts' professionally trained to work with 'dysfunctional families' and 'co-dependents'. The personal narrative can rapidly become an expert's narrative.

There are then significant differences in the stories, and a final caution is in order. Although it is possible to detect a broad patterning at work, the generic stories I raised above are simply paradigms; they are not meant to capture all those experiences commonly known as 'homosexuality' or 'rape' or 'dysfunctionality'. Rather, they simply isolate one particularly prevalent genre of narrating these experiences: there are, for instance, many same-sex experiences that fall outside of this pattern. Here I am discussing what I take to be a relatively new historical story-form (although there are roots in the past). In the next few chapters, I examine examples of this story with a particular interest in the conditions that made the story possible at this particular moment. In one sense, because the stories fit so well into the widely-held narratives of taking a journey, suffering and finding a home, it is easy to see why they have become so pervasive. There is a fit; they sit well with what we already know. But the question then, surely, is why such stories did not come about earlier? Why did these stories come into their own during the last few decades of the twentieth century in the western world? A little historical background is crucial to an understanding of this – locating the development of new communities waiting to hear these stories.

In the next three chapters I look at the ways in which the stories of coming out as gays and lesbians, the 'breaking the silence' of female rape victims and the recovery tales of the sexually dysfunctional come to flourish during the latter part of the twentieth century. What conditions allowed these new voices to appear, and for their stories to take root? Although at an earlier stage the religious confession, the medical case study and the courtroom testimonies certainly had their role to play in all this, the chief feature of all three experiences by the late twentieth century is that the stories were usually being told *not by the expert voices from above but by the participants themselves from below*. New stories were created through the work of both the gay and lesbian movement, the women's movement and the self help movement which directly challenged the medical and legal stories of the recent past. The professional formal elite worlds of doctors and lawyers had been telling different stories about these 'other's' experiences, but now they came under challenge: gays harangued the doctors so that by 1973 homosexuality was declassified as a 'sick tale', whilst women harangued the courts and the police so that rape was no longer minimised.[42] These are textbook case studies of social movement change where official, dominant stories are challenged.

Although the stories of rape, being gay and recovering are indeed very different in substance, they do have many common features – enough to constitute a basic form of story. They are part of a wider social process facilitating new talk about sex, providing blueprints for many sexual experiences to be modeled upon. I consider these stories and their communities because they have helped shift our understandings of sexualities and serve as paradigms of change around the modern stories of sexual suffering.

Chapter 5

Women's culture and rape stories

I have found my voice. Amen to that.

(Jill Saward in Rape: My Story)[1]

Forty years ago, I was the victim of childhood sexual abuse. I still sleep with a gun under my pillow, get up in the middle of the night to check every noise, and to make sure doors are locked. I thank you for the courage you displayed . . . keep speaking out, perhaps some other person, alone, without the support of a lifemate, needs to hear your words.

(Letter to Nancy Ziegenmeyer in her Taking Back My Life)[2]

Stories of female sexualities have changed dramatically over the past century. In 1890, the lives of most women were largely lodged in the stories told by and about men who simultaneously denied women any autonomous sexuality whilst turning them into obscure objects of desire. Those women's stories that did exist in the world of diaries and autobiographies – which may well have been at that time a more feminine mode of writing – were often lost, silenced or interrupted.[3] Yet by 1990, a generation of women had produced an array of new stories with their own autonomous desires and bodies at the centre. New stories of 'liberating masturbation' and 'female pleasures'; tales of women's erotic fantasy worlds – 'secret gardens' and 'forbidden flowers'; narratives which spoke of 'total orgasm', 'G spots' or desires for 'dominance and submission'; and raunchy tales of 'looking for soldiers'. The change was so visibly significant that some started to speak of 'the feminisation of sexuality'.[4] If ever there was a textbook case of social constructionism – of people constructing and changing sexual meanings[5] – then it is most surely here in the active work of some women, though probably not most, building new stories of the sexual for themselves since the 1960s. A radical reconstruction of women's lives in the western world – but especially North America – starts to appear. Note that I am *not* saying here that whereas women were once repressed, they have become liberated: that would presume a nineteenth-century drive awaiting a late twentieth-century release. I *am* saying that many groups – but particularly feminist groups – struggled to produce new stories about women's sexualities which helped produce a multiplicity of ways for women to be, to relate to and to become sexual. Most significantly, some rescued themselves from stories in which they were simply the 'other', defined by men, male sexuality and the male gaze.[6] Others proceeded to redefine men as the 'other', as in the writings of some 'radical anti-sex feminists' like Sheila Jeffreys, Andrea Dworkin and Catherine MacKinnon.[7] And it is these who most of all heralded the new rape story.

THE CHANGING STORY OF RAPE

The dark side of these new stories was the modern rape story and, along with a host of linked phenomena from child sex abuse to pornography, it became a critical symbol to depict a most dangerous practice. Of course, forced sex and sexual violence towards women (and sometimes men) has probably existed throughout history. But it does not dwell within the same meanings, discourses and stories. Rape is always historically and culturally specific, and how it is understood depends upon a framework of story telling. And rape has a long and classical history of 'being told' as a tale: the Rape of Europa, the Rape of the Sabines, the Rape of Lucretia.

Anna Clark has recently demonstrated these shifting meanings of rape within a relatively short historical time span. Studying rape in England between 1770 and 1845 through media and court records, she suggests how it shifts from being located in a libertine story in the late eighteenth century to being one which located lewd women in the public sphere at the mercy of working-class men by the early nineteenth century. As she says:

> In the late eighteenth century, a libertine discourse permeated slang and masculine popular culture, glorifying rape as a source of amusement, or a way of proving their masculinity to other men . . . in the early nineteenth century, libertinism faded from public view, but continued as a private subterranean stream; instead, men were told to be chivalrous and control their desires. Yet rape only extended to those women seen as chaste.[8]

Stories do not remain static but are lodged in specific (situational, economic, historical) social moments. In what follows, I will suggest several key ways in which both the experience and the stories around rape start to get reorganised from the late 1960s in both the USA and England and how this has provided a model story for other 'defiled groups' to follow.

Early days, early stories   In the nineteenth century, rape seems to have been much less of an issue than it is today for feminists.[9] Then, as now, there were many different factions within feminism, (liberal, socialist and evangelical included),[10] and most of their energy was not devoted to sex, but to the rights of women at work, at home and in the polity. Yet, as Judith Walkowitz, Sheila Jeffreys and others have clearly documented – though from very contrasting perspectives – there were also significant purity crusades.[11] Some of these were scares around sexual violence towards women – the Jack the Ripper murders in London in 1888, for instance.[12]

But more typical of this time was the scare over venereal disease, the abuse of girls, the age of consent and, perhaps most crucially, prostitution, which became the 'symbol of an age'. As Ellen DuBois and Linda Gordon write:

> There is a certain parallel construction between the nineteenth-century focus on prostitution and the modern emphasis on rape. It is remarkable, in fact, how little emphasis nineteenth-century feminists placed on rape. It is as if the norms of legal sexual intercourse were in themselves so objectionable that rape did not seem much worse. Instead, feminists used prostitution as the leading symbol of male sexual coercion.[13]

The 'prostitution story' of this time helps lay out some of the elements that were later to be assigned to rape. For prostitution revealed more clearly than anything else man's defilement of woman. As J. Ellice Hopkins – from whose efforts the White Cross Army and the Church of England Purity Society emerged – asked in a pamphlet entitled *The Ride of Death*:

> For who has driven them [i.e. prostitutes] into that position? Men; men who ought to have protected them, instead of degrading them; men, who have taken advantage of a woman's weakness to gratify their own selfish pleasure, not seeing that a woman's weakness was given to call out a man's strength. Ay, I know that it is often the woman who tempts; these poor creatures must tempt or starve. But that does not touch the broad issue, that it is men who endow the degradation of women; it is men who, making the demand, create the supply. Stop the money of men and the whole thing would be starved out in three months time.[14]

In all these debates, the problem slowly emerges: how to stop male lust and keep women pure? All the problems around sexuality are connected to the man's desire for the woman's body. Instead of keeping it pure – 'The Temple of God, The Holy Fame of Life, The Fountain of Health to the Human Race' – men have turned it into 'the refuse heap of sexual pathology'. At its mildest, it was the recognition by Elizabeth Cady Stanton that 'man in his lust has regulated this whole question of sexual intercourse long enough'. More forcefully, Frances Swiney wrote that 'woman's redemption from sex-slavers can only be achieved through man's redemption from sex- obsession'. The solution to the problem? 'Votes for women: and chastity for men.'[15]

Out of this evangelical crusade against male sexuality many towns in England and America started to develop their own anti-vice organisations alongside elementary support systems for women. Sheila Jeffreys, in a fascinating account of women's campaigns around sexuality between 1880 and 1914, has described Ellice Hopkins's 'grand plan . . . to cover the country in a safety net which would include three types of specialised organisation in every town.' These were Ladies' Associations – to look after girls who were homeless and vulnerable to drifting into prostitution; Vigilance Associations – to serve as watch-dogs for any kind of indecency and to act as prosecutors of sex offenders; and the Men's Chastity

League.[16] A new culture appears to be in the making, struggling to redefine the sexuality of men and women. New communities emerge listening to new stories. In the end, like the prototypical gay culture which we shall also see emerging in the nineteenth century, the culture does not achieve its fuller fruition till the second wave of feminism erupts in the 1960s, accompanied by the full flowering of a mass media able to carry messages more speedily and more globally. And by then, prostitution and venereal disease were no longer to be the central unifying stories around sex. Instead, that function was to fall upon rape, and sexual violence in its myriad forms. However, elements from the past were lying in the wings waiting to assist in assembling the modern story of rape.

The classic rape story   In her study of rape legislation and practice in England, Susan Edwards has documented the male construction of rape laws and medical intervention from 1800 onwards – highlighting the view of woman embodied in such practices. Typically, 'female sexuality was not defined in its own right but was instead regarded as a response to male sexuality. Sexual asymmetry in social, medical and legal relations emanated from these fundamental dissimilarities in genitalia.'[17] At base the man was active, driven by sexual need and justified in 'taking sex' as a right from his spouse. The woman, by contrast, was passive, ignorant and uninterested in matters of sex, and yet willing to submit to her husband's desires. The male was sexualised while the woman was desexualised. Once inside marriage, it was the duty of the wife – that 'angel in the house' as the nineteenth-century story had put it – to please her husband. In England, the Hale doctrine had classically enshrined this 'right to rape' in 1736: 'The husband cannot be guilty of a rape committed by himself upon his lawful wife, for by their mutual matrimonial consent and contract the wife hath given up herself in this kind unto her husband which she cannot retract.'[18] Since the woman was not interested in sex, it could hardly be the case that she wanted sex from her husband. But to submit was her duty. And in a sense this helped turn her into her husband's property (an issue well discussed in the 1970s, but one which was so taken for granted prior to this that it could not even be raised).

But if rape was the natural entitlement of the man inside marriage, what were the conceptions held of rape occurring outside of marriage? For both men and women there were two contrasting stories. The normal man was active sexually and that, while often seen as regrettable, was unavoidable; the abnormal man had excessive desire and was a monstrous sex fiend or pervert, fresh from the pages of Krafft-Ebing. The normal woman was pure and passive and hardly likely to be raped because she would be loyal to her husband and would never be in positions or places where her honour could be at risk; the abnormal woman was a whore – enticing the man, leading him on and then saying no, thoroughly enjoying the forced attentions on her to the point of a deeply rooted masochism! Of course these are simplifications, but they embody images of men and women at work in stories of rape before the feminist critique. Whilst they still remain (especially in the minds of many men), the women's movement has brought about a number of critical changes – creating their own new stories and challenging the older ones wherever they prevailed. Prior to 1970, it meant that much rape could be simply dismissed and not taken seriously: only if the woman was very clearly not a whore and the man was very clearly some kind of pathological freak could a clear case of rape emerge. And this was probably rare.

All this is revealed in the way women were typically handled in the judicial process. Rape laws emerged as the only major laws where the victim was assumed guilty until proven innocent. Typically, for an act of theft or violence, the victim who reports the offence is more or less assumed to be telling the truth. For the rape victim, by contrast, there is likely to be an interrogation to establish her credibility – an interrogation which can go right through the judicial system. The ancient assumption seems to be that you 'can't put a pencil in a moving bottle'; in some way the woman consents. But it often went much further than this. As Susan Edwards says, 'From Hale to Hailsham, it is invariably the case that a model of female sexuality as *agent provocateur*, temptress or seductress is set in motion'.[19] There is a whole branch of criminology – victimology – which has often implicated the victim in their own crime; here it becomes 'victim-precipitated' rape. This may be very blunt – the woman was a 'prick-teaser' and knowingly led the man on; or it may be more sophisticated – the woman's behaviour, dress or speech unwittingly enticed the man to believe she really wanted sex and the rape was a faulty communication. In any event, the victim provokes the rape.

Another dimension of the judicial process was the frequent attempt in the court to assassinate the woman's character. Edwards suggests three major stories are evoked to weaken the woman's case: first, that she was a prostitute – hence as a woman of ill repute got her just deserts; second, that she had in fact a past relation with the accused, and hence really consented; or third, that she had had previous sexual experience – was promiscuous – and hence less likely to be the good girl who was really raped.

All of these factors helped throughout the nineteenth and twentieth centuries to maintain the distinction of good girls – pure, chaste, asexual – and bad girls who seduced, provoked, lied and even enjoyed the attentions of male lust: the madonna/whore story. It was an image also seeping through literature and ultimately film.[20] From the 1970s, however, significant changes took place. Whilst the traditional ideas certainly did not vanish, and are indeed still very prevalent, the second wave of feminism would work assiduously to redefine the issues and stories surrounding the rape experience. As Susan Brownmiller could say by 1975: 'That women should *organise* to combat rape was a women's movement invention.'[21] A new story of rape accompanied this invention.

MODERNISING THE RAPE STORY: AN EMERGING NARRATIVE

Prior to 1970[22] the story of rape was predominantly the province of men: they created laws around it, developed medical theories about it, wrote literature about it. Of course a few women were involved; but overwhelmingly to talk of rape was to enter a world of male stories, a world which drew upon and helped to reinforce the prevailing assumptions about men and women. After 1970, rape was increasingly talked about by women, often the very women who had been raped, speaking in their own personal narratives in books, rallies and consciousness raising groups. The narrative comes to assume a fundamentally different form: the story becomes one of power and gender rather than sex and desire. It was a story of women's lives under male power and regulation rather than a story of male sexual release and woman's provocation. The stories of rape – whilst full of variety – fundamentally shifted.

Change is not usually abrupt. Rather bit by bit shifts started to occur around rape which were to move it from being the province of male talk, male theory and male definitions – the male story – to a position increasingly within feminist discourse, a discourse which in turn shaped the way some men thought about rape.[23] For women living prior to the 1970s, it was probably impossible to find 'texts' that would enable them to locate what might have been dimly sensed as their *own* experiences. But since that time, there has been a constant stream of pamphlets, manuals, theoretical analyses and empirical researches written from within a contrasting range of feminist perspectives that have told a new story. In one of the trail-blazing articles of the early 1970s, 'Rape: The All-American Crime', Susan Griffin captured the blend of personal and analytic when she said:

> I have never been free of the fear of rape. From a very early age I, like most women, have thought of rape as part of my natural environment – something to be feared and prayed against like fire and lightening. I never asked why men raped; I simply thought it one of the many mysteries of human nature.[24]

From the earliest days of the second wave women's movement, rape has been discussed by women in ways that merge the private with the public, the personal with the political. Early books gathered together the testaments of women, and early meetings facilitated consciousness raising.[25] Elements of this new story stretch back to the nineteenth century at least, as we have seen, but in the second wave of the women's movement there was much concern about rape from its earliest meetings. Three important strategies in the creation of the new story were (1) the debunking of myths, (2) the creation of a history and (3) the writing of a political plot.[26]

The first strategy is crucial in eliminating the old story. Until this is effectively undermined, it is hard for the new tale to take root. Thus, many early writings of the 1970s attempt to 'demythologise' the earlier assumptions around rape, taking the form of broadsheets and leaflets which challenge the conventional story-line. The classical story has to be challenged, undone, so the new story can be written.[27] One sample of these myths to be attacked runs like this:

- Victims are young, careless, beautiful women who invite rape.
- Victims are 'loose' women who provoke rapists.
- No healthy woman can be raped, and any woman can avoid it.

- A woman who goes to a man's house on the first date implies she is willing to have sex, and if she refuses is inviting sex.
- Women charge rape to cover accidental pregnancies or to take revenge.
- No woman can do much about rape, so she might as well lie back and enjoy it.
- Rapists are sex-starved men.
- All rapists are sick, or had crazy or sick mothers.
- Otherwise decent men are spurred to rape by the clothing or behaviour of women.
- Rapists act on uncontrollable sexual impulses.[28]

This is a major rhetorical ploy. It takes all the elements of the old narrative and in one sweep undoes them. It provides in effect the tightest, most minimal account of the old narrative structure, and by placing them in a frame of 'myths' immediately discredits them. Indeed, by simply inverting each myth the key elements of the new story are provided: thus, all women are potentially victims and they never invite rape is the inversion of the first myth. The whole list may be followed this way. This is a classical rhetorical ploy: to see that every position is constructed out of a sense of opposition. Stories are not formulated in isolation, but through antagonisms. 'Myth debunking' makes this very explicit.[29]

The second key strategy involves the building of a universal story. Indeed, it was Susan Brownmiller in her pathbreaking, best-selling, now classic 'pop' story of rape, *Against Our Will*, which brought the story to the fore. Synthesising the stories of rape of Huguenot woman in sixteenth-century France, the rape of the Sabine women in early Rome, the rape of black women slaves on the plantations in the southern United States, the gang-bang of the modern Hell's Angels and the mass rape-murders of a psychopathic Boston strangler, she constructed the large-scale grand historical narrative so necessary for the telling of a major new rape story. Her book brings together a past, provides a collective memory and sets an agenda for sexual politics.[30]

Finally, the story turns to a political plot. I will briefly outline some of the themes of this story and then see how the development of story depended upon the growth of both a woman's culture and new identities, which in turn helped strengthen the story, making it more visible and open to more women. As the story changed, so too did many aspects of the social reality of rape. Experience, identity, story, community, politics all co-mingle and feed on each other.[31] Several key features of this developing new story stand out.

First, rape is seen as power and aggression. One key and dramatic act of story rewriting stressed that rape had little to do with sexual drives *per se* and much more to do with power and aggression. This was argued both psychologically and socially. Thus rather than seeing rape acts as simply being motivated by male sex drives or 'lust', it became increasingly common to link it to aggressive or dominance motives. It enabled men to express anger and assert control. Although there are different kinds of rape, there is clearly a prevalent and distinctive pattern in which the whole experience is engulfed in the man's sense of rage. The woman is not even simply a sex-object (though she is surely that), but she also becomes an object of the grossest defilement – to be spat upon, urinated upon, fucked and finally carved up. Sexual motives may well co-mingle and for the victim it is clearly experienced as sexually-linked, but overwhelmingly it is experienced as about power and violence. Susan Griffin's 1971 *Ramparts* article, 'Rape: The All-American Crime', was probably the first widely-read statement of this view. For her rape was 'an act of aggression in which the victim is denied her self-determination. It is an act of violence which, if not actually followed by beatings or murder, nevertheless always carries with it the threat of death.'[32]

Griffin tells her own powerful story. Of how, at the age of 8, her grandmother told her that 'strange men wanted to do harm to little girls'. Of her initiation to sexuality through abusive men – 'every woman has similar stories to tell'. And how, piece by piece, an elaborate array of stories and myths are built up around rape. This original and highly political view of rape initially came from feminists; slowly however it has become almost commonplace in academic research. When rapists are studied, their motives are firmly linked to power.[33] And it is a persistent theme in survivor narratives. Nancy Ziegenmeyer writes of learning this new story in her much-publicised account:

> The most important thing I started to learn during those early days was what rape is and what it is not. What it is not, I heard over and over, is sex. What it is, is violence. The man may use sex, his own and the victim's own, as a weapon against her, just like he'd use a gun: to frighten her, to dominate her, to threaten and terrify. But ultimately what had happened to me was an act of violence, not an act of sex. The struggle for most victims, I learned, was to separate out the two, and to try to remove self-blame and self-doubt from the equation entirely.[34]

It is then a narrative of *overt abuse*, highlighting power and violence. At its most basic and brutal it entails the stark physical horror of bloody bodily pain: cutting, choking, beating, stabbing, throttling, gagging. In the name of sexuality and hate, violators may murder and maim their victims. But even if no blood is drawn the body may be violently abused: it may be penetrated orally, anally, genitally – by any unwanted object, a bottle, a fist, a penis; it may be touched by uninvited and fumbling hands; it may find an unwelcome and stinking tongue inserted into a mouth; there may be the unsolicited wolf-whistle, the lecherous stare from afar, the homophobic slander: all can violate and defile and leave scars in their wake. The range of desecrations is enormous.

A second feature of the new story highlights the extensiveness of the damage done. Rape cannot be taken lightly – ever. For the surface abuse is matched by a *psychological damage*. Whatever physical abuse may be generated (and this may be enormous), these are the surface scars: 'danger stories' always sense a hidden and deeper psychological damage. As Andrea Rechtin says: 'Rape injures the core of your being. You can be robbed and beaten but rape indicates something very primitive and basic to your psychic being.'[35] Of course there is the sheer psychological horror of actual violation – but the psychic pain spreads out in a ripple of questions and worries. What made the attacker choose *me*? Am I in some way responsible? Did I dress provocatively? Should I never have hitched that lift? Maybe I should never have gone out on my own? At least in the past, blaming oneself has led to new anxieties and fears. Perhaps most common though is an experience with a lover, friend, father, husband where a sense of trust in a relationship is ruptured.

For those who actually endure the direct pain of violation, many years of subsequent, sometimes silent, suffering may await them. There is *long-term damage*. For rape, Burgess and Holmstrom have identified this as the 'rape trauma syndrome', suggesting it has an acute phase of disorganisation immediately after the act, but also a longer-term impact affecting the sufferer's lifestyle physically (e.g. genito-urinary difficulties), psychologically (nightmares, phobias), socially (minimal social functioning) and sexually (a fear of sex, an avoidance of men).[36] Similar traumas have also been found with child abuse victims – it has been suggested that it is not unlike the Vietnam survivor syndrome. It is the post-traumatic stress disorder. There is a sense of a close brushing with death and a deep sense of psychic harm that bottles up from within. Some of the women in Russell's study comment:

> I went completely inside myself. I'm only now beginning to come out after five years of intensive therapy. There probably isn't one area it hasn't touched because without a solid family foundation you don't have anything.
>
> (Victim of father–daughter incest at age 15)

> I can't seem to get over it. It's so deep-seated, even now at forty-three I'm still affected.
>
> (Victim of attempted rape by brother-in-law at age 16)

> It had an extremely great effect. . . . Everything that's happened to me since in my life has been a result somehow of that experience.
>
> (Victim of stepfather–daughter incest at age 14)

> It changed my way of thinking. I think now that all men are out there for what they can get. You can't even trust your own brother.
>
> (Victim of brother–sister incest at age 16)

> Sexually I was very messed up for a long time. I feel that I could have ended up in a mental hospital from the experiences. I'm lucky I didn't, but it will affect me forever.
>
> (Victim of stepfather–daughter incest at age 9)[37]

Very frequently this suffering may not just happen once, but repeatedly; wife-battering is often sexually linked and rarely happens just on one occasion. The *daily* threat of violence in many homes is very real to many women. Yet there is also often nowhere to turn. For notoriously, after one act of defilement women may find themselves open to further defilement from people who are supposed to help:

the cop who refuses the woman's credibility, the surgeon who inspects her body, the courtroom officials who cast doubt upon the integrity of her character.

The abuse and the psychological trauma may be extended to create a *pervasive fear*. Pain stretches way back before any such explicit isolation occurs and way forward after it has happened. The new stories tell of a whole culture of fear haunting the minds of many women who may not actually even experience it. Doors are locked securely; weapons are taken to bed; empty public spaces become awesomely fearful. Even the most trivial experiences may be turned into a nightmare. Carole J. Sheffield tells her story of a trip to the launderette thus:

> The concept of terrorism captured my attention in an 'ordinary' event. One afternoon I collected my laundry and went to a nearby laundromat. The place is located in a small shopping center on a very busy highway. After I had loaded and started the machines, I became acutely aware of my environment. It was just after 6:00 p.m. and dark; the other stores were closed; the laundromat was brightly lit; and my car was the only one in the lot. Anyone passing by could readily see that I was alone and isolated. Knowing that rape is a crime of opportunity, I became terrified. I wanted to leave and find a laundromat that was busier, but my clothes were well into the wash cycle, and besides, I felt I was being 'silly', 'paranoid'. The feeling of terror persisted, so I sat in my car, windows up, and doors locked. When the wash was completed, I dashed in, threw the clothes into the drier, and ran back out to my car. When the clothes were dry, I tossed them recklessly into the basket and hurriedly drove away to fold them in the security of my home.
>
> Although I was not victimized in a direct, physical way or by objective or measurable standards, I felt victimized. It was, for me, a terrifying experience. I felt controlled by an invisible force. I was angry that something as commonplace as doing laundry after a day's work jeopardized my well-being. Mostly I was angry at being unfree: a hostage of a culture that, for the most part, encourages violence against females, instructs men in the methodology of sexual violence, and provides them with ready justification for their violence. I was angry that I could be victimised by being 'in the wrong place at the wrong time'. The essence of terrorism is that one never knows when is the wrong time and where is the wrong place.
>
> Following my experience at the laundromat, I talked with my students about terrorization. Women students began to open up and reveal terrors that they had kept secret because of embarrassment: fears of jogging alone, dining alone, going to the movies alone. One woman recalled feelings of terror in her adolescence when she did child care for extra money. Nothing had ever happened and she had not been afraid of anyone in particular, but she had felt a vague terror when being driven home late at night by the man of the house.[38]

A fourth feature of the new story, then, involves seeing this fear as a mode of regulation and control in women's lives. Rape becomes part of an ideology which serves important social functions in keeping women in their place: it is a deeply punitive action which men can hold as a constant threat to women if they were to step beyond the confines of their presumed female role. It 'keeps women off the streets at nights. Keeps them at home. Keeps women passive and modest for fear they may be thought provocative.'[39] Rape is 'man's basic weapon of force against women, the principal agent of his will and her fear'. Susan Brownmiller's *Against Our Will* became crucially famous for this argument:

> Man's discovery that his genitalia could serve as a weapon to generate fear must rank as one of the most important discoveries of prehistoric times, along with the use of fire and the first crude stone axe. From prehistoric times to the present, I believe, rape has played a critical function. It is nothing more or less than a conscious process of intimidation by which *all men* keep *all women* in a state of fear.[40]

This fear of rape – 'the female fear' – has entered public consciousness more and more in recent years. It has been testified to, analytically described, researched. One study suggests six out of every ten women in the USA feel 'very unsafe' or 'somewhat unsafe' being out alone in their neighbourhoods at night.[41] And it haunts the new story.

Brownmiller's argument stretches beyond this and suggests a fifth main shift in rape stories. Tracing the punishments for rape from the Babylonian code to English common law, she shows how typically punishment was usually brought by one man against another for damage to his property – rape was a 'male protection racket'. Women become the property of men – fathers and husbands – who 'own' their virginity and sexuality: if 'stolen', then it is these men who need compensation, retribution and revenge, not the woman herself. 'Rape is simply theft of sexual property under the ownership of someone other than the rapist.' Of course, not all 'sexual properties' are equally valuable: virgins are worth more than whores, and those higher up the socio-economic ladder are worth more than the poor. Gradations of the seriousness of rape are locked into this view of rape as property violation.

This kind of understanding has brought with it a critique of 'rape in marriage' along with a woman's right to compensation in rape cases.[42] Both of these issues signpost very significant change. Most legislation until very recently denied the possibility of rape in marriage – thereby clearly reinforcing the view that a woman has no right to consent to sex in marriage. She must submit to the husband's sexual demands and in a very real sense is his 'chattel'. If rape was simply about coercive sexuality or even violence, there would be no legitimate rationale for excluding marital relations from rape laws. But until the late 1970s in the USA, when the women's movement launched a bitter attack on rape laws along with research to show just how much rape in marriage there was, it was taken for granted that rape was impossible inside marriage. By the early 1980s, about ten states in the USA – including California, Florida, New Jersey, Connecticut and Oregon –[43] had deleted the spousal immunity clause; and in 1980 in England, the Criminal Law Revision Committee – in its *Working Paper on Sexual Offences* – recommended abolition of the immunity clause, arguing that a husband's immunity to rape charges 'does not rest on any sound basis of principle and is in some quarters much resented'.[44]

Finally, in the new stories rape becomes a common feature of everyday life. It is no longer extraordinary but can be found everywhere. Contemporary rape stories increasingly enter discourse as 'the mirror image of our ordinary folkways'.[45] The view that rape is an exceptional act perpetrated by unusual men for bizarre reasons and in peculiar circumstances has been directly challenged. For many years it was 'the crime in the closet', but recently it has 'come out' – a soaring rape rate with a large undetected and unreported 'dark figure' is matched by a corresponding degree of public discussion and concern.[46] Not only has it become statistically common, the analysis of it has increasingly stressed just how 'normal', 'everyday', 'common' and bound up with ordinary everyday life it is. Thus, 'the basic elements of rape are involved in all heterosexual relationships'.[47] There is no reason for surprise, since as Germaine Greer put it: 'A man is, after all, supposed to seduce, to cajole, persuade, pressurise and even actually overcome.'[48] Whilst not all men rape – and neither are all women victims – the institutional expectations of male and female roles actually embodies the imagery of rape: of active dominance and passive compliance. At its most extreme then rape becomes a paradigm for sexism in society.[49] And the rape story is turned into a story of everyday folk in everyday life, a story which no self-respecting soap opera can now afford to ignore.

CULTURES OF RESISTANCE AND SURVIVAL STORIES

Since the early 1970s, then, and largely through the work of the women's movement, rape has been given a new story. No longer is it the story of an unusual sexual occurrence including only the odd pathological man; instead it has come to be seen more and more as a widespread, common experience that embodies power, violence and women as men's property and which creates a pervasive fear for many women.

These ideas have been at the centre of putting rape on to the political agenda, where a new culture of resistance and survival has emerged. Its most manifest sign was the rapid growth of the Rape Crisis Centre movement: of hot-lines, support groups, advocacy, self-defence, 'Take Back the Night' rallies, counselling, campaigning, pressure groups and just plain simple 'angry' women who were not willing to let the rapist – or the legal system – have its own way in 'blaming the victim' or failing to provide justice and support. In the late 1960s there was no such culture; in 1970, a first centre was established in the USA and in 1976, the London Rape Crisis Centre came into being; by the late 1970s, such centres were 'to be found in at least one community of every state in the United States'.[50] Such centres proliferated all over the (largely western) world, wherever women were no longer willing to be helpless victims: a culture of resisting and surviving was in the making. Although the Crisis Centre movement is a diverse one, it has been strikingly innovative and crucial in the reconstructing of the rape experience. Like most such movements, it can be seen as having a long-term political goal, a medium-range goal of lobbying and practical change, and an immediate task of providing support.

The *long-term goals* are preventive ones and seek to change the nature of patriarchal society. This is often too global – some texts like Brownmiller's on the universality of rape under patriarchy can leave a sense of the impossibility of change, and have made some feminists simply 'withdraw'. But many centres have set about challenging the myths about rape, rapists and rape victims – along the lines suggested above – with a view to at least making society recognise the connections between rape and male power, and hence the critical area for social change. Campaigns have brought new areas of rape into focus: 'sexual harassment', 'child sexual abuse', 'marital rape', 'date' and 'acquaintance rape' have all become known about since the growth of the crisis movement, spreading the range of concern. Some have coined generic terms – sexual exploitation, sexual terrorism, the continuum of sexual violence[51] – to further stress the pervasiveness but interconnectedness of the problem.

Middle-range practical goals have included a proliferation of new stories: education tales on self-defence and risk reduction;[52] rewriting the stories told to relevant professional service groups such as police, courts, doctors, social workers – bringing about changes in police interview techniques and medical examinations; advocacy stories which challenge psychiatric and pathological interpretations of 'victims'; innovating changes in treatments for victims – such as the now quite widespread account of the rape trauma syndrome and the linked post-traumatic stress responses (often derived from Vietnam survivors and now freely applied to many groups); and the challenging of court stories which perpetuate the polarised 'madonna/whore' narrative.

But the most *practical and immediate response* of this movement has been to provide support and empowerment to victims: to highlight that 'a woman has the right to choose what happens to her'.[53] The experience of suffering rape, hardly documented before the 1970s, has now been described in great detail. For the London Rape Crisis Centre, it may entail any of the following: shock, loss of control, nightmares, a need to carry on 'as normal', fear, shame, guilt, power-lessness, physical repulsion, depression and anger.[54] This process of making public the rape victim's suffering has been crucial to the generation of a culture of resistance. It parallels the coming out process in the creation of gay culture. Women have moved from a private experience – trapped in pain and guilt – to a more publicly shared one. As Jill Saward remarks in her painful story of rape:

> The trauma associated with rape is very great. Anyone who does not believe that should try living through it. There are definite stages, though nobody really explained that to me at first. That's one of the reasons I want to share my experi-ence. So nobody need feel she is cracking up, or going mad, when she is sitting there feeling the greyness, the nothingness. If someone else has gone through similar feelings there can be some form of reassurance that it is all part of a normal

pattern, however abnormal it feels. . . . Women need to be able to talk about their experience to get it out of their system. Trying to ignore the fact that it's happened can create far more problems. . . . My advice to . . . any woman is simply TALK, TALK, TALK. There has to be someone somewhere who will listen.[55]

Thus at 'Rape Rallies' and 'Reclaim the Night' marches women find a public voice to tell their story. Here is an extract from a rally in 1978 (with eight women wearing masks):

My name is Wanda Carr. I am 40 years old. My husband beat and abused me for years. I shot him. I was acquitted.

ALL: I AM A WOMAN. I FOUGHT BACK.

My name is Inez Garcia. I killed the man who held me down while his friends raped me. I spent nineteen months in prison, my case was three years in the courts. I was found not guilty.

ALL: I AM A WOMAN. I FOUGHT BACK.

My name is Gloria Maldonado. I am 32 years old. When my husband attacked me and our son, I shot him. I was not prosecuted on grounds of 'insufficient evidence'.

ALL: I AM A WOMAN. I FOUGHT BACK.

My name is Virginia Tierce. I shot the man who raped me. I was found guilty of manslaughter. I was granted a retrial. I was acquitted.

ALL: I AM A WOMAN. I FOUGHT BACK.[56]

Here, in the briefest of stories told publicly, lies the strongest of emancipatory claims.

IDENTITY STORIES: VICTIMS OR SURVIVORS

Within this new culture, many women – whether raped, in fear of rape or simply 'aware women' – have forged new identities, found new voices. The massive literature on all aspects of rape has helped provide 'texts' from which a new stronger identity can be forged: raped women have started to 'come out'. Many women in the past kept their rape a secret, often blamed themselves, felt guilty about it, often denied that it had ever happened, and sometimes failed to recognise what had taken place (especially in those areas like acquaintance rape or date rape which had not been publicly labeled as rapes): 'I never told anyone I was raped. I would not have thought that is what it was. It was unwilling sex. Today, at 29, I know it was rape.'[57] 'Well, I was raped twenty-five years ago. I never told *anyone* until now. It was in Germany. He was an American soldier.'[58]

But the existence of a new feminist-inspired culture of rape survival has provided the means for many women to identify what has happened, communicate with sympathetic others about it and to construct narratives to make sense of the experience in much more positive ways. No longer does a woman have to stay with secrecy, guilt and self-blame; instead she can, for a while, build an identity around being either a victim or a survivor, or both. This is an important identity distinction and is embedded in the coming out process. One step in this is for a woman to see herself as not being in any way responsible for the rape, and to see herself hence as a victim. She escapes the blame she was once given. Another (and often later) step is to see herself as a person with control over her responses to the victimisation – to enter a survivor identity, more determining than determined. It is a distinction which can easily be found in the feminist narratives of rape.[59]

Women as victim is a theme which riddles many traditional stories of womanhood. Here, women are 'bound by love', are indeed 'victims of love'. Stories here locate women in a cycle of self-denial, compliance with men, suppression of their own anger, a more general male submission and of 'loving too much'. In the full-blown story, women are indeed masochists. By contrast, the existence of a new women's culture, a new social world, enables identities to be built in new ways as 'survivors'. Here women come out into a survivor world which provides new stories of women's strength and resistance: new meanings, legitimations and rules await that can transform the experience. Many feminist cultures may be seen as a cultures of resistance, organised as a protest against dominant forms which are perceived to be oppressing them. But they are more than that, for they are each concerned with discovering a past that celebrates their experience – a woman's history. A political analysis holds it altogether. As the identity and the culture become stronger, they both justify their resistance and affirm their valid difference. 'Rape stories' help develop a new politics. Talking in the context of 'surviving sexual abuse', Liz Kelly has articulated the links in this political process very succinctly:

> It has been the contention of a number of political theorists that an oppositional political consciousness and organised resistance can develop out of oppressive social relations and conditions ... it involves at least three stages of understanding and action. Individuals must see that the cause of their personal experiences is oppressive social relations. This understanding must be accompanied by a belief that social change is both necessary and possible. Individuals must then come together in some form of collective organisation which is directed towards achieving the necessary stage.[60]

She stresses that there is no automatic move from one stage to the other, and finds in her own small sample of abused women that the 'third stage' had not occurred. 'Very few of the women were involved in collective action to achieve social change.'[61] But, one might add, the new stories are now in place should they wish to do so. Survival stories usually bring with them more positive identities.[62] And indeed, survival stories embraced at one moment by some need not remain as the story of a life: survivors can become post-survivors.[63]

A final caveat is in order. I have been focusing on the *new* stories of rape emerging from within the women's movement, not the old stories of rape which have dominated in the past. Many of the 'classic' stories, indeed, continue to be told about rape, and they are particularly prominent in much of the mass media. Often selecting the most sensational cases involving extreme or untypical features, focusing upon street attacks, 'sex fiends' or serial killers – the 'Railway Rapist', the 'Bible Beast', the 'Dracula Fiend' – they send out highly selective and distorted messages.[64] These classic stories are still pervasive, but there are signs that even here in the heart of mass culture, shifts in the stories are happening. The much-reported case of Nancy Zigemeyer's brutal rape followed by her own self-action in writing a book, making a docudrama and appearing on TV chat shows is part of this change.

PROLIFERATING STORIES, CHANGING STORIES

The 'story of rape' that was given its voice by the women's movement in the early 1970s has now moved out beyond this into much wider communities, creating a rich mine of new, but linked, narratives. A crucial new language has been created through which lives are being lived and transformed. The story is now of a 'continuum of sexual violence' towards women – which moves all the way from the 'lust murders' that receive prominent (maybe too prominent) coverage as sensational stories in the media through a myriad cluster of abusive acts newly named or reidentified: *wife-battering, incest, child sexual abuse, daughter-rape, date rape, acquaintance rape, marital rape, indecent exposure, sexual harassment*; on to a range of 'little rapes' – *wolf-whistles, lookism* and *voyeurism*; and through to a general climate of *sexual fear*. A network of new sufferings, new stories and new groups ripples outwards: *nursery crimes, child sex rings, Satanic abuse, fraternity gang rapes* and *children who molest children*. Such stories become criss-crossed with race: black women speak out about incest, Latinos tell of wife-battering. And eventually it is not just a continuum of violence for women but for men too: *male rape, male sexual harassment, abused boys, male-battering*. And not just heterosexual victims but gays and lesbians too: *lesbian and gay battered partners, same sex-sexual harassment, same-sex rape* and *hate crimes*. Twenty years ago almost none of this had found its voice, and much of it is still silent.[65] All these acts of coercion use sexuality as a means to abuse, pollute and desecrate: they generate enormous sexual suffering. Unsolicited and undesired, sexuality becomes the tool to defile and a source of danger.

The language of sexual danger and defilement is now enormous. Shades of such language existed in the nineteenth-century women's evangelical movement, but it was then a much muter story (as all sexual stories were). Today, however, a multitude of dangers and defilements brings their own biographies, their own chat-show presentations, their own docudramas, their own research programmes. The story is told. And the stories are fed by social worlds and into social worlds to shift along the understanding and experience of sexual suffering as sexual danger. Of course all these experiences are very different – a 'lust murder' is not a 'wolf-whistle', and each unique experience brings its own unique pain. But the power of stories here can clearly be seen. For although the story of another person's sexual danger may not be exactly our story, it provides signs and clues for us to make sense of our pains. As always, sexual stories aid in the creation of a past, a present and an anticipated future – marking out histories, differences, unities and agendas for action.

THE FATE OF A STORY

This then has been an account of proliferating stories, multiplying stories, dispersing stories. Just a quarter of a century ago, the narrative of rape I have been discussing here hardly existed except in private, often hidden, form. But now such stories are everywhere: indisputably in the western world, and possibly being globally transported to much of the rest of the world.

But as such stories proliferate, dividing and sub-grouping into more and more stories, with more and more communities to hear and interpret, is there an end point? What is the fate of stories?

For some – Baudrillard would probably be amongst them – the stories will go on unfolding but they will be of little consequence. There is an excess frenzy of story telling which in fact now signifies nothing. A spectacle that makes no difference. There has been story telling overload: and as a parade of stories pass before us every day on *Oprah* and *Donahue*, in cheap paperbacks and sensational tabloids, in newspaper problem pages or the latest hyped best-selling survey, they count as nothing. Mild amusement, mild diversion; here today, gone tomorrow. If this is so, it does not augur well for the modernist stories of rape.

Louise Armstrong, one of the first to produce a book on incest and child sex abuse, senses the clear failure and the potential for overload leading nowhere. She writes:

> When we first spoke out, ten years ago, on the subject of incest, of our abuse, as children, by fathers and stepfathers, of our childhood rape by older brothers, stepbrothers, funny uncles, grandfathers – there was, for all the pain, sometimes humor.
>
> And there was, even through the anguish, a terrific mood of ebullience, of fantastic hope. Not only was it thrilling to pull insight and clarity from turmoil. But then – in the late 1970s – there was that sense of empowerment, of possibility for real change.
>
> In these ten years, things have become unimaginably worse – for child victims, now, and for the women, their mothers, who try to protect these children. And for survivors, who now find the very stuff of their trauma, their degradation, their violation as children, the common currency of talk show guest 'experts' and 'professionals'; find their courageous speaking-out transformed into no more than a new plot option for ongoing dramatic series.
>
> People say to me: 'Well, but at least we're talking about it now'.

Yes. But it was not our intention to start a long conversation.

In breaking the silence, we hoped to raise hell. Instead, we have raised for the issue a certain normalcy. We hoped to raise a passion for change. Instead, what we raised was discourse – and a sizable problem-management industry. Apart from incest educators, we have incest researchers, incest experts, incest therapists, incest awareness programmes, incest prevention programmes.[66]

One things is clear: there is no automatic 'safe place' in the world for stories. As societies change, so stories change. The rewriting of 'Holocaust history' is a major and timely reminder of what can happen. Just fifty years after the Holocaust, strong claims are made by large numbers of people that it never actually happened! Holocaust revisionism has its parallels in some of the stories I have been considering.[67]

At the same time, overload of stories could also be seen as an increasing refinement of our grasping of some aspects of the social world: more and more details are given allowing more and more identities and communities to grasp the sense of proliferating differences. There may be a 'natural cycle' – or a historical circulation – of stories by which they move from silence to a few utterances, to peak moments, to routinisation, to various appropriations and misappropriations and – maybe – ultimate disappearance. The major peaks are witnessed through a media explosion: the routinisation takes place in small worlds of daily activities. The 'sexual harassment' tales of Anita Hill move out into a much more pedestrian day-to-day awareness of harassment and an increased ability for both many women and many men to locate their lives and their actions mundanely in a frame of harassment stories. In a quarter of a century's time, there may be less need to shout the story of rape and harassment because it will have been incorporated into the taken-for-granted stock of stories of everyday life.

But, after a while, when new stories have become old stories, their very claims may have to change. Stories are a never-ending stream. And a story told in the 1970s may need drastic revision for the 1990s. The 'all women are victims/all men are bastards' themes implied by some early rape stories gives way to a much more nuanced account: not all men are rapists, some women do lie. In the early 1990s, the 'political correctness' movement was challenged from a number of sources – the Anita Hill story may be seen as a prime example of this – and new 'less correct' stories came in their wake. Katie Roiphe's *The Morning After* argued that many of the stories around 'date rape' for instance may actually have worked to weaken women's position. The culture of rape stories may have gone so far as to actually scare women and weaken them. As she says:

> Combating myths about rape is one of the central missions of the leaders of the rape crisis movement. . . . But with all their noise about rape myths, rape-crisis feminists are generating their own. If you look at the scenes described in the plays, the poems, the pamphlets, the Take Back the Night speak-outs, the stories told are loss-of-innocence stories. We all know this plot: I trusted him – I thought people were good – then I realised – afterward I knew. The rape or

sexual assault is the moment of the fall. It is the isolated instant, when, in one victim's word, they 'learn to hate'.[68]

And from this, Roiphe produces her own new narrative. Thus, just as new voices soon become old voices, so more new voices will appear. Just what may be lying in store for us is a major theme of the next part of my account in Part III.

Chapter 6

The modernisation of gay and lesbian stories

My cousin loaned me THE COMING OUT STORIES a week ago, and it has been great. I have been struggling with my lesbian identity – am I gay? am I bisexual? is it that I love women or is it just that I hate men? etc. Reading this book has helped me to realize (1) that yes, I do love women and that (2) I don't have to make excuses for it, that I do not have to take responsibility for other people's homophobia, that being a lesbian is a positive life-affirming thing, not a sickness. And realizing the power and strength in that knowledge. By reading about these other women and what they have gone through it helped me to see that the choice of whether to act upon my being a lesbian or not comes down to me, and that, yes, I can choose to do so – here are people that have done so, they DO exist. I am just beginning to see that being gay does not necessarily mean something is wrong with me.

I don't know how I would have fared if I had been born twenty years earlier. My coming out, which will be a life-long process for me, is so much easier because of the women's movement, the gay movement, and most of all the literature and music that is available for lesbians. And your book is one of those experiences that someone like me, a 21-year-old who's finally beginning to realize her gay identity, can grab onto like a rock in the ocean.[1]

Stories of 'homosexuality' have recently changed. Once upon a time, in the western world, there were the Greeks and their loves.[2] Then came the ganymedes, ingles, buggers and catamites.[3] A little later found the mollies; and then the inverts, urnings, homosexuals and queers.[4] The male gay, the clone, the macho man appeared from the 1970s onwards.[5] During the 1980s, the post-Stonewall 'Aids' gay has appeared, and even now as I write in the early 1990s, the story of the new Postmodern/New Age queer is in the making.[6] Lesbians too have their own 'mother tongue': stories of Amazons, Sapphos, romantic friendships, boarding school loves, mythic mannish lesbians, women-identified women, radicalesbians and lipstick lesbians.[7] Throughout time and space the pleasures and displeasures of erotic experience between the same genders have certainly existed; but in every culture such experiences both create and respond to a wider set of cultural meanings. In Ancient Greece, it was partially the story of a noble camaraderie between adult male tutor and beautiful youth – a militaristic and pedagogic sensuality that firmly excluded women, and which was locked into a deeply stratified order of freeman and slave. In Renaissance England, it was partially the story of a world of drunken and sexual excess – surrounded by werewolves, antichrists and witches. In the early western twentieth century, it was partially a story told by 'sexperts': of pathologies, conditions, continuums, disorders and disease, side by side with the eventual creation of a distinct homosexual identity and the elements of a diverse homosexual culture with a unique sensibility. There are many signs – not to mention academic treatises – that suggest the past century has witnessed the slow construction of distinctively new stories around 'homosexualities' alongside distinctively new cultural forms – lesbian and gay social worlds – which exploded, symbolically if not in reality, into the public consciousness through the Stonewall riots in Greenwich Village, New York, in June 1969. Images of erotic desire, camp sensibility and political anger become fused and a distinct past – from Whitman and Wilde to the Nazi extermination of gays[8] – is discovered, re-called and re-membered. Not everyone who seeks same-gender eroticism will be connected to this new culture: small towns, people of colour and some of the elderly may often be much less well served.[9] But for many, it will become the shifting, emergent focus around which their lives are to be organised in the late twentieth century.

COMING OUT: A DOMINANT NARRATIVE

The most momentous act in the life of any lesbian and or gay person is when they proclaim their gayness – to self, to other, to community. Whilst men and women have been coming out for over a hundred years, it is only since 1970 that the stories have gone very public. The full cycle of private, personal, public and political tellings has become possible. Thus, not only have gays and lesbians started to tell the story of their lives to themselves, they have started to tell their stories face to face to each other – in bars, in rap groups, in lesbian and gay centres. More: they also now only too willing to tell their stories to the media. In biographies, edited collections of letters and interviews, in poetry, on tapes, on film, on chat shows, in newspapers there has now emerged a plethora of coming out stories.[10] Every major city in the western world has its own gay and lesbian bookstore which stands as a testament to this explosion of tellings. Just like the modernist rape stories of the previous chapter, the coming out stories have 'demythologised' early stories, built a story of the past, finding a gay and lesbian history.[11] It is a new story – of identities, coming out, gay culture and politics; and its power has been enormous. As Adrienne Rich writes (for lesbians, but it applies to gay men too) in an early and influential anthology of *The Coming Out Stories*:[12]

> Cultural imperialism . . . [is] the decision made by one group of people that another shall be cut off from their past, shall be kept from the power of memory, context, continuity. This is why lesbians, meeting, need to tell and retell stories

like the ones in this book. In the absence of the books we needed, the knowledge of women whose lives were like our own, an oral tradition – here set down on paper – has sustained us. These stories, which bring us together and which also confirm for each of us the path and meaning of her individual journey, are like the oldest tribal legends: tales of birth and rebirth, of death and rebirth; sometimes – too often – of death without rebirth . . .

I keep thinking about power. The intuitive flash of power that 'coming out' can give: I have an indestructible memory of walking along a particular block in New York City, the hour after I acknowledged to myself that I loved a woman, feeling invincible. For the first time in my life I experienced sexuality as clarifying my mind instead of hazing it over; that passion, once named, flung a long, imperative beam of light into my future. I knew my life was decisively and forever different; and that change felt to me like power.[13]

The coming out stories which were heard especially during the 1960s and 1970s (but which started to change with a new cohort appearing through the 1980s and 1990s)[14] are usually 'modernist tales' in that they use some kind of causal language, sense a linear progression, talk with unproblematic language and feel they are 'discovering a truth'. Most typically, the genre of coming out writing does the following:

1 It starts in childhood and follows in a linear progression. Many gay narratives come to assume the same sequenced, causal, rational and linear pattern that is a feature of much modern biography. Robert Musil has put this well: 'it is . . . the simple order that consists in one's being able to say: "When that had happened, this happened." ' The stage models of coming out are the sociologist's version of this, while the sequences of early childhood life are the production of psychiatrists. Chance and contingency is usually overrun by cause and continuity.

2 Childhood is usually seen as an unhappy time, often the source of being gay or lesbian. There is often a strong sense of difference: 'I never felt as if I fit in. I don't know why for sure. I felt different. I thought it was because I was more sensitive.'[15] A deterministic tale suggests that something happens at birth or childhood which sets up this 'difference'.

3 A crucial moment appears – often in early adolescence – where problems appear that lead to a concern – or discovery – over being 'gay'. Problems abound and are usually documented: secrecy, guilt or shame, fear of discovery, suicidal feelings.

4 Problems are resolved in some fashion, usually through meeting other lesbians or gays in a community.

5 A sense of identity or self is achieved as gay or lesbian, along with a sense of community.

This is too simple, but the elements are there. As I suggested in Chapter 4, the narrative can be seen as a journey, starting out from an uncharted shore with a host of problems and gradually arriving home. Earlier this century, novels about coming out frequently went through the same list of problems but the journey did not lead to satisfactory solutions – indeed most such novels became tragedies: homosexuality was viewed so negatively that coming out often led to misery, suicide, madness or at the very least a life of loneliness. There was no such thing as a 'happy homosexual' and early century narratives were often moral warnings of the journey. But this changed from the 1960s onwards – a progress, a future, a world of solutions was increasingly found. 'Coming out' now becomes the central narrative of positive gay experience.[16]

Finding the 'coming out' story is usually the most momentous moment in any gay or lesbian life. Given both heterosexism and homophobia at work, those who may later in life 'go gay' will initially be socialised to believe that they are heterosexual; nagging feelings of being different may emerge very early in childhood or adolescence, but a clear sense of being gay will only unfold later. Gays and lesbians typically feel that they have been given all the wrong stories and that they are living a lie. The opening passages to Paul Monette's eloquent account of his life, *Becoming a Man*, captures this experience perfectly:

> Everybody else had a childhood, for one thing – where they were coaxed and coached and taught all the shorthand. Or that's how it always seemed to me, eavesdropping my way through twenty-five years, filling in the stories of straight men's lives. First they had their shining boyhood, which made them strong and psyched them up for the leap across the chasm to adolescence, where the real rites of manhood began . . .
>
> And every year they leaped further ahead, leaving me in the dust with all my doors closed, and each with a new and better deadbolt. Until I was twenty-five, I was the only man I knew who had no story at all. I'd long accepted the fact that nothing had ever happened to me, and nothing ever would. That's how the closet feels, once you've made your nest in it and learned to call it home . . .
>
> I speak for no one else here. . . . Yet I've come to learn that all our stories add up to the same imprisonment. The self-delusion of uniqueness. The festering pretense that we are the same as they are. The gutting of all our passions till we are a bunch of eunuchs, our zones of pleasure in enemy hands. Most of all, the ventriloquism, the learning how to pass for straight. Such obedient slaves we make with such tidy rooms.[17]

Ventriloquism. The mouthing of other's stories in the absence of your own. This is what makes the coming out tale so momentous. Gay and lesbian 'coming out' refers then to this complex process of moving from a heterosexual (and confused) identity, telling the stories of others given in childhood, to a strong, positive and accepting sense of identity as gay being given to one through awareness of the gay community in later life. It is a momentous, frequently painful, experience in any gay person's life – comparable in impact perhaps to the birth of one's first child in the heterosexual cycle. Experiencing it will dramatically reshape the life-route: life will never be the same again. Quite when the new coming out story will become available in any particular life is unpredictable; many find it occurring during their first heterosexual marriage, some may find it taking place in mid-adolescence and others can move through it during their retirement. And the times change: in America during the 1970s it seemed to occur most typically somewhere between the twenties and early thirties. More recently, there are clear signs that coming out is happening earlier – and in some ways more easily.[18]

The first step is often the hardest, since it usually has to be taken alone without support from others: the whole weight of cultural indoctrination has to be broken down. This, to engage in understatement, is not easy. At home, at school, with one's peers or confronting the media the message has insidiously been the same: the only story is the heterosexual one, and the tales learnt in school or street are tales of 'queers' – few, sick, dangerous. 'How can I – in spite of vague feelings and fantasies – be one of that sick few? I can't – and even if by some freak chance I was, it must be kept as a dark and hidden secret to be carried quietly to my grave.' Yet to even start to have such ponderings is to set in motion the spiral of signification by which the idea that you could indeed be gay or lesbian slowly becomes more and more central to your life. At what point the fuller story breaks through – 'I am like that, I must do something about it' – is largely unpredictable; but that this breakthrough does happen – against all odds – is unmistakable. An open mind, a liberal peer group, access to gay books, articles and films, the sight of a Gay Switchboard sticker, knowledge of a homosexual person may all play their contributory roles in facilitating this self-awareness.

A critical component for many is the *textual search*: a scanning of the stories available to help see who one is. Lesbians who came of age in the immediate post-war period frequently tell of scanning *The Well of Loneliness* and *finding themselves in the text*. Later generations scan different texts – now increasingly in film and video – but scan they do. As one gay man remarked:

> Like so many other bright children growing up in the inarticulate world of the poor, books fueled my imagination, answered my questions, led me to new ones, and helped me conceive of a world in which I would not feel so set apart. . . . Early on I acquired a taste for reading history, particularly ancient history. . . . I was fascinated by pictures of the nude male torsos. There was something about smooth, headless torsos, the irisless eyes of ephebes that made me stop flipping through pages and touch the papers where these things were depicted. By the time I was twelve I understood that my fascination was rooted in my sexual nature. One day, walking to school, clutching my books to my chest, girl-style, I heard myself say, 'I'm a queer'.[19]

These first painful experiences of coming out can usually be resolved speedily once other lesbians and gays are met and their stories heard. Earlier doubts – the guilt, identity confusions, secrecy and sexual frustrations – can begin to be faced once others are met who can tell the story of being 'glad to be gay', living contented and productive lives.

Ultimately, the coming out story is a tale concerned with establishing a sense of who one really is – an identity which ideally exists not just for oneself alone, but which is also at home in the wider world. In coming out to him or herself, to the gay community and to the wider environment, the lesbian and gay can develop a consistent, integrated sense of a self.

CREATING THE TALE

To understand just what has happened to same-sex experience during the past century it may help to start with an exercise in imagination. Picture, if you can, a microscopic experience of homosexuality: an erotic eye for the same sex, two people – or more – responding with their genitals to each other's bodies, two people of the same sex feeling emotionally content when close to each other. Such experiences are probably ubiquitous and universal. Imagine you were born in the nineteenth century and have wandered into the late twentieth century. A wholly different world appears before you: what has happened to such microscopic experiences? In many big cities, you will find that a massive network of talk and activity has flourished around these seemingly small and personal experiences. There are bookstores and video shops, magazines and newspapers, books on every conceivable subject linked to lesbian and gay life: from lesbian erotic tales to gay detective stories, from medical texts to science fiction comics. Gays in film, gays in art, gays in poetry, gays in theatre.[20] Alongside all this are a host of new cultural inventions and forms;[21] there are bath-houses and porno-houses, bars and clubs, hi-energy discos and low-energy poetry readings, theatre companies for lesbian and gay theatre, bookstores and strip clubs, health clinics and restaurants, gay men's choruses and lesbian communes; there are groups for every conceivable interest – politics, sport and spirituality; and magazines and newspapers to accompany each. Hundreds of thousands of men and women have come over the past two decades to live their whole life from within this world, and millions have come to live adjacent to it. A small experience has become a major cultural form.[22] It is a form under constant change: throughout the 1980s it became more and more a culture under the spectre of Aids, and at the same time it continued to proliferate into satellite cultures embracing much difference and diversity.[23] The experiences and the stories change dramatically even within a few years.

But more than this: the experience has also been transformed into a major way of *being* in the world. For in every major western city throughout the world, people have become 'gay' or 'lesbian' or even, since the late 1980s, 'queer' all over again! Identities are built around sexuality; an experience becomes an essence; *and the new stories that are told and written about homosexuality hold it all together*. Of course this is just what the medical practitioners were doing in the nineteenth century when they created their rogue's gallery of perverts. But now the identity is no longer imposed, stigmatisingly, from without. It is instead embraced, willingly, from within. This, the story goes, is what that microscopic experience 'really' meant all along: it was a sign of a deep-seated, truly different nature. For many, it is a biological story of natural difference.[24] It is a culture creating its own essentialist story of identity – 'Homosexuals are born, just as heterosexuals are born. This is what I think, feel, know, and there has been no evidence to prove otherwise', says Larry Kramer – a leading gay activist. And when in 1991, Simon LeVay (re)discovered the biological basis of homosexuality through his study of the shrinking hypothalamus, he became a celebrated character of gay culture.[25]

Alongside these new cultures and new identities also comes a new political story: a digging around in the past to create a history of the new 'species'. A scanning of the present connects a multitude of contemporary political rhetorics – socialism and Marxism, libertarianism and ecology, feminism and anti-racism, conservatism and evangelicalism, deconstruction and postmodernism – to the gay personhood. An elaborate theory and politics of homosexuality becomes organised, with its intellectual workers, its schismatic social movements, its codifying pamphlets, newsletters, journals and books. The sexual story becomes a political story.

From a microscopic experience, then, a vast social world of new stories has been created: identity stories telling who one is, political stories telling where one is going, cultural stories that weave the gay life into the fabric of the social. Those men and women of the early twentieth century who lived in 'queer' and shadowy worlds furtively reading their Oscar Wilde, their Krafft-Ebing, their *Well of Loneliness* would scarcely believe what has been created. They would ponder why an experience so tinged with secret and silent stories of suffering and stigma in their day has for millions been transformed into a public and political story of positive well-being, something to be proud of, to shout about and to enjoy. How is the rise of the story of 'the making of the modern homosexual'[26] to be explained?

THE DYNAMICS OF MAKING STORIES: POLITICS, COMMUNITY AND IDENTITY

My argument is simple. I will suggest – just as I have for rape stories – that for narratives to flourish there must be a community to hear; that for communities to hear, there must be stories which weave together their history, their identity, their politics. The one – community – feeds upon and into the other – story. There is an ongoing dynamic or dialectic of communities, politics, identities and stories which have their roots in the nineteenth century but which reach a critical 'take-off stage' by the middle of the twentieth. At this point, it becomes a global phenomenon.[27] But there is nothing inevitable about this and nor can it be simply projected into the future: my view of change and history is contingent and piecemeal.

It may help to see a parallel development between the biographical hi*story* of a gay identity and the social hi*story* of a gay culture. Both the development of a gay personhood and a gay culture proceed incrementally, in tandem and feeding upon each other. As gay persons create a gay culture cluttered with stories of gay life, gay history and gay politics, so that very culture helps to define a reality that makes gay personhood tighter and ever more plausible. And this in turn strengthens the culture and the politics.[28] Put simply, small sufferings seek solutions, both on a personal and social scale; successful solutions generate stories, cultural resources, that can be drawn upon by successive generations facing similar sufferings; a snowball, amplifying effect follows. Although, since each generation faces a different historical milieu, the sufferings and the stories will also shift.

Elsewhere, and in some detail, I have discussed the evolution of modern gay identities – 'going gay'.[29] Briefly, I suggest four loose phases: sensitisation, signification, sub-culturalisation and stabilisation.

In the first stage, a person becomes *sensitive to difference*: they start to develop thoughts that they could be a certain kind of sexual person. That is, they become sensitive to their sexuality: they do not automatically know that they are gay: they must cue themselves on to the potential that they could be this kind of person. They do this by looking around the culture for certain interpretations of their previous history. They scan their past lives, trying to make sexual sense of them and in the process of doing this they start to totter towards the construction of a sexual story telling them who they are. For some people this may be relatively unproblematic, but for those who start scanning their sexual histories to find anomalies, or curiosities, or worrying matters the potential is set for the emergence of troubled labelling. Things just do not seem to match up with the conventional commonsense culture. This process can last a lifetime and as we shall see there are some people's lives where the struggle is on from adolescence onwards to make some kind of coherence out of their sexuality.

The second step however is much bigger: a smaller group of people will have to confront it. This is the phase known as *signification* – a term originally coined by David Matza in *Becoming Deviant* to indicate how consciousness changes when it is confronted with stigma and ban. At this stage there is not just a sensitivity to anomalies, but an overwhelming awareness of the possible nastiness, the sordidness, the wrongness of it all. The stigma attached to potential identity starts to take its toll. The experience starts to become trapped in the key defining problems of stigmatised sexualities. These are:

1 Devaluation: 'Am I wrong; Am I bad?'
2 Secrecy: 'Dare I tell anyone?'
3 Solitariness: 'Am I the only one in the world?'
4 Self consciousness: 'What's this all about?'
5 Identity: 'What kind of person am I?'

Such problems can loom large in consciousness, making it more and more significant and central; and these worrying thoughts may last a long time, even a lifetime. In the earlier part of this century, many men and women who wanted homosexual experience got no further than this. Yet, once these problems are identified, there is a potentiality for finding a solution. And the solution lies in finding the right story.

The third phase is critical: it is quite literally a *coming to terms*. It is associated with coming to work out fairly clearly the nature of sexuality: to give a label, to resolve the problems posed through signification, to find the story which explains it all. The most common strategy for doing this is to gain access to new social worlds – an access to story tellers open to coaxing and coaching into the tales of gay and lesbian life. Here, secrecy and isolation will be broken down, legitimations and justifications for the new way of life are found, and a sense of who one is will finally be arrived at.[30]

Clearly, what I have described is a cumulative series of phases – there is no reason why people should pass through them all. The critical phase is perhaps the signification phase: if the problems are too great, people may be unable to go on. They may attempt to turn back, to resolve their problems by blocking them out, by seeking cures and therapies to give them a sense of identity that is different from the one they were heading towards. Presumably, the greater the stigma experienced, the greater the problems and the less likelihood of moving along through these phases. The shift that I am describing is centrally a shift in consciousness in which the emergence of stories plays a crucial part. The awareness of stigma that surrounds homosexuality leads the experience to become an extremely negative one: shame and secrecy, silence and self-awareness, a strong sense of differentness – and of peculiarity – pervades the consciousness. At another point in time, the engulfing stigma gets neutralised through an appropriate tale: the ability to experience sexuality positively comes to exist.

These shifts in consciousness and identity have their parallels in the shifts in community and culture on a wider scale. The history of gay community passes through complementary stages: three main 'waves' can therefore be detected. The history of this new culture is now well documented.[31] In an early first wave – exploration – covert meeting places and networks were established. As early as the eighteenth century, taverns existed where homosexual men – often effeminate men – gathered. They had a slow growth, and often were akin to brothels or, at the other extreme, gentlemen's clubs. For women, the culture was less evident: romantic friendship seems the major pattern of this time. Whilst some homosexuals could meet, such encounters were strictly taboo and their hallmarks were probably secrecy and silence. By the middle of the nineteenth century, a few groups in Europe and American attempted to organise themselves more politically; in France, André Gide's 1911 defence of homosexual love, *Corydon*, and the subsequent *Arcadie* group; in England, Edward Carpenter's 1894 pamphlet *Homogenic Love*; in America, more ambivalently, the work of Walt Whitman – especially his 1860 *Leaves of Grass* and the much later Chicago Society for Human Rights;[32] in Germany, the creation by Magnus Hirschfield of the 'Scientific Humanitarian Committee' in 1897 and later the first Institute of Sexual Science (to be destroyed when Hitler came to power). Bullough comments of the latter: 'In a sense, the committee, the group behind the clinic, journal and research centre, came close to being an association of homosexuals, and it has sometimes been regarded as the first effective organisation of homosexuals'.[33] During this period, then, there was a covert coming together of some elements, and the beginnings of a text. Much of it was to be destroyed however with the dramatic emergence of fascism in Europe in the early twentieth century.

A second wave, around the end of the Second World War, started to make the experience more and more socially significant. Europe and America witnessed a slow and cautious proliferation of homosexual movements and law-reform lobbies (the latter often arising outside overt homosexual groups). In America, a social club – the Veteran's Benevolent Association – was established in 1945 and lasted until 1954, by which time many organisations had been founded: SIR (Society for Individual Rights), Mattachine and the Daughters of Bilitis being the longest lasting and each producing their own fairly continuous (but much harassed) magazines.[34] In England, the Homosexual Law Reform Association was set up in the wake of the Wolfenden Report[35] and worked assiduously so that a decade later the Sexual Offences Act was finally passed decriminalising homosexual acts by men over 21 in many circumstances. The final symbolism of nearly thirty years of organisation came in the Stonewall riots, 28 June 1969. This marked a distinctive change from the days of the early homophile movement – gays showing active resistance to police harassing a local Greenwich village bar, with a two-day street battle following. From this moment on the approach to homosexuality shifted. Whereas before it had largely been apologetic, it was now 'glad to be gay'; whereas before it had been secretive, now it was 'coming out'. Homosexuality drastically increased in visibility and the language surrounding it began to shift from one of disease to one of politics and 'rights'.[36]

The story of Stonewall has been much rehearsed: it has become a major organising 'social memory' of many lesbian and gay stories, found in film, in books, on rallies, in exhibitions. The fact that it was certainly not the first radical action by lesbians and gays; the fact that in the USA the West Coast may have had a stronger tradition of radicalism than New York;[37] the fact the shifts in the women's movement played at least as central a part in gay liberation; the fact that in some other countries of the western world – notably the Netherlands – gay liberation was already much further advanced[38] – all these 'facts' are beside the point. Stonewall became a galvanising symbol: a crucial memory in the recon-struction of lesbian and gay stories from the late 1960s onwards. How 'Stonewall' provides a narrative thread for lesbian and gay lives has been brilliantly shown in Martin Duberman's account of Stonewall.[39]

From the 1970s onwards, then, a third wave of modern lesbian and gay life is reached. The central issue here was 'coming out' and a politicalisation of sexual difference, and it has led to an ever-increasing proliferation of gay institutions.[40] Whereas once the secret bar and the clandestine 'cottage' were all that existed for homosexuals, the 1970s witnessed the growth of gay publishing, gay industries, gay bath-houses, gay counselling services, gay switchboards, gay churches, gay trade unions, gay political parties, gay fashion, gay discos, gay ramblers – gay everything. Sexual diversity had become the explicit, overt organising point of hundreds of thousands of lives.[41] Whole communities in America and Canada became colonised into 'gay ghettos'. Whatever evidence there was for 'gay sub-cultures' in the Middle Ages or for institutionalised homosexuality amongst certain tribes, it seems likely that world history has never seen the organisation of stigmatised sexual diversity on such a massive scale before. It is out of this third phase that more stable and enduring structures start to evolve. Just as 'coming to terms' in the personal history leads to a gay identity as a foundation for subsequent life choices, so too the 'coming out' of gay culture leads to a baseworld for the proliferation of gay institutions.

Arguably, 'gayness' has set a model for other sexually diverse experiences to follow. The model suggests that in a first phase there must be minimal conditions for some like-minded people to come together – usually in secrecy and shame. From this, a gradual case can be made for changes in attitudes or law: this will be a low-key debate, virtually silenced in the public sphere. By now, though, two crucial conditions will have been established: that people experiencing diversity can meet and that arguments can be made in their defence. It becomes therefore increasingly plausible to accept and extend the diversity until a third phase is (unexpectedly) reached: the take-off into coming out and mass political protest. Once sexuality enters this sphere, the conditions are ripe for the proliferation of many institutions for the sexually different – and coping with such diversity ostensibly becomes much easier.[42]

EMERGENT CULTURES, EMERGENT STORIES

Why and how did this new culture emerge?[43] Gay worlds came into being through a number of coinciding conditions brought about by modernity. I do not suggest any inevitable evolution or history here: there is always human agency intervening, making outcomes less than predictable. Nevertheless, many broad changes identified with the modern world do seem to have produced a climate very conducive to gay identities and gay culture; none on their own would have worked. Although the agency of the gay movement is necessary to activate change, there are many preconditions which are closely connected to the rise of an advanced form of capitalism and a technological society. A leading historian of gay communities, John D'Emilio, has summed up some of these factors very lucidly, and signposted the way:

> During the second half of the nineteenth century, the momentous shift to industrial capitalism provided the conditions for a homosexual and lesbian identity to emerge. As a free-labor system, capitalism pulled men and women out of a household economy and into the marketplace, where they exchanged their individual labor power for wages. Throughout the nineteenth and twentieth centuries, as the socialized production of commodities spread, goods formerly made in the home could be purchased. The family, deprived of the functions that once held it together as an economic unit, became instead an affective entity that nurtured children and promoted the happiness of its members. Birth rates declined steadily, and procreation figured less prominently in sexual life. In place of the closely knit villages, the relatively small seaport towns, and the sprawling plantations of the preindustrial era, huge

impersonal cities arose to attract an ever larger proportion of Americans. The interlocking processes of urbanization and industrialization created a social context in which an autonomous personal life could develop. Affection, intimate relationships, and sexuality moved increasingly into the realm of individual choice, seemingly disconnected from how one organized the production of goods necessary for survival. In this setting, men and women who felt a strong erotic attraction to their own sex could begin to fashion from their feeling a personal identity and a way of life.[44]

Crucial to this, then, was a free labour system which emerged under capitalism. In much of the pre-capitalist world, life was usually local, centred upon family units that had to be self-sufficient and autonomous. Children were a central component in this work situation, as was the husband–wife complex: but the structure was typically patriarchal. There was little room for men or women to wander away from their families and few reasons for not having many children. A tight world was created. But capitalism necessitated wage labour and a free market: work was now bought and sold, and workers had to go where the market sent them. The once tight unit of household production slowly became looser. Systems of transport and travel improved so that men and sometimes women could wander further afield; children and procreation were increasingly less necessary – indeed in the evolving system children became increasingly costly. Increasing mobility attracted more and more men and women to the growing urban centres – where work and wage could be found. The birth rate started to fall. Here then are the first cluster of elements, well known to historians: wage labour, shifting family relations of shrinking size and greater flexibility, the possibility of singlehood, the growth of urban centres and a declining birth rate.

But it is more than this: for along with shifts in material relations came shifts in ideology – most noticeably the rise of possessive individualism.[45] Capitalism in part depends upon the idea of the free individual – free to sell his or her labour on the open market, free to achieve, and free, ultimately, to lead a private life. Of course, it is a double barrelled freedom – free to fail miserably as well as to succeed. But the notion of an autonomous individual achieving is a crucial idea. It is the rise of the modern self: a self that has to be much more flexible, mutable, protean than the self in a pre-capitalist order where identities were fixed, stable and largely God-given. Modern identities, as so much writing has documented, become[46] uprooted, less stable, often trivialised, existing in a supermarket of choice. As we can change our jobs, so we can change our identities; as we can fail or succeed at work, so we can fail or succeed with our identities. Some contemporary commentators – like Lasch and even Sennett – suggest that this individualising of the self has gone too far: a narcissistic, minimal self has emerged with little sense of history or collective life and a preoccupation with one's own survival. And others have taken it still further: to a postmodern breakdown of all identity, to a post-identity world. Whether it has gone too far or not, and I will discuss this further in later chapters, I am sure that individualistic notions of the mutable self have been another precondition for the emergence of gay culture. Indeed, the *notion of gay identity only becomes a possibility once there has been a breakdown in traditional notions of the self. In the past, the possibility to choose to possess a gay identity simply did not exist.* Ironically, it was in part the work of the medical experts in designating the homosexual type during the late nineteenth and early twentieth century that provided the backdrop to the creation of the new gay identity. The ideology of individualism provided the context for choice; the medics provided the role models.

Although the medicalisation of homosexuality has been much attacked by the contemporary gay movement (indeed their protests played a key role in the 1973 decision by the American Psychiatric Association to no longer define homosexuality 'in itself' as a sickness), the actual process has really been a double-edged one. For whilst much writing has been about sickness (providing a sense of apprehension for gays around which they could mobilise for change), much writing has also been about a condition which is not of the individual's own choosing – a disadvantage, maybe, but no sickness. This latter argument was historically important in liberalizing laws; but it was also crucial for the evolution of gay culture – men could come to identify themselves as 'born like that' and hence 'essentially' gay. The old sodomites of the seventeenth century hardly had the basis for such an identity.[47] And although the modern story of homosexuality firmly disavows 'sickness', it regularly affirms an essential and deterministic causality – a fixity of desire.

A further symbiotic change must be mentioned as crucial: the shifts in communications and mass media. Cultures of the past were largely oral cultures, bound into worlds of face to face talk and for a few, usually elite groups, the world of writing. The possibility of communicating homosexuality to wide groups was non-existent. Yet the past century or so has experienced the proliferation of new communications: shifts in modes of travel and the rise of the tourist gaze; shifts in access to print – the cheap paperbacking of the world and the emergence of newsletters and desk-top publishing; new media – radio, film, television, video; and shifts in technologies – telephones, faxes, computers – making the world a global village. All the many new technological inventions have brought with them new social inventions: independently of what we communicate, we now communicate in ways that are fundamentally different from earlier centuries.[48] And whilst this has brought great fears of 'mass society', it has also brought a diversity of communication in segmented social worlds that was simply inconceivable in earlier times. The development of gay cultures has been massively aided by this.

The impact of all this cannot be underestimated for the creation of lesbian and gay stories. For although it is possible to trace an underground literature on 'homosexuality' being developed in the earlier part of this century (much of which was destroyed in the bonfires of Germany in the 1930s), the publication of lesbian and gay magazines is usually dated from the early 1950s – with the regular appearance of *One Magazine: The Homosexual Viewpoint* in 1952 (and later *Mattachine Review* and the *Ladder* in 1956) along with *Vriendschap* in the

Netherlands.[49] In tandem with these 'more political' magazines, emerged a market in soft-core paperback gay and lesbian fiction,[50] and a more limited world of homo-erotica – often in the guise of 'physique' magazines. All of this served as a means for creating an emerging and elementary sense of community – an interpretive community where a sense of belonging to a a gay social world becomes more and more possible. And in all these emerging media, stories of lesbian and gay life were being told.

The quantum change, however, comes in the early 1970s. During this period a number of major lesbian and gay magazines start to emerge – *The Advocate*, published from Los Angeles and possibly the world's longest-running gay magazine, first appeared in 1968. In the UK, popular magazines like *Jeremy* make an appearance (often very briefly), and a leading national newspaper – *Gay News* – is established in the UK in 1971. Gay publishing houses – some of which had existed in the clandestine 1950s – start to become more prominent during the 1970s: Naiad Press and Alyson Publications in the USA, Gay Men's Press (GMP) in the UK. Lesbian publishing houses develop often in tandem with the new women's presses. And throughout this period more and more media forms develop on an international basis: the growth of gay film (with their own film festivals), of gay theatre, of pornography, of video. By 1987, some 1, 924 magazines could be listed in an *International Directory of Gay and Lesbian Periodicals*.[51] Gay bookstores proliferate: in 1977 there were eight such stores in the USA whereas by the early 1990s there were around thirty-five – many with their own catalogues. And even mainstream booksellers have developed gay and lesbian sections. By the 1990s, it was clear that a new 'niche market' had come of age in an era when other markets were floundering in a depression. The lesbian and gay market – the pink economy – had become identifiable as a 'dream market'.[52] There has also been a pronounced interest in the more academic 'lesbian and gay studies'. And more recently still we have seen the emergence of gay and lesbian computer bulletin boards alongside gay and lesbian e-mail networking.

Over the past twenty years or so, then, lesbian and gay stories have proliferated in the lesbian and gay media – itself largely an invention of the past two decades. But such story tellings as are found there then ripple out into the wider community: whereas once a silence pervaded film, press and TV, now lesbian and gay issues get regular airings. Most soaps have at least introduced one gay or lesbian character – from *Eastenders* and *Brookside* in the UK to *Dynasty*, *The Golden Girls* and *Roseanne* in the USA. There is also a large market for mainstream lesbian and gay publishing, and lesbian and gay films have increasingly entered the mainstream culture.[53]

Finally, one of the most striking developments in the modern world has been the emergence of new social movements. As a key dynamic in opposing the domination of states, social movements have proliferated around a number of cultural struggles: race and ethnicity, ecology and the earth, nuclear energy and disarmament, sexism and the women's movement. These are not just marginal to the workings of modern societies: they are central oppositional forces. Whilst

many of them had their 'moment' in the counter-cultural 1960s, they all have roots
going back into the nineteenth century, and they have all sustained themselves and
proliferated in the closing decades of the twentieth century. There is, then, a
historical affinity for the gay and lesbian movement. As gay culture emerges through
modernity, a political wing also is created with strong symbiotic relationships with
other social movements: strategies, struggles, ideologies all have to be worked on,
and feed into each other.

There is no one factor then that has given rise to the emergent gay and lesbian
communities: it is the coalescence of many, which then feeding off each other set
up recurring collective actions, social worlds, habits. The stories of the community
are a crucial part of this world – feeding into it, strengthening it, but very much
dependent upon it for a space where they can be said and heard.

PROLIFERATING STORIES, CREATING DIVERSITIES

Once gay culture has taken hold, it is not hard to explain its persistence and
amplification; and like all cultural forms it is constantly shifting and reorganising
itself. Coming out stories which were told in the early 1970s take on new forms
during the 1980s. A plethora of publications make it a more and more readily
accessible story; and the stories multiply so that mothers, fathers, daughters,
sisters, brothers can all have their coming out stories too.[54] Counselling books
telling people how to come out appear, alongside advertising campaigns on
coming out. In the United States, for instance, there has been, since 1988, a
National Coming Out Day – 11 October. And of course there are the inevitable
coming out workshops.[55]

And the stories keep changing. Aids brought about a now well-documented
change in both lesbian and gay communities, including a proliferation of new
institutions of care, support and activism.[56] This change was rapid: Aids was only
announced in 1981/2, but by 1985 a vast network of Aids organisations had sprung
up throughout the world. For instance, San Francisco, like many major cities had
produced a chain of Aids organisations: The Aids Foundation, Shanti, The Aids
Alliance, Bartenders against Aids, Stop Aids Project, Aids Hotline, Aids Health
Project, etc. To this was added an output of Aids narratives: 'personal dispatches',
'reports from the front line', 'borrowed time', not to mention a new world of
drama, poetry, film, biography. A new genre of Aids writing was in the making.[57]
And with all of this, of course, the stories told of coming out were given new –
often tragic – dimensions. Neither the stories nor the communities remain static.

But not just Aids. Throughout the 1970s and the 1980s, the critique from people
of colour became more vocal. Although there remains an overwhelming
dominance of white, middle-class narratives, others voices have slowly come to be
heard. Jospeh Beam's two anthologies, *In the Life* and *Brother to Brother*, both
start by decrying the total silence of stories being told outside the white world.
Reading many gay books, one writer observes: 'The books made no reference to
black men . . . nor were there black case studies for me to examine, and in the few

pictures identified as homosexual, not one was black.'[58] But likewise reading books by black authors led to an omission of any gay stories: 'The modern Negro texts of protest and the black writings of the 1960s never acknowledge homosexuals except as negative, tragic or comedic characters.'[59] Amongst women, there are some fragments preceding the 1970s, some of which have been claimed through oral history,[60] but the major change came with the publication of *This Bridge Called My Back* in 1981. In 1993, with the publication of *A Lotus of Another Colour* [61] the South Asian gay and lesbian story started to be told. In each case, a silence is broken, a new story appears and a potential source for political change becomes more and more pronounced.

The stories, then, have snowballed. Not just white gay men and lesbians 'coming out', but black men, black lesbians, Hispanic lesbians, Hispanic men, Asian men, Jewish women, elderly gays, ageing lesbians, deaf gays and lesbians. And, as we shall see later, the coming out of children to their parents, of parents to their children.[62] And it is a global story, since many of the tales told criss-cross their way around the world.[63]

The Story of Coming Out is a story in its time.

Chapter 7

Recovery tales

*The question was, why was no one talking about this? How many women might
be suffering in silent confusion? . . .* Maybe if I described the experience I would
find there were others out there like me.

(Colette Dowling)[1]

Without my suffering, I would not be able to bear witness to an addictive society
and the pain it is causing people.

(John Bradshaw)[2]

I'm Oprah Winfrey and like millions of Americans, I'm a survivor of child
abuse. I was only 9 years old when I was raped by my 19-year-old cousin. He
was the first of three family members to molest me. I kept the abuse a secret
over twenty years. Every year in America nearly three million cases of child
abuse are reported. Who knows how many go unreported? We are here tonight
to face this national epidemic of child abuse and neglect. You're about to meet
six perpetrators . . .

(From the *Oprah Winfrey* Show)

In North America up to fifteen million Americans participate in half a million self
help/recovery groups.[3] Based loosely on the original success of Alcoholics
Anonymous, founded in the 1930s, such groups now include meetings for debtors,
cocaine users, overeaters, smokers and a host of less well-known problems such as
credit abusers, shopaholics and trichotillomaniacs (people who pull their hair too
much!).[4] At the forefront of this 'recovery' movement are the 'sexual sufferings'
of the 'relationship' and 'sex' addicts. It is these latter groups and their stories
which are the focus of a third major modernist tale of 'sexual suffering': one which
hinges around 'therapy' and 'recovery'. These are the stories told by the 'sex
compulsives', the 'love/relationship addicts', the 'sexually dysfunctional' and all
their 'co-dependents'.[5] They are told in self help books, on chat shows, in therapy
groups and on that curious new phenomenon, tele-advising: *Donahue*, *Oprah* and
the proliferating talk-lines and chat shows.[6] Such stories can clearly overlap with
both gay and rape stories, focusing as they also do on 'breaking the silence', on
'coming out' and on 'surviving'. Indeed, these are all staple features of

tele-advising shows. They all involve a very similar process, of moving from a secret, solitary, even shameful world into a more public one. They all involve a clear transformation of the self, usually overcoming denial and seeking a path to 'recovery'. Yet whereas for the first two, the tales are centrally about a much-needed *political change*, recovery stories have a much stronger narrative about the need for *personal change*. They are much less concerned with politics, and become embroiled in the more personal self help worlds rather than the more political worlds of social movements. Often they shun wider political change. The dividing line is not always tight: clearly gay coming out stories and rape survival stories are also personal transformations of the self, and they can be, and often are, told within therapy groups.[7] But they are very commonly collective, participatory political projects too. The rape movement clearly sees aspects of patriarchy as the problem and orchestrates public protest (in 'Reclaim the Night' rallies, for instance). The gay and lesbian movement sees heterosexism and homophobia everywhere. But the recovery movement rarely looks outwards: its focus is the personal problem, personal pathology, personal shame. Here is the world of individualised and individualising change; a largely – though not exclusively – 'woman's world'.[8] We are also much more in the world of 'experts' stories'. These stories still tap into community, but it is a community which is much less concerned with radical change and more likely to listen to the expert's voice. As Wendy Simonds says, in her study of self help books, 'the ideology of self-help books, like the capitalist and patriarchal ideology that is dominant in our culture, denies connection and community-based action. Self-help books rarely recommend socially-oriented solutions.'[9] Of all the stories being raised in this book, recovery tales are probably the most widespread and accessible. Although they are found throughout the western world, they are especially prominent in North America – a fact that is linked, as we shall see later, to the long existence of a self help culture. Here the self help paperbacks and self help popular television programming are at their most advanced. Much of this chapter will hence be about North America.

TELLING RECOVERY TALES

Just what do these stories look like? Although every tale is a unique one, as before there is a generic pattern which emerges. Indeed, although the stories told may sometimes seem extraordinary, even 'freakish', they are all held together by certain common expectations. Before looking at these generic features, a few examples may help clarify the nature of these stories.

A best-selling story: women who love too much

Mass-market paperbacks are central to these stories. Pocket Books started in 1939, and 'democratised reading in America'[10] and self help books have always been its staple. Starker sees them as a 'distinctively American phenomenon' growing out of 'seventeenth-century notions about self-improvement, Christian goodness and otherworldy rewards',[11] from early marriage manuals and spiritual advice books to a parade of best-sellers in the 1970s. As Starker says: 'In the early 1970s, sexual self-help books were among the leading non-fiction works, reflecting and reinforcing a dramatic liberalisation of moral standards and modification of social values.' Between 1970 and 1975, the following works appeared on best-seller lists, selling millions of copies: *Everything You Always Wanted to Know about Sex but were Afraid to Ask* (1969) and *Any Woman Can* (1971), both by David Reuben, *The Sensuous Woman* (1969) by 'j', *The Sensuous Man* (1971) by 'M', *Open Marriage* (1972) by Nena and George O'Neill, *The Joy of Sex* (1972) and *More Joy* (1975) by Alex Comfort. Such books became blockbusters, courted by mass marketing, the 'personality-author-star' syndrome and synchronised television circuits.

Robin Norwood's best-seller and highly influential *Women Who Love Too Much* (along with its sequel, *Letters from Women Who Love Too Much*) exemplifies the book form of this tradition. It is immediately recognised because of its slick marketing and somewhat extravagant praise on the cover: this is a book that will change your life![12] The body of the book is then composed of personal stories: here, a new person and their story appears in each chapter. These are the stories of the 'women who love too much'. Based upon interviews, the women speak in their own voice. 'In the chapters that follow, each of the women you meet . . . has a story to tell about loving too much. Through their stories perhaps you will be helped to understand the patterns of your own life more clearly.'[13] Out of these stories, Norwood assembles the identification checklist – the characteristics 'typical of women who love too much'. In this case, fifteen items are described ranging from '(1) Typically you come from a dysfunctional home in which your emotional needs were not met' through to '(15) You are not attracted to men who are kind, stable, reliable, and interested in you. You find such "nice" men boring'.[14] This checklist is in turn amplified through more and more stories. The checklist may be seen as harbouring the generic plot of these stories stripped to the bare bones and is a staple feature of this mode of story telling: Norwood provides frequent checklists – of the woman's characteristics before recovery[15] or of 'The relationally addictive woman'.[16] The stories take on a repetitive style: it is the same story being told over and over again, though through different voices. The narrative is a well-rehearsed one by the end of the book.

As is common with most 'sexual stories', the narrative 'fits' well into a pre-existing narrative ideology; it is not a threat to existing stories in any major way. Indeed, Norwood recognises this:

> This theme of women redeeming men through the gift of their selfless, perfect, all accepting love is not a modern idea by any means . . . (it goes back to fairy tales, like 'Beauty and the Beast'); like every fairy tale that has endured centuries of telling and retelling, [it] embodies a profound spiritual truth in the context of a compelling story.[17]

Other books in the genre clearly play on this mythology – *The Cinderella Complex*, *The Peter Pan Syndrome*, *The Wendy Dilemma*.[18] But the stories 'fit' into more than one major narrative structure: there is also a strong congruence with the rhetorics of addiction, co-dependency and self-shame that is part of the framework of therapeutic thought that guides similar texts. The texts can easily feed off each other. Likewise, the narratives fit Elsbree's classic structures: of suffering, journeys, contests, consummation, home. And more: the stories also sit easily with the standard frames of women's melodrama – found in gothic writing, romance novels and most recently soap operas. Clearly, then, stories of 'women who love too much' are not complex ones: they mesh so well with other common frameworks of story telling that they can be readily and easily assimilated.[19]

The stories told are, however, never just stories. They are part of a strategy of self help and advocacy. The self is evoked to bring about the required change: 'She (the woman) is the one who must change ... her recovery must begin with herself.'[20] A programme of action is laid out for recovery – often based upon the twelve-step programmes initiated by Alcoholics Anonymous, but in this case it is collapsed into ten tasks:

1 Go for help.
2 Make your own recovery the first priority in your life.
3 Find a support group of peers who understand.
4 Develop your spiritual side through daily practice.
5 Stop managing and controlling others.
6 Learn to not get 'hooked' into the games.
7 Courageously face your own problems and shortcomings.
8 Cultivate whatever needs to be developed in your self.
9 Become 'selfish'.
10 Share with others what you have experienced and learned.[21]

Finally the appendices offer more practical help: setting up support groups, providing a series of 'affirmations' (e.g. 'Twice daily, for three minutes each time, maintain eye contact with yourself in a mirror as you *say out loud* [Your name] I love you and accept you exactly the way you are')[22] and listing further sources – books and groups. Ultimately, a quasi-religious zeal is to be found in the book – a mission to change that borders on the spiritual. Norwood's book provides a story-line in which many women say they have subsequently been able to find themselves. We know this, because three years later, Norwood published a series of letters she received around the book – most of them very positive. Just like lesbians and gays, here are people 'finding themselves in the text':

> I fit the prototype in your book quite exactly, and if I had known about you, I would have been quite upset that you wrote about me and spread my intimate thoughts and feelings on the pages of your book for the world to see ... the knowledge I have gained ... has enabled me to have strength in this ongoing struggle.[23]

I hated *Women Who Love Too Much.*
I hated it so much that it took me months to read it.
I hated the women you wrote about. I hated the stories.
And then I finished the book.
And then:

> I went to my first Overeaters Anonymous meeting.
> I found Al-Anon.
> I joined ACOA.
> I got into group therapy.
> I found VOICES and for the first time in my life talked about
>   having been sexually abused.
> I stopped binge-eating.
> I got a new job.
> I made a budget for the first time (I'm thirty- three).
> I have begun a new life.

I thank you.[24]

Telling the television tale

Confessional television has been around since the 1950s, but it is with the arrival of *Donahue* in the mid-1970s[25] that it is transformed into a pervasive public forum. Day-time television in the USA can now boast dozens of such shows, with *Oprah* currently being the most popular.[26] In England, there are far fewer, with *Kilroy* being the prime day-time example. It has developed into a distinctive mode of story telling in which 'before a live audience', as well as a hidden audience of a good few million, people provide narratives of their innermost lives. Sex is one of the most recurrent themes, and as the years have moved along, the topics chosen have become more and more 'unusual'. Again, the narrative structure remains constant but it is more evidently 'polyvocal' than the self help book. In general, a suffering is revealed publicly; a voice is shared; and a language connected to addiction, dysfunctionality, recovery appears. More than any other stories raised in this book, these raise issues about the turning of the private life into a very public one: both how can people tell so much in public, and how can other people listen? Wendy Kaminer hints at the dark side of all this when she comments that: 'Watching strangers on television, even responding to them from a studio audience, we're disengaged – voyeurs collaborating with exhibitionists in rituals of sham community. Never have so many known so much about people for whom they cared so little.'[27]

Good sex and Dr Ruth   *Dr Ruth's Good Sex* is one example of the medium. Dr Ruth Westheimer started her therapeutic media career in August 1980 with a New York phone-in radio programme (*Sexually Speaking*). Her book, *Dr Ruth's Guide to Good Sex* was published in 1983. The radio programme was syndicated in 1984 and turned later into a national TV show (*Good Sex with Dr Ruth*). In 1985 it was renamed the *Dr Ruth Show*, and it ran for four to five years, also being relayed to the UK (where it did not survive very long). In a cheery, chirpy (even giggly) manner, being oh so positive about good sex (and much more negative about bad sex), she deals with 'clients' who write letters and ring her with their 'problems' – impotence, frigidity, orgasm, masturbation, affairs, perversions. She simulates therapy sessions, and has a celebrity guest. It is a programme based upon confessional stories in which therapy tales are provided as the solutions to problems. They are essentially individualistic therapy tales. Dr Ruth is firmly located as an expert. Each opening of the programme makes this clear: the credits say – 'The programme is hosted by Dr Ruth Westheimer, noted sex therapist and adjunct associate professor in the sex therapy teaching programme at New York Hospital – Cornell Medical Center'. In the programme, she problematises – a problem story is told; and then either normalises – a story of normality – or excludes – a story of bad sex. Dr Ruth watches over the viewer. As LaFountain has argued in an intriguing Foucauldian analysis of Dr Ruth, she has a panopticon-like gaze, a look of surveillance over the sex habits of a nation. She looks right into the camera – right into the eyes of the viewer – and tells the sexual story, the story of 'good sex'. It is a woman's voice: not a feminist but a 'diminutive, pleasant, friendly, and frank woman [who] recreates the code of the relationship of helping'. LaFountain suggests that she may be directly linked to Foucault's repressive hypotheses: 'Dr Ruth operates more as an unwitting ideologue and perpetrator of power than as a liberator or critic . . . her dialogues with her "patients" are in reality monological recitations of the discursive apparatus of sexuality'.[28] Her 'good sex' is clearly a judgemental story which implies its opposite: stories of 'bad sex'. Indeed, Mimi White sees two 'simultaneous and intertwined discourses'[29] – one focusing on the body and sex, the other upon 'morality and limits'. It is indeed about 'Good Sex', harbouring several key views: the 'natural' view of sex – a biological process from 'natural functioning'; the view that much damage has been done to sex by repression, negativism, hypocrisy – and it needs to be 'normalised', seen as a healthy part of life. Yet at the same time there are dangers and limits. In the end, she normalises a relatively conventional system of sexual values: 'good sex' is needed, with awareness, liberation, discussion and enjoyment. If all else fails, the therapist should be approached. And there is a real need to continue talking.

Chatting away   The television talk show is another example of this medium. Guests, host and audience all sit together and traditional television boundaries are often broken. Topics chosen for discussion usually bring some area of controversy – and many feature sex. It brings together a mix of three genres: debate, romance and therapy.[30] And it typically displays a strong populist feel. Donal Carbaugh, writing specifically of *Donahue*, sees the talk show as symbolising American culture. It is less what is said, but how it is said. 'Individuals' on these programmes have 'rights': the rights 'to state almost any opinion';[31] the right to choose. There is he says 'a tyranny of personal opinions, uniqueness and openness'.[32] The mode of speaking highlights 'honesty', 'sharing' and 'communication'.

Increasingly, too, the world of television has come to play a major therapeutic role – as Mimi White argues, tele-advising therapy has been invented. She comments: 'Television provides simulated and degraded replacements of experiences that are somehow more "authentic" or valuable in their original or previous cultural manifestation than in their current, deformed, consumerized expression on television.'[33]

She extends the discussion to a wide array of new shows: phone-ins, date-ins and match-making, tele-evangelical programmes, sex shows and shopping lines as well as chat shows. In part this may be 'degradation', but it may also raise the possibility of a more active viewer participating in media worlds. For some, *Oprah* heralds a more radical text of the day. For it encourages a 'shifting or participatory subjectivity'; a 'privileging of the storied life over the expert quest'; it displays an 'exponential chaos of difference'; and it keeps permeable the voices of audience, subjects, Oprah. As Gloria-Jean Masciarotte writes, in a powerful feminist defence of *Oprah*:

> Could it be that all these women talking on, talking to, and talking about television talk shows frighten cultural critics because they have invaded the Symbolic register and suggest a reconstellation of individual and asocial agency? 'The Oprah Winfrey Show' functions as a new *Bildungsroman* that charts the irritant in the system through an endless narrative of discomfort, instead of an individual in the system through a balanced narrative of incorporation.[34]

Into the group   Recovery groups are centres of sexual story telling. There are two main and linked sexual stories that appear in these groups: tales of sex addiction and tales of relationship addiction (although abuse stories and survivor stories overlap greatly). People join groups like Sexaholics Anonymous (SA), Sex Addicts Anonymous (SAA), Sex Anonymous (S-Anon) and Co-Dependents of Sex Addicts (COSA), which started to appear from late 1970s, and have now proliferated[35]

It is a key part of the culture of recovery self help groups to move around the circle of participants who confess their problems, tell their secrets and seek help from a higher power. Wendy Kaminer, who has critically studied such groups, suggests that

> The format of the groups is constant. (They're like 7-11 stores; you can walk into a twelve step group anywhere in the country, I suspect, and feel at home.) Members take turns leading the meetings; usually they begin by reading the Alcoholics Anonymous Serenity Prayer.[36] Then the leader reads a mission statement, also taken from the AA, affirming that the group is 'a fellowship of men and women who share their experience, strength and hope with each other that they may solve their common problem and help others to recover.'[37]

Most of the groups then follow a twelve-step model borrowed from the AA but modified. Starting with a statement of 'loss of control' ('We admitted we were powerless over our sexual addiction – that our lives had become unmanageable') they build up to the twelfth step as a statement of success: 'Having had a spiritual awakening as a result of these steps, we tried to carry the message to others and to practice these principles in all our affairs.'[38] Along the way, the members are asked 'to believe in a Power greater than ourselves'; 'to turn our will and lives over to God as we understand him'; 'to make a searching and fearless moral inventory of ourselves'; 'to admit . . . our wrongs'; to be ready to 'have God remove all these defects of character'; 'to make amends to everyone we've harmed'; to continue to take a 'personal inventory'; and to keep in 'conscious contact with God, as we understand him' through prayer and meditation. These twelve steps are the core of most recovery groups. As Anne Wilson Schaef, one of the leaders of the movement, has remarked: 'As I travel around the country I am amazed at how many people are actively involved in a Twelve-Step programme as the result of one addiction or the other. In a way, this is a great Cosmic joke.'[39]

Therapy is built into the American culture, but it often takes a peculiar form. Unlike Freudian analysis which requires time and money (and lots of both, making it the refuge of the wealthy) much more popular 'instant' therapies have developed in the USA which allow for quicker, more instant 'solutions'. They are immediate, dealing decisively in the 'here and now', and pragmatic.[40]

THE GENRE OF SEXUAL RECOVERY TALES

In books, on television and in groups, then, people are telling their sexual recovery tales. The generic characteristics of these tales are not hard to delineate. Indeed, it is one of their features that they should provide clear and simple messages: complexity is not usually part of their style as they work for instant appeal and immediate recognisability. They are part of what Ritzer has referred to as the McDonaldisation of Society.[41]

In most of this story telling, there is a distinct and common pattern, and readers approach the stories with a clear expectation of what is to be found: standard routines are the norm. The genre often starts by *identifying a new problem*: 'it' will break 'the last taboo', find the 'final frontier', uncover the 'hidden dimension'. A telling *new term* will be invented. Sometimes this may be clinical but usually a catchy new complex will be unearthed – *The Cinderella Complex* (Dowling), *The Casanova Complex* (Trachtenberg), *The Soap Opera Syndrome* (Davidson). Often the title of the book catches the theme – *Men Who Hate Women, The Women Who Love Them* (Forward), *Women Who Love Too Much* (Norwood), *Men who Can't Love* (Carter and Sokol), *Smart Women, Foolish Choices* (Cowan and Kinder), *The Sexual Addiction* (Carnes). At the core of all these tales will be the *personal narrative* – in letters, in interviews, in workshops and group meetings 'testaments' are given of the experience. The author, or therapist, or facilitator, will usually have had first-hand experience of the problem themselves, and so the *author's testament* is usually part of all this. Indeed, the personal narrative is often seen to be the only reliable form of knowledge – abstracted 'male' thought is often seen as dangerous and deadly.[42] Sometimes, though, there is a curious blend of personal talk about experience blended into a distancing language of dysfunctional systems, addiction, 'little children within' and trauma – a quasi-objective language reasserts itself over the personal story. From the stories told there usually emerges a *personality profile*. Often a checklist is constructed in which the recoverer is invited – from a long list of possibilities – to spot whether they are part of this problem. Melody Beattie's influential and best-selling *Codependent No More*[43] lists fourteen major characteristics – caretaking, low self-worth, repression, obsession, controlling, denial, dependency, poor communication, weak boundaries, lack of trust, anger, sex problems (miscellaneous and progressive); and under each of these headings finds no less than three other attributes. In all, the checklist provides 238 items to watch out for! Likewise, Joy Davidson's *Soap Opera Syndrome* asks sixteen questions to discover if the reader is a 'drama-seeker'.[44]

All this leads to *the diagnosis*. Most stories converge into a childhood tale of dysfunctionality and abuse connected to 'a lost child' and a world of hidden shame and secrets. The stories return to the *childhood* of the teller where something traumatic happens. In the fullest versions of the stories there is always a *dysfunctional family* at work and a trauma is experienced – even though it is usually so deeply denied that it cannot be readily recognised (it will be the task of the author or facilitator to help bring this 'repression' to the surface). From this a *linear* – or *cyclical* – model of some pattern of abuse starts to unfold. The story most frequently is seen to be emerging in stages, or cycles. Thus, for Patrick Carnes, one of the inventors of the sex addict and sex compulsion movement, the key stages that the tellers of sex addiction stories move through are: preoccupation, ritualisation, compulsive sexual acts, despair and back again to preoccupation.[45] Again, the *checklist* is a common feature of much of this writing and talking. Much of the story needs bringing to the surface by an expert, and part of the pattern of denial and delusion to be found in the story will be the workings of co-dependents – those who help cover up the real story and who help to reinforce the problems. The rhetoric used in the story is drawn heavily from the metaphor of addiction – usually 'any process over which we are powerless'. Life is 'out of control'.[46]

Finally *the solution* is proposed, most commonly as a form of 'spiritual growth' through a series of stages. Out of the suffering, a new self is born. As John Bradshaw puts it:

> In my own case, I'm beginning to see that everything that I have gone through had to be. From the perspective of my unity consciousness, I see that my parents were perfect. I needed to become a drunk so that I could have the experience for understanding the kind of suffering addiction causes. Coming out of a dysfunctional family, I could learn about the rules which create dysfunction in families. All this is part of my self's purpose for being here.
>
> Had my dad not been a drunk and my system not been dysfunctional, I could not have created a television series about families' dysfunction and I wouldn't

be writing a book. My life was just what it needed to be for me to be able to evolve and expand my consciousness through suffering. . . . Once the contact was made with my lost child, I began the journey to discover my true self.[47]

Throughout, denial, self-exploration and recovery are key themes. Most frequently the rhetoric that is used here depends upon an amalgam of therapeutic language matched with religiosity and spirituality. The twelve-step programme developed through the Alcoholics Anonymous programmes are often the bases for such solutions. Here, classically, a formal story is provided for people to follow.[48]

RECOVERY TALES AT WORK

All this story work is aimed at helping people find their proper place in the social order – to find out who they are, construct identities, assemble a new subjective world. It provides a language in which folk can partially dwell, and a narrative structure which can frame lives. Sexual problems are framed into a therapy story which in turn becomes the story of a life.

These stories are usually very different from those of gay culture and rape politics. For whilst the story makes a sexual issue a public concern, it is in the very nature of the self help culture not to make them political. Instead, a central organising idea of therapeutic culture is the individualisation of problems. The self creates the problem and the self must solve the problem; the self should be explored and the peaks reached; the unconscious masks the problem which is an inner one. Unlike the other two stories, therapy stories do not often lead directly to political action, social movements or social change.[49] There is in principle no reason why such stories cannot be political. Indeed the prominent black feminist scholar, bell hooks, has made very clear the links between emotional and personal change alongside political and collective change. She argues that 'when wounded individuals come together in groups to make change, our collective struggle is often undermined by all that has not been dealt with emotionally'.[50] There is room for individual therapy to enhance collective change. But my point is that in practice most recovery tales lead away from politics and maintain a concern with the individual. And in their individuation they lead to less clear communities of support. Stories 'land' in smaller, less identified groupings.

The self help culture is ubiquitous and takes many forms. Some are clear group forms: counselling, therapy, self help groups, survivors' groups, coming out workshops, addicts anonymous all lead people to tell their stories to each other in face to face encounters. When this happens there is a direct community of support – people to talk with, people to ring up, friendship networks. But what is also at work here is a much more impersonal *imagined community of support*: the 'tele-advising', the self help book, etc. take people out of a solitary experience into a shared collective world where others with similar problems exist, even when they may not be known on any face to face basis. Simonds, who interviewed a number of women who read such books, concluded that: 'Reading self-help books allows women to feel part of an invisible, and thus somewhat illusory, community of other women readers who have the same concerns and problems.'[51] Some readers of self help books may indeed share books, recommend books, talk about the books and in doing so create a new network of friendship and support. Others may actually use the books as a basis for joining a group – reading about sexual addiction, for instance, leads to joining S-Anon.[52] But for others, books can provide a general awareness without having to confront actual others: especially 'authority figures' like therapists.[53] Hence there is less cost, less risk, and a person can go at their own speed.

Whilst both men and women are involved in therapy stories, there is a stronger link to women's culture. Women in general report more reading of self help books,[54] have been identified as having their own self help culture, are more likely to watch the TV day-time talk shows which serve as a major new means of telling therapy stories, and indeed seem more prone to going to therapists generally.[55] More books seem to be written with women in mind, both the tellings and the readings seem gendered. In many ways, these stories connect to what has already been identified as women's stories – gothic tales, romance novels, soap operas. Indeed, much of this writing brings into therapy exactly what is seen on the soaps – and one author, Joy Davidson, has even called it *The Soap Opera Syndrome*, a book which writes the story of the stories. Here many women's lives parallel the soap opera themes in a search for drama, relationships, constant emotional conflict. There is 'tragic structure of feeling' at work.[56] Simonds's study makes a wider point: from her study of women reading self help books, she suggests that women may often describe their reading of self help books as providing an 'emotional security', to assist in 'confronting problems', to enhance a 'live inner space'.[57]

This is not, however, just a woman's world: there are some books by, for and about men. It is true that many of the books on men are by women decrying men, and are probably written with a female readership in mind! The titles are suggestive: *The Peter Pan Syndrome* (1983), *Men Who Can't Love* (1987), *Men Who Hate Women and the Women Who Love Them* (1987), *Secrets About Men Every Woman Should Know* (1990). In the 1990s, however, a new style of self help book for men appeared – guided by the new men's movement. Robert Bly's *Iron John* was the most celebrated.

In all of this there is a complex process of sexual lives entering stories, only to find the stories creating the lives. At base, story telling becomes a commodity. It enters media worlds and sells. The texts so produced become narratives that people find themselves within. A circle of production and consumption is created which amplifies and highlights certain stories. Denzin has provided a number of valuable discussions of this process, but here he states the problem:

The dividing line between public and private lives has dissolved; anyone's personal troubles can now serve as a front-page story couched as banal morality tale with a happy ending. But as this erasure occurs, groups like ACOA, AA, NA, Adult Children of Sex Addicts, Child Abusers Anonymous and Adults

Recovering from Incest appear and take their place within the fractured fabrics of the American social structure. In these groups, members attempt to take back their lives and make sense of the experiences they encountered while being raised in their particular family's version of the American dream. They thus make public, in a limited way, the very secrets they felt the public had held against them. But along with releasing talkers from an oppressive morality that had previously trapped them in a private hell, the very moment of their talking turns their stories into commodities sold in the public marketplace.[58]

THE CONDITIONS FOR TELLING

We have seen how coming out stories were contingent upon the rise of a lesbian and gay movement and how rape stories were contingent upon the development of a woman's culture. Just what has led to this array of public story telling around 'sexual recovery'? What brings people to write their stories to an anonymous editor? What makes a person go on TV to announce they are a sex addict, that they are abused, that they are an 'older woman in love with a young man'? Of all the three case studies – gay, rape and recovery stories – the role of the mass media becomes most obvious with this case. But, again, there is a longer history that needs examining.

These stories have grown, historically, from three interrelated sources: the formal, elite and 'expert' worlds of medicine, the less formal worlds of self help and therapy, and the ongoing 'purity tradition'.[59] The roots may differ somewhat in the UK and the USA: medicine may be more prominent in the UK, whilst the USA has a longer and much stronger tradition of self help and therapy. And this in turn may account for why these kinds of stories are much more prevalent in the USA – whilst they exist in the UK, the USA is the stronger case.

One root, then, is the distinctive tradition emergent in the nineteenth century in which sex became entrapped in a *medical* metaphor. Whilst much of the medical diagnoses of the nineteenth-century medics like Acton, Benjamin Rush or even Krafft-Ebing may have long since become discredited and anachronistic, the paradigm lives on in the medicalisation of sex. The stories which emerge within this tradition centre on the failure of the sexual body and are told in deadly serious tones. They are exemplified in the work of the sex therapy business, and have led to an array of stories around erectile dysfunction, premature ejaculation, orgastic dysfunction, frigidity, anorgasmia, vaginismus, hypersexuality and the like.[60] This has become the 'objective world' of sexological science, found in the proliferation of Institutes of Medical Sexology, academic journals, professional trainings. Personal narratives of dysfunction will be found here, but usually embedded in texts written by experts. The subjective narrative gets trapped in an objectivist science. Personal experience tropes wrestle with scientific metaphor.[61]

A second distinctive tradition has its roots in a broader *therapeutic and self help discourse*, linked back to religion, Freud and most recently the counter-culture. It now blends into much New Age thinking.[62] Some versions – steeped in the rigidities of formal psychoanalysis – depend upon 'expert systems' and parallel sciences for blending the analysand's narrative with that of the patient. But others, derived usually from some strands of humanistic psychology and New Age philosophies do not claim the same objectivity as the scientific tradition, but provide instead guidance, steps, advice, support groups which will assist in personal recovery. Much of the group work here is modelled upon the success of the Alcoholics Anonymous movement.

Steven Starker and others have traced the development of self help in the USA back to the traditions and values of Protestant New England.[63] In these early, largely religious, settings people learned through appropriate instructions that they could achieve salvation through leading a good and pious life. Early writings advocated self help. Cotton Mather's *Bonifacius: Essays to Do Good* (1710) and Benjamin Franklin's *The Way to Wealth* (1757) set a mould of writings, carried on through de Tocqueville's admonitions a little later. Lears, likewise, has traced a culture which moves from 'salvation' in the late nineteenth century – where Christian spiritual values dominated – to an increasingly secularised culture based upon 'New Thought' in the late nineteenth century 'and increasing self-revelation' throughout the twentieth. The 1920s (in the USA at least) saw a notable increase in sexual awareness and self help books were published with titles like *Sex Problems Solved*.[64] The story from the 1950s is well known and indeed, by the 1960s this self-revelation and 'self-actualisation' had become so widespread that it could ultimately lead to accusations in the 1970s of ushering in the 'culture of narcissism', 'the awareness trap', the 'me-decade', the 'greatest age of individualism in American history', even an 'orgy of self- gratification'.[65]

This critique has always struck me as a little odd since it fails to take into account a third tradition which impinges upon the recovery stories: that of 'purity' and 'temperance'. This is a very strong tradition, again visible from North America's early days with the founding 'Puritan Fathers' and the spread of the Protestant Ethic, highlighted through its persistent war on alcohol and the development of The Temperance Movement. All of this suggests that much self help is not so much about the unleashing of a potential self but about restraint, regulation and control. Indeed, an underlying fear – embodied in the 'addiction' metaphor – is the fear of a 'loss of control'. Self-control is seen to be extremely important. Most of the recovery stories are hence highly prescriptive: most of the books end by telling the reader exactly what to do, whilst therapy groups provide a strong programme of what must be done (and they will not usually tolerate 'deviance'). As Reinarmand and Phillips have observed: 'Addiction, the defining feature of which is "loss of control" has become the reigning metaphor (the meta-metaphor) for personal troubles in the 1980s'.[66]

A SORT OF CONCLUSION . . .

As this section of the book comes to a close, a summary may be useful. I have argued that through a cumulative process of change whose roots seep back to the nineteenth century, communities were slowly emerging that would eventually be ready to both create and consume the stories of gay and lesbian lives, as well as those of rape survivors and twelve-step recoverers. I have suggested that 'pains' linked to these experiences earlier this century were personal, private and pathologised; they were usually solitary, secretive and sick. It doesn't matter whether the concern was rape, homosexuality or 'women who love too much': these were the modes of apprehending such experiences routinely. And they fed into a wider understanding of our sexualities in general as being morally individualistic, personally private and medically comprehensible. If you could bring yourself to imagine you were homosexual, you certainly didn't announce it: priests would have little compassion, doctors would put you in a mental hospital, the law would arrest you. Hence it was largely unheard of and lived in silence. Likewise, in most circumstances of being raped, it was also kept quiet, and indeed even when recognised, the victim frequently blamed herself, afraid of what others might say. And if you were a 'sex addict', you certainly had no language for it and no means of talking about it. But, with roots going back much further, significant changes have happened in the last quarter century. In fits and starts, with uneven development, a shift is identifiable. *The private pains increasingly become public ones; the personal sufferings become collective participations; the pathological languages turn to political ones. Stories of private, pathological pain have become stories of public, political participation.* The 'old worlds' of course remain, but progressively the late twentieth-century experience of being gay, being a rape victim, or being a relationship addict have all become very different stories.

Looking formally at the stories being told, these modern tales of desire, danger and recovery can be seen to work on three levels. Solitary 'experiences' are converted into 'beings' through the construction of *stories of identity*. Private spaces are reorganised into public ones through the construction of active groups, communities and *culture* – the personal/public distinction of the past no longer holds. And personal sufferings are (often) transformed into political ones through an emerging *political narrative* and rhetoric. These changes are common to both gays and rape survivors. With recovery groups, the political dimension is less clear.

The idea that the late twentieth century has witnessed the growth, proliferation and consolidation of new identity stories, cultural stories and political stories around both desires and defilements seems unmistakable – simply inspecting any feminist, gay or recovery bookshop will make this apparent. Homosexuality, rape and recovery stories are the major paradigmatic examples, the strong cases which signpost the emergence of new underlying forms for reconstructing the sexual sufferings. But this analysis cannot end here. For rape and gays are really only the clearest, surface tip of social worlds of new sexual story telling that have emerged over the recent past. They simply signpost a much wider range of stories.

Part III

Sexual stories at century's end

We need to become awash in tellings.

(Miller Mair)

When people define situations as real, they are real in their consequences.

(W.I. Thomas and Florian Znaniecki)

Oppressed people resist by identifying themselves as subjects, by defining their reality, shaping their new identity, naming their history, telling their story.

(bell hooks)

Chapter 8

The tale and its time

If I see a girl that most people would find attractive, I immediately tend to imagine that she has in fact wet herself and that her underclothes are wet. And instead of saying, there's a pretty girl, I desire her – I do it in two stages. This is a pretty girl. Let us imagine that she has just wet herself. Therefore I desire her.

(Cedric)

When you see someone on the streets and television – a good-looking girl that most people would look at – I don't think to myself about sort of normal sex with that girl. I will just think of, you know, being down at their feet.

(Glenn)

... shades of stockings and also shades of skin, and shades of shoes and a combination of shoes with the shape of the foot. I've noticed that some women seem to excite me tremendously for no apparent reason at all. And it appears to be because they have a certain shade of stocking on which suits their particular shade of skin, and they've got a certain fat or muscle layer in a certain form of the foot itself. That's why muscular feet seem to excite. A skinny bony foot will do little for me, usually. I'm learning how complex it is.

(Bert)

Here are more sexual tales gathered from research. In the late twentieth century, it could seem as if every sexual story that could be told is being told. Many desires have found a voice in the recent proliferation of sexual stories. Some of the newer stories have been about desires for a cross-gender experience – to be a bit, or a lot, like people are sensed to be from the other gender: the cross-dressing tales, the transvestite tales, the transexual tales. Some have simply been for any erotic desires at all: women who have been encouraged to talk about their sexual lives and desires in ways that thirty years ago was denied them. Some have been about desires in different contexts: to be a sex worker, to be a sex consumer. Some have been for special kinds of relationships – often simply ones that 'work'. Some have been for erotic desires not within their reach, or, when in their reach heavily devalued: sadomasochistic, 'fetishistic' of all kinds, high desires and low desires, adolescent and child desires and desires for adolescent and child, pornographic or representational desires, desires for sounds, and smells, and touches and tastes.

From the well-rehearsed tales of coming out, surviving abuse and recovery found in every bookstore to the continuing babble on *Donahue* or *Oprah*, the swirling simulacrum of story telling seems everywhere. We have arrived in the sexual tower of Babel where a world of past silences has been breached. How have we come to this curious situation, what has led to this new culture where sexual stories are everywhere, and is it possible to find stories that still have not been told?

Certainly, there are stories – important stories at that – which remain largely hidden from sight. Much of the sexual can still not be said, and there are stories that may well be awaiting their time. The late twentieth century has not yet easily told the stories of sexual-religious abuse: of the millions of children brought up in authoritarian families where religion circumscribes their moves, prohibits the sexual, turns their understanding of the sexual into something negative and vile and potentially leaves scars for life. Nor has it easily told the personal narrative of those millions of young women and girls whose lives are transformed through having a child and raising it, outside of traditional families.[1] It has not yet easily told the tale of the millions of boys who undergo circumcision at birth and adolescence, and may consequently experience trauma.[2] Nor has it told the personal story of erotic smell;[3] of obscure fetishism, or even the story of what it is like to masturbate. Indeed, many worlds of 'obscure' desire and dreadful thwarting are still often unmasked. And further: very rarely does the late twentieth century tell the tale of a paedophile, a rapist or even a serial murderer from their point of view. Indeed when these latter stories are found, they are trapped in the language of authority which pathologises, demonises, trivialises, or sensationalises. They are the 'horror stories' and the 'atrocity tales', not stories told as personal narratives whose time has come.

Consider, for instance, the personal story of Scott McDonald, the tale of a radical man who consumes pornography.

> The frequent contempt of 'intelligent' people for those who 'need' pornographic materials has always functioned to keep me quiet about my real feelings, but a screening of *Not A Love Story* and a series of responses to it have emboldened me to assess my attitudes. . . . From the instant my car is carrying me towards pornography, I feel painfully visible, as if everyone who sees me knows from my expression, my body language, whatever, exactly where I am going. The walk from the car to the door, and later from the door to the car, is especially difficult: will someone see me? . . . I always fear the power of the social stigma against such experiences. Unless the people who see me have been in my situation, I'm sure they deduce my visit to the arcade reflects my inadequacy. . . . Once inside an arcade . . . this anxiety continues.[4]

What is it like to buy porn, read porn, masturbate with porn? In 1990, Michael Kimmel published a series of essays like the extract above in which some men tell their stories of pornography. It was unusual, because although the story of pornography is polyvocal – it is certainly not a silent story, as the volumes written about it will amply testify[5] – certain story telling modes about it have been more or less silenced. We can certainly hear the voice of the pornographer speaking through the text; we can hear the voice of the scientist telling the story of its 'effects'; we can hear the story of the women abused through pornography; we can hear the voices of 'community standards'; we can hear the voices of anti-porn feminists risen against it. But only very recently are the voices of the people who actually read and look at pornography being heard. Even though millions of people look at pornography every day, very few have been willing to talk about this experience. The pornography consumer is only just starting to 'come out'.

Men (and now women) have generally been silent about consuming pornography. The whole experience has been deeply shrouded in stigma and hence silenced. In the Attorney-General's Commission on Pornography, instigated by President Reagan in 1985 (The Meese Commission),[6] the only people who speak out about using porn are the men who say that it has ruined their lives.[7] Likewise, in the sex addiction stories published in the 1980s, we find men telling of their compulsion towards pornography, of obsession, of escalation, of tragedy. But the 'sad tales of porn' are all we seem to hear, a story which reinforces shame and guilt and prevents other tales from being heard. Pornography is revealed in the biographies of serial sexual killers. But rarely is the everyday story told of everyday folk who 'just like pornography', who use it for erotic delight! Can it all be so unmitigatingly bad? Why don't people tell any good stories? Why is this world of stories so silent? Just what is the role of pornography in many personal lives? How is it obtained? Where is it stored? How is it read? Is there a history to the reading of certain images? Why is there often a silence? What happens once disclosed? How – in short – does pornography feature in the everyday lives of everyday men (and increasingly, it seems, women)? Where are the personal narratives of all this? Curiously, as I am writing this, a new tale is starting to appear. But it is a tale being told largely by women, not men. It is a tale told of women who have decided to make their own porn, consume their own porn, delight in their own porn. There may be a new story – of *women liking porn* – in the making.[8]

Many stories, then, are still largely untold and many voices have not yet been heard. Although a chorus of new voices around sexual stories has been emerging throughout this century, it is still not all said and done. Most stories that 'take off' in a culture do so because they slot easily into the most accepted narratives of that society: the dominant ideological code. Others that are still not heard may fit less easily. And in the closing chapters of this book, I will be increasingly concerned with the making of some of these newer stories. When, then, does a story come into its time? When can a voice and a claim about sexuality be heard?

In this chapter I will look briefly at some sexual stories whose time has not yet come and ponder why this is so. Building upon this, I will examine the circumstances that lead stories to 'come out' into their time, as both historical process and situational contingency.

SILENT STORIES OUT OF TIME

Here is a fragment of another research story, one gathered from an intensive life history over several years. It is a voice that is not heard that often: that of a 70-year-old man, William White, who has spent his life as a paedophile:

> The main problem is the sort of longing, the sort of eternal longing, for a companion, for somebody you can love and somebody who'll love you in return. This is a problem common almost to anybody, whatever their sexuality, but it's ever so much more difficult in the case of a pederast. Because he knows that if he is lucky enough to find this person, it's only going to be a thing which lasts for a very short time. Very, very short time. Just between certain ages and then the boy is going to develop and go away, we're hoping as a normal boy, as a heterosexual. He ceases to be a boy and therefore ceases to be attractive to me, and similarly he is beginning to be attracted by girls. So the problem is almost insoluble. Yet you never give up hope. You can go on even to the age that I am at the moment and you're still telling yourself all the time that you are going to find the one. You convince yourself that you are, but you damned well know it isn't so.
>
> A thing that has always puzzled me immensely is that you see this beautiful boy, and the original thing that one wants to do is not to have any sort of violent sex with him – the thing that you find you most want to do is to kiss and cuddle him and lie in a naked embrace – which is to what he responds and he responds to your kisses. And you kiss his face and his eyes and his ears and you're content with the embrace and the kissing which in many ways seem to be the first things which seem to be more important. Getting down to any sort of grim sex – well you hope this will happen and it does eventually happen, but the urge in the first place, I think, my urge is always just to have him in your arms and have him respond to you.

I first met William White in 1976, as he was coming to the end of his working life. Born in a southern town, he was widely travelled and had had a successful career (in weights and measures inspection) until he was convicted of a sexual offence around the time of the 'Wildblood-Montagu' homosexual witch-hunts in the mid-1950s.[9] He was sentenced for a year, and although, perhaps surprisingly, he was not treated too badly by the authorities inside the prison, it did permanently damage his career. (He turned to sales work subsequently.) Although he was actually arrested on a false charge, he had prior to this period organised his life so that older boys would come and stay in his house in the country and he would teach them swimming, fishing, hunting and the like and have the 'pleasure' of getting close to them. The boys were never under 13, as he regarded this as a risk; and the boys would always want to engage in the experiences, or so he argued. Ironically, though, he did not go to prison for this – but for a 'false allegation'.

William's interest, then, was focused primarily on boys around pubescence – a little before and a little after. Like so many, he recalled this interest as developing fairly early in life and it had stayed with him. Rarely had it resulted in any sexual acts with boys. His sex life was usually by necessity limited to older males who, if less satisfying, were at least safe. His conception was a 'romantic one' – his desires were much more than 'lust' and he spoke at great length about the desire for the young person's welfare and how indeed those with whom he had formed a relationship had been helped and were often still in contact with him.

His whole life had, however, been haunted – not only by the desire, but also the ban:

What I think is such a terrible thing is that a man has to go his entire life in fear, solely because he lives in a country where ignorant people have made laws which he has to abide with. And so, all these law-makers and judges and magistrates and people judge you, and punish you. They have a free sex life. I often wonder how many times an ordinary normal married man, well it doesn't matter if he's married or not, how many times he has sexual relations in his life. Now those ones that sit and make the laws, they say about people like myself, you're not allowed to do this at all. Ever. In other words, I'm born in such a way that the law doesn't permit me to ever have any sexual relation which I enjoy. And so I do of course – I can't stand the temptation for ever and ever, so I sometimes have a little illicit sex, which is punishable. Punishable by law. Laws made by people that don't know what the hell they're talking about. And you couldn't have anybody put it better than Masefield did:

> The laws of God, the laws of man,
> Let them keep that will and can, Not I
> Let God and man decree laws for themselves,
> but not for me.
> And if my ways are not as theirs,
> Then let them mind their own affairs.
> Their deeds I judge and much condemn,
> But when did I make laws for them
> But no they will not, they must still
> Wrest their brother to their will,
> And make me dance as they desire,
> With Gaol and Gallows and Hell Fire.

It's exactly what he meant . . . I remember an enormous amount of poetry, it wasn't Masefield, it was Housman. A.E. Housman. . . . There are many poems he wrote on the same sort of theme. Little lines come to mind. 'They hanged the poor fellow for the colour of his hair.'

Here is a tale of suffering, of a desire sensed to be damned. It was a highly articulate version of damnation as the poetic lines often rolled from William's tongue. But then, as is so common, he had had many years to reflect on his damned desire and to rehearse his story. William's is not a gay story: indeed he is hostile to gays and it forms part of his story to make this clear and to mark himself off from these 'others'. But his is a story with a familiar ring. Others may not have his desires, but they share his stories. They recognise a desire for some kind of satisfaction in their personal (emotional, erotic, intimate?) life which is persistently thwarted. Yet whilst these other stories may be told, that of William is much rarer.

The story of the adult male who professes and sometimes practices a sexual desire for children is an instructive case of a story that has dimly tried to be told by a few and yet has generally not been heard. There are very few stories from identified 'child sex abusers'; once caught their own story goes silent and instead their tale gets incorporated into the tales of critics, researchers, analysts.[10] Their own story in their own voice is not heard.[11] In part this is clearly because nobody will allow it to be told and nobody wishes to hear. It is simply implausible that paedophiles have a story, and inconceivable that they should be allowed to speak it. And, indeed, few 'child lovers' would even be willing to tell it. For their own story is not told because of their own shame, their own need for secrecy, their fear of ostracism and indeed, their potential for imprisonment. It cannot be heard because of all the 'sexual differences', this is the one which seemingly creates greatest anger and concern in the wider communities of interpretation. It cannot be received easily. It is hence a good test case for sensing when stories may be told.

Silence voices/created communities   There is one strained voice trying to tell personal stories around this painful and explosive experience. This strand does not take on the language of child sex abuse, for this is after all a negative language. Instead, it takes a more positive voice: as paedophilia, as child love, as children's sexual rights and liberation. It seeks to debunk the myths that surround it. It claims its own history in strands of thought and politics which can certainly be taken back to the nineteenth century in several countries, and even to the Ancient Greeks.[12] An overt, political movement starts to emerge most forcibly in the early 1970s. In England, it was through PAL (Paedophile Action for Liberation) and PIE (the Paedophile Information Exchange) – breakaway groups from The Gay Liberation Movement. In North America, the prime group was NAMBLA – the North American Man Boy Love Association. Finding their desires for young men being rejected from within the gay movement, of which they were originally a part, they created their own, new political groupings with meetings, newsletters, magazines, agendas, stories. In the Netherlands and Scandinavian countries other small groups appeared, often earlier. But small they have always been.[13] In the UK, for instance, PAL went defunct within two years, and PIE never had a membership beyond 200 and had ceased altogether by 1985.

What are the claims they made and the stories they wrote? It is possible to place their stories on a spectrum which is arrayed from the conservative to the radical. Some speak in Boy Scout Leader tones about the purity of the man–boy relationship and whose stories provide manuals of etiquette for behaviour between adult and child. Others see the adult–child relationship as a revolutionary act.[14] A paedophile who enters this world has an array of stories that can be drawn upon in making sense of the experience. They exist within these elementary social movements and they also exist in the wider culture of fictional stories. The stories are there, but they have not been assembled into the lives of paedophiles. Why?

These were not stories whose time had come for several reasons. First was the sheer strength of taboo against paedophilia. This story is taboo. Indeed, paedophilia is a criminal act. Unlike the gay story of coming out which starts to be told loudly at the very moment when decriminalisation becomes more common, the paedophile relationship remains a criminal offence. Most countries not only have laws, but strong penalties, for adult–child sex. Closely linked to this, prosecutions were made against most of the major paedophile groups and many of its leaders were imprisoned. Tom O'Carroll was the leading spokesperson in the UK and wrote a book that aimed to provide a radical defence of his position. He was also prosecuted for conspiracy to corrupt public morals, his case was heard at the Old Bailey, and he was sent to prison. He was not sent to prison for paedophile acts, but basically for paedophile *talk*.[15] Overt hostility, then, inhibits story telling.

Second, there was no media support and amplification on behalf of paedophiles: indeed the reverse took place, as the mass media presented periodic but cumulatively more intense moral panics against child abuse. Paedophile stories of 'the most evil men in the world' fed directly into a much larger narrative plot that was unfolding from the early 1970s onwards: the story of 'threatened children'.[16] The media serve as gatekeepers, transformers and amplifiers of stories: their stories are purposive behaviour. They work to carve out fields and expand some rhetorics while ignoring others. Certainly the media has covered paedophilia but nearly always in a negative/hostile fashion within the ever-expanding story of threatened children. This begins with the concern over child abuse in the 1970s but spreads out to capture an ever-widening domain: 'kidnappers, child molesters, child pornographers, drug pushers, pimps, Satanists, Halloween sadists and other deviants who victimize children ... abortionists, drunk drivers, people with Aids ... missing children, abused children, sexually exploited children, and other child victims.'[17]

And third, alliances between paedophile and other groups were few, usually non-existent. There were 'children's sexuality lobbies', a few 'anarcho-libertarians', even the odd feminist,[18] but there was really very little by way of support. All the fashionable literature on marginality/outsiders/silenced voices allows no space for these marginal voices to be heard. They were an embarrassment to even the most liberal of voices. They should be silenced. And all of this meant that there was no sustained community of support, no place for coming out, and secrecy was maintained. Without a community 'fattened up' to hear the story and receive it, the story could not be told.

THE SOCIAL ORGANISATION OF SEXUAL STORY TELLING

If there are lessons to be learnt as to how stories cannot be told, there are also lessons to be learnt as to how they can. *What are the social conditions that have facilitated the emergence of the new stories being heard in the late twentieth century: how do these new stories come to be told and heard?*[19] This is not quite the same as asking why specific people can or cannot tell their tale. Brave (or foolish) folk may tell a story 'out of time'; many folk may not be able to tell their tale even when the story is being widely told. I am asking about stories whose time has come.

Thus, for instance, lesbian and gay coming out stories could hardly be heard publicly before the 1970s, although they may have been secretly said. Likewise, the stories of the survivors of child sexual abuse were largely silenced till the 1980s, although there is much evidence of child abuse being common before this time.[20] They were dormant stories. But since then there has been a flood of tellings – in books, in therapy groups, in TV shows – for those who would hear. Even more recently, would the damagingly different stories of sex and harassment told by Clarence Thomas and Anita Hill in the autumn of 1991 have been heard at all in, say, 1960, or 1860? And who could have said – and who could have heard – the stories of 'Women Who Love Porn' on *Donahue* in 1975? And on an even wider scale, who could imagine the performance-stories of a Prince or a Madonna being told in the 1950s, when the wiggle of an Elvis was just entering the world of possible public movements? Or what sense might an audience have made of the film *sex, lies and videotape* in 1940, even assuming it could have been made – which it couldn't, as its very premise about the videotaping of sexual stories was technologically impossible at that time.

Stories can be told when they can be heard. There is usually no point in telling a tale without a receptive and appreciative listener, and one who is usually part of a wider community of support. (Although sometimes, as in masturbatory stories, the teller and appreciative hearer may be the one and the same solitary person!) To publicly tell a story to someone who will then mock you, disbelieve you, excommunicate you, sack you, hospitalise you, imprison you or bash you bleeding senseless to the ground may be brave but foolhardy: it is not a fertile ground for the amplification of that story. It may well be better to be silent, at least for the moment.

What has happened over the past few decades is the proliferation of an array of different audiences willing to hear some different voices and some different stories – and some of these audiences may then become tellers themselves, adding to collective communities of story telling. I do not wish to suggest some inevitable determined 'cause' of such story telling but an imagery instead of facilitating conditions, stumbling affinities, precarious emergence. The contemporary growth of sexual stories – through books, media, new social movements – can perhaps best be seen through the shifting of social spaces in which listeners and audiences break down traditional boundaries around stories. Whereas once stories were largely part of a localised oral culture, told in small bounded worlds, the nineteenth century witnessed stories moving into mass print – into the tabloids, penny press and scandal sheets;[21] and the twentieth century has seen them become television docudramas, talk-show fodder and self help manuals available for mass consumption. Modern mass media organisation has shifted access to worlds that may not have been visible, accessible or even thinkable before. Whilst in one sense it has rendered the world *mass*, in another it is has rendered it segmented, fragmented, dispersed.[22] In *No Sense of Place*, Joshua Meyrowitz has argued that the new electronic media have blurred previously distinct spheres, such as those between men and women, young and old, gay and straight, black and white, making what were once segregated worlds more pervasively accessible. Yet the media also bring homogenising, mass tendencies too. When our central media was face to face talk, separate worlds could be created in which 'special informations' were kept away from others or, indeed, not permitted at all. Modern media breaks down such boundaries: telephones make sexual communication across place more easy, travel and tourism opens wider vistas of sexual possibility, television chat shows enable one to hear about the sexual problems of all manner of groups over breakfast, whilst MTV can tell its postmodern sexual story twenty-four hours a day. In England a child being sexually abused can come to hear of Esther Ranzen, ChildLine, where to ring, what to say. For many, these stories fall into an impersonalised mass: to hear a story of sexual impotence does not lead you to a community of impotence sufferers – or even to a community of men keen to swap stories of their impotence.[23] But for others, communities of support do exist. So, simultaneously, mass undifferentiated audiences are created side by side with new segregated worlds of specialist consumers. The neophyte young gay man who may first find himself through a gay pop star on TV, may then find 'his story' in the more segregated world of the gay community – with its own fictions, memories and magazines stuffed full of the stories of gay life. Modern audiences for stories are both more *and* less segregated.[24]

Stories come into their time when a community has been fattened up, rendered ripe and willing to hear such stories. Whilst they can be heard amongst isolated individuals, they can gain no momentum if they stay in this privatised mode. Many personal narratives hence remain in the private sphere of dim inarticulateness, having no group to sustain and strengthen them. For stories to flourish there must be social worlds waiting to hear. Social worlds are not like communities of old: no locale is required, only a sense of belonging, sharing traditions, having common memories. As I have argued earlier, a key point about the coming out stories is that they progressively acquired an *interpretive community of support* which enabled them to flourish. There is historical amplification and feedback at work here. For sure, people could come out as gay in the 1960s and before: but then it really meant in isolation, to oneself, a solitary lover or in the disguised, furtive 'twilight' worlds of the secretive homosexual underworld. As the artist F.O. Matthiesen wrote to his new lover in 1925:

> Of course this life of ours is entirely new – neither of us know of a parallel case. We stand in the middle of an uncharted, uninhabited country. That there have been other unions like ours is obvious, but we are unable to draw on their experience. We must create everything for ourselves. And creation is never easy.[25]

To turn this tale from a private, personal tale to one that can be told publicly and loudly is a task of immense political proportions. It requires a collective effort, creating spaces in the wider social order and the wider story telling spaces. Bit by bit – through the leaflet, the pamphlet, the booklet, the book, the meeting, the recording, the newspaper, the television programme, the film, the chat show, the video – the voice gains a little more space, and the claims become a little bigger. There will always be counter-stories too, but these may also have their part to play.

BACK TO THE FUTURE: HISTORY, CONTINGENCY AND STORY TELLING

A full social history of the rise of these new stories and audiences awaits writing. But the fragments for assembling it already exist, and come in several waves. Foucault, for instance, has charted the long revolution. Starting somewhere back in the eighteenth century in the western world, he locates the paths through which the modern period brought a 'discursive explosion', an 'incitement to discourse', a desire to 'tell everything'.[26]

> Western man has been drawn for three centuries to the task of telling everything concerning his sex; that since the classical age there has been a constant optimisation and an increasing valorisation on the discourse on sex; and that this carefully analytical discourse was meant to yield multiple effects of displacement, intensification, reorientation and modification of desire itself. Not only were the boundaries of what one could say about sex enlarged, and men compelled to hear it said; but more important, discourse was connected to sex by a complex organisation with varying effects, by a deployment that cannot be adequately explained merely by referring it to a law of prohibition. A censorship of sex? There was installed rather an apparatus for producing an ever-greater quantity of discourse about sex, capable of functioning and taking effect in its very economy.[27]

Foucault's compelling account of the workings of power through this apparatus has been extremely influential and may now be too well known to repeat. Of course, it is possible to take Foucault further and further and argue – with Baudrillard – that all the stories that are now told bear no relation to reality at all, that anything and everything can be said about sex, that it is all simulation, play, hyperreality, simulacrum. Discourses have imploded into themselves, sex is dead, simulations are all we have. And anything can be said because it means nothing. A take-off point for this process would probably be the late 1960s – the high point of expressivism. For Baudrillard, 'everything is sexuality' and by the same token, nothing is. Everything can now be said. But can it?[28]

I think both Foucault and later Baudrillard go too far. Baudrillard is the philosopher of excess, and provides little real aid in understanding the direct empirical world (not that he would want to: as he turns it all into a hyperreality). It is not the case that everything can now be said about sex – much has been said, but not everything. And indeed many stories are a long way from the hyperreal – tell an abuse victim or a young woman coming out as a lesbian that their stories are mere simulations, mere excrements of a hyperreal reality, with no links to real pains, sufferings, life! But even the (slightly) more measured and much cited account of Foucault is couched at a level of generality – of the deployment of discursive strategies and power/knowledge spirals – which is too opaque. Yes, sexuality has been thoroughly reconstituted for the modern period and, indeed, the sexual stories of this book could slot neatly into his schema. Yet his account neglects the rise of mass media in all its diverse forms, and it provides little space for the generation of particular kinds of stories at particular moments: it is all strangely undifferentiated. Stories about sex have not all been fashioned from the same cloth in the modern world. Indeed, to hark back to the gay and lesbian story, there is a world of difference between the morbid pathological stories so prevalent in the nineteenth century, and the 'liberating' coming out tales of the late twentieth. Power may be ubiquitous – for Foucault, as for me. But some forms of power expand choices (coming out stories) and are empowering; whilst other forms reduce choices (pathology/victim tales), and lead to control and domination. What hence needs to be explained is why specific stories have their specific times, whilst others do not. Why do some stories lie *dormant*, some become *dominant* (at particular moments), some take on a *dissident* position, whilst yet others become *dead*, moving out of their time? And many stories, possibly most, undergo *recycling* – for example, the narratives of sexual danger so popular in late Victorian England returned to popularity in the late twentieth century, as did narratives of decadence and disease.[29]

A first step in this task is to avoid talking in such grand historical sweeps as Foucault, and to turn to a more specific time. Whilst the seeds of modern sexual stories are there in the nineteenth century, it is to the last four decades of the twentieth that real attention must be paid. Whatever changes occurred in the nineteenth century to establish preconditions of sexual story telling, a qualitative shift occurs in the mid-twentieth. Most analysts of sexuality agree that something dramatic happened to sexuality during the 1960s and 1970s. For some, it is simply 'the "permissive" watershed': 'commentators of all political persuasions are inclined to agree that it was the "sexual revolution" of the "fab" and "groovy" 1960s, myth or reality, which served as the sea-change in the sexualisation of modern capitalist societies.'[30] More specifically, shifts have been detected in the swings towards a libertarianism where sex is 'viewed as a positive, beneficial, joyous phenomenon . . . connected to personal health, happiness, self-fulfillment and social progress';[31] towards a feminisation of sex;[32] towards a recreational sex;[33] and ultimately towards a democratisation of intimacy.[34]

There is no one reason for these changes. One factor is surely the growth and proliferation of communications. Not only have the major means of mass communication been put into place so as to be widely available to most (from mass paperbacking to records, TV, telephones, videos, etc.), but enough stories have been told publicly and circulated freely to reach a critical take-off point. Freud's stories, for example (his dreams, Dora, Hans, the Rat Man, Oedipus and all the rest) ooze through much of the early decades (becoming a consistent narrative plot to be reworked and reanalysed into many sexual stories – personal tales, fiction, film, even social science!). A string of important narrative tales around the intimate pile up in the latter part of the twentieth century, each one making it more and more plausible for others to emerge.[35] In the late 1930s, the cheap popular paperback was invented and 'the world of books – like the world itself – would never be the same'.[36] By the late 1940s, the Kinsey Reports on *Human Sexual Behaviour* – turgidly taxonomic and ponderously long as they were – had become scandalous best-sellers.[37] And then a steady flow of major books raised their own story: Betty Friedan's *Feminine Mystique* (tales of invisible and oppressed womanhood), Masters and Johnson's *Human Sexual Inadequacy* (scientific tales of sexual dysfunction), Alex Comfort's *Joy of Sex* (tales of love-making practices), Nancy Friday's *My Secret Garden* (tales of woman's fantasies, updated seventeen years later as *Women on Top*), Susan Brownmiller's epic *Against Our Will* (tales of rape) along with *The Sensuous Woman*, *The Happy Hooker*, *The Total Woman* and hundreds of other delights. All were paperback best-sellers in the USA before the mid-1970s. But the list could be much extended.[38] Indeed, throughout the 1980s one sexual paperback after another became a best-seller: *The Intimate Male*, *The Hite Report on Male Sexuality*, *Pleasures*, *Swept Away*, *Sweet Suffering*, *Women Who Love too Much*, *Rediscovering Love*, *Remaking Love*, *Men Who Hate Women and the Men Who Love Them*, *The Casanova Complex*, *Looking for Love in all the Wrong Places*, *Escape from Intimacy*, *Smart Love*, *Sex for One*, *Nice Guys Sleep Alone* – to name but a few!

Yet whilst the spread of the media and the cumulative proliferation of stories provide a context ripe for more and more sexual stories, other factors have played a part in creating a culture of sexual story telling. First is the major spread of consumerisms. The post-war period is marked increasingly by the rise of a logic of consumerism, which leads to increasing advertising and marketing. 'Consumption objects' become a means to demarcate lifestyles and hierarchies.[39] 'Sex' in all it forms is manifestly part of this Big Sell. Newspapers seek out sex stories, willing to pay a high price, because of the likelihood of increased circulation; publishers pursue more and more outrageous stories – Madonna's *Sex*, for instance – because they often sell well, and especially in the USA frequently head the best-seller charts; advertisers head for the chat shows and the soaps that peddle sex; therapists and sexologists may be less commercial, but still know where the money is.[40] Everywhere, the expansion of capitalism brings with it the expansion of sex consumerism.

An important part of the consumerist culture has been the rise of 'youth culture' in the post-Second World War period. Of course, 'youth' existed before, but not within the space of such a well organised market – of magazines, films, television programmes (the whole of MTV seems marketed for youth). An array of super pop stars singing of sex and writing their sexual stories. From the early furore that surrounded Elvis Presley's appearance on the *Johnny Carson Show*; through the

1960s with Jimi Hendrix copulating with his guitar and simulating masturbatory ejaculation on stage; through to the banning of the Sex Pistols, Frankie Goes to Hollywood, and on to the ubiquitous Madonna scandals, sex stories have never been far away from the youthful consumer.[41]

Alongside the rise of both media and consumerism, a new infrastructure of 'cultural intermediaries' has developed. This large occupational culture connects to media, advertising and 'para'-intellectual information, and generates a proliferating industry concerned with the production and selling of 'symbolic goods'.[42] There were, for instance, no talk-show hosts who could invite you on to television to tell your sexual story before the 1950s; there were few 'celebrity intellectuals'. But in the late modern period, people with a word processor or a video or simply an enthusiasm can decide to tell their sexual stories and indeed to sell their sexual stories – making themselves into part of the sexual 'chattering classes'! Everyone seeks their Warholian fifteen minutes!

Closely allied to this rise of new cultural intermediaries is the acceleration of the individualistic 'therapeutic/expressive culture' which fosters the telling of self-narratives. As discussed in Chapter 7, there is a long history in the USA of self help development. Reaching back to Benjamin Franklin, amplified by Freudian thought, developing through the therapies of the 1960s, symbolised momentarily by the counter-culture and drifting into the New Age, this whole modern period has been characterised negatively as the *Culture of Narcissism*, and, more positively, as the *Psychological Society*. Another whole field of work has been generated around therapy and self-exploration: the creation of the *Secular Priests*, a belief in the *Faith of the Counsellors*, the *Triumph of the Therapeutic*.[43]

All this telling of sex has consistently been surrounded in controversy, moral panics and a stream of moral crusades which have tended to polarise positions, keeping 'sex stories' as contested stories well in focus in public debate.[44] Indeed, without polarities the stories may have lost much of their potency: ironically, the protests may well have amplified the context for more and more stories, by bringing them constantly into sharp public attention (even if just to denounce them). The right contest the left; the orthodox contests the progressive;[45] the romantic contests the libertarian;[46] the right-to-lifers contest the right to choose; the moralists contest the causalists;[47] and the traditionalists, modernists and postmodernists are all at odds with each other. Conflict and contest each serve to extend and highlight the power of sexual talk, pushing the stories further and further.

This, then, is the backdrop to the creation of the culture of sexual story telling. The growth of mass media, the expansion of consumption, the rise of new cultural intermediaries and the expansion of a therapeutic culture – all locked into conflicts which highlight stories in their warfare. It is against this backdrop that more and more stories can be told.

MAKING STORIES HAPPEN

Sexual stories told in the past may have little relevance for today, just as stories told today may have little relevance for the future. Stories have their times. But the question that has concerned me over the past few chapters has been how certain stories of suffering and surviving have come into their time. The reason for my concern with this question is a frankly political one: I worry that just as some voices from the past were not heard, some voices of today remain mute. Many of the silenced voices of the past – of women, of blacks, of gays, of ecologists, of 'the other' – have created some spaces, told some stories, brought about some change; and there are lessons to be learnt from this. But there are also stories that still we have not imagined. In the last two chapters, I will be touching upon some of these unimagined, even unimaginable, stories. But before doing this, I want to bring together a number of themes which might suggest when stories can be told, what I will call *the generic process of telling sexual stories*. I put them in a rough sequence, but the sequences should not be taken too seriously: the world is not that linear. Still, they do indicate necessary conditions for the full-blown 'successful' telling of a sexual story (or indeed any story): for a story 'finding its time'.[48] These generic processes are:

1 Imagining – visualising – empathising;
2 Articulating-vocalising – announcing;
3 Inventing identities – becoming story tellers;
4 Creating social worlds/communities of support;
5 Creating a culture of public problems.

The process can be pictured as a move from an 'inner world' of telling stories to the self privately to an increasingly public one where the circle of discourse becomes wider and wider. In the earliest moments, the story can hardly be imagined: it may be told privately as a tale to oneself. Later it gets told to a few people – a lover, a friend, a psychiatrist. Slowly it can move out into a public domain where it comes to take on a life of its own. It becomes part of a public discourse.

First, then, there are processes of *imagining – visualising – empathising*. Something – a feeling, a thinking, a doing – is to be envisioned. This can be a very simple task – an issue is felt, experienced, found and is brought into focus as a story. *But I am thinking also of a whole world of feelings and experiences about which we may not even initially know.*[49] They inhabit worlds where it seems that nothing unusual is happening at one moment, and then some kind of trouble appears at another. This 'trouble' has to be recognised – by self or other. Just as in the past rape happened in marriage but was hardly recognised, just as child abuse happened in families and was taken for granted, so what is taken for granted now will not necessarily be in the future. 'Nothing unusual' will become 'trouble'. Betty Friedan, over a quarter of a century ago, could sense 'the problem that has no name'. Oscar Wilde, over a century ago, could speak of the 'love that dared not speak its name'. And Rousseau, over two centuries ago, could save the unnameable for after his death! Good stories of course are intimately connected to the imagination; but much of modern life is also trapped in the conventions and rituals of pre-existing stories which prevent, conceal and block other ways of seeing. There is a need to recognise *the blocks to imagining* stories that could be told but are currently not.

I am speaking here about experiences hidden from awareness and part of this means entering the world of the unconscious: of repressions, masks, denials. Much of the inner life is kept at bay, sealed off from any potential for story telling. But it also means understanding better the processes of feeling helpless, incapacitation and loss of control. Traditionally, for example, women have sensed less control over their lives than men, and may have been less able to voice their stories because of this. In any event a crucial emergent from this process must be a growing awareness of languages that mask, hide, deny or erase experiences. To take a major example: menstruation. All girls experience this, and yet it exists largely in a world of silence. Girls may experience a shock, a pain, a concern and yet the public narratives of menstruation are few. Much of the existing story telling around menstruation often cloaks it in myth and danger – the film *Carrie* opens with a menstrual scene, but this in turn places it firmly in a world of danger. Some girls may find communities of support but there is little public discourse that facilitates this often isolated experience.

A myriad of little sexual stories may be imagined – stories of intrigue and romance, stories of extreme eroticism thwarted in everyday life, stories of unhappiness built up through frustrations, stories of wives leaving their partners, tales of divorce through 'bad sex'. But such stories, whilst commonplace, remain culturally insignificant as long as they fail to enter the more public domain: as long as they are silent. Hence, crucially, a second generic process – of *articulating – vocalising – announcing* becomes crucial in the making of stories. To breathe life into the imagination, a language must be found for it. For what has to be seen, there may often not be words. Or if words exist, they may be the wrong words – words which place a wedge between the being and the telling. A space needs to be found where languages can be invented, words can be applied, a voice can be found, a story can be told. This will be a language explosion; from small words whispered alone to the self to whole rhetorics shouted in public spaces – from the trauma of naming your abuse to yourself to the public story at a 'Take Back the Night' rally. Language may not just be a matter of words said, but how the words are said: the *ways* in which stories are told. Thus some words may become little crimped tales told in small corners whilst others become shouted expansive stories told by people aware of power-dressing. Here are matters of control over space, body, face, dress, eyes and touch. Likewise, there are many possible languages, rhetorics, stories that could be told. For instance, imagine that someone somewhere comes to see that there is a 'problem' or 'trouble' in the number of poor, unmarried, young women having babies and raising them. The story could be told as an instance of pathology (disturbed family backgrounds), of moral decline (the weakening of family values and chastity ideals), of education (failure to educate young women), of feminism (of patriarchy putting women at a disadvantage), of racism (the 'black girls' are targeted), of fundamentalism (God's wrath is evoked), of social policy (advocating adequate welfare benefits) or of victim-blaming (it's their own fault in some way). And, of course, within any of these few themes there are many possible sub-stories. In other words, imagining and identifying concerns says nothing in itself of the kinds of languages, claims and stories that will then be produced around them. And there is no one story that is fixed into the 'trouble' we imagine; gay stories of the nineteenth century, rape stories of the eighteenth century were very different. And these days, many stories compete with each other.

Third, there are processes of *inventing identities – becoming story tellers*. The image I have is that bit by bit stories move out from a small space of imaginings into a language, through a few tellers and into a community ripe and ready to hear. Crucial in this process therefore must be a time when story tellers come into public view: writing books, magazines, appearing on other media, etc. To work at their best they will be 'the stories of our lives', not stories of others co-opted, although in early stages these may be of value.[50] Hence the stronger stories will be those of community – providing programmes and maps where others may be able to sense themselves. Highly individualistic stories without a sense of community will just 'float', with less chance of reaching a critical take-off point. Grounded in this will usually be a story of identity – of who one is, of a sense of unity yet difference. At this moment, the experience and a faltering language gains a voice and a person-hood. The 'gay', the 'survivor', the 'recoverer' becomes recognisable, an identity emerges with a sense of past, present, future: history, difference, anticipation. And the narratives of this new personhood start to enter public worlds of talk. The basis of a politics of identity is formed.[51]

Fourth, then, this implies *creating social worlds*.[52] The story has moved out beyond the individual story teller to a community of reception. It is being heard by others. As we saw clearly in Part II, social worlds must be invented which will hear the story. These 'others' must in some way identify with it, feel it to be part of their 'story'. The correct audiences become crucial. Some of these social worlds may already exist, whilst others may actually be formed by the stories. Thus, many pre-existing social worlds of age (youth worlds, childhood worlds), of race (black worlds/Hispanic worlds/Asian worlds), of gender, class, etc. provide forums for talk and telling stories. Often such worlds are segregated – the stories young men tell each other in the factory are not to be shared with parents or female friends.[53] Other 'worlds' seem to come into being around the stories.

The critical take-off point comes when social worlds come together around the story, which clearly starts to become a public matter. Earlier, I discussed some of the factors which helped shape the emergence of gay and feminist social worlds – urban life, shifting families, media messages, consumer markets – as well as factors which have impeded others developing – strong taboos, overt hostility, minimum media, few alliances.[54] Yet these interpretive communities exist in and through social worlds of power: they are hierarchically arranged, and some are marginalised whilst others are prioritised. Thus, just having a community will not be sufficient: the more power the community has, the greater the story's chances of taking hold. Hence the story needs a visible public community of alliance and allegiances which facilitate the telling of the tale.

Fifth, and finally, then, are the generic processes involved in *creating a culture of public problems*. Here the story moves out of a limited social world and enters an array of arenas of public discourse. Sociologists have long studied the mechanisms through which social problems are socially constructed:

> How the dimensions are carved out, how the number of people drawn into concern about these discussions is increased, how a common pool of knowledge begins to develop for the arena participants, and how all these subprocesses increase the visibility of the problem.[55]

Telling personal stories is a crucial part of this public process: the human interest story is one of the key foci in getting issues on agendas. A 'good personal story' will advance a social problems agenda significantly. For the culture of public problems is a competitive one: many stories are available, but few are chosen. How stories get selected for public attention will depend upon such matters as novelty, drama, saturation, the 'carrying capacity' of media and the competition from other stories.[56] At this stage the kind of stories being told will matter enormously, for the story has to attract allies and fend off opponents. It is at this stage that rhetorical work matters most (although clearly it comes into play with most of the other processes, cutting across them). It has now entered a wider discourse, which will involve claims, grounds and warrants pitched against counter-claims, grounds and warrants.[57] Stories whose time have come will be those that have entered this culture of public problems, the political spectacle. With this, there will be (1) a large number of people willing to claim it as their own, (2) a willingness to tell the story very visibly so that others can identify with it and (3) the presence of alliances who do not claim the story as their own, but who are keen to give it credibility and support. Indeed, it is in part a measure of political success when allies claim its legitimacy and give it support in large numbers.

PUBLIC PROBLEMS, PERSONAL STORIES AND CONTESTED LIVES

Public problems do not, as Gusfield notes, 'spring up full-blown and announced into the consciousness of bystanders'.[58] Rather, they have to become infused with life – animated, legitimated, demonstrated – through argument, statistics, rhetoric. And one of the central strategies of infusing life is to tell a life: many problems require a strong personal story to become well established. The public domain cannot take too much abstraction: it needs a 'life' to make the elements of the story cohere into a public issue. A contested sexual life story is usually to be found at the heart of the culture of sexual problems. In the early 1990s, for instance, major issues became focused upon Clarence Thomas and Anita Hill (sexual harassment), Jason Donovan (gay outing), Magic Johnson, Arthur Ashe and others (Aids),

Jeffrey Dahmer (sexual murder and serial killers), Madonna (sadomasochism and female sexuality), Michael Jackson (child sex abuse) as well as on an array of political celebrities.

HIV-related illness, for instance, may have existed since at least 1981, but it received relatively scant media attention until a major public figure died from it in 1985. This was the story of Rock Hudson; and as Randy Shilts comments in his narrative of Aids: 'Rock Hudson riveted America's attention upon this deadly new threat for the first time, and his diagnosis became a demarcation that would separate the history of America before Aids from the history that came after.'[59] In the half-year following Hudson's death, the media coverage of Aids more than tripled.[60] Hudson's body image became the icon of 'dying from Aids' – contrasted as it often was with his earlier wholesome and handsome 'beefcake' body of the 1950s. The September 1985 Life magazine printed the face of Aids via Rock Hudson, saying:

> Aids was given a face everyone could recognise when it was announced that Rock Hudson, 59, was suffering from the disease. The quintessential 1950s leading man . . . had looked ill when he appeared with Doris Day in July at a press conference.'[61]

The stories centred, over and over again, upon the issue that Rock Hudson was a secret homosexual – 'the all-American boy had another life, kept secret from the public: that he was almost certainly homosexual'.[62] Often this issue was implied rather than overtly stated. Indeed, the secrecy of Hudson's life, a secrecy through stigma and shame, is an organising feature of many of the narratives of his life at this time. Hudson's life was a 'stunning lie'. His sexual story was used as a major focus for HIV and Aids, and many other stories have followed in his wake – highlighting different aspects of the issue. Nowhere is this clearer than in the *politics of the Quilt*. The Aids Quilt was a major strategy to use personal narrative and a linked iconography to turn Aids-awareness into a major public discourse.[63]

Some of the stories we have heard through the book so far are evidence of the full scale of the generic process of story telling (e.g. gay stories, rape stories) which is already part of the culture of public problems. Others have not really got beyond creating identities or widely establishing their social worlds (e.g. sadomasochism). Still others have not yet been imagined! The remainder of the book enters the worlds of these possibilities.

Chapter 9

The shifting sexual stories of late modernity

Social change is woven into the very fabric of modern life. It is not something that intrudes to interfere with the operations of modern society; instead it represents modern society in action. Instead of decreasing or tapering off, every reasonable sign points to the certainty that in the developing future social change will increase ... sharp breaks with what is cherished as part of traditional local cultures will probably be the most startling differences in the new mentality.

(Herbert Blumer)[1]

The world is always different. Each morning we open our eyes upon a different universe. Our intelligence is occupied with continued adjustment to these differences. That is what makes the interest in life. We are advancing constantly into a new universe.

(George Herbert Mead)[2]

Modernist stories of sexual suffering and sexual surviving have been strikingly well rehearsed over the last decades of the twentieth century. They are stories with driving, coherent and linear plots – of suffering, of coming out, of survival – which ultimately fit into major archetypal forms of story telling: journeys, homes, consummation. They fit into the narrative plots of both the great literature of the distant past and the trashy Hollywood tales of redemption that have swamped this century. And they have become almost commonplaces: in the recovery and therapeutic literatures, in lesbian and gay studies, in women's studies. They are stories that have been well told and whose time has clearly come.

But we are now at century's end. We may be entering a shifting historical period where some of the old stories are partially and slowly losing their obdurate grip upon the narrative world. If, as so many have been suggesting for the past decade, we are now moving into a different kind of social order, then we may expect different kinds of stories to be emerging *alongside* the older ones. As we enter the so-called 'post-paradigmatic' era – of post-modernity, post-Fordism, post-feminism, post-history, post-sexuality, post-everything! – then we could expect a post-narrative to be emerging. Indeed, some of the modern stories discussed so far throughout this book may well have become so tired and clichéd that their imminent death can already be sensed in some circles. Some may have been said so often that they are reaching exhaustion. Thus, many a self- reflecting lesbian may well have started to ponder whether her life is quite as neat as her narrative of it, and indeed books have already appeared in which *Sisters, Sexperts and Queers* tell new stories in all their emerging differences![3] Bonnie Zimmerman, for example, writes at the end of her major study of lesbian fiction that:

> it is . . . a newly established truth that we have 'gone beyond' the coming out novel. We have dealt with that, the received wisdom intones, and are on to bigger and better subjects. Lesbian fiction 'is finally growing up' because it no longer focuses on coming out and falling in love.[4]

But it is not just the lesbian story. Many people who have heard the repetition of 'abuse survivors' stories in therapy groups must begin to wonder at the curious sameness of so many stories. Is the pattern *so* clear? Is the truth of abuse *so* manifestly causal, linear, driven? How have these dreadful secrets remained *so* hidden throughout most of history?

Certainly, most modernist stories of sexual suffering can be fairly readily slotted into the wider scientific tales of sexuality that have engulfed us over the past century or so: the beliefs in the naturalness and givenness of sex; the beliefs in being able to find out the truth of our sex; the belief in some unitary, essential, core experiences which connect in some deeply patterned fashion capable of discovery. Yet increasingly, and from many sources, the world may no longer always be seen in such straightforward, transparent terms. We are tottering to the Far Side of Modernity – what some writers insist is postmodernity, and what I will call here late modernity[5] – where stories and the whole process of story telling may be in transition. If there is change in social worlds, then the sexual stories we tell may well be starting to shift too. There is something afoot. It is the aim of this chapter to ponder a little of these new kinds of sexual stories that may be in the making.

A caveat is in order. One of the odd things about much of the new 'postmodernism' is its claim to have ruptured wholly from the past. Yet the several theoretical baselines of this book – interactionism, constuctionism, pragmatism – converge in this period of late modern theorising, suggesting a longer history. There is an undeniable coincidence of drift between those theories of sexuality developed in the past twenty years and now called constructionist theories (from all their diverse backgrounds), the general theoretical stance of symbolic interactionism, the philosophical position of pragmatism and the tottering towards a kind of social thought and social world which has been called postmodernism. They are not synonymous, but there is an affinity. And it is all far from new. All these positions deny the absolute essentialist world of foundational truth – of nature, of psychology, of history. All deny any 'strong truth' (some deny all truth), and seek pluralities and multiplicities. All highlight the role of language and symbols, signs and signifiers. Thus, for the pragmatist, there has been a hundred year war on foundational truth and grand theory alongside a concern with 'plural universes', an avoidance of essentialists and 'totalisers', dualists and 'splitters'. In the interactionist version, there has long been a concern with the plurality of truths, the ambiguity of meaning, the struggle of a social self in the dialectics of 'I and Me', the ceaseless flux, the localised context, and the deconstructed, decentred life in story telling.[6] Likewise, in the more general constructionist account of sexuality,[7] an 'extremely outrageous idea' has been proposed: that 'one of the last remaining outposts of the "natural" in our thinking was fluid and changeable, the product of human action and history rather than the invariant result of the body, biology, or an innate sex drive'.[8] Pragmatism, interactionism, constructionism and postmodernism all throw into doubt grand stories of sexuality.

THE RISE OF THE LATE MODERNIST SEXUAL STORY?

What, then, are late modernist sexual stories starting to look like? I do not want to create a sense of anything too sure, stable or solid about these transformations; every small trend detected here must be counterposed. Modernist stories certainly still predominate, and are likely to continue well into the future. But they may well be harbingers of change.

For there are signs of newer and diverse stories in the making which shun unities and uniformities; reject naturalism and determinacies; seek out immanences and ironies; and ultimately find pastiche, complexities and shifting perspectives. Jencks says in general about the postmodern, what is equally true of the late modern sexual story, that it

is a time of *incessant choosing*. It's an era when *no orthodoxy* can be adopted without *self-consciousness and irony*, because *all traditions seem to have some validity* . . . [It] is fundamentally the *eclectic mixture* of any tradition with that of the immediate past. . . . Its best works are characteristically *doubly-coded and ironic*, making a feature of the wide *choice, conflict and discontinuity* of traditions . . . [It is a] double coding: the combination of Modern techniques with something else in order . . . [for architecture] to communicate with the public and a concerned minority.[9]

These stories do not replace the modern narratives but run alongside of them, providing a dispersal of critical commentary. Drawing from some of this, in the most general terms, three broad and overlapping shifts may be suggested.

First, sexual stories of authority – given to us from on high by the men in black frocks and white coats – are fracturing in the face of *participant stories*. The past has seen first religion dictating the truth of our sex, then medicine giving rise to the sexological sciences. Sexuality has been trapped in the gaze of science and religion. In part these were at odds with each other – the scientists were a shock to the clergy – and the conflict itself helped highlight the problematic nature of their power. But in the late modern period, many newer voices start to get heard in their own right: rape victims, abuse victims, gay stories, lesbian stories, Aids biographies, paedophile tales, women's sex lives, men's sex lives and so on. Often such tales are still seduced into the voices of authority, and often they may even try to turn themselves into new voices of authority. Meanwhile the old voices of religion and science continue to attempt to shout above the multiplicity of emerging voices. But, and short of a reversion to some central authoritarian regime, the future surely lies with an abundance and proliferation of contested and clashing participant sexual stories.

Second sexual stories of the Essence, the Foundation, the Truth are fracturing into *stories of difference*, multiplicity and a plural universe. As a trend this goes back well into the nineteenth century – when a recognition of perspectivism and pluralism were to be found in some writings (from James to Weber). Nevertheless the dominant stories of the past purported to discover the spiritual or scientific truths of our sexual beings. They tried to lay before us a core, a centre of our sexual lives. But in the late modern period such stories have become increasingly shattered. Sometimes this happens from within – 'progressive religions' want to adapt to the times, and some science – the Kinsey continuum, for instance, hints at pluralism. But usually it happens from outside: the centre no longer holds. The sexual life can no longer be seen to harbour an essential unitary core with an essential truth waiting to be discovered: there are only fragments – disrupting, dissenting, dissolving. The hope for establishing the essential truth of our sex gives way to an awareness of differences everywhere.

Thirdly, sexual stories of the Categorically Clear no longer hold, and in their place come *stories of deconstruction*. In the late modern period, the very language we use to grasp the world comes to the fore as a problem – no longer can it be simply assumed to describe or reflect 'reality'. The old language is seen as clichéd, straitjacketing, empty of meaning. This has become the age of the sign, where symbols, icons, language and stories become increasingly problematic. There has been a 'textual revolution' and sexual stories are part of this. Sexual stories become more and more ambiguous: a lack of clarity, a sense of the power and profound ambiguity of language, mingles with simple-minded borrowings, repackaged into pastiche, reassembled to tell the same old stories in new and ironic ways. The stories are full of indeterminacies; a supermarket of sexual possibilities pervades, with endless choices potentially available and unavailable. Sexual story telling becomes much more self-conscious and much more artefactual. We are dealing in constructions, fictions and the like. Indeed, stories of the controlled and the clear may burst out into a language of excess: hyperbolic madness starts to invade many stories.

There is ample evidence that such shifts in stories are happening, even though they may not last, may not affect all, and indeed may be a passing fad in a few elite intellectual circles. Still, the classic world of autobiographical writing, for instance, which since Augustine (or Rousseau) has chronicled some linear pursuit of an inner self, now seems to be in partial collapse amongst some.[10] And this may be a sign of stories to come.

For instance, spurred through feminist criticism, some men have recently taken to writing their stories in this new key. David Jackson makes the change highly explicit in his own attempt at 'a critical autobiography' of *Unmasking*

Masculinity.[11] Urging that more and more men should 'come out of hiding and . . . start excavating, in public, the sedimented layers of their own particular and diverse life histories', he suggests a rejection of the uncritical, celebratory, confessional mode and lays down some of the key features of a critical autobiography. Amongst the challenges he poses are:

> *Refusing the search for the true self*: . . . transparent recall to reveal a neutral, fixed, absolutely truthful past does not exist. *Rethinking the relationship between past and present*: . . . the significance of past events isn't immutably set for all time, but is constantly being selectively edited and re-focused in terms of my present-day world-view. *Challenging chronological, linear sequence*: . . . narrative time 'springs forth in the plural unity of future, past and present'. . . . *Recognising different voices*: . . . rejecting 'The strong temptation to present the text as a smooth, seamless flow, the product of a unified, consistent, single, voice'. . . . *Refusing a split between the personal and the social*: to attack critically the dichotomies, divisions, separate categories that split the personal and the social. . . . *Seeing political agency, and acknowledging the structural.*[12]

Jackson's autobiography joins the swelling ranks of a wide-ranging new breed of writing, in which many of the writing strategies of the past are self-consciously erased in favour of experiment. It is this theme which haunts the emerging sexual story telling at century's end. What follows is a short glimpsing – a catalogue – of some of the new stories in the making. To repeat: for most people 'modern tales' are still being told, but some of the following are happening for some people. These broad changes can be seen both in terms of *how* stories are told – the shifts in modes, moods, methods; and in *what* is being told – the shifts in narratives, myths, metaphors.

SHIFTING GEARS: NEW WAYS OF TELLING A STORY

As David Jackson's story above demonstrates, the forms of story telling are becoming more and more self-conscious and reflective. For some, sexual story telling is no longer such a straightforward description or discovery of who one is – being a man, being gay, even being a survivor. Instead, these terms themselves become discussed, elaborated upon, contested. For some men, for instance, being a man is not a simple matter of being born that way: the recent proliferation of 'men's stories' – conservative, pro-feminist, Iron Johns, socialist, backlash, gay, black and so on,[13] show there is not one way of being a man. They make it increasingly necessary, for some, to choose and construct a story of what it means to be a man. Likewise, the whole fashion for queer theory throws into radical doubt the existing categories of homosexual or gay. The artifices are visible: the very act of assembling the story becomes part of the story. The discussion in Chapter 3 of this book – which in part shows how we invent ourselves from the contradictory stories around us – becomes common knowledge.

And as some people are becoming increasingly reflective over the way they tell their personal sexual stories, so they also find different ways to tell them. Many sexual stories are now being told in less conventional ways through new means of communication and new strategies of telling: from video diaries and 'zines', through telephone sex, computer sex and video sex, and on to virtual reality and virtual sex.

Telephone sex, for instance, sprouted during the 1980s, creating a wholly new way of communicating sexual stories without direct contact. A new literary tale accompanied it: Robert Cheslsey's 1986 play *Jerker; or the Helping Hand* shows two men conducting an entire relationship over the phone whilst Nicholson Baker's *Vox*[14] was high on the best-seller lists in both the UK and the USA in early 1992. Here, Jim and Abby talk over a telephone sex party line – talk sex, have orgasms, hang up. A post-Aids story of non-connection, yet also techno-sex is at work. They talk sex, tell each other intimacies galore, but we know little about them as people. Likewise, computer sex-lines now enable people to write their sexual stories all over the world to like-minded people, modifying them as they go along.

The music video has become a new erotic/pornographic form for telling sexual stories.[15] Indeed stories have become increasingly visual – and a new 'visual literacy' is required to understand them.[16] Personal narratives now get told through home videos – a major invention of the 1980s, whereby people can tell their stories as they happen through the visual roving eye. Traditional narrative devices break down as the hand-held camera jumps around the life, awaiting or not awaiting the editor's hand. Startling new stories get told this way. There is the possibility of placing a sexual life story on an interactive CD ROM, capable of calling up images, sounds, documentation all around the sexual life.[17] And already, sexual stories flood the computer. There are major networks of electronic mail through which sexual stories are being sent on 'bulletin boards'.

New ways of telling start to creep into academia too. Academics find their formal 'scientific rhetoric' inappropriate as a means of communication and turn to other ways of presenting their 'sex findings': the personal narrative, the play, the poem, the collective story, the chorus![18] For some a 'dialogic' mode of presentation is in the making. Carolyn Ellis and Arthur Bochner, two interactionist sociologists studying abortion, present their stories as a dramatic narrative to be performed. When published it is actually written up as a social drama in key scenes with the women who is having an abortion telling her story side by side with the man telling his.

And at the most extreme edge, a wholly new way of telling personal stories based upon virtual reality may be in the making: encased in computer technology, our bodies may enter three-dimensional fictional worlds where we can invent our own stories and live them out in real-life fantasy! Through pre-coded story lines, we can come to engage 'virtually' in our wildest fantasies. 'Cross-dressers can do so to their hearts' contents, without revealing their sex. Bisexuals can do whatever they wish with other consenting adults, without declaring their position.'[19] This is a highly controversial development – high-tech sex – which may well become a commonplace of the twenty-first century.

Many stories are also directing themselves to differential taste cultures:[20] they are told to groups which are less and less homogenous. The days of the truly mass market, mass culture and mass audiences are declining and stories are being told to specialised audiences.[21] Heaven forbid that the sadomasochist narratives found in sadomasochistic magazines should wander into the confessionals of a fundamentalist church (and vice versa). And yet, ironies of ironies, even though such communities are firmly separated in one instance, they may ultimately borrow from each other: as sadomasochism needs its religious rites, and fundamentalists need their sadomasochistic threats.

And this suggests how stories have become more recursive, more dependent upon borrowings from the mass media especially, but from social science too. Ideas, fashions, trends flood the instant market-place to become part of a new instant narrative. Changing stories travel faster. The signs, symbols and languages given to us through paperbacks, soap operas, chat shows, docudramas, film, video, self help manuals, therapy workshops, music videos and the like become more and more the resources from which we tell our stories. As one woman discovers that 'she has loved too much', and tells it to Oprah, so do thousands of others. The media itself draws upon the media to tell sexual stories – Madonna's 'Material Girl' video drawing from *Gentlemen Prefer Blondes*, for instance, and the constant reconstruction of old film genres in music television. And people in turn draw upon these genres in their sexual story telling. Personal narratives of Aids, for instance, are woven around film texts – such as *Gone With the Wind*.[22] Ideas become more and more recursive, acting back on themselves. Ideas discovered at one moment – the importance of rape trauma syndrome, the idea of the transexual, the notion of twelve steps – become the organising principles of our story telling at a later moment. The works of a Freudian or a Foucauldian or a feminist are consumed avidly, becoming the textual frame of many 'radical' personal narratives. Indeed, a whole strand of social science comes to be presented as stories and framed within these languages.

Not only is the media drawn upon, the boundaries between fiction and 'reality' collapse. Fiction becomes faction. The talk show entertains us through others telling us the truth of their orgasms. The docudrama simulates the sexual story from real life and feeds it back as reality. Nancy Ziegenmeyer's rape becomes a story told on chat shows, paperbacks, serialised newspaper columns and a docudrama. Hence the boundaries between her life and the multiple media events blurs. Any other rape fiction comes to look just like her faction.[23] Foucault's death becomes a biography that links his life to his theory till the contrasts between them fade.[24] Madonna's life become books and films that assume the role of fictional narratives that seem very close to home.[25]

And finally, the stories become more and more likely to challenge authorities and eclipse one standard telling. The Old Gods have had their day. This is linked to all the above. Once stories become more self-conscious, recursive and are told to distinctive audiences, then the stories given from on high are seen to be artefactual. The foundation collapses, and authoritarian stories are only one amongst many. The multiple stories of gays and lesbians simply discredit the stories of scientists, who continue saying their scientific story as before but have manifestly decreasing relevance to gay and lesbian lives. And on chat shows a new pluralised, democratised text starts to emerge where many voices speak at once.

SHIFTING STORIES: OLD TALES/NEW TALES?

Closely linked to all this, the content of some sexual stories may also be starting to differ. At the widest cultural level, a curious change can be sensed in cult popular films like *Blue Velvet, sex, lies and videotape, Paris, Texas* and *The Cook, the Thief, his Wife and her Lover*; in books like *Panic Sex*, and Bret Easton Ellis's randomly violent *American Psycho*,[26] whilst MTV has been championed by many as the sexual embodiment of the postmodern. Dominant genres cease, realist readings end and a multiplicity of ironic, parodic, pastiched, excessive, self-conscious and hence often unintelligible voices start being heard to be simulating sexualities. Todd Gitlin captures much of this writing when he says it is:

> completely indifferent to questions of consistency and continuity. It self consciously splices genres, attitudes, styles. It relishes the blurring or juxtaposition of forms (fiction–non-fiction), stances (straight–ironic), moods (violent–comic), cultural levels (high–low). It disdains originality and fancies copies, repetition, the recombination of hand-me-down scraps. It neither embraces or criticises, but beholds the world blankly, with a knowingnness that dissolves feeling and commitment into irony. It pulls the rug out from under itself, displaying acute self-consciousness about the work's constructed nature. It takes pleasure in the play of surfaces, and derides the search for depth as mere nostalgia.[27]

Since a dominant style of this writing is the list, here is my list of what some sexual stories are starting to look like at century's end.

1 The sexual life is no longer seen as harbouring a unitary core with an essential truth waiting to be discovered: there are only fragments – disrupted and dissimilar, dissimulating and disappearing. The sexual life as a core or essential truth fractures; fragments, slices, surfaces, a multitude of bits or voices is what we are left with. The dominant tales of the modern period do just the opposite. Thus, recovery tales take a delight in labelling new symptoms (via checklists) and new names (e.g. sexual addiction) for new problems, finding coherent causal chains largely through dysfunctional families and abuse. This writing gives a very simple and direct picture; it delights in the most straightforward of acronyms, stages of recovery, checklists. Likewise, lesbian and gay stories are orchestrated most clearly through a lesbian and gay movement which generally believes in an essential gayness. Queer theories start to weaken all this. Newer stories sense differences as everywhere, and listen to the differences. Multiplicities abound.

Carol Rambo Ronai, for instance, has attempted to capture her experiences as an exotic dancer, who is also a researcher. Night after night she stands on the bar with men looking at her, harassing her. How is she to recall all this? She writes:

> According to one editor, I'm having a problem with my 'voice'. She tells me it is not clear who is speaking at various points in the text I have produced. I need to clarify when the dancer is speaking and when the researcher is speaking. Here's the problem. My voice is cracking as I write this. My identity is fracturing as I spill my guts while trying to produce in my audience an emotional knowing of my experience as a dancer/researcher. I cannot smoothly switch hats and write, 'Here is how the dancer in me feels, and here is how the researcher feels, and here is how the wife feels, and so on'. It is dishonest and contrived to separate out influences and label them, though occasionally one voice will speak out loudly and clearly. My perception of my 'self' incorporates influences from these roles, but the end result is not compartmentalised around them.[28]

2 The stories to be told are borrowings, reassembled into pastiche, never-endingly being reassembled to tell the same old new stories in ironic ways. It is as if a generation has simply grown tired with the old stories and now plays ceaselessly with them. Much social science and literary theory now tells stories that suck the past into a new (often incomprehensible) tales. And even a story as deadly as Aids can find its past narratives to borrow from – as Arnie Kantrowitz does when he relates the painful story of gay communities dealing with Aids interspersed with whole commentaries and texts from *Gone With The Wind*. A brief exchange between Ashley and Scarlett captures the pains of Aids in the gay community:

> Ashley: I'll always be haunted by the memory of a charm and beauty that are gone forever . . . oh, the lazy days and warm still country twilights . . . the golden warmth and security of those days!
> Scarlett (tears in her eyes): Don't look back, Ashley. Don't look back. It drags your heart till you can't do anything but look back![29]

3 The stories are full of indeterminacies; a supermarket of possibilities can start to pervade, with endless choices potentially available and unavailable. The old linear narratives – first this, then that – and the old causal stories – the childhood fix – break down. Thus the old coming out stories which used to outline stages – sensitisation, signification, sub-culturalisation and the like[30] are now in dispute. We know that younger gays and lesbians are telling their tales in different ways, at earlier ages, criss-crossed with class and race, and in a much less linear fashion. Indeed, coming out stories as widely documented in the 1970s and 1980s may sign-post a distinct historical period: said much less, if at all, in the twenty-first century. This is not to suggest a free-for-all, that anything can happen. It is to suggest that a wider more diffuse set of stories for coming out are becoming available.

4 Identities blur and change. We may be entering a different historical period where the old identity stories that researchers heard, myself included, are slowly losing their dominance upon narrative reconstruction. The psycho- social plots of Eric Erikson and others who suggested the importance of identity crisis in mid-century may now be losing their wider grip. There is a new intensive fashionability which seems to require a change in 'who one is' regularly: the videos of a Madonna or a Michael Jackson show identities shifting not just across videos but within the same one. Jackson's 'Black and White' provides images of constant and flittering identity *shift* as a man becomes a woman, a black becomes a white, an old person becomes a young person. This is part of a wider story now well documented in social science: of the Protean Self, The Mutable Self, The Homeless Mind, The Narcissistic Personality, The Saturated Self. Here identities in the late modern world are no longer so stable or fixed.[31] In the most extreme versions of this story, we move beyond human beings altogether ('The Death of the Subject') and identities (the word 'post-identitarian' has already been invented).[32] The 'human being' vanishes altogether from the story.

5 Any sense of a grand story breaks down. Lyotard suggests, in probably his most famous line: 'I define postmodernism as incredulity towards meta-narratives.'[33] It is the 'loss of master narratives'.[34] All master narratives are dead. The old language is clichéd, empty of meaning.

6 A language of excess is ever-present. Hyperbolic madness starts to invade the stories. We see this in the writings of the Krokers when they talk about 'panic sex' and 'excremental sex'. They write:

> When we have passed beyond . . . sex as nature and sex as discourse, to sex as fascinating only when it is about recklessness, discharge and upheaval – a *parodic* sex, then we have broken beyond the analytics of sexuality and power to *excess*; beyond Foucault's language of the 'care of the self' to *frenzy*; beyond the 'use of pleasure' (Foucault again) with its moral problematisation of the ethical subject in relation to its sexual conduct to a little sign slide between *kitsch and decay*. Not then the nostalgia for an aesthetics of existence today or for a hermeneutics of desire (these are passé and who cares anyway?), but parodic sex as about the free expenditure of a 'boundless refuse of activity' (Bataille) pushing human plans; not the coherency of the ethical subject (that has never motivated anyone except in the detrital terms of the subject as a ventilated reminder of death), but the excitation of the subject into a toxic state, into a sumptuary site of loss and orgiastic excess. Not, finally, a productive sex, but an *unproductive* sex, a sex without secretions, as the site of the death of seduction as that which makes sex bearable in the postmodern condition.[35]

Just what is this 'unproductive sex . . . without secretions' that awaits us? Whatever else is here, this is certainly no straightforward modern tale of the kind I have been researching and describing. They get worse. On panic sex, they have this to say:

What is sex in the age of the hyperreal? A little sign slide between kitsch and decay as the post-modern body is transformed into a rehearsal for the theatrics of sadomasochism in the simulacrum. Not sadism any longer under the old sign of Freudian psychoanlytics and certainly not masochism in the Sadean carceral, but sadomasochism now as a kitschy sign of the body doubled in an endless labyrinth of media images, just at the edge of ecstasy of catastrophe and the terror of simulacrum.[36]

This voice is not exactly new – there are shades of de Sade, Nietszche, Bataille, Genet and others floating around here. But it is certainly one that disrupts the major narrative conventions of our modern period. There is a drive towards telling the excess tales – of serial killers, of satanic rites, of Madonna's *Sex.* Indeed, there is the evocation of a nightmare violent 'post-future' landscape – the Armageddon backdrop of *Terminator* starts to emerge as part of these scary late modern tales of sexual excess.

7   Yet many stories also become glitzy, glossy, high-tech, commercial, consumerist. Pornography, for instance, takes on new forms – as one advertising catalogue for 'trendy gay men' put it in 1992:

FreshMEN redefines gay erotica for the nineties. The look, the feel, even the taste of FreshMEN is out there on the cutting edge. It's just what these wild Los Angeles art guys wanted. . . . We've got fresh reading, too . . . only the ferociously horny young writers of FreshMEN can help you get a handle on your hippest fantasies with their New Age sextalk and radical sexplay. The salacious Newsex pages are to other gay erotica what MTV News is to the MacNeil-Lehre Newshour. These sexy news bits cover items you'll never read in USA Today – from the most outrageous 'try-sexual' performance art from Clubland to the trend in Queer Nation jack-off fundraisers.[37]

At its most extreme, we enter the world of cyborgs – Sterling's post-human 'clades'. Sex becomes 'high-tech', lodged in a world of chemical implants, programming of brain electrons, of computers matched up to persons, of electronic surveillance, of science fiction.[38]

8   The stories become retextualised, revisioned. Since the idea of a fixed meaning is dissolved, new readings of all manner of cultural phenomena become possible. Lesbianism, once an act of passion between women, now become a complex metaphor: not a simple sex act, nor a simple way of being, but a profoundly complex symbol anchoring a range of concerns, pleasures and anxieties. It feeds into a radical revisioning, a task already started by the new queer theorists.[39] In the late 1980s and early 1990s this was the stance that increasingly came to dominate lesbian and gay studies conferences, often leaving the earlier challenges of the social sciences looking quaintly old-fashioned. Newer stories then are in the making. These newer queer theorists – or, dare I say, story tellers of late modernity – draw much from feminist postmodernism, and examine 'the complex entanglements of identity,

voice, intersubjectivity, textualities, and sexualities'. They see 'Writing as Re-Vision', as 'the act of looking back, of seeing with fresh eyes, of entering an old text from a new critical direction'. It is an 'act of survival'. Just as 'every text is written from a gendered consciousness, just as every reading is a gendered experience', so is every text open to a gay or lesbian reading.[40]

9 And herein lies a clue as to another coming change. Whereas my subjects read texts to find out truths about themselves, however complex that process may be, the future may bring readings that are more akin to endlessly playful/ironic layers of narratives. The texts for reading other texts are shifting ground. Indeed, just as the produced narratives start to become less coherent and more multiple, so too do the readings. Indeed, they almost certainly feed into each other.

I do not think there are as yet many everyday folk – outside of the art and intellectual worlds – telling stories like those I have just described. I have yet to meet people who clearly account for their lives as being 'post-gay' or 'post-abuse', for instance. But these kinds of stories are present already in the worlds of fiction, film and 'postmodern academia'. As the dominant metanarrative gets fractured, dispersed or even eliminated, it may become easier for personal stories to be told in a more pastiched, potpourried, pluralistic, polycentric, polysemic mode in which narratives are assembled with a less clear driving, linear force behind them. Thus, for example, the search for the truth of a unitary phenomenon designated 'homosexual' will become discredited precisely because there is no such unitary phenomenon. The most astute observers of homosexuality have known this for a long time – from Freud through Kinsey to Foucault. What we have are a multiplicity of feelings, genders, behaviours, identities, relationships, locales, religions, work experiences, reproductive capacities, child-rearing practices, political disagreements and so forth that have been appropriated by a few rough categories like 'homosexual', 'lesbian', 'gay'. They may have served the dual functions of control and support in the early modern period, but they certainly don't cohere around a fixed or given phenomenon. In the late modern world, the very idea of 'being gay' may increasingly get transformed into the idea of a multiplicity of sexual/gendered/relational/emotional, etc. beings in the world. Enter the time of the post-gay and the post-lesbian? And, as importantly, the awareness of a dispersal of homosexualities must also mean the awareness of a dispersal of heterosexualities. Indeed, late modernist stories dissolve such distinctions at base. The separate genders and their separate sexualities cannot so clearly be sustained.

THE OBDURATE GRIP OF THE MODERN

This chapter has examined a few of the many shifts detectable in a few emerging sexual stories in the late twentieth century. But some caveats are in order. First, shades of all the above seep back into the whole modernist project – there is little that is really new. Self-reflection is there in the modernist novels of Proust, Woolf or Musil. Machine folk start to appear with a vengeance in *Frankenstein*, or *Metropolis*. Visual imagery, especially in the new story telling medium of movies, has been a preoccupation of the twentieth century. Excess is Sadean. And so on. There is little that can claim to be really and distinctively new in these themes, although it is all pushed much further. I am unhappy with those positions that think that late twentieth-century life is the grand or final rupture with the past; or that think that the possibility of any kind of truth at all has now gone; or that think the only way to deal with the new order is to construct a new language of ever-increasing bizarreness: or that see a 'urinal politics' as the key to the future; or that suggest that David Lynch's *Blue Velvet* is the text of the times; or that sense the cyborg as being just around the corner. This is not to minimise such ideas, but it is to worry about their more omniscient claims. I have glimpsed some new stories in the making but they remain rare. Indeed, however dramatic the tales above may look as signs of change, *most of the tales I have heard and studied at least continue to talk as if they had an authority, told a truth and believed in clear categories*.

Ponder the stories told in Part II: of abuse survivors, of gays coming out, of recovery. Some of these, for sure, can totter to the far side of late modernity and adopt a certain postmodern craziness. But most do not. In all of this widespread sexual story telling modernist conventions remain at the forefront. Most stories I have examined are still very much alive and well, and at root (1) they are still claiming to be the truth – the truth of coming out, the truth of abuse; (2) they still have conventional narratives of time and cause: such stories are usually linear and suggest antecedent factors in shaping the problems – be they genetic (as in many gay coming out stories) or psychodynamic (as in many abuse stories – cycles of violence, little girls within, etc.); (3) they still have some conception of Enlightenment progress: amelioration, often via therapy or counselling, is hailed as the outcome: the world seems to be developing much more optimistically than in many of the postmodern accounts where we are the end of progress; and (4) they still suggest that talk is talk: what people say in their stories may be quoted as in some way representative of the truth. The words are what they say they are! Coming Out is Coming Out. Abuse is Abuse. In these stories, the world of the late modern is, then, still a long way off.

If there is a lesson of modernity, it is perhaps a slow and painful awareness throughout the past two hundred years of the relativisation of truths – there is no 'absolute' as the early scientists thought, but neither is anarchistic and epistemological nihilism the way ahead. The voices – the story tellers, the coaxers, the readers, the texts – that have revealed sexual stories over the past two hundred years may have struggled to provide a dominant story which is now visibly crumbling. Hopefully the future will bring wider, richer, more imaginative, more complex sexual stories from many more voices, hence adding further to the repertoires of narratives available for twenty-first-century life. The time may have come for a wider proliferation of stories. A glimpse of the issues this may raise will bring the book to a close.

Chapter 10

Intimate citizenship
The politics of sexual story telling

There can be no esoteric 'truth' of sex to be discovered by diligent research; only perspectives on contending 'truths' whose evaluation is essentially political rather than scientific.

(Jeffrey Weeks)[1]

But I who am
bound my mirror
as well as my bed
see causes in Colour
as well as sex

and sit here wondering
which me will survive
all these liberations
(Audre Lorde)[2]

As postmodernism pushes itself into everyday life, old political ideologies are collapsing. The boundaries and borders between national states are being redrawn. Traditional meanings of health, illness, Aids, the human body, reproduction, medicine, sexuality, the family, intimacy, love, education, work, leisure, science, religion, art, entertainment and the private and the public are being swept aside. Even as this occurs, fits of nostalgia for the past lead to its re-enactment in contemporary popular culture.

(Norman K. Denzin)[3]

Stories, narratives and discourse have all recently started to play a prominent role in understanding the workings of the political and moral life of societies. From many different persuasions, the argument has been made that the stories we tell of our lives are deeply implicated in moral and political change. For the moral philosophers, the sense of self and the meaning of virtue cannot exist outside of webs of narratives.[4] For the political scientist, we have come to inhabit worlds of discourse which regulate lives and where the ability to take control over the story of one's own life may be seen as a major mode of empowerment. Indeed, 'education is systematic storytelling'.[5] For the social scientist, the shifting tale of self and identity is leading to a radical transformation of the social order.[6] There are sharp disagreements between many of these thinkers, but the following quote from a leading feminist philosopher captures the kinds of concerns that have become central. Seyla Benhabib writes:

> The self is both the teller of tales and that about whom tales are told. The individual with a coherent sense of self-identity is the one who succeeds in integrating these tales and perspectives into a meaningful life history. When the story of a life can be told only from the perspective of others, then the self is a victim and sufferer who has lost control over her existence. When the story of a life can only be told from the standpoint of the individual, then such a self is a narcissist and a loner who may have attained autonomy without solidarity. A coherent sense of self is attained with the successful integration of autonomy and solidarity, or with the right mix of justice and care. Justice and autonomy alone cannot sustain and nourish the web of narratives in which human beings' sense of selfhood unfolds: but solidarity and care alone cannot raise the self to the level not only of being the subject but also the author of a coherent life story.[7]

This book has argued that stories and narratives depend upon communities that will create and hear those stories: social worlds, interpretive communities, communities of memory. The telling of sexual stories that can reach public communities of discourse has been a central theme. Without lesbian and gay stories the lesbian and gay movement may not have flourished. Without the stories told by abuse survivors, the whole rape movement would probably have floundered. And recovery tales identified in their narratives a whole scenario of hitherto undetected concerns that have entered a public arena of debate. And these stories work their way into changing lives, communities and cultures. Through and through, sexual story telling is a political process.

Hence the analysis of sexual stories is not just a quirky interest, or even a titillating, voyeuristic one. It is central to an understanding of the workings of sexual politics in the late modern world. In these closing chapters I look a little more at the changing character of politics, examine the workings of stories in this climate, and suggest an increasingly growing zone of political and moral activity that I will call 'intimate citizenship'.

THE SHIFTING SOCIAL WORLDS OF POWER

The sexual stories found in the late modern world are part of the process through which contemporary politics is being rewritten. Abounding with contradictory tendencies, one strand of modern politics (replete with its counter-strand) is an emancipatory and democratising impulse which has progressively weakened the political claims of earlier periods and cultures embroiled in tradition, elite rule and authoritative stories.[8] This is not to be unduly optimistic or champion a Whig view of history as inevitable progress. There are still many anti-democratic counter-trends strongly at work. There are still massively structured social inequalities around class, gender and race across the world. And this is still the century that has witnessed holocausts, world wars, nuclear explosions, eco-catastrophe, and – at century's end – a proliferation of tribal wars, based on religion, ethnicity, nationhood. It is still the case, then, that many people's lives are trapped in inequality and oppression, subject to exploitation, marginalisation, powerlessness, cultural imperialism and violence.[9] To say less would be naive. But at the same time this is a period of history when the claims being made about empowerment and emancipation have also grown. There are still many authoritarian voices of tradition,[10] but this has also been an historical era when claims are regularly made for oppressed groups by both liberals and radicals. Giddens has called this stage of history a period of 'emancipatory politics'. As he says:

> From the relatively early development of the modern era onwards, the dynamism of modern institutions has stimulated, and to some extent has been promoted by, ideas of human *emancipation*. . . . Emancipatory politics [is] a generic outlook concerned above all with liberating individuals and groups from constraints which adversely affect their life chances. [It] involves two main elements: the effort to shed shackles of the past, thereby permitting a transformative attitude towards the future; and the aim of overcoming the illegitimate domination of some individuals or groups by others. . . . Emancipatory politics is concerned to reduce or eliminate *exploitation, inequality* and *oppression* . . . [it] makes primary the imperatives of *justice, equality* and *participation*'.[11]

However much these imperatives have failed or remain in jeopardy, over the past two centuries this language and its claims have become the increasing currency of diverse strands of political talk: around religious tolerance, anti-imperialism, the search to eliminate class and economic inequalities, trade union activism, aboli-tionism and slavery, the civil rights movement, an awareness of racialisation, women's emancipation, the idea of citizenship and most recently sexual liberation. Although they have often depended upon grand stories – from Marxist to liberal accounts of justice and freedom – they have, ironically, progressively punctured any sense of one sole narrative or story. These changes do not just mean shifts in political cultures, but also shifts in ways of relating which have become more infused with equality and empowerment. For many people there has been the beginnings of a 'democratization of personhood'.[12] Lives can be lived with a greater sense of personal control and equality for many more people than was possible in the past. Again, it would be naive, given the history of the twentieth century, to see this as a necessary progress[13] or, indeed, as in any way complete. Rather these are small changes created in some small spaces – possible signs of futures, no more. And they are mirrored in the diversities of sexual stories that are starting to appear. For some, all this marks the collapse of civilisation as we know it, a decline of moral standards has occurred that presages a call to return to an authoritarian set of values from the past.[14] But the call to return to 'traditional values' or 'family values', or to get 'back to basics', is a call that has no grasp of modernity, as we shall see later.

BEYOND EMANCIPATION TO LIFE POLITICS?

For the late modern world is moving beyond 'emancipation'. Whilst 'emancipatory politics' is still in the foreground, a new (and even more 'liberating'?) 'life politics' has also been identified as emerging. In making this distinction, there are no grounds for political complacency about the devastations reaped upon many people and groups, even as I am trying to see in this chapter other issues. Change is everywhere, and whilst the last chapter suggested we are entering a new era of late modernity, so this chapter suggests *this era brings with it the potential for new sexual stories that harbour the potential for political change*. At its worst, it is claimed we have entered the stage of post-politics. Certainly some of the champions of so-called postmodernism are reactionary, indifferent, tired libertarians or nihilists who see no future. And many of the male writers about postmodernism blithely ignore feminist or gay (or race) arguments.[15] But for others, there are also signs of a new pattern of politics emerging, slowly and with difficulties. There is a weakening of a single-minded and often absolutist concern with the now traditional politics of emancipation (whilst still assuming it as a vast backdrop) and a suggestion of a multiplicity of new projects, new constituencies, new strategies for the future. Again, there is no need to engage in the obtruse language of postmodernism to recognise that *something new is afoot*.

Put simply, the new politics comes in a plethora of forms and labels, moving under various, often contradictory, names: a politics of difference, a radical and plural democracy, radical pluralism, communitarianism, new liberalism, ironic liberalism, cultural politics, life politics, civic liberalism. In short, *a radical, pluralistic, democratic, contingent, participatory politics of human life choices and difference is in the making*.[16] For convenience, five major themes can be indicated here – each having radical implications for the nature of story telling in a late modern world.

First, there is *the eclipse of the essence*. Much of the older politics struggles over some abstract notion of the good life, of principles of justice. But the new politics brings a recognition that the modern world is now too complex, too pluralistic, harbours too many competing claims to truth to believe any longer in any foundational authority or wisdom that transcends all practical situations. Neither abstract philosophical thought, nor notions of pure rational debate, nor 'science' can save us, or, indeed, serve as *the* foundation for this politics. This is not to deny these forms of thought any role at all; but it is to weaken their claims to an absolutely binding higher authority. Much that has passed in the name of science over the past two hundred years has been a form of technical control, even repression. It has therefore to be challenged and contested. Nor is there any straightforward core. The political cannot be simply connected to traditional 'male' concerns of government and state. Instead, it is everywhere, circulating around housework, school life, ethnic relations, art, music and, of course, 'sexualities', as well as domains hitherto unspecified. Practical, and inevitably ambiguous, contingent and contested, activities involving thought, feeling, talk and action are the basis of this new politics. Politics hence becomes a matter of possibilities and pragmatics. 'The Truth', grand and abstract, is contested; partial 'truths' are now always part of situated, contingent knowledges. And politics itself can no longer make grand claims or set up global agendas for action.

Second, there is *the delight of differences*. Much of traditional politics is concerned with 'the other'; with those outside our boundaries who need to be co-opted into our life or banished altogether from it.[17] But the newer politics increasingly brings a recognition that the differences found between experiences, people and groups are not to be lightly wished away, coercively co-opted or summarily assimilated. Instead, there is an acknowledgment of difference – sometimes differences that may be so great as to make communication very difficult, if not impossible. This is a challenging politics: not one that sees an inevitable coming together of different positions, but one which acknowledges that differences are omnipresent and not simply capable of being co-opted. Queer fundamentalists have no way of reconciling their differences with Christian fundamentalists; anti-porn feminists are divisively at odds with those feminists who celebrate erotica and sadomasochism or sex work; pro-life feminists are at odds with pro-choice feminists. Even greater differences might be found across race or class lines, fissures which cannot be easily or lightly blended. Politics has now to work out some way of acknowledging fundamental differences. The traditional 'emancipatory' concerns of 'oppression' and 'inequalities' remain important; but through this focus on differences, there has also been a widening of concerns to take into account people's desire *to live different kinds of lives*.

Third, there is the *power of participation*. In the older politics, democracy is often given from on high, not claimed from below. In contrast, the new politics brings a recognition of the importance of active and local participation of people in bringing about the changes they seek in their lives. Politics hence becomes a matter of active participation. People are world-makers now in new ways, being able to build more diverse communities and identities than possibly ever before. The rule of the old-fashioned expert and elite is coming to a close; and intellectual work is work more closely concerned with action than before. With this comes a focus on the new social movements, the value of community and an awareness of the ways the politics of identity works. Academics are no longer simple Ivory Tower folk but instead are often associated with the new social movements, communities of action and critical pedagogy. They may also become part of 'cultures of resistance'.[18]

Fourth, there is the *significance of the sign*. Language and signs are not simply vehicles for conveying political wisdoms, but are themselves constitutive of the political process. There is a recognition of the widening of the goals, strategies and constituencies of political action to incorporate the importance of the political spectacle – the role of symbolism and the sign, and the importance of mass communication within this. There has also been an increased awareness of the role of language, argumentation, discourses, meanings, claims and, of course, *stories* in assembling political debates and constructing discursive democracies. And a core challenge has been to speak the unspeakable and represent the unrepresentable, to create a world of different images and signs that transgress, regress, progress and ingress.

And fifth, there are *the tactics and strategies of time and space*. A recognition that the old order where both time and space were usually perceived as relatively stable and structuring is rapidly giving way to a world where political actions are both intensely local yet also global, and where momentous political changes along with awareness of such changes can occur in very rapid time-spans. Politics must now take into account the rapidity of movements across time and space, and hence the greater interconnectedness both of social orders and political actions. Indeed, for some, the 'globalization of contingency is the defining mark of late modernity'.[19] Along with this is the creation of new local spaces that are also interconnected globally: voices in small corners of the world have the potential to be relayed immediately all over the world.[20]

THE NEW SOCIAL WORLDS OF SEXUAL POLITICS

What has all this to do with my account of sexual story telling? At base, I want to argue that the new politics has one major axis in gender/sexual/erotic politics, and that the workings of such politics is heavily dependent upon the kinds of stories invented about the roles of intimacy within it. The 'coming out' narratives of gay and lesbian personal experience, just like the 'breaking the silence' stories of rape survivors, played crucial and critical roles in the development of gay and feminist politics. Moving out of a silence, the stories helped shape a new public language, generating communities to receive and disseminate them on a global scale, ultimately creating more and more spaces for them to be heard. All this must be seen as political – as empowering. Of course, much sexual politics is traditionally also found in the arena of emancipatory politics: the work of the women's movement from the early nineteenth century onwards has done much to set new agendas for the liberation of both women and the relations between the genders more widely. Women have, at least in parts of the western world, gained citizenship rights in many areas: e.g. the right to vote, some equality before the law, some welfare rights. As with all emancipatory politics, it has not extended far enough; but these issues are firmly on the agenda and firmly discussed. But the modern women's movement – perhaps more than any other of the new social movements, and despite a widespread sense of a backlash[21] also hurls us into the world of a new sexual politics. Here is a concern not just with the emancipation of women from all forms of oppression and exploitation, important as that is: rather the concern now is to see that 'the political is the personal', and to sense a politics about much more than inequalities. Rather, the politics of feminism is about the *kinds of lives women can choose to live during an emerging era of history.* And with this, inevitably, come new ways for men to live too. New issues enter the political agenda. Feminism is a model for much of this new politics at work. It has battled both internally and externally over fundamental differences; it has been a model of participatory politics (with all the problems of leaving some groups out); and it has established new and powerful discourses over how life should be lived. In doing this, it has staked out the claims for a future, better world of both gender and sexuality. As this book has shown, however, the women's movement – in all its diversity – has not been alone in this. Most notably, the lesbian and gay movement has established gains that would have been largely unthinkable a century ago. And in their wake, a whole string of smaller, less organised and less powerful communities and claims have developed which speak to a wider range of differences. In Part II I hope to have demonstrated the role of these movements in shaping new stories of identity, and new cultures of political action. Rape stories and gay stories were taken as emblems of many other potential stories that could be told in the future. And I have suggested that new forms of being have emerged alongside these new stories. Indeed, the (late) modern period has invented stories of being, identity and community for both rape survivors and gays that has made it increasingly possible to claim rights in ways that could not be done until these stories were invented.

Rights and responsibilities are not 'natural' or 'inalienable' but have to be invented through human activities, and built into the notions of communities, citizenship and identities. Rights and responsibilities depend upon a community of stories which make those same rights plausible and possible. They accrue to people whose identities flow out of the self-same communities. Thus it is only as lesbian and gay communities started to develop and women's movements gathered strength that stories around a new kind of citizenship became more and more plausible. The nature of our communities – the languages they use, the stories they harbour, the identities they construct, the moral/political codes they champion – move to the centre stage of political thinking. Michael Sandel writes:

> Open-ended though it may be the story of my life is always embedded in the story of those communities from which I derive my identity – whether family or city, tribe or nation, party or cause. On the communitarian view, these stories make a moral difference not a psychological one. They situate us in the world, and give our lives their moral particularity.[22]

What has become both visible and practical over the past two decades (although the roots go further back) is the creation of these new communities of discourse and dialogue championing rival languages, stories and identities which harbour the rights and responsibilities of being sexual, pursuing pleasures, possessing bodies, claiming visibility and creating new kinds of relationships. The old (and still important) communities of rights spoke of political rights, legal rights or welfare rights of citizenship: the language of women's and gay communities certainly draws upon this – such gains should not be lightly lost – but takes it further. A new set of claims around the body, the relationship and sexuality are in the making. This new field of life politics I will call 'intimate citizenship'.

STORIES OF INTIMATE CITIZENSHIP

Be careful what you wish for, you might get it.

(Delia Ephron, *Funny Sauce*)

We are what we pretend to be, so we must be very careful who we pretend to be.

(Kurt Vonnegut, *Cat's Cradle*)

Citizenship has been a major concern of western-style democracies throughout the twentieth century. In the classic formulation of T.H. Marshall, three clusters of citizen's rights have emerged chronologically during the past two centuries to deal with concerns over civil, political and social rights – to justice under the law, to political representation, to basic welfare.[23] Despite many criticisms, it remains a useful model to sense a general and slow expansion of the idea of the citizen in modernity.[24] In my view, it should not be seen as a necessary, evolutionary or essential concept, but a loose conglomerate of spheres of action whereby communities are developed which attribute certain rights and responsibilities to human beings around the zones of law, politics and welfare. Telling the personal stories of 'their rights' is a crucial part of this. There is hence nothing inalienable or given about such citizen's rights: they are, rather, heavily contingent and dependent upon the communities through which they grow. And, in turn, the stories such communities create help to shape the rights which develop.[25]

To the existing three realms of citizenship, a fourth could now be added at century's end: that of intimate citizenship. This speaks to an array of concerns too often neglected in past debates over citizenship, and which extend notions of rights and responsibilities. I call this intimate citizenship because it is concerned with all those matters linked to our most intimate desires, pleasures and ways of being in the world. Some of this must feed back into the traditional citizenship; but equally, much of it is concerned with new spheres, new debates and new stories. For many people in the late modern world there are many decisions that can, and increasingly have to, be made about a life. For some, natural hierarchies of order and dominance, of a fixed place in the world with a fixed agenda, of a stable story, are visibly crumbling. Now, and I suspect increasingly in the future, people may have to make decisions around the *control (or not) over* one's body, feelings, relationships; *access (or not) to* representations, relationships, public spaces, etc.; and *socially grounded choices (or not) about* identities, gender experiences, erotic experiences. In line with the general feature of life politics I have outlined earlier, there can no longer be an expectation that blueprints pure and simple will be found. Intimate citizenship does not imply one model, one pattern, one way. On the contrary, it is a loose term which comes to designate a field of stories, an array of tellings, out of which new lives, new communities and new politics may emerge.

New claims and new stories, then, can be sensed as in the making which touch on many areas of intimacy. The major stories that I have considered so far – the modernist tales of suffering – are established, and will probably continue to proliferate. The late modernist stories I started to hint at in Chapter 9 are still being written. Seven areas seem crucial in shifting the content of the stories of intimate citizenship. In what follows I signpost very rapidly new stories of intimate citizenship that are starting to appear at century's end. In short: what kinds of new stories are in the making around our bodies, our reproductive capacities, our relationships, our ways of raising children, our feelings, our representations, our identities, our genders, our sexualities?[26] For all these concerns, the traditional modern stories are well known and well bounded. I am hence more interested here in the shifts.

'Family' stories

A major story of our times has been that of *the* traditional nuclear family, of 'traditional family values'. It is heavily reflected in many media stories – TV sitcoms, soaps, romantic novels, popular film, and it finds a daily voice in personal narratives, harbouring a sense of nostalgia for romantic times past. It is in the old film world of *It's a Wonderful Life* or *Meet Me in St Louis* and in the old television world of *Little House on the Prairie*.[27] There is the happy and devoted family: a male breadwinner, a full-time home-maker wife, several dependent children and a general contentment. It is a family of nostalgia, a family that purportedly existed in a 'world we have lost', a family based upon the sentimentalisation of a presumed white middle-class lifestyle, yet a family that in reality reflects 'the way we never were'. Stephanie Coontz, in a book of that name, has shown very clearly how many of our 'memories' of families in the past function primarily as mythical stories. But, as she says,

> Families have always been in flux and often in crisis; they have never lived up to nostalgic notions about 'the way things used to be'. But that doesn't mean the malaise and anxiety people feel about modern families are delusions, that everything would be fine if we only realised that the past was not all it's cracked up to be. Proving that there was no 'Golden Age' of the family is in one sense a debater's point that rightfully leaves most audiences unsatisfied. Even if things were not always right in families of the past, it seems clear that some things have gone newly wrong.[28]

Tellingly she says:

> Not all myths are bad. . . . People need shared stories to bring them together and reinforce social solidarity. But myths that create unrealistic expectations about what families can or should do tend to erode solidarities and diminish confidence in the problem-solving abilities of those who 'fall short'.[29]

Right-wing politicians still cling to the story of a traditional family and the espousal of family values is still everywhere heard.[30] The debate is a regular feature of political campaigns. In the run-up to the 1992 presidential election, for instance, Vice President Dan Quayle attacked the fictional TV character Murphy Brown, played by Candice Bergen. The programme displayed a 'poverty of values' through its glamorisation of a career woman positively giving birth out of wedlock.

Yet however much the presumed traditional family and its values is championed by some, it has become one narrow option from a range of possible strategies for living together. In much of the western world it has already ceased to exist as a dominant form, if indeed it ever did in the highly romanticised ways of some depictions. By the 1970s it was common to hear talk of 'alternatives to the family'; by the mid-1980s in the USA, 'only 7 per cent of households conformed to the "modern" pattern of breadwinning father, homemaking mother and one to four children under the age of eighteen'; by the 1990s the range of experiences had become an accelerating commonplace and there was talk of the 'postmodern family':[31]

'The family' is *not* 'here to stay'. Nor should we wish it were. The ideological concept of 'the family' imposes mythical homogeneity on the diverse means by which people organise their intimate relationships and consequently distorts and devalues this rich variety of kinship stories. And, along with the class, racial and heterosexual prejudices it promulgates, this sentimental, fictional plot authorizes gender hierarchy. Because the postmodern family crisis ruptures this seamless modern family 'script', it provides a democratic opportunity. Feminist, gay liberation activists, and many minority rights organizations' efforts to expand and redefine the notion of family are responses to this opportunity. These groups are seeking to extend social legitimacy and institutional support for the diverse patterns of intimacy that Americans have already forged.[32]

The first zone of intimate citizenship hence centres around new personal narrative stories of living together. Hearing the tales of lone mothers and fathers, step-children, being single, divorcees, new couples, serial relationships, etc. will all help clarify the domain of rights and obligations in new communities living together. We need to hear these stories. But in addition it may go much further. Homosexualities, for instance, reach out and touch family life in a myriad of forms. These stories have hardly been heard. Gays and lesbians grow up inside families, usually having to keep their emerging sexuality a secret and often facing abuse once it is discovered, a form of sexual abuse never mentioned by the child sex abuse lobby. Gays and lesbians often get married to heterosexual spouses and raise families, only to decide later that a gay or lesbian relationship is preferable. Gays and lesbians may be uncles and aunts, brothers and sisters, sons and daughters or grandparents. Gays and lesbians may foster children. Gays and lesbians may embark upon relationships that are as enduring and as fulfilling as any heterosexual ones, and in some countries such relationships have become legitimated by religion, or law or both. And gays and lesbians may provide mutual networks of support, care and friendship that are as strong as any family, and maybe stronger because they are chosen rather than simply given. The lives of lesbians and gays touch upon 'family' in every direction, but stories of this diversity have rarely, until recently, been told.[33] The ideology of *the* family engulfs too many people and provides a distorted mirror; but the realities of diverse fami*lies* are very different. Here gay and lesbian experiences must be increasingly recognised in all their rich and diverse forms. Gayness is not a simple threat to the family, but a sign of the increasingly rich and diverse ways in which late modern societies are coming to organise ways of living together, often in mutual support.

The very concepts of kinship and family, then, are becoming increasingly contested: only some families need be linked to biology and blood. New personal stories have emerged around 'families we choose or create' rather than 'biological/blood families'.[34] The question now has increasingly become: how am I to live my life with others? Should it be with a single person of the opposite sex with marriage and children, or should it be with several and mixed, or on my own? More, how am I to be involved with children – with their conception, their birth, their care – and indeed with the elderly, and other generations: am I to live in an age-segregated world, or in one where age dissolves as such a key organising feature? The future may well lie in the proliferation of more and more stories of differing ways of living together that help provide new understandings and communities of citizenship.

Emotional stories

Much of story telling deals with the worlds of emotions, and yet often whole worlds have been left out. Lots of feelings – including ways of feeling not even recognised as feeling – can get written out of the stories we tell of our lives. And more. Feelings are also part of politics – of empowerment and diminution: the social worlds of passion, esteem, rage and love. These matters that often go to the heart of a personal life and, dimly sensed, may be closely related to empowerment and feelings of powerlessness. Some of the stories of our feelings have started to become more visible and public as rape victims and other survivors speak out about their sense of powerlessness on a public stage. The short tale of one victim of an acquaintance rape can stand for many:

> There's no way to describe what was going on inside me. I was losing control and I'd never been so terrified and helpless in my life. I felt as if my whole world had been kicked out from under me and I had been left to drift all alone in the darkness.[35]

Here is a previously hidden world of emotion, emerging in confusion through a story, and helping to provide a language for someone to find their own experience. Once, bit by bit, it is rendered public, it becomes easier for others to adopt the story, to locate their feelings through this frame.

Throughout this book, a new world of emotional story telling can be seen as in the making. I ponder what happened to some feelings before they were spoken about. Listening to the stories of incest survivors which have appeared in the past twenty years, a world of feelings is now spoken about: of deep repressions, of disassociation, of traumatic flash-backs, of protection of personal boundaries, of fear, anxiety, terror and rage. This is 'PSTD' – or post-traumatic stress syndrome. What happened to all this previously? And most significantly, since this very emotional experience is now so often seen as the key to the whole workings of a life, what happened to these victims before they were able to put their feelings into words and tell their stories? There is much evidence that incest is not new, but that the story telling around it is new.

Incest survivors are just the public tip of whole worlds of unspecified feeling stories. As Chapter 7 showed, there has been the growth of a major industry devoted to telling us all about our feelings: the recovery industry. The new men's movement has enabled men to weep and wail around the campfire telling their innermost feeling tales.[36] And the sense of anger, fear, grief, suffering, bereavement and loss has surfaced often in the stories of Aids and HIV.[37] Within these narratives, worlds of feeling become specified for others to grasp. And at the same time, social scientists have started to take this more seriously, writing about their constructed nature.[38]

One part of intimate citizenship is 'feeling worlds' and many more stories of these feeling worlds await telling.

Representational stories

How the intimate can be imagined, portrayed, represented has traditionally been at the centre of the regulation of the intimate. There is a long history of people being kept away from dangerous stories of the intimate life. It is nowadays omnipresent in art, film, writing, music, theatre, dance, advertising. What can be said about the intimate, how it may be imagined and depicted, is curiously the parallel story of censorship and freedom of speech and expression. How can we learn to talk about what images we see, want to see, do not want to see? What kinds of stories will emerge around this? There has been a long controversy around art and media, and in recent times it has become acute: with controversies in art, as Serrano's *Piss Christ* dangles in the artist's urine or as Robert Mapplethorpe photographs 'fist-fucking'; or in pop music, as the Beastie Boys or Madonna or Prince mime masturbation and simulate intercourse on stage; or as Michael Jackson or Marky Mark unzip their flies on prime-time video; or as the 2 Live Crew rap group use the word 'fuck' over 200 times on one record. What, one may well ask, is the contribution of all this to citizenship?!

The need is for readers' tales. Censorship is usually the tale told from the prohibitionist's story. What is needed are readers' stories: just what sense do people make of Madonna's simulations or Mapplethorpe's fist? In an important study of the workings of the Meese Commission on Pornography, Carole Vance suggests the meagreness of our language to describe visual pleasures and the erotic. Even those who claim to be opposed to censorship often shy away from the defence of erotic imagery: when witnesses saw some during the Meese hearings 'they were unprepared, speechless, and unwilling to defend anything so patently sexual'. Arguing that our frame for thinking about the visually erotic has been defined by the right wing as danger in need of censorship, she pleads for a new kind of story:

> We need to offer an alternative frame for understanding images, one that rejects literalist constructions and offers in their place multiplicity, subjectivity, and the diverse experience of viewers. We must challenge the conservative monopoly on visual display and interpretation.[39]

Some of the challenges can be heard in the new voices of feminism, of the women who find erotic pleasure in the visual, and who see the prior feminist story of single-minded 'danger' as a far too simple one. Linda Williams, for instance, in *Hard Core* analyses a range of heterosexual pornography – from the earliest stag movies through to the explosion of the 1970s and through the 'snuff' and sadomasochism era to a more recent trend for feminist-inspired erotica.[40] Throughout, she stresses – contrary to Andrea Dworkin[41] – the diversity of meanings inherent in pornography rather than the unitary structure which Dworkin found in her earlier radical feminist analysis. But what is still missing though, even from Williams's analysis, is a sense of the varying voices that watch and read and consume this material. What stories can be told about visual pleasure – what one sees, how one sees, how one feels what is seen?

Bodily stories

For most of the modern period, stories of the body have placed 'it' primarily in a fixed, well-bounded, causal and 'natural' framework: the body has been separated from mind, culture and science, and seen to rigorously shape our lives from within – through gender, through age, through disease and ultimately through death. Anatomy was Destiny. It was the story of the Natural Body. There have always been challenges to this of course, but only very recently have significant changes emerged. Now the story of what we may do with our bodies has firmly entered the agenda of politics and daily life – in science, in medicine, in sport, in health and exercise, in reproductive (or generative) technologies, in the eco-movement. No longer can the meanings and stories of the body be simply assumed as given, bounded, natural. New narratives of the body are in the making.

Is there a way of telling stories about the body that enable us to see it not simply as a bounded, 'there', 'in us' but something which resonates socially? To see perhaps the deeply interconnected social nature of the body – how something like childbirth, for instance, is not 'in' the body and then 'out' of it, but permeated at every stage with the social. The body is part of the social and not cut off from it.

The body hence becomes a central site of concern for stories of intimate citizenship. Stories of the body need to be told, especially, that will connect to *reproduction* (reproductive politics, abortion, reproductive rights, pregnancy, genetic engineering and all the new technologies of reproduction).

Gender stories

Running through almost all our stories is a tale of gender – a tale which organises difference and 'others', setting up boundaries and otherness. Throughout history, gender seems to have been a key organising metaphor – through legend and myth across time and space. It is hard to believe that such a story is in decline, especially when new stories of masculinity from the men's movement assert a return to these old tales – of Iron Johns and warriors. It is clear that this major narrative will not collapse. The former tribal stories speak of men and women as if they were separate tribes. They base their foundations on biology, nature and religion, suggesting the natural man and the natural woman within, often struggling to get out in these dangerous times. The most conventional versions of this story are told by 'conservative' men and women, along with the socio-biologists. Here, men are by nature 'barbarians' (aggressive, lustful, competitive) and societies can only survive if they are regulated by the more nurturing hand of women. 'Women control . . . the life force in our society and in our lives . . . [shaping] the level of happiness, energy, creativity and solidarity in our lives.'[42] Yet in different guise this is a tale stated not just by conservatives and some scientific socio-biologists, but also by major wings of both feminism and the men's movement. Here there is a critical recognition that women's and men's true and essential natures should be explored more fully. Thus women come to perceive worlds of men as violent, dangerous and sex-driven, and simply leave them behind in order to explore through each other their own loving, nurturing worlds of spinning and weaving, of herstory and mother goddesses: of gyn/affection.[43] Meanwhile (back in the cave so to speak) the men recognise their frailties, huddle together and return to the wild in order to find the deep roots of their male souls. There is a need to find the 'wild man within', the reservoir of deep masculine emotion that has been lost in the modern world. As I write, these stories have become something of a best-seller!

But a wholly different set of emerging stories speak as if there will be no such thing as gender in the future, indeed there really is no gender now. For gender is really a 'science fiction', a 'discourse', even a bad habit: 'the repeated stylization of the body, a set of repeated acts within a highly regulatory frame that congeal over time to produce the appearance of substance, of a natural sort of being.'[44] Usually amassing cases of transexuals, transvestites or even homosexuals across different cultures to prove the point, gender gets deconstructed. Of course gender has been *made* to exist throughout history; but the point is that it does not have to. A false binary split has been created in which social life has become encoded, entrapped: the task is to break beyond, transgress. Nor is this just the task of 'radical theory'. In a much more modest tone, the liberal humanist feminist Susan Moller Okin can produce a social policy agenda which claims:

> A just future would be one without gender. In its social structures and practices, one's sex would have no more relevance than one's eye colour or the length of one's toes. No assumptions would be made about 'male' or 'female' roles; childbearing would be so conceptually separated from childrearing and other family responsibilities that it would be a cause for surprise and no little concern if men and women were not equally responsible for domestic life or if children were to spend much more time with one parent than the other. It would be a future in which men and women participated in more or less equal numbers in every sphere of life, from infant care to different kinds of work to high level politics.[45]

This is certainly not a radical deconstructionist case: rather it is a story of 'humanist justice'. But it starts with imagining that 'a just future would be one without gender'. Maybe this is a story whose time has come?

I have sketched two contrasting stories freely circulating at the end of the twentieth century: *a narrative of polarised gender*, one which finds communities in the past and draws upon them to assert the power of a dualistic gender in our lives for the future; and *a narrative of abolished gender*, one without much of a tradition to draw upon, but which seeks to provide new stories of the ways in which lives can be lived without the 'tyranny of gender'. There are many positions in between and all the stories need telling.

Erotic stories

Since at least the late 1960s new stories of sexuality have been in the making. The dominant narrative which placed the world of the erotic largely within a framework of procreation, coitus and family life has clearly been dispersed, much to the horror of traditionalists. I have shown at many points in this book how new meanings have been given to sexualities and how new patterns have emerged in pockets of the western world, especially amongst women.[46] With profound changes in family, media, economy, polity and urban structures all taking place, it was a period when new sexual stories could be told, new sexual identities could become solidified and new sexual institutions could emerge. By the 1980s the sexual world of the west was extremely different to the world a hundred years earlier. This book has hinted at an array of newer and proliferating erotic tales that are developing at century's end. New sexual stories have been in the making. A few can be mentioned here.

A first striking set of new stories are emerging around 'safer sex'. A new language of sexual experience is in the making which shifts emphasis away from the traditional tale of penis–vagina procreational sex. In its place, it advocates bodily pleasure without the exchange of bodily fluids. First suggested by some New York gay men around 1982 in the publication *How to Have Sex in an*

Epidemic, 'safer sex' soon became the organising theme of gay health campaigns and was subsequently adopted on a broader scale throughout the world. It is an attempt to deal with the negative meanings of Aids – the 'stop sex' view – by maintaining positive images of sexualities and being innovative about sexual practice. For some the emphasis is placed on *safe*, with all sexual practices being classified as high, medium and low-risk activities. But for others, the emphasis is placed on *sex*, with the task of 'eroticising safe sex'; of keeping the body erotic whilst playing safe. In North America, this has meant many new practices proliferating alongside their accompanying tales: 'telephone sex', 'buddy jerkoff groups and jack and jill jerkoff groups', 'the eroticising of the condom', 'safe sex porn' and 'new styles of bodily intimacy' have all established themselves. A new world of innovative 'outercourse' has emerged.[47]

A further cluster of new personal narratives emerging at century's end are those of sadomasochism, S/M, leatherfolk. Various compilations of writings have appeared over the past decade or so which describe the experience of *leatherfolk*, suggesting an emerging history of community and identity whilst detailing its practices in first-person stories, and often providing a political rationale: *Coming to Power, High Risk, Modern Primitives, TRUST/The Handbook, Learning the Ropes, S-M: The Last Taboo, Urban Aboriginals, Hard Corps, Leatherfolk*.[48] At their broadest, these stories explore the full potential of human sexualities – a wide-ranging 'radical sex'. As one anthology, *Leatherfolk*, waxes:

> S/M can serve deep spiritual needs for wholeness and completion. . . . Radical sex practice is about the exploration of eros. . . . Being playful with sexuality – entertaining our fantasies, enriching our lives with pleasure – is an essential freedom. The look, scent and feel of black leather sexualizes everything it comes in contact with. Liberating erotic potential from the dour puritanical ethics that still rules our culture, and our libidos, is prerequisite to establishing a more sane and forgiving society. S/M practice, composed of highly potent sexual games, increases awareness about ourselves and others. . . . S/M play is about healing the wounds that keep us from fully living.[49]

The women's movement has also, and perhaps curiously, contributed to these newly emerging narratives of the erotic. Whereas the 1970s largely saw a feminist ethic emerging that was very heavily anti-sex, a strain of thought has also developed which highlights the diversity of the erotic. Initially through the controversial movement of lesbian sadomasochism (SAMOIS) and the writings of Pat Califia, Gayle Rubin and others, new personal experiences were described for women. By the late 1980s, these stories had gone much further and a whole new world of women's sexual narrative had emerged in the writings of Suzie Bright, Joan Nestle and others.[50]

There are many other attempts to create new erotic worlds for the future, and with them has come much writing on sexual guidelines for the future. Some feminist writers have come up with lists of 'safe, forbidden and risky sex practices', not in terms of HIV risk but in terms of 'politically correct sexuality'.[51]

Others have returned to classic liberalism.[52] Still others such as Peter Tatchell are attempting to develop broad strategies of sexual rights, linked to principles of diverse equalities for many groups.[53] If the shifts of the past decade prefigure the future, sexuality in the early twenty-first century will look very different to what it was in the mid- twentieth. I do not wish to suggest that such changes can ever be easy, because sexual cultures have histories, structures, institutions and ideologies which give them a semi-permanence; people become committed to their particular forms of sexuality, and there is usually resistance in both culture and personal life to change. But change is nevertheless, now, omnipresent. Although the old narrative of procreation may still be one in dominance, the past decades have produced a miracle of diverse campaigns that have shifted the languages and stories through which we understand the complexities of our sexualities and politics. In a further proliferation of new languages and stories, claims and counter-claims may well lie the future. We are in the middle of a living experiment in rewriting our sexual stories.

Identity stories

It is a cliché of sociology that whereas once identities were stable, fixed, bounded, ascribed and taken for granted, in the modern world they have become increasingly fragmented, destabilised, trivialised, mutable and problematic. There is now a massive set of writing which analyses the shifts in the stories of our identity over the past several hundred years, but especially the past thirty years, and at its most extreme it places the very notion of the human being, 'the human subject', under question. What kinds of persons are we, who are we to become? 'What to do? How to act? Who to be?', as Giddens puts it.[54] Traditional identity stories of gender stability, age boundaries, religious tribalism, family lineage and moral character start to shift ground dramatically for some people. The old identity stories of family or gender are shifting ground. Once clear and fixed, identities are increasingly destabilised.

Identity stories at century's end – like all the other stories – move in many directions. Asking the basic question of who we are – our sense of boundary, of difference, of destiny – some stories move in very bleak directions: with portrayals of the future in which identities become manipulative, pure pastiche, narcissistic, even non-existent. But equally come stories in which new identities take us beyond the limiting categories of the past, and start forming identities which are forged around relationships and conscious choices over the life one wishes to live and who one wishes to be. This means that identities may be more self-consciously constructed, and that they can indeed change; but not that they are mere ephemeral, chameleon-like empty fabrications. Identities may well matter more once they are an issue of self-construction; they even become a basis for politics as the recent developments in the women's, gay and black movements show most clearly.

THE WAR OF THE INTIMATE TALES: FROM TRIBALISM TO DIFFERENCE

The past two chapters have introduced the possibilities for an array of new personal narratives that may be told around the intimate and the sexual: stories which suggest new living arrangements, new families, new ways of thinking about feelings, bodies, representations and identities, and new modes of the erotic. We can see a proliferation of stories in the recent past, and there is no reason to think they will suddenly cease. Old stories will however remain side by side with the new. And in this lies a major source of conflict.

For with every new story, there is a rival old one. Tales of new families are countered by tales of 'family values'; tales of new bodies are countered by traditional values of the 'natural'; tales of new ways of being men and women – even to the point of their dissolution – are countered by 'backlash stories' with the reassertion of traditional masculinity and femininity;[55] and tales of the new sexualities generate intense anxiety over traditional standards of sexuality. Traditional values and absolutist moralities are evoked in the presumption of decline and relativity.

The ideas of life politics and intimate citizenship are not the ideas of a relativistic moral vacuum. They lead to new sexual stories and new communities of support, championing new ways of living together. With this does come a danger. For often the voices and stories to be heard lead to sharp conflicts. The eclipse of the essence, the delight in difference, the emphasis on participation – all this will inevitably mean that traditional and largely authoritarian stories of the past are placed severely under threat from a multiplicity of conflicting voices. Will one drown the other out? Can they coexist, and if so how? What are the possible relationships of different stories to each other? A difficult period awaits.

One recent account by James Davison Hunter has presented the clash in stories as a 'culture war': as the latest manifestation of a religious and moral combat. In the past, the battle grounds were drawn up *between* religions – Protestant versus Catholic, Catholic versus Jew. But now the battle grounds are being drawn up between those of different moral and political visions which cut *across* past schisms, suggesting new alignments. On one side are those of religious orthodoxy – Protestant, Jew, Catholic, Buddhist, Islamic alike – who continue to seek the truth in a fixed authority, usually through a canonical scripture. On the other side are those who look more pragmatically to the shifts in the modern world for clues as to how to live the new moral life. It is a divide between *cultural conservatives/ moral traditionalists*, and *liberals or cultural progressives*. As Hunter says:

> What is common to approaches to orthodoxy is the commitment on the part of adherents to an external, definable, and transcendent authority . . . [defining] a consistent, unchangeable measure of value, purpose, goodness, and identity, both personal and collective. It tells us what is good, what is true, how we should live, and who we are. It is an authority that is sufficient for all time.

By contrast, what is common to the progressivist is:

> the tendency to resymbolize historic faiths according to the prevailing assump-
> tions of contemporary life. . . . Traditional sources of moral authority, whether
> scripture, papal pronouncements or Jewish law, no longer have an exclusive or
> even predominant binding power over their lives.[56]

In my terms, the former cling to the old stories, the latter are writing new ones even
with a sense of their past. But they are telling very different kinds of stories.
Whereas the traditionalists tells stories which attempt to encompass all within an
obdurate framework of authority and received truth, to lay out the one story which
all should adhere to, the progressivists attempt to open up the range of stories, of
possibilities. Hunter's account fails to clearly acknowledge, however, that some
groups want to tell others what to do: their moral code is a code for themselves, it
is true, but they wish it to be extended to others. It is a politics of prohibition: they
wish to stop abortion, single-parent families, pornography, sex education, diverse
sexualities, gay rights, etc. The other position is more pragmatic – looking for
spaces to open up it is a politics of possibilities – no one has to have an abortion,
but it is possible to. As such the latter is more open and more pluralistic. It is, of
course, a story of the right to choose.[57]

The problem of conflicting and competing stories is a central political issue for
the future. Can the divergent stories manage to coexist or will certain tales
triumph? Ultimately, we enter here many of the classic problems of contemporary
political philosophy – where issues of democracy, freedom, community,
participation, empowerment, equality and justice have been paramount concerns
in a theory of citizenship. There are a range of responses to the problem of
competing stories – from fundamentalism and tribalism to a more pluralistic and
participatory culture.

The first, and in my view the most dangerous and pessimistic response to the
problem of conflicting stories, is the reassertion of *tribalism, fundamentalism* and
separatism. Here is the affirmation of stories which are exclusive, closed,
authoritarian. They prioritise one group, culture and identity over others, and
provide one essential or foundational truth over and above others. In many ways it
is the politics of the past, still alive in the present: it is the politics against which
emancipatory models came to fruition. Some of its arguments may be vital in
shaping debates, but their triumph would see the closure of proliferating stories and
the triumph of *the* story. It has and will lead to tribal warfare. Today it can be seen
in the dissolution of old nation-states, and it is present in religious fundamentalisms
of all sorts. Likewise, both sexual and gender fundamentalism (so common in the
past) is still on the agenda: with the potential for sexual and gender tribes to assert
their own fundamentalist stories. Some of the new social movements around these
matters generate 'true believers' in single stories which themselves create a new
essentialism: women as superior, gayness as radical transgression, men as
warriors. The late modern world here will become an increasingly risky place.
Giddens ends his recent book on modernity with such concerns:

How can we moralize social life without falling prey to prejudice? The more we return to existential issues, the more we find moral disagreements; how can these be reconciled? If there are no transhistorical ethical principles, how can humanity cope with clashes of 'true believers' without violence?[58]

A more benign response may be that of *communitarianism*. This is most clearly exemplified in the philosophy of Alasdair MacIntyre, and in the sociology of Robert Bellah and Etzioni. Here is asserted the need for 'tribes' with their own 'traditions' but it is a model of the tribes at least managing to live together. The source of moral value is to be found in the community. Here, as in the earlier tribal response, communities will build their own collective stories in which people can locate the shared traditions of their lives; but unlike the tribalism, their stories will not assert a moral superiority.

But with such a model, how are people to live together without the conflicts becoming unbearable? The traditional liberal response to this has been to establish some sense of a *common framework*, a *minimum of ground rules* through which stories can be told. An intriguing variant on this is the necessary *constraining and limiting* of truly discordant voices. Becoming aware that some stories are so different, so at odds with each other, one suggestion is to create a silent pact: some things are best left unsaid, best left unspoken. It is easy to see how this works on the personal level: millions of people who see themselves as gay may simply avoid coming out to non-gays; and non-gays just elect to ignore it. This way (gay) life goes on and nobody is (too) threatened. People can live together through simply ignoring fundamental differences! It is simply better not to know, even when we might really know all along. At a wider level, this is the liberal political strategy advocated by Bruce Ackerman with his idea of 'conversational restraint':

> When you and I learn that we disagree about one or other dimension of the moral truth, we should not search for some common value that would trump this disagreement; nor should we try to translate our moral disagreement into some putatively neutral framework; nor should we seek to transcend our disagreement by talking about how some hypothetical creature would resolve it. We would simply say *nothing at all* about this disagreement and try to solve our problem by invoking premises that we do agree upon. In restraining ourselves this way we need *not* lose the chance to talk to each other about our deepest moral disagreements in countless other, more private, contexts. . . . Having constrained the conversation in this way, we may instead use dialogue for pragmatically productive purposes; to identify normative principles all political participants find reasonable.[59]

Again, this is an empirical reality: a great deal of social life is conducted through a tacit agreement of silences, and is likely to continue. The lesbian and gay coming out story is often a story that others simply do not want to hear. Whilst many gays and heterosexuals may be able to coexist by ignoring or not hearing each other, they may well find the telling of the story too much to bear. Here, 'keeping certain secrets secret is important to . . . the general balance of life, the common utility'.[60] But this is not always a very hopeful strategy – it means many voices will continue to be unheard, and for reasons implicit throughout this book I think this will be increasingly difficult in the future.

Tribalism, communitarianism, constraint are all possible futures, but they all work to remove threatening or new stories: tribalism through its appeal to authority, communitarianism through its appeal to tradition, constraint through its tacit agreement that some things are best left unsaid. A range of other responses, however, place the greatest emphasis upon different aspects of communication, dialogue and discourse. One strand draws from Habermas and stresses a communicative theory of ethics. In a universal and seemingly ahistorical 'ideal speech situation', all must have equal chances to make their voices heard; it takes a 'pragmatic turn'. Deception, including self- deception is eliminated, domination is removed and intersubjective communication becomes purer. But communictive competence free from deception and domination is ideal, and although Habermas's view has its followers it 'ignores the contingent, historical and affective circumstances which made individuals adopt a universal-ethical standpoint in the first place'.[61] The whole theory is too homogenising, too objectivist, too close to making external (and internal) elite claims.[62]

AN UNSURE FUTURE: A DIALOGUE OF STORIES

> I remember when I first met Myra and I was really enjoying her and when I found out her position I was really surprised, you know, but I was able to say, OK, I understand. I respect Myra's position and she respects mine and neither of us have any fantasies about changing the other. And I think we both recognise that it's a very complex and difficult issue. I find with Myra there is unity on other values, or at least nothing that leads to conflict.
>
> (a pro-choice woman describing her relationship with a pro-life woman)[63]

> You know liberal and conservative doesn't make sense any more, it really doesn't.
>
> (A right-to-life Democrat)[64]

To take a challenging example: abortion stories. In the last quarter of a century, there has probably been no one story to have aroused such polarised passions as abortion. The claims made by pro-lifers seem irrevocably at odds with pro-choice activists. A movement of fundamentalists find abortion as embodying the killing of a living foetus. Meanwhile, an older generation of feminists can see and hear only one story: the right for women to choose. It is a bloody conflict – not without its share of abortion clinic bombings and vitriolic attack. The stories of activists on both sides have been told many times and they are in stark contrast to each other. It is a tension documented many times.[65]

So what could possibly be the way ahead? The fundamentalisms on either side are now a dead end. Though they may have once been important in clarifying issues, they are now too well known to need such polarities. Conversational restraint is probably, in practice, what is taking place in many places: a tacit agreement to live together and ignore differences. Traditional communitarians – perilously close to fundamentalisms – seek out the history of their ethics through the religious or feminist community. An ideal speech situation where a communicative ethics may be established remains just that: an ideal. There is not a lot of guidance here.

An intriguing, though controversial, study by Faye Ginsburg points in one direction. Interviewing a number of grass-roots activist women living in a small town in America (Fargo) over a controversial abortion clinic which opened in 1982, she found two sets of polar but linked narratives of the women's lives. A moral drama is re-enacted as a small town finds itself confronted with an abortion clinic. Women tell their life stories about abortion as 'procreation stories' centred around issues of pregnancy, childbirth and nurturing. Both sides were engaged in activism; both sides saw themselves as under attack; both sides felt their story was the truth.

For pro-choice activists, their experiences were primarily grounded in the women's movement activism of the 1960s and 1970s. They stress the right for women to work, but do so in a context of female values of nurturing. They recognise the key role women play in birth and reproduction, but wish to extend it. Pro-life activists are largely younger, usually also with strong feminist sympathies (as opposed to the way they are usually represented), and have often changed their views when confronted with a changing time and morality. They are not 'straightforward' mothers, but women who are 'astute, alert to social and political development, and on many issues are not anti-feminists. They approve of and endorse women seeking political and economic power.'[66] Nevertheless, 'the unborn child' was their 'root metaphor' which helped organise most of their story telling. Here then are enemies: each side depicts the other side as 'the other'. But at the same time, Ginsburg charts how there is a lot of mutual respect, understanding, tolerance going on between the groups here. It led, briefly, to setting up a pro-dialogue group where both sides could get together and at least listen to each other's tales.

This is no solution, but there may not be a solution. What we are left with is the proliferation of stories, recognising stories not yet told and creating new spaces. This is a task that postmodernism has claimed for itself, but of course it is one that goes back further. Following this line, there can be no grand conclusion to this book – no final story to be told. Indeed, if one analysis has come through it is surely that in the late modern period such grand stories are no longer possible. Indeed, such claims must be looked upon with suspicion. What we are left with are fragments of stories. What seems to be required is a sensitivity to listen to an ever-growing array of stories and to shun the all too tempting desire to place them into a coherent and totalising narrative structure. Indeed, as Jane Flax has so clearly suggested, it may be that 'structures' only appear clear from the false perspective of the single unitary story of dominant groups.[67] I have tried, in these closing pages, to turn from the simple modernist narratives discussed earlier, and whose time has now come, to open up an array of potential stories and voices that are emerging at century's end. It is not an easy option to keep the pluralistic, polyvocal potential of proliferating stories open; but it is probably a very necessary one.

Following the pragmatist tradition, we need to hear new stories and anticipate how they might change our lives if we do. Although there is much I would disagree with, Richard Rorty is the contemporary heir apparent to the pragmatist heritage. He has argued that human sufferings can only be reduced through an improved sensitivity to the voices of the suffering, and that this is 'a matter of detailed description'. The search for such narratives of self is the work of much popular culture, which cannot therefore be lightly dismissed. For him, 'the novel, the movie and the TV programme have, gradually but steadily, replaced the sermon and the treatise as the principle vehicles of moral change and progress'.[68]

Other writers on sexuality and intimacy have recently converged on a position not wholly dissimilar to mine. Steven Seidman's study of *Embattled Eros* leads him to a 'postmodern position' which advocates a 'pragmatic ethical strategy'. This shuns strict moral hierarchies, and grants respect to differences:

> Unless we are prepared to exclude all those sexual constructions that differ from 'our own', or to deny difference by interpreting them as minor variations of an identical phenomenon, we must concede that groups evolve their own sexual culture around which they elaborate coherent lives.[69]

Likewise, Jeffrey Weeks has, for over a decade, espoused a position of 'radical pluralism' which pays partial attention to contrasting meanings and situations over sexuality.[70] A dialogue around a multiplicity of stories needs to be established.

A final word can be left, for the time being, with the prescient William James:

> No one of us ought to issue vetoes to the other, nor should we bandy words of abuse. We ought, on the contrary, delicately and profoundly to respect one another's mental freedom: then only shall we have the spirit of inner tolerance without which all our outer tolerance is soulless, and which is empiricism's glory; then only shall we live and let live, in speculative as well as practical things.[71]

Chapter 11

Epilogue

Beyond stories? The pragmatics of story telling

It may not be exactly true, but it makes a great story.

(Sarah Schulman, *The Sophie Horowitz Story*)[1]

When talking about their lives, people lie sometimes, forget a lot, exaggerate, become confused, and get things wrong. Yet they are revealing truths. These truths don't reveal the past 'as it actually was', aspiring to a standard of objectivity. They give us instead the truth of our experiences. Unlike the Truth of the scientific ideal, the truths of personal narratives are neither open to proof nor self-evident. We come to understand them only through interpretation, paying careful attention to the contexts that shape their creation and to the world views that inform them.[2]

To talk of stories and narrative has become very fashionable in the world of academic cultural studies. But to talk of stories is to sense an invented world of fantasy: of fiction, of fabrication, of 'making up'. As children we come to see stories as an escapist world of make-believe. Thus, when social scientists of all persuasions come to use the term – as they recently have – they implicitly suggest that the world of story telling is not quite the world of truth. At their worst, they even seem to suggest that all we have are stories.

Such arguments are dangerous and have the most serious consequences for any analysis. For instance, to sense that people raped, or people with Aids are 'simply' telling stories may well be taken to imply something less than serious: that they too, like children, are 'making up tales'. Rape victims know only too well the frequent charge that they are simply making up stories. This is not my argument. Likewise, to sense the importance of stories in social life is never to suggest that stories are all there is: the telling and reading of stories is always grounded in social processes that by definition are 'beyond the stories'. There is more, much more, to life than stories.

And hence, although my concern throughout this book has been with stories, it has always also been with more than that. I have tried to show how stories are truly sociological phenomena – rather than mere narratives or texts in the abstract. I have asked how they get produced socially; how they get read socially; how certain kinds of stories can only be told at particular social moments; how they change socially; and how they are part of socio-political argument. In this concluding epilogue, my concern lies with the ways in which sexual stories connect to a world that lies beyond stories: an obdurate empirical world 'out there'.

As usual, it is helpful to start with a story. This time, it comes from a 22-year-old black science fiction writer Samuel R. Delany who is reflecting on telling his coming out tale for the first time inside a therapy group. As he ponders what he has said, he feels the story, told only a few hours earlier, does not ring true:

> I'd talked like someone miserable, troubled and sick over being gay; and that wasn't who I was. On the contrary . . . the gay aspects of my life, from the social to the sexual, were the most educational, the most supportive, the most creative, and the most opening parts of my life. . . . Where had all the things I'd said that morning come from?
>
> I began to understand where they'd come from that night. They'd come from a book by the infamous Dr Bergler I had read as a teenager that had explained how homosexuals were physically retarded. They came from a book by Erich Fromm that told how homosexuals were all alcoholics who committed suicide. They had come from *Psychopathia Sexualis* . . .
>
> When you talk about something openly for the first time – and that, certainly, was the first time I'd talked to a public *group* about being gay – for better or worse you use the public language you've been given. It's only later, alone in the night, that maybe, if you're a writer, you ask yourself how closely that language reflects your experience. And that night I realised my experience had been betrayed.[3]

Here Delany becomes aware of a 'truer' story and a betrayal. *Whatever else a story is, it is not simply the lived life.* It speaks all around the life: it provides routes into a life, lays down maps for lives to follow, suggests links between a life and a culture. It may indeed be one of the most important tools we have for understanding lives and the wider cultures they are part of. But it is not *the* life, which is in principle unknown and unknowable. Hence a key concern in looking at stories must be with the kinds of relationships the story bears to a life. How indeed does a sexual tale link to a sexual life? How does the story told by Delany at one moment bear false witness to his life at another? How might the tale of a Rousseau connect to his 'sadomasochist life'? And that of an abused or raped woman link to her story of abuse?

Throughout this study, I have been stressing the socially constructed nature of the story telling process. Story telling and story reading are indeed social inventions, fictions, fabrications. They cannot be otherwise. None of this means that people are lying, deceiving, cheating (though of course they can be!): for at the moment a story is told or read we may come to 'own' it. People believe in it and its veridical power. Only later, might it be sensed as a construct. Nevertheless, some of these story tellings may come very close to the life as experienced; others much less so. Some may be said in full conviction that 'the truth' is being told; others are defences, denials, repressions, lies. Some may be 'false memories' and many are 'screen memories'. Some may be told as if manifest truths for all times and places, others hold only for the here and now, and fragilely at that. Some stories are told unreflectively; at other times the speakers are only too aware of the artifice involved – of how the stories we tell of our lives shift so much with who might hear. Likewise, readers with differing interpretive frames make sense of the stories they hear in different ways: nowhere is this clearer than when a story is contested. Anita Hill tells her story against Clarence Thomas, or Mia Farrow tells her story against Woody Allen, or the Bobbits argue in court against each other. Stories clash, sides are taken, different patterns of interpretation are evoked, stories are reread, retold, reclaimed.

The case of Anita Hill and Clarence Thomas is exemplary on all this. These Supreme Court appointees' hearings gripped the USA in October 1991, when accusations appeared of nominee Thomas's imputed sexual harassment of Anita Hill ten years earlier. Each told their 'story' before the Senate Judiciary Committee of Inquiry, and the whole proceedings were nationally televised. The sexual stories of Thomas and Hill riveted the nation for several days, breaking conventional codes of media story telling by providing accounts of the sexual usually cut off from public view. It was a 'media event, a milestone in TV history'.[4] They are a famous set of stories, shown at the time, reprinted in many places, documented and re-documented, debated and redebated. Hill tells of how Thomas made sexual overtures to her when she worked for him a decade earlier; how he had spoken of 'pornography', 'group sex' and his 'own sexual prowess'. In several famous remarks, she testified that he once asked her 'Who has put pubic hair on my Coke?'; and also told her of 'the pleasure he had given to women with oral sex'.[5] Thomas categorically denied everything, and said this was a 'high-tech lynching for uppity blacks who in any way deign to think for themselves'. The stories here then are directly at odds with each other, and the Senate Judiciary Committee was charged with ascertaining the truth. Such investigations of stories is the commonplace task of all court situations where stories are in contest and truth is sought.

At the time of the hearings everybody that I spoke to thought Hill must be telling the truth and that Thomas was not – but the people I spoke with were largely students on a sexual politics course I was teaching and colleagues in a social science department. Nationally, it appears, Thomas was believed more than Hill. In any event, the Senate narrowly confirmed Thomas who now sits (for life) on the Supreme Court. But since that time, public opinion has turned more and more in favour of Hill and against Thomas. The story has spawned dispute after dispute.[6]

In April 1993, David Brock published the best-selling *The Real Anita Hill: The Untold Story*.[7] In great detail – culled from court records and interviews – he concludes that Hill was not telling the truth. For him she is not a conservative black Baptist Reaganite (as was usually claimed) but a radical – certainly liberal – feminist Democrat who fabricated charges and was herself obsessed with sex! Jane Mayer and Jill Abramson have refuted all this.[8] They show that Brock's evidence rests on confusions, false memories and errors. This in turn set off a proliferating correspondence in the *New Yorker*, and elsewhere.[9] Orlando Patterson contextualises the stories as process: they both could be true, and ten years is a long time to ascertain the truth of such tales. Sexual harassment occurs in the workplace, and ten years ago – and maybe especially in a black context – it may have been little more than routine, hardly noticeable in a culture where such harassments had not yet been defined. Sexual banter may be part of this context and Hill and Thomas would have known it: maybe even going as far as a way of 'affirming their common origins'. Hill may not have liked it, but it was common. Thomas could forget because it was common. It was after all ten years ago, a different time and place. The meanings of the story are not fixed for all time. Hence ten years on, Thomas would not remember what might have been the cultural air he lived in; Hill may recall a mode of speech removed from its context.[10] But in Capitol Hill, the community and the language changed: and with it the stories.

It is hard to produce a firm conclusion from the myriad of arguments developed around the stories. The sexual stories of Anita Hill and Clarence Thomas are thoroughly contested. It is unlikely that the 'real truth' will ever be wholly clear. But what is clear is the way the stories have been used – overwhelmingly taken as metaphors that help focus on feminism, racism, elitism; race, class, gender, power; the law, the media, the workplace; sex, danger, rape, harassment: even the meaning of 'American life' itself.[11] The Hill–Thomas affair was a highly dramatic, widely publicised and fateful story told to millions and having a global impact. Several years after the stories were told and the official conclusions reached, it remains the topic of endless debate. It is unusual in a number of features, but it illustrates the socially organised nature of the whole story telling process. It is not that there is no 'truth': all the debates about this story are about how to access the truth. The truth of the story is itself socially organised, contextually bound, a matter for contestation. And whatever story is told, or believed, it spills out into the wider social world with far-reaching consequences. And in this, through more dramatically, it is like all stories.

THE TRUTH OF THE MATTER

I have slowly come to believe that no stories are true for all time and space: we invent our stories with a passion, they are momentarily true, we may cling to them, they may become our lives and then we may move on. Clinging to the story, changing the story, reworking it, denying it. But somewhere behind all this story telling there are real active, embodied, impassioned lives. Is this a process of peeling back stories to reveal better and better ones? And if so, when do we know a story is better? Or is it a process of constant readjustment of stories to be aligned with the time and the place of their telling? I am here suggesting that multiple stories engulf us, and we need tools for distinguishing between layers of stories, or even layers of truth.

Whilst accepting the inevitably fictional nature of all stories – they are by definition fictions, made up, invented – we can and must move beyond. But does that thereby make them all equally valid, or indeed, invalid? To say that a person with Aids tells a story could sound trivialising. To say that a victim of abuse tells a story could imply she is lying. To say that a woman's experience of abortion is recounted in her story of it may be too weak. The real pains experienced can get transformed into so much light, and fabricated, talk. The personal narratives of the kind discussed in this book are surely not just fictions. So what criteria might we have to assess the claims of stories?

The classic way of approaching this might be through the correspondence theory of truth. At one extreme, questions can be asked whether the story may be taken as a mirror on reality, as in some way reflecting it. When Germaine Greer or Gail Sheehy decide to tell the stories of their menopausal changes, in the same year (1992) but in different countries (the UK, the USA), we may see these stories as mirrors to the pains of their lives, told as accurately as they can. But at the other extreme, we may see the stories as unrelated to reality: as speech acts or language games, even as simulacra that fly off into their own make-believe worlds, having little correspondence with the worlds they describe. The most cynical might see them as pitches for the best-seller market!

Still, in time-honoured ways, stories can be appraised through checking their correspondence to other events. There are many ways of validating parts of stories and they should not be lightly ignored – papers, diaries, books read and underlined, friends, newspapers cuttings and of course day-to-day experience. All the stocks-in-trade of historians and social scientists who don't simply want stories but truth can be brought into play – though this time with a much greater self-reflexivity. This then is a most straightforward criterion: there is a matching of the story with things that can be documented.

But others have located an aesthetic connection: the realm of aesthetics gives a concern with the grace and beauty of the story. Stories that enrich our imaginations, help us to see wider and further, that stir the spirit or that may capture sensed nuggets of wisdom. These are the poetic and creative texts that pull us into them so that we may savour the new understandings and sensibilities of them. Much story telling (especially in social science) does not do this at all – it is almost ugly in its stark, clichéd, monotone manner. Much sociology, for instance, tells the dullest stories in the most dreary ways – and often deliberately so, for this is the mantle of scientific story telling: it is supposed to be dull.[12] But it is possible to seek fresher and more inspirational ways of telling our stories – in part, this has been my project in this book, and it is certainly one of the aims of the so-called postmodern project, which is not just exploring new kinds of stories but new ways of telling them.

A third stance to story telling is to take them seriously in their own right – not as historical truth but as narrative truth. In a psychoanalytic interpretation, Donald P. Spence has distinguished between 'narrative truth' and 'historical truth'.[13] Whilst the latter has been seen as the traditional mode of 'hearing stories' in which some kind of historical truth is dug out, Spence sees 'narrative truth' as being more valuable. Here the focus turns to the narrative fit of what people say in the here and now: the work of stories in lives in the present.

And this leads closely to the point of view of this study, a symbolic interactionist analysis which I will call the pragmatic connection. Here the concern is less directly with matters of truth, and more with matters of consequence: to consider the consequences of saying a particular story under particular circumstances. In this lies much of the power of story analysis. Stories help people to say certain things at certain times and in certain places, and likewise not to say them at others. Sexual stories can now be examined for the roles they play in lives, in contexts, in social order. What role does a certain kind of story play in the life of a person or a society?

THE SOCIAL PRAGMATICS OF STORIES

Sexual stories in lives

Recently, and from different academic disciplines, a number of writers have converged on the same basic idea: we tell stories about ourselves in order to constitute our selves. In modern experience this indicating to oneself 'the life', this 'story telling', may be a major clue to understanding identity. Dan McAdams, a leading psychologist for this position, has put the argument persuasively:

> An individual's story has the power to tie together past, present and future in his or her life. It is a story which is able to provide unity and purpose. . . . Individual identities may be classified in the manner of stories. Identity stability is longitudinal consistency in the life story. Identity transformation – identity crisis, identity change – is story revision. Story revision may change from minor editing in an obscure chapter to a complete rewriting of the text, embodying an altered plot, a different cast of characters, a transformed setting, new scenes and new themes. . . . Identity is a life story.[14]

People tell sexual stories to assemble a sense of self and identity. *Sexual stories lay down routes to a coherent past, mark off boundaries and contrasts in the present, and provide both a channel and a shelter for the future.* If they do their work well, sexual stories will give us a sense of our histories – partly of our own life and where we've come from, but no less a sense of a collective past and shared memories. They will provide a cause, a sequence, a history. As a collection of lesbian oral histories puts it:

> We need the past in order to be able to understand ourselves. We need it in order to believe in our future. If we have come from nowhere, where are we going to? . . . It is important for lesbians to tell stories to each other . . . for we cannot rely on our families to pass on our stories and validate our lives.[15]

But such stories also give a life a sense of present difference – of being marked off from the 'other'. There is unity in the story which harbours a difference. Stories from rape survivors provide identities which establish boundaries; who indeed we are not, and who by contrast our enemies – or 'the other' – may be. And further, sexual stories are maps for action – they look into the future, tell us how we are motivated, guide us gently into who we will be. They make certain worlds more plausible. They signpost directions to be taken – personal stories lead the tellers in some directions and not others. As one of the letters in Robin Norwood's collection of *Letters From Women Who Love Too Much* put it:

> My name is Ramona A. and I'm not only a recovering alcoholic but I'm now also a recovering woman who loves too much. . . . Somehow in my emotional hell I found your book and read it. There I was on every page and there was what was wrong with me. Only then could I accept and see that there was hope. I started a group based on your book.
>
> I can't begin to tell you how my life has changed since then, how the doors have opened for me, how my self-esteem has grown, how my faith has grown, or how I have grown.[16]

Sexual stories, then, may provide a history, a unity and difference, and a motive for the future.[17] All these elements get fashioned into our stories through 'self work': the active process of assembling all the signs around a life into an ongoing, emergent narrative. Core stories may be established to give a coherence to the disparate elements sucked out of the wider narrative bricolage found in the culture.[18] 'Modernist sexual tales' seek to find these unities, integrations and cores; they search out an *essence of the self*. And, as we have seen, many social movements and therapies are engaged in the very task of providing cultural accounts of history, coherence and identity which themselves create an essence – of abuse survivor, of gay, of sexual addict – that fashion further the modernist tale. Other kinds of stories – late modernist sexual tales – are, by contrast, more and more aware of the reflexive nature of much story telling, where the centre cannot hold, the essence disappears and a dispersal of identities becomes more and more likely. They are 'blurred genres'. And with that, the burdens of self work become correspondingly greater.[19]

Therapy provides a major instance of the power of essentialising stories in personal lives, where sexual stories weave together past, present and future into an identity. They help to clarify personal problems, the story lending a (maybe only momentary) coherence to a life. As Arthur Kleinman has shown for illness and David Payne and Judith Herman have shown for therapy, narrative plays a key role in the healing process. It can provide answers to the questions 'Why me?' (what Kleinman calls 'the question of bafflement') and also 'What can be done?' ('the question of order and control').[20] Therapy provides a vocabulary that enables people to cope with inadequacy, to manage failure and to gain a sense of esteem.[21] ' "The action of telling a story" in the safety of a protected relationship can', says Judith Lewis Herman, 'actually produce a change in abnormal processes of the traumatic memory'.[22] Dr Ruth, twelve-step programmes and *Oprah* serve to affirm therapy and recovery. The truth of these tales may not really be the issue: the work they do in the lending of coherence to a life and its problems is what matters. But this has its dangers: too often the self found may become standardised.[23]

Coherence and catharsis then are key functions of story telling revealed in many places: therapy, self help, consciousness raising, speak-outs, public rallies. The story is told that facilitates power in the life.

Sexual stories and community building

The coming out, surviving and recovery stories discussed earlier, reveal the key role community plays in the process of story telling. Stories need communities to be heard, but communities themselves are also built through story tellings. *Stories gather people around them*: they have to attract audiences, and these audiences may then start to build a common perception, a common language, a commonality.[24] Typically, stories that are not involved in community-building do not become strong stories. Although, for instance, the American therapist Gabrielle Brown became a celebrity telling her tale of 'celibacy' on US talk shows and through her book *The New Celibacy*,[25] it did not really achieve the popular status of many other sexual stories. It never seemed to achieve a community of story tellers. The same is true of a great many individualised worries such as impotency, infidelity or intercourse itself where there is typically no coming together to tell stories.

By contrast, the stories of Aids were indisputably community-building. A huge literature on Aids has emerged over the long decade since its discovery, and part of this has been an outpouring of literary narratives. From the Names Project Memorial Quilt where each patchwork signifies a personal story of Aids, through edited collections of 'personal dispatches' where writers confront Aids, to personal biographies such as Barbara Peabody's *The Screaming Room* and Paul Monette's *Borrowed Time*, the personal tale of Aids has played a pivotal role in reshaping the gay community.

As one man said at an Aids Memorial Day Rally in 1988:

What Aids has done is to reacquaint a community with the expressive function of life. No community has had to do so many artistic things, for their original purposes, so quickly and for such pressing reasons . . .

We need the stories, the feelings, the situations, the characters, the humor, the romance, the memories, and the affirmation of the recent sexual and communal and emotional past that novels and poets can give us. We need the stories the Aids Memorial Quilt collected. We need the voices of PWAs, the stories of the tending and the tended. We need our formidable imaginations and the resources of our style, our aesthetic sense, our sexual memories, as much as we need our other resources. We need what makes life good.[26]

And the bridge here is between story and community. Stories help organise the flow of interaction, binding together or disrupting the relation of self to other and community. Rape stories, coming out stories and recovery stories feed upon and into community – shifting the spheres of what is public and private, secret and known about.

Telling sexual stories may work a myriad of tasks in interactions. They may be told as a challenge: to threaten parents, to go against the grain of a social order. They may cement relationships: bonding together a peer group with stories of sexual camaraderie, strengthening a loving couple with shared tales of sex. They may be a means of gain: the story is told for money, status, immortality. Or more simply as a form of play: the sexual story is playful, a part of recreation, pleasure, novelty. Or they may be told as a means of expressing anger: the story gives vent to rage, hostility, aggression. Or as a habit: the story enters the vast flywheel of habit. Or finally the story may be told as a form of transcendence: the story is a means of breaking beyond. Not all stories are preservative. Some are threatening, and indeed it may well be that this is the characteristic of postmodern stories. They do not return to ritualised, conventionalised, habitualised forms of story telling: instead they seek to break asunder, to challenge dominant narratives, to be a threat. Such stories harbour change.

Sexual stories in culture

At the broadest level, stories have an important task to perform in the wider culture. Most self-evidently, sexual stories provide information, even education, in the service of reform or change. They can work a quiet 'catharsis of comprehension'.[27] Abstract arguments and dense detail are no substitute for 'human interest stories' that may ultimately bring about greater understanding or social transformation. Most writers recognise this. The academic arguments around transexualism or transvestism, for instance, can be very dry: but the personal narratives of a Christine Jorgensen, a Jan Morris or a 'Julia' give flesh and blood to the issues. Autobiographies of transexuals and transvestites can work a gradual comprehension on their readers, paving the road for greater acceptance and understanding. This of course is an obvious, even banal, function of story telling; but it should not be overlooked. It is one that story tellers themselves recognise over and over again:

From Christine Jorgensen:

[I hope that] a clear and honest delineation of my life may help to a greater understanding of boys and girls who grow up knowing they will not fit into the patterns of life that is expected of them; of the men and women who struggle to adjust to sex roles unsuited to them; and the intrepid ones who, like myself, must take drastic steps to remedy what they find intolerable.[28]

From an anthology of women and Aids

For many years I have worked in alternative media, exploring issues important to women's lives. I approach these concerns through the writings and testimonies of women, since their words yield a certain depth and honesty absent in an impersonal approach. . . . I hope that by reading this book more people will be encouraged to realise their own connection to the epidemic and integrate this understanding into their personal and work lives.[29]

Or from the editor of an anthology of lesbian and gay police officers talking of their experiences:

> It is the goal of this book that both the police and the lesbian and gay communities learn something of the problems faced by the other, and give recognition to those lesbian, gay or bisexual officers who, as part of each community, are often comprehended by neither and persecuted by both.[30]

Or, as a final instance of the obvious, the editor of an anthology of 'writings by women in the sex industry':

> Prostitution will remain a crime . . . so long as there is no identifiable voting bloc that clamours for changes in the law. As it stands now, horrible police abuse can be reported in the newspapers and just as quickly forgotten. Prostitutes get scapegoated for Aids and few people cry out. Prostitutes are murdered and the police tell no one until ten or more have been murdered. And even then there is little outcry in the square world. None of this will change, it seems to me, until prostitutes speak out in all their varied voices. . . . I hope this book helps the struggle along.[31]

This then is a very straightforward task of many sexual stories. But there are deeper issues here. The telling of sexual stories can ultimately move beyond the life of a person or a community, and beyond an informational educational role, and become a clue to the wider symbolic workings of whole cultures. The stories told in daily lives flow from the culture and back into it: they are major resources for comprehending a culture and its dynamics, values and changes.[32] Randolph Trombach, a leading historian of sexuality, has remarked how 'sexual behaviour (perhaps more than religion) is the most highly symbolic activity of any society. To penetrate to the symbolic system implicit in any society's sexual behaviour is therefore to come closest to the heart of its uniqueness.'[33] Sexual stories are a major key to this system. Not only do stories work pragmatically for the people who tell them, so too they feed into and perform major tasks for societies and groups within them.

And they work in many ways: indeed, 'narratives reinforce the dominant culture and put it into question, all at the same time'.[34] They have conservative, preservative, policing control tasks – as well as transgressive, critical, challenging tasks. 'Sex stories' have frequently become the basis of hysteria, moral outrage and heated political argument over the past hundred years because their potency speaks to highly ambivalent and much wider cultural concerns than the 'merely' sexual. All that confessional sexual story telling on *Donahue* or *Oprah* cannot surely *just* be about our genitals?

Many stories for instance perform conservative and preservative tasks: often the same stories are told over and over again, and they fit into broad patterns that have been detected over centuries. Part of the appeal of contemporary rape stories and lesbian and gay stories lies in their fit with major narrative tales of 'going on a journey', 'enduring suffering', 'finding a home' and the like. Some stories work so well because they fit easily into the major rituals of story telling. Socially and personally, they find a congruence with the world. Their ultimate pragmatic function is to make the world safe for us, to keep the threat and terror of life at bay. Even seemingly radical stories, such as those originally told in lesbian and gay coming out stories, take on conservative functions once they assume traditional narrative forms.

Stories in symbolic systems

Human sexualities wander in a world of ambiguity, disorder, potential chaos. William James once located the whole of human life in a world of 'big blooming buzzing confusion',[35] and in one sense sexuality is just a part of this. Sexualities need their stories to provide a coherence.

Thus sexual story telling is part of the elaborate symbolic systems endemic to social life. Both in the public culture and in the personal mind, a sense of order comes to be imposed on what would otherwise prove to be inchoate disorder – unmanageable, unpredictable, unstable. Imposing a sense of order on the world means constructing and organising a symbolic system in which stories come to play an important role – in the naming of parts, the creation of a cosmos, the making of a 'natural order', the assembling of a world taken for granted, the creation of characters and plots. A process of ordering and organising becomes necessary for human life, and stories are part of this order. As a leading narratologist remarks:

> Reordering by narrative may therefore have its functions . . . the affirmation and reinforcement, even the creation, of the most basic assumptions of a culture, about human existence, about time, destiny, selfhood, where we come from, what we ought to do whilst we are here, where we go – the whole course of human life.[36]

Such a reordering is artificial and imposed and always implies an underlying disorder: ambiguities will emerge, phenomenon will not fit, new stuff will emerge which threatens the purity of the existing order. Stories function to gloss over disorder. Indeed, the greater the sensed disorder, the stronger may be the need for stories to create tighter classification, stronger boundaries, rules for living. Modernist tales largely provide this sense of order, whereas emerging late modernist stories are drenched in ambiguity.[37]

Some of the major sexual narratives of the late twentieth century have been clearly linked to this wider symbolic analysis. Aids, for instance, has come to be seen as a major narrative that is not simply about sex (although it is also about that). As I have argued in detail elsewhere, Aids has:

> come to assume all the features of a traditional morality play: images of cancer and death, or blood and semen, of sex and drugs, or morality and retribution. A whole gallery of folk devils have been introduced – the sex-crazed gay, the dirty

drug abuser, the filthy whore, the blood-drinking voodoo-driven black – side by side with a gallery of 'innocents' – the haemophiliacs, the blood transfusion 'victim', the new-born child, even the 'heterosexual'.[38]

It connects back to a rhetoric that conveys a major stigmatising message. Likewise, personal narratives over abortion are more than just about abortion: they touch on the nature of motherhood, birth, procreation, nurturance. Abortion narratives can be seen as 'procreation stories', for instance, which are hence not simply about abortion but stand for the much wider concern over the 'future of motherhood'. An ideal narrative of what it is to be an American 'mom' is constructed and stories compete around it, with pro-choice activists subverting 'the conventional story of reproduction as "natural" to women's lives.'[39] And the Hill–Thomas affair opened up a major debate around race, sexuality and power. Thus Anita Hill and Clarence Thomas provided contested stories around sexual harassment. This was a story that first started to be heard in the early 1970s – that got a voice and carved out a problem in books such as Lin Farley's *Sexual Shakedown*. Progressively what was once seen as office dating and male pickup stories became transformed into sexual harassment stories: a narrative that recasts the ways in which men and women relate. Hill and Thomas brought different personal narratives to this problem and turned it into a contested narrative.

Sexual stories are widespread in modern culture because they perform major tasks in providing information, establishing contested territories and clarifying boundaries. At both millennium and century's end, when a strong sense of massive and rapid social change is in the air, stories take on a crucial symbolic role – uniting groups against common enemies, establishing new concerns, mapping the social order to come. Stories mark out identities; identities mark out differences; differences define 'the other'; and 'the other' helps structure the moral life of culture, group and individual. Stories are often, if not usually, conservative and preservative – tapping into the dominant worldview.

But, as a number of the stories discussed throughout this book have shown, stories can also be radical in their implications. Gay and lesbian tales have brought about a major change in same-sex experience. New rape stories have helped many a woman and shifted many institutional approaches to rape. We have to see how people read their stories: the same tale may be taken as an instance of conservative thought, or turned into a radical moment. The tale told of Michael Jackson in 1993 – of scandal and child sex abuse – was, for most purposes, read as slotting neatly into the moral panic over child sex abuse that has been a central staple of media work over the past fifteen years. But for a few the story was an occasion to debate issues of intergenerational sexualities and the like. The same broad story may be conservative and transgressive. This theme is a persistent concern of media research. For some the media stockpiles conservative ideas: it is a tool for lethargy, brainwashing, trivialising of important issue, mass society and ultimately moral decline. But for others, it can take on a more active role. It can be used critically –

there are possibilities at least for 'active viewers', 'citizen viewers', even 'readers' liberation fronts', a source of public debate and a stimulant for participatory democracies. Throughout this book, both possibilities have persistently been apparent.

NO CONCLUSION

This book is very much an introduction to all the issues it raises. I am only too aware that I pose many more concerns than I resolve, and that at times I have lapsed into far too much superficial brevity. A kindly reader will at least sense a world of important new questions.

In the end, I can see four books struggling to get out of this one and none of them has anything specifically to do with sex. Indeed, whilst sexual stories have been my case study, this has not been a 'sexy' book. I have used sexual stories as my peg to develop questions about story telling as a sociological phenomenon. But it could have been about any kind of story – near-death stories, holocaust testaments, slave narratives. The issues – though not the details – would have been the same.

Hence the main book struggling to get out of this one is a much fuller account of the powerful role of the story telling process in the everyday life of everyday societies. It is a plea for the development of a sociology of stories: nothing to do with sex at all, just simply the need for sociologists to see and analyse grounded story telling activities and their links to social structures. Part of this task is self-reflexive: to see that much social research is itself a story telling process and can be analysed in the same generic fashion as other stories. This is the task I started in Chapter 2.

A second theme that emerges quite specifically in Part II of this book is the analysis of specific story genres: not simply as narrative forms, but as tales which have their time. Much more attention needs to be given to the historical production of stories and the communities from which they are generated and to which they subsequently return. In this book, I make a small contribution to the analysis of coming out stories, rape stories and survivor stories; but there is much more that could be said.

A third book struggling to get out of this one concerns social change, one key theme of Part III. Much has been written on the drift to postmodernity at century's end, maybe even too much. Too often there is a sense here of the 'end of the narrative', whereas what I have suggested is that new narratives are appearing to run alongside the older ones. If it is true that we live our lives in the stories we tell of them, then it behoves us to understand more about the ways in which story telling is changing.

And finally there is a work of political theory struggling to appear. Many political theorists of recent times have sensed the links between narrative, voice, identity, community, citizenship and differences: my treatment of such arguments has had to be skimpy. But here is the idea of developing a politics of intimate citizenship. And second a wider claim: to examine the role of stories in building diverse, pluralistic moral communities which may be radically at odds with each other and yet somehow manage to coexist.

Notes

1 PROLOGUE: THE CULTURE OF SEXUAL STORY TELLING

1 Rousseau's story is usually cited as one of the foundations of modern autobiography, though this has often been refuted by feminist scholarship. See Personal Narratives Group, *Interpreting Women's Lives* (1989), p. 104.

2 For instance, see *Walter: My Secret Life – The Unique Memoirs of England's most Uninhibited Lover*, edited by the Kronhausens (1967) and the critical discussion of it in Steven Marcus's *The Other Victorians* (1966), Chs 3 and 4. It should not pass without remarking that some people regard the book as a fantasy fiction and not as a personal narrative. Until recently it is possible the book was more referred to than read, as was the fate of many other texts like Richard von Krafft-Ebing's *Psychopathia Sexualis*. For an overview of many of these nineteenth-century texts, see Jeffrey Weeks, *Sex, Politics and Society* (1989). Fascinating accounts of some late nineteenth-century narratives of sex include Elaine Showalter's *Sexual Anarchy* (1991) and Judith Walkowitz's *City of Dreadful Delight* (1992).

3 See Michal McCall, 'The Significance of Story Telling' (1990).

4 See Barbara Myerhoff's *Number Our Days* (1978). The concern with 'stories' seems prominent in a range of different intellectual disciplines which generally do not speak enough to each other. Common to all is the critique of the externalist, mechanistic, objectivist mode of thinking which has dominated the human sciences. A long list of examples of this 'new turn' could be given, but representatives of this shift in psychology include J. Bruner's *Actual Minds, Possible Worlds* (1986), R. Romanyshyn's *Psychological Life* (1982), T. Sarbin's *Narrative Psychology* (1986) and K. Gergen's *The Saturated Self* (1991); in history, a key contribution comes from Hayden White – *Metahistory* (1973) and *The Content of the Form* (1987); in the developing 'cognitive sciences' see the work of G. Lakoff and M. Johnson in *Metaphors We Live By* (1980) and G. Lakoff in *Women, Fire and Dangerous Things* (1987); in philosophy, N. Goodman's *Ways of Worldmaking* (1978) and R. Rorty's *Contingency, Irony and Solidarity* (1989) are important. Cultural studies has been to the forefront of breaking down traditional disciplinary studies, although in the end much of it acts as a revamped literary theory. The fields of feminist theory, black theory, lesbian and gay studies and psychotherapy are also relevant.

5 Clifford Geertz, *The Interpretation of Cultures* (1975), p. 448.

6 Barbara Hardy, *Tellers and Listeners: The Narrative Imagination* (1975), p. 4.

7 I use these diverse phrases but generally not the term 'the postmodern'. Although I am referring to similar things as the postmodernists, it is an overused term that reeks of a certain intellectual style and fashion that I wish to avoid until its future is clearer. I am reluctant to plunge at this stage into the abyss of modern/postmodern arguments, important as they are, and will deal with some of these issues in Part III. For the time

being, I will use these terms as a social historical classification to recognise two things: first, the period between, say, 1960 and 2040 can loosely be seen as a rare historical moment when people are at the brink of a new millennium, and when dramatic change – continuous with the past – is 'in the air'. Of course, time itself is a social product – there is nothing in nature or inevitable about periodisations, be they weeks or decades or millenniums. (See for instance Eviatar Zerubavel's *Hidden Rhythms* (1981).) But people sense the importance of time through such things as decade plotting, turn of the century crises, and especially the 'end of the millennium'. See also Showalter's *op. cit.* for a discussion of sexual change at *fin-de-siècle*: as the late Angela Carter has epigramatically remarked: 'the *fin* is coming a little early this *siècle*.'

But second, and independently, I suspect the last decades of the twentieth century did see changes of an extraordinary kind around politics, technology, communications and the like. These changes will be partially considered in Part III in order to assess their implications for sexual story telling. I will leave this matter for the time being.

8 And indeed, some commentators have noted that sexuality is really pre-lingustic: once spoken about, sex becomes flattened: 'the charm is broken.' See Paul Ricoeur, 'Wonder, eroticism and enigma' (1964), p. 141.

9 I have discussed the link between the personal life and social science in my *Documents of Life* (1983). On coming out stories, see Chapter 6 and the references therein.

10 For those whose cultural life has led them to miss *Donahue*, this has been running in the USA for twenty-five years as the major talk show (recently usurped by *Oprah*) and is nationally syndicated. It has also been shown around the world, including England. For an interview with Donahue which provides some background to the long-running television show, see Arthur Unger, 'Phil Donahue: "I cannot be the BBC in an MTV world" ' (1991). The key texts on the chat show are Donal Carbaugh, *Talking American: Cultural Discourses on Donahue* (1988), Sonia Livingstone and Peter Lunt's *Talk on Television* (1993) and Mimi White, *Tele-Advising: Therapeutic Discourse in American Television* (1992).

11 See *USA Today*, 'Today's Talk Show Highlights', 18 February 1992.

12 This comparison between the UK and the USA is brief. A sampler of similar programmes in the UK shows a smaller number of 'talk shows' but still an emphasis on sex. One listing in Livingstone and Lunt (*op. cit.*, appendix) lists twenty-two programmes over two weeks, twelve of which are connected in some way to the sexual. Although I focus on the USA and the UK, this phenomenon seems widespread in the western world. The same modes get recycled – sometimes in more extreme forms – in Italy, Greece, Turkey, the Netherlands, Sweden, etc. A full-scale comparative study is needed of this globalisation of sexual stories!

13 The television programme was screened by CBS on 15 March 1992; the book was published by Summit as *Taking Back My Life* (subsequently in 1993 an Avon paperback).

14 *TV Times* (US, California), 15 March 1992, p. 4.

15 I am not alone in this wonderment. Lilian Rubin in *Erotic Wars* remarks:

> At last count, the Doubleday bookstore on Fifth Avenue in New York City had almost two hundred volumes in its section on sex alone, not to mention the hundreds more elsewhere in the store that deal with sex as one of many issues that beset our relationships.
>
> (1990: p. 188).

This is a point that need not be laboured: evidence is everywhere.

16 More and more commentators have noted this, but the original phrase comes from Foucault. See also Gayle Rubin on 'Thinking Sex', in Carole S. Vance (ed.), *Pleasure and Danger: Exploring Female Sexuality* (1984), pp. 267–320.

17 On the Martian method, see Fred Davis, 'The Martian and the Convert' (1973).
18 This material is discussed more fully in Ken Plummer, *Symbolic Interactionism and Sexual Differentiation: An Empirical Investigation* (1979).
19 On this transformation see J. Clifford and G. Marcus (eds), *Writing Culture* (1986); J. Van Maanen, *Tales from the Field* (1988); Norman K. Denzin, *The Research Act* (1989a); John M. Johnson, 'The Third Generation of Field Research Conduct' (1987); Paul Atkinson, *The Ethnographic Imagination* (1990); Jaber F. Gubrium and David Silverman (eds), *The Politics of Field Research* (1989); John M. Johnson and David Altheide, 'Reflexive Accountability' (1990).
20 This raises questions of pedagogy more generally. For some interesting discussions of 'critical pedagogy', see Patti Lather, *Getting Smart* (1991) and the work of Henry Giroux, especially *Border Crossings* (1992).
21 See Ann Barr Snitow's 'Mass Market Romance' (1984), Janet Radways's *Reading the Romance* (1983) and Linda Williamson's *Hard Core* (1989) for 'readings' of these other kinds of sexual stories.
22 See Norman K. Denzin's *Interpretive Biography* (1989) p. 48 for these distinctions.
23 See Michel de Certeau's *The Practice of Everyday Life* (1984).
24 These stories are part of a bureaucratic, coercive chain and have been well discussed sociologically by Mike Hepworth and Bryan Turner in *Confession* (1982). Their prime focus is upon the rituals of inclusion found in religious and courtroom confession. They place a lot of emphasis on confessions to murder, and very little upon sexuality.
25 Generic social processes are at work here. There are patterns that can be captured. In literary theory, film theory and television theory, genre is an important issue in which types of narratives become clearly identifiable – as comedy or tragedy, as musical or western, as soap opera or chat show. See, for example, the discussions by Feuer and Fiske, in Robert Allen (ed.), *Channels of Discourse* (1987). 'Stories' may clearly be classified into genres, and 'sexual stories' may thus become one kind of story. Within such a broad genre, many sub-genres may be detected; personal narratives are one such sub-genre and the key focus of this book. Yet here again further sub-genres can be detected: the tales of suffering, surviving and surpassing is the specific sub-genre I treat.
   The plot, however, thickens. For social life also has its forms, and for this a better concept than genre is probably *generic social practices* – how life congeals into certain basic interactional forms. This is a fundamental idea in Simmel, through Park and on to the modern interactionist writings of R. Prus, J. Lofland, J. Wiseman and C. Couch. See, for instance, Robert Prus, 'Generic Social Processes' (1987). Story telling would seem to be one generic social practice, and this will be my focus in Chapter 2.
26 Something of the range of writing around Aids may be gleaned from Judith Laurence Pastore's edited collection *Confronting AIDS through Literature*, (1993).
27 See, for instance, Norman K. Denzin, *Symbolic Interactionism and Cultural Studies* (1992).
28 In an earlier book, I introduced the term 'sexual citizenship' (*Modern Homosexualities* (1992), p. 21–4). I now think this is too limiting and specific and that a better term would centre around the many facets of the intimate – the kinds of relations we choose to have, the gender we express, the feelings we explore, the body, identity and the imagery we construct and gaze at. I discuss all this in the latter chapters, but wish now to counteract the idea of 'sexual citizenship' which seems to create an exaggerated concern with the erotic. On the latter idea, see the book by David T. Evans *Sexual Citizenship* (1993).

2 AN INVITATION TO A SOCIOLOGY OF STORIES

1 As an instance of each of these points, see: in anthropology, Clifford Geertz, *The Interpretation of Cultures*, (1975); in psychology, Dan McAdams, *Power, Intimacy and*

the *Life Story* (1987), Jerome Bruner, 'Life as Narrative' (1985), *Actual Minds, Possible Worlds* (1986), and the essays in Theodore Sarbin, *Narrative Psychology*, (1986); in history, Hayden White, *The Content of the Form* (1987); in oral history, Paul Thompson, *The Voice of the Past* (1978); in psychoanalysis, Donald Spence, *Narrative Truth and Historical Truth* (1982); in philosophy, Alasdair MacIntyre, *After Virtue* (1981), Richard Rorty, *Contingency, Irony and Solidarity* (1989) and Nelson Goodman, *Ways of World Making* (1978); in economics, D.N. McCloskey, *The Rhetoric of Economics* (1985).

2 Patricia Ticineto Clough, *The End(s) of Ethnography* (1992), p. 2.

3 See David R. Maines, 'Narrative's Moment and Sociology's Phenomena' (1993), p. 22.

4 Maines, *op. cit.*, p. 21. For others in sociology advocating a narrative turn see the works cited in the bibliography by Laurel Richardson, Norman K. Denzin, Patrica Clough and Richard Brown. There is a strong link to sociology's renewed interest in auto/biography: see for instance Liz Stanley and David Morgan's specially edited issue of the journal *Sociology: Biography and Autobiography in Sociology* (1993).

5 Suzanne K. Langer, *Philosophy in a New Key* (1942), p. 10).

6 The more generic discipline is 'narratology', the study of narratives and stories. For a guide to this whole field, see W.J.T. Mitchell (ed.), *On Narrative* (1981); Donald E. Polkinghorne, *Narrative Knowing and the Human Sciences* (1988); Catherine Kohler Riessman, *Narrative Analysis* (1993); Theodore R. Sarbin (ed.), *Narrative Psychology* (1986); Donald P. Spence, *Narrative Truth and Historical Truth* (1982). In the USA there is a National Association for the Preservation and Perpetuation of Storytelling, with its own magazine *Storytelling*; as well as a new academic journal called the *Journal of Narrative and Life History*, vol. 1 (1992).

7 Although I use the term symbolic interactionism here, the term has acquired a somewhat passé meaning in recent sociology, what some have referred to as the 'greying of symbolic interactionism'. Indeed, it seems to me that sociology has difficulty sustaining any of its original theorisations for too long – all extant theory undergoes constant modification and reformation into 'new' (and more fashionable) theories. Each generation of students seems to want to 'reinvent' theory, and maybe this is a direct consequence of living in a constantly changing social world. No theory, no language can settle down for too long! These 'fads and fashions' were noted many years ago by P. Sorokin in his *Fads and Foibles in Modern Sociology and Related Sciences* (1956), and also by C. Wright Mills in *The Sociological Imagination*, when he remarks that 'Nowadays, it is true that many intellectual fads are widely taken up before they are dropped for new ones in the course of a year or two', p. 13. This prescient observation was made in 1959. Symbolic interactionism has indeed undergone something of a renaissance and revitalisation in recent years, and has taken on board a wide range of new and emerging positions, but the term itself still seems antiquated. Denzin has tried to rename it 'interpretive interactionism', without much success, and others have linked it to the sociologies of everyday life. Whatever name one adopts, there is now a flourishing body of very diverse work loosely informed by what was once called symbolic interactionism. For recent reviews, see Gary Alan Fine, 'Symbolic Interactionism in the Post-Blumerian Age', in G. Ritzer (1990), and his 'The Sad Demise, Mysterious Disappearance and Glorious Triumph of Symbolic Interactionism' (1993); and Norman K. Denzin, *Cultural Studies and Symbolic Interactionism* (1992). The yearbook of interactionism – *Studies in Symbolic Interaction* – documents, especially in recent years, some of this change. Volume 10, edited by Noman K. Denzin, provides a series of essays which discuss the 'critique and renewal in symbolic interaction', and subsequent volumes become increasingly concerned with the development of a 'postmodern sociology'.

8 See Stuart Hall's work on ideology, especially his celebrated 'encoding/decoding'

article (1981). One of the more developed sociological accounts of stories is to be found in Michel de Certeau, *The Practice of Everyday Life* (1984).

9 See Goodman, *op. cit.*.

10 The resonance here with Marx will be apparent. There is in fact a great deal of affinity between much of the earlier Marx and the ontology of interactionism. See, for example, Tom W. Goff's *Marx and Mead* (1980). Blumer's persistent repetition of the notion of an empirical world highlights a real and material external reality. Some critics have charged interactionism with extreme solipsism, idealism and subjectivism, but this is most decidedly not a view I share.

11 See the essays by Howard S. Becker gathered together under the title *Doing Things Together* (1986).

12 I have discussed the theory more fully in a number of places, but see most recently 'Introductions' Plummer (ed.), *Symbolic Interactionism: Volumes 1 and 2* (1991), which also contains an extin ensive guide to further reading, and a selection of key articles which exemplify the growth and traditions of interactionist inquiry. This is a view of social life whose roots seep back into many traditions, of which pragmatism, humanism, relationalism, formalism and empiricism are its most common harbingers. *Pragmatism* teaches us to shun vast abstractions and grand theories and to return to local experiences in a plural universe. Truths are never fixed, absolute or essential but are always shifting, multiple and contested. Likewise, the grand metaphysical dualisms so beloved of philosophers – determinism/voluntarism, mind/body, individual/group, nominalism/realism, idealism/materialism – should be shunned in favour of inspecting activities in practical situations. It asks: what are the practical consequences of holding this view or doing this action? *Humanism* teaches us to take seriously the human subject who acts in the world, and in this it is decidedly out of fashion with the current postmodern proclamations of the 'death of man'. It directs the interactionist to see that in matters of morality and politics, the embodied, passionate and thinking human being remains our best guide. This does not have to collapsed into an essence of man, as so many critics have falsely proclaimed: instead, many humanisms insist upon the historical specificity of our 'humanities' and their interconnections with wider social, global and animal worlds. *Relationalism* teaches us to acknowledge the inevitably varying 'perspectives' on the world, that there is no core and always a multiplicity of emergent meanings, whilst shunning the nonsenses of a blind 'anything goes' relativism. It encourages us to seek out 'perspectives' that are many and varied, but at the same time stresses the need for them to be related to each other in order to gain a wider picture. *Formalism* teaches us to at least attempt to search out the patterns of social life, even whilst recognising the difficult and recursive nature of the enterprise: are there elementary and generic, though soon to change and never fixed, patterns to be detected in social life? *Empiricism*, finally, believes that there *is* a world 'out there' which con- strains us and is open to exploration and inspection. The world, in truth, is a hypothesis. Like all the above 'isms', empiricism harbours many positions, and for me should not be readily equated with positivism. Nevertheless, the fleeting but grand judge of human inquiry is the world of human activities, not disembedded philosophical speculation.

13 The term 'joint action' is Blumer's reworking of Mead's 'social act'. He discusses the idea in very similar terms in a number of places, but notably in Herbert Blumer, *Symbolic Interactionism* (1969), pp. 16–20 and 70–2. The quote is from p. 70.

14 From sociology, a key sourcebook on the dramaturgical method is Dennis Brisset and Charles Edgley (eds), *Life as Theater: A Dramaturgical Sourcebook* (1990). Intriguing remarks on gender and performance are to be found in Judith Butler's celebrated *Gender Trouble* (1990).

15 These classics are Robert Bogdan (ed.), *Being Different: The Autobiography of Jane Fry* (1971); Michael Foucault, *Herculine Barbine* (1980); and The Pelican Sigmund Freud Library, *Case Histories: Little Hans, Dora* (1977).

16 See Donald P. Spence, 'Turning Happenings into Meanings: The Central Role of the Self' (1987).

17 The term 'social worlds' is sociological and coined by Anselm Strauss, in 'A Social World Perspective' (1978); I discuss it more fully in Chapter 9. 'Interpretive communities' is a term derived from the literary theory of Stanley Fish: *Is there a Text in this Class*? (1980). They point to different, but closely linked, phenomenon.

18 Robert Bellah *et al.*, in *Habits of the Heart* (1985) talks of 'communities of memory' and William Simon of 'audiences of memory'(personal conversation). 'The audience' is fast becoming 'the community'. Memory is also moving from being a topic that is the prime concern of psychology to one which may be analysed by historians and sociologists – as 'social memory'. See for instance: James Fentress and Chris Wickham, *Social Memory* (1992) and Elizabeth Tonkin, *Narrating Our Pasts* (1992).

19 His story was widely reported internationally, and for a short while Magic Johnson joined President Bush's task force on Aids. His autobiography was subsequently published.

20 For a discussion of all this see P.M. Hall, 'Interactionism and the Study of Social Organization' (1987).

21 See, for example, David Morley's *Family Television* (1986), as well as his later *Television, Audiences and Cultural Studies* (1992).

22 Angela McRobbie's study of *Jackie* and *Just Seventeen* – two leading UK 'teenage girl' magazines – is to be found in her illuminating *Feminism and Youth Culture: From Jackie to Just Seventeen* (1991), p. 142. It is a useful source for understanding teenage girls' sexual stories.

23 I refer to *Oprah* throughout this book because it is the main example of the talk show. *Kilroy* is a day-time downmarket UK equivalent.

24 These distinctions are central to the work of Carl Couch and Shing-Ling Chen, 'Orality, Literacy and Social Structure' (1988); Harold Innis, *Empire and Communication* (1972), Marshall McLuhan, *The Gutenberg Galaxy* (1962); Joshua Meyrowitz, *No Sense of Place* (1985); and the work of Walter J. Ong. (See Bruce Gronbeck et al., *Media, Consciousness and Culture: Explorations in Walter Ong's Thought* (1991)).

25 See Walter Benjamin in 'The Storyteller' (1970), who suggests that 'the art of storytelling is coming to an end. Less and less frequently do we encounter people with the ability to tell a tale properly' (p. 83).

26 See my earlier article which develops these ideas: Ken Plummer, 'Herbert Blumer and the Life History Tradition' (1990a).

27 In a most curious fashion it is possible to see the broadest tenets of symbolic interactionism joining with some aspects of postmodernist theory, or what I prefer to call 'late modernist' theory. On postmodernist theory, see especially the work of Lyotard, Jameson and Baudrillard. See my brief debate with Denzin in Ken Plummer, 'Staying in the Empirical World' (1990b).

28 See Judith Williamson 'Every Virus Tells A Story' (1989) and Linda Williams *Hard Core* (1989).

29 These are the kinds of questions that have become popularised in literary analysis (through reception theory) and most recently in audience ethnography.

30 See Constance Penley, 'Feminism, Psychoanalysis, and the Study of Popular Culture' (1992).

31 Power is one of the most central, but hotly contested, concepts in the social sciences. Even the new postmodern theorists whose task, in at least one reading of their texts, seems to be the disposal of all grand metanarratives or foundational truths, still seem to devote much time to its nature, and for some, like Foucault and the postmodern

feminists, it seems almost pivotal: the concept has not gone away. Over the past several decades a serviceable and sensitising concept of power has emerged in symbolic interactionist writings which can be laid out quite simply (and which, by the way, is not incompatible with much other analysis). See P. Hall, M. Edelman, T. Scheff and R. Emerson, along with my brief discussion in Plummer (1991), *op. cit.*, vol. 2.

32 Elizabeth Janeway in *Powers of the Weak* (1981) talks of 'a limiting power to compel and a liberating power to act', p. 87.

33 On all this, see Randall Collins, 'Micromethods as a basis for macrosociology' (1983), p. 184.

34 See Chapters 4 through 8 for a fuller discussion of these issues.

35 On the politics of emotion, see T. Kemper (ed.), *Research Agendas in the Sociology of Emotions* (1990).

36 On the power of the 'Closet', see Eve Kasofsky Sedgwick's *Epistemology of the Closet* (1991), and Richard Mohr's essay on 'The Outing Controversy' in his *Gay Ideas: Outing and Other Controversies* (1992).

37 Again, this process is discussed more fully in Chapters 4–8. The issue of coming out and outing is a prime model for the telling of sexual stories in the latter part of the twentieth century. It is a central ingredient in the analysis of modern homosexuality – for example from Jeffrey Weeks's *Coming Out* in 1977 through Eve Kasofsky Sedgwick's *Epistemology of the Closet*, first published in 1990. For a general review of this theme, see Roy Cain, 'Disclosure and Secrecy among Gay Men' (1991). Much of the second section of this book is concerned with aspects of this issue. For the most recent controversies, see Richard Mohr's *Gay Ideas* (1992), Michelangelo Signorile's *Queer in America* (1993) and Larry Gross's *Contested Closets* (1993). The main drift of each of these books is to support 'outing'.

38 The work of S. Retzinger and T. Scheff on the 'shame-rage' spiral could be instructive to develop in this regard.

39 See for instance the compendium edited by John Preston, *Personal Dispatches* (1989).

40 ibid., pp. xii, xviii.

41 Nancy Fraser's 'discourse ethic of solidarity' sees people and political debate as being 'members of collectivities or social groups with specific cultures, histories, social practices, values, habits, forms of life, vocabularies of self-interpretation and narrative traditions'. She sees these discourses around needs as crucial in positioning spaces. She makes a useful distinction between the 'oppositional talk' (from below, of excluded and marginalised groups), and 'expert talk' (from above) attuned to social problem-solving. For Fraser's discussion of this, see *Unruly Practices*(1989), p. 174. See also the earlier classic statement of 'the hierarchy of credibility' by Howard S. Becker (1967) which I evoke here, and the prevalence of such an argument in the constructionist account of 'social problems claims making' that I discuss much more fully in Chapter 8.

42 The classic discussions of this are in Leonore Davidoff's 'Class and Gender in Victorian England'(1979) and Liz Stanley's *The Diaries of Hannah Cullwick* (1984). For a discussion of the 'Arthur Munby' problem, see Julia Swindell's 'Liberating the Subject?' (1989).

43 Alice Jardine in *Gynesis* (1985) has sensed the radical importance of these spaces. She says

> To give a new language to these other spaces is a project filled with both promise and fear . . . for these spaces have hitherto remained unknown, terrifying, monstrous: they are mad, unconscious, improper, unclean, nonsensical, oriental, profane. If philosophy is truly to question these spaces it must move away from all that has defined them, held them in place: Man, The Subject, History, Meaning.
>
> (p. 73).

44 See, for instance, Anita Cornwall, *Black Lesbian in White America* (1983) and Joseph

Beam (ed.), *In the Life: A Black Gay Anthology* (1986).

45 The literature on this draws ideas from E. Goffman, T. Scheff, the work of the ethnomethodologists, etc. There is an interesting summary of a number of gender-linked issues in Hilary M. Lips, *Women, Men and Power* (1991), esp. Chs 4 and 5.

46 The classic statement of this is Carol Gilligan's (1982) discussio of abortion and moral argument in her book *In A Different Voice*. It is however a position which has been much contested, and Gilligan's own position seems to have shifted several times. The danger lies in essentialising male voices and female voices: it may help to see this as a tendency, but not as an inevitable essence.

47 For a review of this literature, see Mary Field Belenky *et al.*, *Women's Ways of Knowing: The Development of Self, Voice and Mind* (1986), p. 5. This important study interviews 135 women around their experiences of 'knowing') of being silenced, of listening to others, of reasoning.

48 See bell hooks (1989), p. 43, my italics. This last point has been well documented in women's studies and in black studies. For a long time, the voices and stories of women, and especially black women, were simply *erased* and *denied*. They were *invisible*, with the odd token *gesture* being made. Kum Kum Bhavani has nicely named this process as the 'editing of women's studies' in 'Talking Racism and the Editing of Women's Studies' (1992).

49 See Gayle Rubin, 'Thinking Sex' (1984), p. 279. In this article, she parts company with her earlier, equally influential article, 'The Traffic in Women', and focusing upon the system of sex/erotic subordination she outlines the ideological formations 'whose grip is so strong that to fail to discuss them is to remain enmeshed in them'. She outlines six of these ideologies, I am mentioning just one of them here. The other five ideologies are: essentialism, sex negativity, the fallacy of misplaced scale, the domino theory of sexual peril, the lack of a concept of benign variation. All six, it seems to me, help shape our narratives of sex, along with who can tell the stories.

50 As revealed tellingly in the film *Paris is Burning* (1991), set in New York City.

51 Many linked terms capture this such as Adrienne Rich's 'Compulsory Heterosexuality' (1980); Jeff Hearn's 'hierarchic heterosexuality' (in *The Gender of Oppression* (1987), p. 91); R.W. Connell's 'hegemonic masculinity', capturing the admittedly ambiguous 'global domination of men over women' (in *Gender and Power* (1987), p. 183; Sylvia Walby's conceptualisation of patriarchy in *Theorising Patriarchy* (1990), and Judith Butler's 'compulsory order of sex/gender/desire' linked to a heterosexual matrix, in *Gender Trouble* (1990), pp. 6 *et seq.*, p. 151, n. 6.

3 MAKING SEXUAL STORIES

1 The project was funded by the (then) SSRC and was called 'Symbolic Interactionism and Sexual Differentiation' (1980). The research officer for that project was Annabel Faraday and the research secretary was Janet Parkin. Most of the material from these interviews has never been published.

2 There are a substantial number of transvestite and transexual biographies. The 'TS/TV story' has become one of the more popular 'intimate stories' of the past twenty years or more, possibly because it goes to the heart of gender issues. See, for example, Robert Bogdan (ed.), *Being Different: The Autobiography of Jane Fry* (1974); Julia Grant, *George and Julia* (1980) which was also the basis of a BBC TV *Inside Story* documentary in 1980; *Christine Jorgensen, A Personal Autobiography* (1967) (the first and perhaps the most famous case study, also made into a film); Jan Morris, *Conundrum* (1974). For an excellent analysis and lengthy discussion, see Dave King's Ph.D. thesis 'The Transvestite and the Transexual' (1986, University of Essex), and his book of the same name (1993); and also the inspired work of Richard Ekins, 'On Male Femaling' (1993).

3 A key phrase here is 'coming out', which will be discussed much more fully in Part II.

4 On Shere Hite, see her *The Hite Report on Male Sexuality* (1978). See also two best-sellers in the USA, much feted on chat shows: Robin Norwood's *Women Who Love Too Much* (1985) and Peter Trachtenberg's *The Casanova Complex: Compulsive Lovers and Their Women* (1988). There are hundreds of such titles. Such books do however seem less pervasive (or persuasive) in the UK, where the 'self help/recovery' movement seems altogether weaker. I discuss these more fully in a later chapter.

5 See Gordon Allport, *The Use of Personal Documents in Psychological Science* (1942), Ch. 5.

6 These terms derive from the key works of Kenneth Burke, John Gagnon, Nelson Goodman, Bill Simon, W.I. Thomas and others. The term 'programme' is used in Robert S. Perinbanayagam, *Signifying Acts* (1985) – a sophisticated but too-neglected backdrop to this whole discussion. See also his *Discursive Acts* (1991).

7 The idea here is derived from George Herbert Mead, as reworked in the various writings of Herbert Blumer. See the latter's *Symbolic Interactionism* (1969).

8 See Ann Swidler, 'Culture in Action' (1986).

9 See Madonna, *Sex* (1992).

10 This short quote comes from a much longer interview with a couple of masochists who enjoyed being fully encased in rubber. The link between armour and rubber is not clear– the key theme, though, seems to be 'encasement'.

11 For an unusual listing of such collections see the discussion by Ann W. Burgess and her colleagues in *Child Pornography and Sex Rings* (1984), esp. Chs 4 and 5. Prominent in this discussion is the idea that many 'abusers' keep detailed records of their sexual fetishes and indeed their sexual exploits.

12 See David Morley, *Television, Audiences and Cultural Studies* (1992), p. 95.

13 Cf. Richard Brown, *Society as Text* (1987).

14 On all this, see for example, E. Ann Kaplan, *Rocking Around the Clock: Music Television, Postmodernism and Consumer Culture* (1987).

15 See Anthony Giddens, *The Transformation of Intimacy* (1992), p. 29. Giddens is one of the world's leading social theorists, but only in his most recent works has he turned to the analysis of the more intimate worlds. See also his *Modernity and Self-Identity* (1991), for a powerful account of how 'texts' are read into the workings of the self. For a critical discussion of this late turn in Giddens' work, see Ian Craib's *The Importance of Disappointment* (1994).

16 Nelson Goodman, *Ways of Worldmaking* (1978), p. 105.

17 See Radclyffe Hall, *The Well of Loneliness* (1950); (originally published in 1928); Rita Mae Brown, *Rubyfruit Jungle* (1973); and Pat Califia, *Macho Sluts* (1988). See also Karla Jay and Joanne Glasgow, (eds), *Lesbian Texts and Contexts* (1990).

18 Bonnie Zimmerman, *The Safe Sea of Women* (1990), p. 232.

19 See Patricia Hill Collins, *Black Feminist Thought* (1990).

20 Robert Bly's *Iron John* (1990), topped the best-selling lists in the USA for much of 1991 and early 1992. It provides myths and poetry which can assist the new man in developing. In its wake, a number of books have attempted similar tasks.

21 Bly, op. cit., p. 5. The connections between the Grimm fairy tales and patriarchal structures has not escaped a number of critics. See Kenneth Clatterbaugh, 'Mythopoetic Foundations of New Age Patriarchy' (1993).

22 This term is Gayle Rubin's in her classic article, 'Thinking Sex' (1984).

23 Cf. Bryan Taylor, 'Guilt-Free Motives for Pederasty' (1976).

24 And sometimes, these sources are much more explicitly the providers of rules and guidance. For instance, Parker Rossman's checklist for paedophiles in *Sexual Experience Between Men and Boys* (1979); or in Marshall Kirk and Hunter Madsen's moral guidelines for gay men in their *After the Ball* (1990). This is an important issue in establishing intimate communities, and one I will return to in part III.

25 The phrase has been popularised in the fiction of Armistead Maupin (notably in his *Significant Others* (1987)), but its origins lie deep in symbolic interactionism and especially the philosophy of George Herbert Mead, who seems to have coined the term. Now it takes on quite a different meaning, so that by the 1990s the American *Heritage College Dictionary* could define 'significant other' as a person with whom one shared a long-term sexual relationship. This is *not* the way I am using it here.

26 The concept of 'vocabularies of motive' was first introduced by C.W. Mills and Kenneth Burke. During the 1970s a minor but important literature developed around case studies in this field – focusing upon many sexual stories. Amongst the most prominent were those of sex offenders (L. Taylor), child molesters (C. McCaghy), lesbians and gays (K. Plummer), prostitutes (J. Bryan), nudists (M. S. Weinberg) and rapists (S. Jackson; D. Scully). A prime focus was the fashion in which such stories or accounts served to justify, excuse and legitimate various patterns of stigmatised sexual conduct. On all this, see Ken Plummer, *Sexual Stigma* (1975), pp. 81–2, 137–41; Diana Scully, *Understanding Sexual Violence* (1990); and Laurie Taylor, 'The Significance of Replies to Matrimonial Questions: The Case of Sex Offenders' (1972).

27 A clear sourcebook and paradigm statement of this is John Bradshaw, *Bradshaw on the Family* (1988), also a public broadcasting service TV series and a best-selling paperback (my copy says: 'National Bestseller: "Over 500,000 Copies sold!" ' on the cover).

28 Witness the way in which Simon LeVay's account of the biological basis of homosexuality was so popular in the lesbian and gay communities. See LeVay's *The Sexual Brain* (1993) for his account, and the commentaries in the *Advocate,* and in *Newsweek* in late summer 1991 for the original enthusiasm from the gay community.,

29 See Scully, Op. cit., esp. Chs 4 and 5.

30 As George Herbert Mead says:

> history serves the community in the same way as the memory does the individual. A person has to bring up a certain portion of the past to determine what his present is, and in the same way the community wants to bring up the past so it can state the present situation.
>
> *(The Philosophy of the Act* (1938)).

31 See Jerome Bruner's important discussion in 'Life as Narrative' (1987), p. 31, my italics.

32 Quoted from Saul Bellow, *Mr Sammler's Planet* (1970) and cited in the excellent discussion of nostalgia in the role of shaping identity by the late, and much missed, Fred Davis: *Yearning for Yesterday* (1979), Ch. 2, p. 30.

33 This 'functional autonomy' of stories parallels Gordon Allport's 'functional autonomy of motives'. Allport in a classic statement suggests that 'Past motives explain nothing unless they are also present motives' (in his *Pattern and Growth in Personality* (1961), p. 220.

34 See David Middleton and Derek Edwards (eds.), *Collective Remembering* (1990), p. 3.

35 On social memory, see James Fentress and Chris Wickham, *Social Memory* (1992). This tradition has strong links to oral history and to narratives of the past. On all this, see the work of Paul Thompson, *The Voice of the Past: Oral History* (1978); Jan Vansina, *Oral Tradition as History* (1985); and Elizabeth Tonkin, *Narrating Our Pasts* (1992).

36 These two phrases are drawn from Jack Katz's important study *Seductions of Crime* (1988), pp. 4–8. Here he taps a major neglect in sociological writing– the moment of true creativity (in his study the focus is upon the authenticity of some criminal actions). See also William James, *The Varieties of Religious Experience* (1952).

37 In one instance, Annabel Faraday and I borrowed some of the books of an interviewee in order to 'reread' what he had considered important – through the underlinings, notes

in the margins, etc. He highlighted in the text a number of names he mentioned in the interview. On this process more generally, see Judith Okely's fascinating account of her reading and rereading of *Simone de Beauvoir* (1986), and of the significance that *The Second Sex* had on her life.

38 Helen Roth, cited in D. Billings and T. Urbam, 'The Socio-Medical Construction of Transexualism' (1982), p. 274. See also the sophisticated work of Richard Ekins who links transexualism to Habermass's 'double hermeneutic' (e.g. 'The Assignment of Motives as a Problem in the Double Hermeneutic' (1983)).

39 Norman Fiske, cited in Billings and Urban, op. cit. p. 274.

40 Maria Marcus, *A Taste for Pain* (1981), p. 20.

41 Ibid., pp. 25–6.

42 Ibid., see pp. 46, 53, 55.

43 See for example discussions on the way women consume self help books and their stories in Wendy Simonds, *Women and Self-Help Culture* (1992), romance stories in Janice Radways's *Reading the Romance* (1984) and soap operas in Christine Geraghty's *Women and Soap Opera* (1991).

44 See the work of Constance Penley on the *Star Trek* fanzines for an account of producers who become consumers. See Constance Penley, 'Brownian Motion' (1991) and 'Feminism, Psychoanalysis and the Study of Popular Culture' (1992).

45 See Philip Schlesinger *et al., Women Viewing Violence* (1992).

46 The term 'community' probably still implies something too stable, solid, bounded, shared. It also brings with it a certain nostalgia for things past. I do not believe that 'community is in decline' but rather it is taking on new, even exciting, forms. People still strongly identify with shared meanings, senses of history, 'communities of memory' but they do it in different ways to the past. Following Anselm Strauss, I prefer to talk of 'social worlds', but these are worlds which bring forth new senses of community. The term can encompass:

i   Interpretive communities. For Stanley Fish, the key organising term is 'interpretive communities', by which he means 'a set of community assumptions so that when they read [the reader] will do what I did'. It is concerned with depicting reading strategies held in common amongst specified groups, and is a part of a 'reader-oriented' literary analysis. See *Is there a text in this class?* (1980).

ii Communities of memory. This is the key term for Robert Bellah and his colleagues in *Habits of the Heart* (1985).

iii Imagined communities. A term coined by Benedict Anderson to highlight the ways in which media, especially the newspapers, serve to create a sense of national identity; it has been broadened out by other commentators. See his *Imagined Communities* (1983).

iv Audience community. Part of the task of understanding these new communities centres around 'audience ethnography' – studies of communities of media consumers.

On all this, see Morley, op. cit. and Shaun Moores's *Interpreting Audiences* (1993).

47 Extracted from the magazine *Magpie,* no. 2 (1977), April, p. 1. This was the house magazine of the Paedophile Information Exchange, which ran for approximately sixteen issues till Autumn 1981 – by which time the organisation had effectively ceased through prosecutions.

48 There are many different audiences. For an interesting case of racialised audience, see J. Bobo's 'black women as cultural readers':

a Black audience, through a history of theatre-going and film-watching, knows that at some point an expression of the exotic primitive is going to be offered to us. [There are hence two options:] one is never to indulge in media products, an impossibility in an age of media blitz. Another option, and I think this one is an unconscious reaction to and defence against racist definitions of Black people, is to filter out that which is negative and select from the work, elements we can relate to.

J. Bobo, 'The Colour Purple: Black Women as Cultural Readers' (1988)

49 This awful word seems to have been invented by John Thompson in his *Ideology and Modern Culture* (1990). I wish there was a better word to catch this process, and I hope this one does not catch on!

50 Colette Dowling, *The Cinderella Complex* (1981), p. 13, cited in Simonds, op. cit., p. 123.

51 See Robin Norwood's *Robin Norwood Answers Letters from Women Who Love Too Much* (1988).

52 See Nancy Ziegenmeyer, *Taking Back My Life* (1993). Chapter 22 provides a number of readers' responses to her original story which was published as 'It Couldn't Happen To Me: One Woman's Story'– a five-part series in the *Des Moines Register*, 25 February 1990 onwards.

53 Although books on sexual harassment appeared during the 1970s (see Lin Farley, *Sexual Shakedown* (1978); Catherine MacKinnon, *Sexual Harassment of Working Women* (1979), many new books appeared after the Thomas–Hill affair, not only on the affair itself but also as 'speak-outs' on harassment. See for instance Amber Sumrail and Dena Taylor's *Sexual Harassment: Women Speak Out* (1992).

4 COMING OUT, BREAKING THE SILENCE AND RECOVERING: INTRODUCING SOME MODERNIST TALES

1 Wayne Curtis (ed.), *Revelations – A Collection of Gay Male Coming Out Stories* (1988), p. 5.

2 See Paula Webster, 'The Forbidden', in Carole Vance (ed.), *Pleasure and Danger* (1984), p. 385.

3 I am very aware that this is only one kind of personal narrative, but it is the one that has most absorbed me. Other types must await further consideration.

4 See Sandra K.D. Stahl on 'personal experience narratives', in 'The Personal Experience Narrative as Folklore' (1977).

5 On epiphany, see the discussion in Norman K. Denzin's *Interpretive Biography* (1989c).

6 These key phrases reccur in many places. See for instance the introduction to Toni McNaran and Yarrow Morgan (eds), *Voices in the Night* (1982), one of the first speak-outs about incest. As the editors say, 'This book is about breaking the silence', p. 11.

7 See, for examples, Andrea Parrot and Laurie Bechofer (eds), *Acquaintance Rape* (1991) and Robin Warshaw, *I Never Called it Rape* (1988).

8 Griffin wrote a very influential article in the early 1970s, 'Rape: The All-American Crime', which signposted so clearly what so many women had felt before. It is reproduced as the first essay in her 1979 collection, *Rape: The Power of Consciousness*.

9 See ibid., pp. 27–8.

10 There is now a voluminous literature debating these ideas – setting different dates, places, meanings, etc. See, for instance, David Greenberg, *The Construction of Homosexuality* (1988), Ken Plummer (ed.), *The Making of the Modern Homosexual* (1981b) and references cited later in Chapter 6.

11 As I write the story is changing: 'Queer' is now the favoured word, and a range of possibly new meanings are being given to the story. I will turn to this issue in a later chapter.

12 Donald Webster Cory, *The Homosexual in America* (1951), p. 11–13.

13 Aaron Fricke's story became a *cause célèbre*, a court injunction being taken out to allow him to attend the senior prom with his gay partner, Paul. Fricke subsequently published a further biography, concerning his relationship with his father. See *Reflections of a Rock Lobster* (1981) and *Sudden Strangers* (1991). The quotes are from *Rock Lobster* pp. 31–3, and 109.

14 Generic analysis is discussed by Robert Prus in 'Generic Social Processes' (1987). This strand of interactionist analysis seeks out the underlying forms of social life. Links can readily be made with genre analysis.

15 In many stories I was struck by an image of linear narrative, childhood determinism and sexual 'drivenness' which links to the broader metanarratives and allow little room for drift, contingency, chance and choice – that is until one enters more modernist metanarratives. I have discussed this issue more fully in Plummer, 'Beyond Childhood' (1987); and so have chosen not to consider it further here. But it is a central matter.

16 See Lawrence Elsbree, *The Rituals of Life: Patterns in Narratives* (1982), p. 36.

17 Ibid., p. 51.

18 Ibid., p. 25.

19 Ibid., p. 76.

20 Ibid., p. 16.

21 See the following for a sample: Curtis, op. cit., Sarah Holmes, *Testimonies* (1988); Julia Penelope and Susan J. Wolfe (eds), *The Original Coming Out Stories* (1989), Meg Umans (ed.), *Like Coming Home: Coming Out Letters* (1988).

22 E.g. Curtis, op. cit., p. 17.

23 See Curtis, op. cit.

24 See Bonnie Zimmerman, *The Safe Sea of Women* (1990).

25 More detail of the kind of story I am outlining here is provided in Chapter 7, where I depict an ideal type of recovery story.

26 And not just sexual stories – there are others like 'imagined ugliness', 'paranoia' etc. There are thus wider implications than I can deal with here.

27 See John Kitsuse, 'Coming Out All Over' (1982).

28 In addition to the coming out literature, signposted elsewhere, there are many valuable general discussions of these areas: amongst them are Sissela Bok's *Secrets* (1983); Kittredge Cherry's *Hide and Speak* (1991); Erving Goffman, *Stigma* (1963); Marty Klein, *Your Sexual Secrets* (1988); David Matza, *Becoming Deviant* (1969), Ch. 7; Adrienne Rich, *On Lies, Secrets and Silence* (1979); Georg Simmel, 'Secrecy', in Kurt Wolff, (ed.), *The Sociology of Georg Simmel* (1950).

29 This brief listing is derived from Cherry, op. cit., Ch. 2, 'The Value of Closed Doors'. A more hostile list is to be found in Klein op. cit. Ch. 3 'The Value of Sexual Secrets'. Both of these books act as 'recovery' manuals for avoiding secrets and coming out, though the latter incorporates a much wider range of 'everday sexual secrets' including secret fantasies and fears over arousal and response.

30 Bok, op. cit., p. 19–20. Klein however, op. cit., suggests much of this is 'pseudo-power', p. 47.

31 See Klein, op. cit., Ch. 2.

32 For discussions of consciousness raising, see for instance, the New York Radical Feminist's *Rape: The First Sourcebook* (1974), p. 9 on consciousness raising on rape, and p. 31 on the importance of personal testimonies.

33 Sara Evans, *Personal Politics* (1980), p. 134.

34 See the section on consciousness raising in Leslie B. Tanner (ed.), *Voices from Women's Liberation* (1970), p. 231–53. See also June Arnold, 'Consciousness Raising', 1970.

35 On these changes, see Gilbert Herdt and Andrew Boxer's *Children of Horizon* (1993) and Kath Weston's *Families We Choose* (1991). Younger men and women who came of age in the 1980s and 1990s started to have a less pronounced coming out experience.

36 I first outlined these processes in 1975, in *Sexual Stigma*, p. 147–50. Most recently, see the general model contained in Rob Eichberg's therapeutic manual, *Coming Out* (1991), p. 41.
37 Eichberg, op. cit., p. 17.
38 See Lillian Faderman, 'The "New Gay" Lesbians' (1984).
39 See Eichenberg, op. cit., special letters, p. 259 *et seq.*
40 For opposing and representative selections see Vance, op. cit., and Dorchen Leidholdt and Janice Raymond (eds), *The Sexual Liberals and the Attack on Feminism* (1990). For the early origins of schisms within the women's movement, see Alice Echols, *Daring to be Bad* (1989).
41 On the notion of 'expert systems' and the role they play in late modern societies, see Anthony Giddens, *The Consequences of Modernity* (1990). More frighteningly, they are also part of the risk society; see Ulrich Beck, *The Risk Society* (1992).
42 See for example the discussions by Ronald Bayer, *Homosexuality and American Psychiatry* (1981), P. Conrad and J. Schneider, *Deviance and Medicalization* (1980) and M. Spector and J. Kitsuse, *Constructing Social Problems* (1987) on the demedicalisation of homosexuality.

5 WOMEN'S CULTURE AND RAPE STORIES

1 Jill Saward, *Rape: My Story* (1991), p. 61. This is a famous UK case of rape, often designated the Vicarage rape.
2 Nancy Ziegenmeyer's rape became a media event in the USA in the early 1990s – with newspaper series, docudrama and book. The importance she places on 'speaking out' is a key theme of the book. See *Taking Back My Life* (1993), p. 151.
3 There are many accounts of this process of silencing, but see Dale Spender, *Women of Ideas and What Men Have Done to Them* (1982). On women's voices more generally, see Mary Field Belenky *et al.*, *Women's Ways of Knowing* (1986).
4 Amongst other sources, see Nancy Friday, *My Secret Garden* and *Forbidden Flowers*, published in the early 1970s, which need to be contrasted with her more recent *Women on Top* (1991). See also Lonnie Barbach *Pleasures* (1984), Rosemary Daniell's *Sleeping with Soldiers* (1984); and of course, Shere Hite, *The Hite Report* (1976). A helpful review of all this is Barbara Ehrenreich et al. *Re-Making Love: The Feminization of Sex* (1987). The assertion of a forceful women's sexuality drips from the pages of the controversial Barnard Conference of 1982 published as *Pleasure and Danger*, edited by Carole Vance (1984).
5 On this position, which informs much of this book more generally, see my earlier 'Symbolic Interactionism and Sexual Conduct' (1982); and the more recent excellent review by Carole Vance on 'Social Construction Theory' (1989). The constructionist debate dominated the 1980s but is much less prominent now. See Diane Fuss, *Essentially Speaking* (1990).
6 Classically, see Simone de Beauvoir's concern in *The Second Sex* (1949). The classic account of the male gaze is from Laura Mulvey, 'Visual Pleasure and Narrative' (1975), though more recently, the male gaze gives way partially to the female gaze. For a valuable, cautious but optimistic, feminist account of all this see Linda Williams, *Hard Core* (1989), Ch. 8.
7 Some major sources of these stories are Sheila Jeffreys, *Anti-Climax* (1990); Dorchen Leidholdt and Janice Raymond (eds), *The Sexual Liberals and the Attack on Feminism* (1990); Andrea Dworkin, *Pornography* (1981); Catherine MacKinnon, *Feminism Unmodified* (1987).
8 See: Anna Clarke, *Women's Silence, Men's Violence: Sexual Assault in England*

1770–1845 (1987) p. 14.

9 Though not, of course, less common – the homes and streets were notoriously unsafe. See Judith Walkowitz, *City of Dreadful Delight* (1992).

10 For divisions in feminism, see amongst others Olive Banks, *Faces of Feminism* (1981) and David Bouchier, *The Feminist Challenge* (1983); and more recently Rosemarie Tong, *Feminist Thought* (1989).

11 Sheila Jeffreys documents them in her dossier, *The Sexuality Debates* (1987).

12 For important discussions of these early narratives, see both Elaine Showalter, *Sexual Anarchy* (1991) and Walkowitz op. cit. See also Jane Caputi's *The Age of Sex Crime* (1988).

13 Ellen DuBois and Linda Gordon, 'Seeking Ecstasy on the Battlefield' (1984) p. 32–3.

14 Hopkins, n.d., cited in Jeffreys, op. cit., p. 5.

15 These quotes are derived from Sheila Jeffrey's discussion in Lal Coveney *et al.*, *The Sexuality Papers*, pp. 26–8 *et seq*.

16 Jeffreys, *op. cit.*.

17 Susan Edwards, *Female Sexuality and the Law* (1981), p. 24.

18 Ibid.

19 Ibid.

20 See Molly Haskell, *From Reverence to Rape* (1987).

21 Susan Brownmiller, *Against Our Will* (1975), p. 447.

22 Here, as throughout the book, I take dates as symbols, not as wholly accurate chronologies of time and place. This is not a work of classical history, and I am only attempting to sensitise the reader to a change rather than to an exact chronology, which I suspect would be impossible anyway.

23 e.g. Harry O'Reilly, 'Crisis Intervention with Victims of Forcible Rape' (1984). I first heard this paper at a 'Victims of Sexual Assault' conference at Teesside Polytechnic in April 1981. As a key worker with the New York City's Sex Crime Unit, he peppered his talk with stories about how he had been influenced by the stories of rape victims and how this had changed his approach to working with rape victims.

24 Originally printed in *Ramparts* (1971), pp. 26–35. It is also to be found in S. Griffin, *Rape: The Power of Consciousness* (1979), p. 3.

25 See for instance the New York Radical Feminists, *Rape: The First Sourcebook for Women* (1974); Andrea Medea and Kathleen Thompson, *Against Rape* (1974).

26 Note the same is true of the gay story too; there are also myths to be debunked, a history to be written and a political analysis to be made.

27 E.g. Julia and Herman Schwendinger, 'Rape Myths' (1974).

28 Margaret Gordon and Stephanie Riger *The Female Fear* (1989), p. 6. This is a brief, but recent listing. There are usually more sustained discussions providing evidence aginst each myth.

29 On all this, see the important work of Michael Billig, *Arguing and Thinking* (1987).

30 See Brownmiller, op. cit. Some writers think this is the truth of rape – a universal essence of male power: Kathleen Barry, in *Female Sexual Slavery* (1979), Ch. 8, for instance, has little time for those who would relativise the problem away. Yet whilst the continuities are important, so too are the differences. As many commentators have now shown, the practice of forced sex can assume many meanings, have many different sources and be organised in fundamentally different ways, See Roy Porter, 'Rape – Does it Have a Historical Meaning?' (1986) and Julia and Herman Schwendinger, *Rape and Inequality* (1983). There are societies where rape seems non-existent; others where it is institutionalised and not seen; and others when it may become a 'public holiday!'.

31 Small sections of this have been previously published in Ken Plummer, 'Social Uses of Sexuality: Symbolic Interaction, Power and Rape' (1984), but this is a substantial rewriting.

32 Griffin, op. cit., p. 3.

33 Nicholas Groth, for instance, has studied rapists and comments:

> Clinical work with offenders and victims reveals that rape is in fact serving primarily non-sexual needs; it is the sexual expression of power and anger. Rape is motivated more by retaliatory and compensatory motives than sexual ones; it is a pseudo-sexual act, complex and multi-determined, but addressing issues of hostility (anger) and control (power) more than desire (sexuality).
>
> (N. Groth, essay in A. Burgess and L. Holmstrom, *Rape: Crisis and Recovery* (1979), p. 29)

At the same time, some feminists have been worried about turning rape into just a matter of power: why is sex the means to establish power?

34 Nancy Ziegenmeyer, *Taking Back My Life* (1993), p. 39.
35 See Andrea Rechtin cited in Tim Beneke, *Men on Rape* (1982).
36 See Burgess and Holmstrom, op. cit., Ch. 3.
37 See Diana Russell (1986).
38 See Carole J. Sheffield, 'Sexual Terrorism' (1987), pp. 173–4.
39 Griffin, op. cit.
40 Brownmiller, op. cit.
41 See Margaret Gordon and Stephanie Riger, *The Female Fear* (1989), p. 9, and the discussion therein. In the UK a smaller-scale study is that by Jalna Hanmer and Sheila Saunders, *Well-Founded Fear* (1984).
42 See Diana Russell's *Sexual Exploitation* (1984) and *Rape in Marriage* (1982).
43 The first in 1977.
44 See paragraph 37. A final report was however more cautious, and in any event it has not to date been implemented. Legal judgements made in 1991 however anticipate a change.
45 Ruth Herschberger, *Adam's Rib* (1970), p. 15.
46 See Vicki McNickle Rose, 'Rape as a Social Problem' (1981).
47 Griffin, op. cit.
48 Germaine Greer, *The Female Eunuch* (1971).
49 See Pauline Bart, 'Rape as a Paradigm of Sexism in Society' (1979) for this argument. Rape has become ubiquitous. Statistically, the USA appears to have the highest official rate (in 1980, 71 out of every 100, 000 females reported being victims of rape or attempted rape – a 38 per cent increase over 1976) and estimates of the true incidence of rape suggest it is occurring in 'epidemic proportions and in a pattern that is escalating over time' (Russell (1984), op. cit., p. 65).
50 Mary Koss and Mary Harvey, *The Rape Victim* (1987), p. 74; London Rape Crisis Centre, *Sexual Violence* (1984).
51 For example: Liz Kelly, *Surviving Sexual Violence* (1988).
52 E.g. London Rape Crisis Centre, op. cit., p. 116–18.
53 Koss and Harvey, op. cit., p. 82.
54 Many of these responses are also found in the USA research of Burgess and Holmstrom under what they call a rape trauma syndrome. This has two phases – immediate, 'in which the victim's lifestyle is completely disrupted by the rape crisis', and long-term 'in which the victim must re-organize this disrupted life style', op. cit., p. 35.
55 See Saward, op. cit. p. 150.
56 Portland Women's Night Watch Second Annual Flashlight March. Cited in Griffin's op. cit., p. 96.
57 In Robin Warshaw, *I Never Called it Rape*, (1988), p. 119–20.
58 In Gordon and Riger, op. cit., p. 43.
59 E.g. Kathleen Barry, *Female Sexual Slavery* (1979), Ch. 3.
60 Kelly, op. cit. (1988), p. 228.
61 Kelly, op. cit. (1988), p. 231.

62 See Trudy Mills, 'The Assault on the Self' (1985), p. 118.
63 'Survivor' stories have become very popular for many experiences. Although I am generally unsympathetic to the ideas of Christopher Lasch, I have found his chapter critiquing the ubiquitous use of the survival metaphor to be of value. See *The Minimal Self* (1985), Ch. 2. His attack is on the overuse of the idea and its limiting function once it becomes an end in itself: 'people only committed to survival are more likely to head for the hills', (p. 78). This is also part of Orrin Klapp's wider argument about the *Inflation of Symbols* (1991).
64 The quotes are taken from a key UK study of this: Keith Soothill and Sylvia Walby, *Sex Crime in the News* (1991). They document the dramatic increase in rape reporting over the past thirty years (Ch. 2), but also suggest ways in which the image of a 'sex fiend' has been created during the 1980s (Ch. 3). For the USA, see Gordon and Riger, op. cit., Ch. 5 where there is a discussion of the 'zebra killings' in San Francisco and the New Bedford, Massachusetts Pool Table Rape which was linked to a fictional account in *Hustler* magazine. A wider discussion of US media is to be found in Helen Benedict's *Virgin or Vamp* (1992).
65 Indeed, bit by bit, the whole world can be turned into a story of sexual danger, and in some radical feminist accounts all of sexuality does becomes just that. A representative sampler of this literature which is now too enormous to include in any detail here could include: Ellen Bass and Louise Thornton (eds), *I Never Told anyone: Writings by Women Survivors of Child Sexual Abuse* (1983); Toni McNaran and Yarrow Morgan (eds), *Voices in the Night: Women Speaking About Incest* (1982); Elizabeth Ward (ed.), *Father–Daughter Rape* (1984); David Finkelhor, *Child Sexual Abuse*, (1984); Diana Russell, *The Secret Trauma* (1986); Gordon and Riger, op. cit.; Warshaw, op. cit.; Peggy Reeves Sanday, *Fraternity Gang Rape* (1990); Sue Blume, *Secret Survivors* (1990); Andrea Parrott and Laurie Bechofer (eds), *Acquaintance Rape* (1991); Claire Renzetti, *Violent Betrayal : Partner Abuse in Lesbian Relationships (1992); Gary Comstock, Violence Against Lesbians and Gay Men* (1992); Richie McMullen, *Male Rape* (1990).
66 Louise Armstrong, 'Making an Issue out of Incest' (1990), p. 43.
67 In the revised tales, Auschwitz offers the luxuries of a country club and gas chambers become mere delousing facilities. See Deborah E. Lipstadt, *Denying the Holocaust* (1993).
68 Her work has since been published as Katie Roiphe, *The Morning After* (1994).

6 THE MODERNISATION OF GAY AND LESBIAN STORIES

1 A lesbian-identified reader commenting on *The Coming Out Stories*, edited by Julia Penelope and Susan J. Wolfe, a year and a half or so after their initial publication in 1980. This comment appears in the second, expanded edition, published in 1989, p. 2.
2 E.g. David Halperin, *One Hundred Years of Homosexuality* (1990).
3 E.g. Alan Bray, *Homosexuality in Renaissance England* (1982).
4 E.g. David Greenberg, *The Construction of Homosexuality* (1988).
5 See Dennis Altman, *The Homosexualization of America* (1982); Michael Bronski, *Culture Clash* (1984); John Marshall, 'Pansies, Perverts and Macho Men' (1981); Gregg Blachford, 'Male Dominance and the Gay World' (1981); and Martin Levine, 'The Life and Death of Gay Clones' (1992).
6 See for example Alexander Doty, *Making Things Perfectly Queer* (1993), and Michael Warner's 'From Queer to Eternity' (1992).
7 The classic statements included Judy Grahn, *Another Mother Tongue* (1984); Lillian Faderman, *Surpassing the Love of Men* (1981) and *Odd Girls and Twilight Lovers* (1991). On lipstick lesbians, see Lindsy Van Gelder, 'Lipstick Liberation' (1992), p. 30–4.

8   On this last point, see Richard Plant, *The Pink Triangle* (1987).
9   See Neil Miller, *In Search of Gay America* (1988); and John Preston (ed.), *Hometowns: Gay Men Write About Where they Belong* (1991).
10 See Ken Plummer, 'Speaking Its Name', in Plummer (ed.) *Modern Homosexualities* (1992) and the references, reading guides, etc. cited within. See also Henry Abelove *et al.* (eds) *Lesbian and Gay Studies Reader* (1993), which provides a good collection of recent articles and debates.
11 See the collection of essays in Martin Duberman, Martha Vicinus and George Chauncey, Jr, *Hidden from History: Reclaiming the Gay and Lesbian Past* (1989).
12 See Penelope and Wolfe (1980), op. cit.. This is a major and fairly typical example of the genre where some forty-one voices tell their story of coming out, having been invited to contribute by the editors in *Lesbian Connection*.
13 Adrienne Rich, foreword to Penelope and Wolfe, (1980), *op. cit.*, p. xii.
14 For accounts of this change, which I turn to in a later chapter, see Kath Weston, *Families We Choose* (1991), Gilbert Herdt and Andrew Boxer, *Children of Horizon* (1993) and Roy Cain, 'Disclosure and Secrecy among Gay men' (1991).
15 Citing Richard Troiden's work in Savin Williams, p. 35. Djuna Barnes in *The Ladies Almanack* (1928) calls the lesbian 'A Woman born with a Difference' (in Bonnie Zimmerman's *Safe Sea of Women* (1990), p. 45).
16 Academics, myself included, have tended to put all this into a sequential model! For a review, see the late Richard Troiden's *Gay and Lesbian Identity* (1988).
17 Paul Monette, *Becoming a Man* (1992), p. 1–2.
18 Again, see Herdt and Boxer, op. cit. and Weston, op. cit. for evidence of this.
19 P. 28. See Michael Nava, 'Gardenland, Sacremento, California', p. 21–9, in Preston, op. cit..
20 Bookstore catalogues are the best guide to the full range of contemporary publications, and most lesbian and gay bookstores produce them. But see for example the Washington-based *Lamda Review*.
21 In a fascinating account of social inventions, Philip Abbott's *Seeking Many Inventions* (1987) suggests a whole array of new items such as quilts, telephones, camps. Surely the book on gay and lesbian inventions must be awaited: but it would have to mention the disco, safer sex, camp and many other items.
22 See Edmund White, *States of Desire* (1980); Altman, op. cit.; Martin Levine (ed.), *Gay Men* (1979); John Alan Lee, *Getting Sex* (1978); Bronski, op.cit.
23 The term satellite culture is used by Laud Humphreys's 'Exodus and Identity', in Levine, op.c cit. For discussions of the ways Aids has impacted gay and lesbian communities, see the contributions by Beth Schneider, Barry Adam and Tim Edwards in Plummer, op.cit.
24 As I write, there is a popularity for the Simon LeVay school of thought (subsequently published as *The Sexual Brain* (1993)). Those with longer memories may recall M. Ruse, K. Dorner, M. Kallman, M. Hirschfield. It is not a new story, but says something of our need for biological stories.
25 See Larry Kramer, *Reports from the Holocaust* (1990), p. 245. On the Simon LeVay 'story', see the account in *Newsweek*, 'Is the Child Gay?', 24 February 1992.
26 The title of a book of essays which I edited in the early 1980s: see Ken Plummer (ed.), *The Making of the Modern Homosexual* (1981b).
27 See the *Pink Book*, published by the International Lesbian and Gay Association, which depicts some of the global trends.
28 'Life history and world history coalesce to transform each other', Phillip Abrams (1982), p. 256.
29 See Ken Plummer, 'Going Gay' (1981c), and the earlier formulations in *Sexual Stigma* (1975).
30 Elsewhere I discuss a fourth stage. Not all one's problems however will be resolved

speedily through coming to terms. In this fourth phase, *stabilisation*, one embarks upon a series of decisions concerning the kind of lifestyle one wants to adopt.

31 Valuable documentation of the rise of the new culture and new movements include Barry Adam, *The Rise of a Lesbian and Gay Movement* (1987); Margaret Cruikshank, *The Gay and Lesbian Liberation Movement* (1992); John D'Emilio, *Sexual Politics, Sexual Communities* (1983b); Faderman, op. cit.; Jeffrey Weeks, *Coming Out* (1990).

32 Jonathan Katz, *Gay American History* (1976), pp. 385f.

33 Vern Bullough, *Sexual Variance* (1976), p. 645.

34 See especially D'Emilio, op. cit., on all this.

35 *The Wolfenden Report* (1957).

36 A year later a small group of students met in a room at the London School of Economics and the English Gay Liberation Front was born. By that time, it had indeed become an international political movement, and it has remained so ever since.

37 It is, however, a part of the myth of origins to say Stonewall. Whilst New Yorkers tell this story, a little travel will soon teach other stories. Both San Francisco and Los Angeles make claims for origins, and in Europe the most common claims can be linked to the Netherlands and Germany. International stories are in the making. In 1989 – the twentieth anniversary of Stonewall – I organised a session on lesbian and gay life at the Annual American Sociological Meetings in San Francisco. When I initially called the session 'Twenty Years after Stonewall', a very informed colleague told me that since gay liberation started in the West Coast of America long before Stonewall, this would be a very insensitive title. I subsequently dropped it! Good accounts of gay and lesbian life on the West Coast include the biography of Harry Hay – Stuart Timmons, *The Trouble With Harry Hay* (1990), Faderman op. cit. and Allan Berube *Coming Out Under Fire* (1990).

38 See Rob Tielman, *Homosexualitiest in Nederland* (1982).

39 See Martin Duberman, *Stonewall* (1993).

40 See the early arguments by Dennis Altman, *Homosexual: Oppression and Liberation* (1971), and his comments a decade later in *The Americanization of the Homosexual*, op. cit., as well as *Aids and the New Puritanism* (1986) after the onset of Aids. Coming out is a central theme.

41 See White, op. cit.

42 Jeffrey Weeks first hinted at these stages in his now classic study *Coming Out*, op. cit., pp. 6–7.

43 See the brilliant discussion of all this by Ann Ferguson in her *Sexual Democracy* (1991), and my brief comments on this in *Modern Homosexualities*, op. cit. Ferguson sees three major accounts of gay and lesbian identity. A first sees gay and lesbian culture as the full fruition of a natural gay sensibility – one that has been with us throughout the ages, and which comes into its own when cities reach a large enough size to bring enough gay people together. In this view, it is the natural evolution of a gay and lesbian people. Another suggests it was centrally the outcome of the turbulent 1960s which saw the counter-cultural moment of feminists, blacks and students protesting against an oppressive order. Both views seem too simple: one posits a gay 'essence' that I have already criticised; the other – while partially true – only locates an immediate crisis in ideas and fails to see wider historical conditions. Her own view, and mine, is a more historically grounded dialectical one.

44 See John D'Emilio, 'Capitalism and Gay Identity' in Anne Snitow *et al.*, *Powers of Desire* (1984). His pioneering and important work is developed in *Sexual Politics, Sexual Communities* (1983), and *Making Trouble* (1992).

45 C.B. Macpherson, *The Political Theory of Possessive Individualism* (1962). For an excellent philosophical exposition of the development of the modern self, see Charles Taylor, *Sources of the Self* (1989).

46 See Antony Giddens, *Modernity and Self-Identity* (1991) and the discussion in the next

chapter of this book, along with the references to R. Baumesiter, L. Zurcher, K. Gergen and others.

47   See P. Conrad and J. Schneider, *Deviance and Medicalization* (1980). They detect a cycle in medicalisation models.

48   See Joshua Meyrowitz, *No Sense of Place* (1985) and John Gagnon, 'The Self, Its Voices' (1992).

49   See Timmons, op. cit., Ch. 9. The *Second ILGA Pink Book* (1988) has an informative account of the gay and lesbian press by Evert van der Veen.

50   Allan Berube is currently working on a study of this 'pulp' fiction of the 1950s and 1960s.

51   See H. Robert Malinowsky, *International Directory* (1987). Although this aims to be a comprehensive listing, some key gay magazines that I am aware of like *Gay Times* in the UK were not even listed. Hence this number is likely to be an underestimate.

52   So much so that a number of articles appeared on its importance. The whole gay market got 'upscale' in the 1990s with magazines like *Out* and *Genre* appearing as glossy gay and lesbian equivalents of *Vanity Fair* or *HQ*, and containing mainstream commercial advertising. See for instance, 'From Closet to Mainstream', *Newsweek*, 1 June 1992, p. 62, and Bob Summer's 'A Niche Market Comes of Age', *Publishers Weekly*, (1992) pp. 36–40.

53   See, for example, Richard Dyer's *Now You See It* (1991).

54   For a series of family coming out stories, see: Loralee MacPike (ed.), *There's Something I've Been Meaning to Tell You* (1989) and John Preston (ed.) *A Member of the Family* (1992).

55   See Rob Eichberg's *Coming Out: An Act of Love* (1991) which describes the Advocate Experience, a coming out workshop, along with the development of the Lesbian and Gay Public Awareness Project, p. 187 *et seq.*.

56   See Barry Adam and Beth Schneider's articles in Plummer (1992), op. cit.

57   E.g. John Preston (ed.) *Personal Dispatches* (1989). See also Philip M. Kayal's *Bearing Witness* (1993).

58   Essex Hemphill, 'Introduction' to Joseph Beam (ed.), *Brother to Brother* (1991) p. xv.

59   Ibid., p. xvi.

60   J.R. Roberts, 'Black Lesbians Before 1970: A Bibliographic Essay', in Margaret Cruishank, (ed.), *Lesbian Studies* (1982), p. 103–9.

61   See Rakesh Ratti (ed.), *A Lotus of Another Colour: An Unfolding of the South Asian Gay and Lesbian Experience* (1993).

62   See Cherrie Moraga and Gloria Anzaldúa (eds), *This Bridge Called My Back* (1981), Evelyn Beck (ed.), *Nice Jewish Girls* (1989), etc. etc.

63   See Julia Penelope and Sarah Valentine (eds), *Finding the Lesbians* (1992) and Jürgen Lemke (ed.), *Gay Voices from East Germany* (1991) as two instances.

7 RECOVERY TALES

1   See Colette Dowling, *The Cinderella Complex* (1981), p. 19.

2   John Bradshaw, *Bradshaw on the Family* (1988), p. 236. This is not just a book, but a television programme, a video, a travelling therapy group, a business.

3   At least this is what *Newsweek* estimated in 1990. See 'Afflicted? Addicted? Support Groups are the Answer for 15 Million Americans', 5 February 1990. Quoted in Wendy Kaminer, *I'm Dysfunctional, You're Dysfunctional* (1992), p. 80.

4   Craig Reinarman and Mary Phillips, 'The Politics of Self-Control in Postmodernity' (1991), p. 13.

5   The literature on all this is now enormous. For a preliminary sampler, see, *inter alia*: Patrick Carnes, *Contrary to Love: Helping the Sexual Addict* (1989); Ralph Earle and

Gregory Crow, *Lonely All the Time: Recognizing, Understanding and Overcoming Sex Addiction, For Addicts and Co-Dependents* (1989); Grateful Members, *The Twelve Steps for Everyone* (1975); Melody Beattie, *Codependent No More* (1987).

6 In an insightful discussion of this phenomenon by Mimi White she defines tele-advising as 'the deployment of therapeutic and confessional discourses on television'. See Mimi White, *Tele-Advising: Therapeutic Discourse in American Television* (1992), p. 7.

7 See for instance Rob Eichberg's *Coming Out: An Act of Love* (1990) which, although political, comes much closer to seeing coming out as a personal issue rather than a political one, and is written by a coming out counsellor who organises coming out workshops. The rape and child abuse literature here is also very substantial.

8 See Wendy Simonds, *Women and Self-Help Culture: Reading Between the Lines* (1992).

9 Simonds, op. cit., p. 227.

10 Kenneth C. Davis, *Two-Bit Culture* (1984), p. xii.

11 See Steven Starker, *Oracle at the Supermarket* (1989), p. 4.

12 See Simonds, op. cit., p. 136 for a discussion of the covers and marketing strategies of these books.

13 See Robin Norwood, *Women Who Love Too Much* (1985), p. 25.

14 Ibid., pp. 7–9.

15 Ibid., pp. 39–40.

16 Ibid., p. 207; cf. Simonds, op. cit., p. 138 on the prominence of the checklist in the whole genre.

17 Norwood, op. cit., pp. 137, 138.

18 Note too that writings from the new men's movement also make explicit references to such folk myths and stories – many of which are not far removed from misogyny and fascism! See Ken Clatterbaugh's 'Mythopoetic Foundations of New Age Patriarchy' (1993), p. 2–13.

19 There is now a substantial feminist analysis of all this congruence. See, *inter alia*, Tanya Modleski, *Loving with a Vengeance* (1982).

20 Norwood, op. cit., p. 218.

21 Ibid., (1985): Ch. 10, pp. 221–2.

22 Ibid., p. 272.

23 Robin Norwood, *Robin Norwood Answers Letters from Women Who Love Too Much* (1988), p. 328, 330.

24 Norwood (1988), op. cit., pp. 3–4.

25 Donahue started local talk shows in 1967, and in 1976 Multimedia started syndicating the show in the USA. It is transmitted to over 200 stations and has won at least twenty Emmies.

26 *Oprah* started in the mid-1980s and by 1993 was transmitted each weekday to more than 200 stations as well as over sixty countries. She is reputed to earn $50 million a year.

27 See Kaminer, op. cit., p. 33. The chapter 'Testifying Television' provides some illuminating comments on this phenomenon.

28 Marc J. LaFountain, in 'Foucault and Dr Ruth' (1989), p. 135.

29 White, op. cit., p. 39.

30 Sonia Livingstone and Peter Lunt, *Talk on Television* (1993), Ch. 3.

31 Donal Carbaugh, *Talking American* (1988), p. 28 *et seq.*

32 Ibid., p. 110.

33 White, op. cit., p. 179.

34 Gloria-Jean Masciarotte, 'C'mon, Girl: Oprah Winfrey and the Discourse of Feminine Talk' (1991), p. 83.

35 Listed in Jennifer Schneider and Burt Schneider, *Sex, Lies and Forgiveness* (1990), p. 15.

36 This runs in part as follows:

> God grant me the serenity
> to accept the things I cannot change;
> Courage to change the
> things I can; and
> Wisdom to know the difference.
> Living one day at a time;
> Enjoying one moment at a
> time; Accepting hardship
> as the pathway to peace.
> (Part of the 'Serenity Prayer'
> by Reinhold Niebuhr)

37 See Kaminer, op. cit., pp. 70–1.

38 Patrick Carnes, *The Sexual Addiction* (1983), p. 145.

39 See Ann Wilson Schaef, *When Society Becomes an Addict* (1987), p. 145. All the quotes are taken from Carnes, (1983), op. cit., p. 145. But they are typical of a very wide spectrum. For the most general model, see Grateful Members, op. cit. This provides a twelve-step model of recovery for almost anything you care to think of!

40 See Hendrick Ruitenbeck, *The New Group Therapies* (1970), p. 62 This is part of the American character of 'getting things done', solving problems and doing it all quickly. In Europe, cultural pessimism leads many to think that problems cannot be solved and common unhappiness is the best we can hope for!

41 See George Ritzer, *The McDonaldization of Society* (1992). Ritzer brings Weber's thesis up to date and suggests McDonalds is the contemporary manifestation of Weber's rational 'Iron Cage'. McDonalds provides the basis for understanding much contemporary social organisation, and it can be seen in many therapy groups. Edwin Schur also recognised this clearly twenty years ago in his *The Awareness Trap* (1976).

42 As Anne Wilson Schaef – a leading 'recovery guru' who claims the whole of society is addicted and co-dependent – says:

> the most reliable information is that which comes from people with personal experience. Objectivity is a myth. The people who can be trusted the most are those who can honestly say 'I know how you feel because I have been there myself'.
>
> (op. cit., p. 5)

43 According to *Harper's* 1991 figures, *Co-Dependent No More* had sold over two million copies by 1991 and had been on the New York Times best-seller list for over a hundred weeks. See Kaminer, op. cit., p. 11.

44 See Joy Davidson, *The Soap Opera Syndrome* (1988), p. 15. An intriguing study which plays back into itself. It sees the soap opera as providing the drama and excitement which may be missing from lives and suggests that this is what people need in their lives; hence their 'addiction' to soap opera where they may be able to find it. Soap opera seems to be problem, solution and problem!

45 Carnes (1983), op. cit., p. 16. This is his earliest statement and he has now published a significant array of books.

46 See Schaef, op. cit. (1987), p. 18. Or as Carnes puts it: 'A moment comes for every addict when the consequences are so great or the pain is so bad that the addict admits *life is out of control* because of his or her sexual behaviour' (op. cit., p. v, my italics).

47 Op. cit., p. 236.

48 For a useful guide to much of this literature, see Barbara Yoder, *The Recovery Resource Book* (1990). See also Wendy Kaminer's amusing but highly critical account *I'm Dysfunctional/You're Dysfunctional*, op. cit. See also the much earlier book by Edwin Schur, op. cit.

49 Even when the problem is seen to be 'society', as in Schaef's condemnation of the

addictive society, the solution is still seen to be a personal one; see Schaef, op. cit.

50 See bell hooks, *Sisters of the Yam: Black Women and Self-Recovery* (1993), p. 5.
51 Simonds, op. cit., p. 43.
52 Cf. Schneider and Schneider, op. cit., p. 46.
53 See Simonds, op. cit., p. 60 *et seq.*
54 Starker, op. cit., p. 152.
55 They also seem to be more interested in 'made-for-TV movies' which have a basis on human drama. See Elayne Rapping's *The Movie of the Week: Private Stories, Public Events* (1992).
56 See Joy Davidson, *The Soap Opera Syndrome* (1988).
57 See Simonds, op. cit., p. 42.
58 See Norman K. Denzin, *Symbolic Interactionism and Cultural Studies* (1992), p. 91.
59 Two of these are clearly depicted in Janice Irvine's *Disorders of Desire* (1992) and experienced by me on my trip around the sexological world in 1976: exemplified in the serious tone of Masters and Johnson and the more playful tone of the then Kinsey Institute of Sex Research.
60 See, as one instance, Helen Singer Kaplan's *The New Sex Therapy* (1978).
61 For a good instance of analysing 'science' as rhetoric, see Joseph Gusfield's 'The Literary Rhetoric of Science' (1976).
62 See Christopher Lasch, 'Soul of a New Age' and Kaminer, op. cit., Ch. 6.
63 See Starker, op. cit.
64 See Starker, op. cit., p. 45.
65 Cf. Tom Wolfe, 'The "Me" Decade and the Third Great Awakening', *New Yorker*, 23 (August 1976), p. 40; Wolfe 1977. See also Christopher Lasch's *The Culture of Narcissism* (1979), and Schur, op. cit. The final quote here is from Starker's *Oracle*, op. cit., p. 120. This culture may be weaker in the UK but it is still there – see the long-lost study of Maurice North, *The Secular Priests* (1972).
66 Quoted in Reinarman and Phillips, op. cit., p. 14. I am grateful to Arlene Stein for bringing this (as yet) unpublished paper to my notice.

8 THE TALE AND ITS TIME

1 I write this as a week-long debate has raged over Dan Quayle's remarks on the television sitcom *Murphy Brown*, which – unusually – featured a single parent, and which the then Vice President, well noted for his gaffes, blamed for the decay of the nation and the LA riots of 1992.
2 Warren Farrell, a leading writer on male liberation, has proposed a need to look at and hear men's voices more generally, and especially on circumcision. It is something about which 'we have not cared to ask'. He writes:

> Within moments after infant boys are born, 80 per cent undergo surgery. . . . Their penises are taken to the blade of a knife and cut. This is done to the male child prior to the age of consent. . . . Doesn't lack of circumcision make a boy child feel different? Yes. Which is why, if circumcision creates birth trauma, it needs to be publicised very widely.
>
> (Farrell, *Why Men Are the Way They Are* (1986), p. 232)

This is challenging – or mildly amusing? – talk, and it is part of Farrell's thesis on what he calls the 'New sexism', where there is a double standard at work. Here he suggests women's voices are heard more than men's on these issues (he singles out the birth pill as a key concern).

3 Sex is generally seen to be a sensuous matter – it taps into all manner of issues around sensuality, arousing our senses. Yet there has been remarkably little focus upon some

of our senses and how they contribute towards a sexual life. Smell is perhaps the clearest example. It is generally one of the most neglected of senses anyway, but some claim it is the most powerful: triggering in a hidden fashion so much of our lives. Yet we haven't even a basic language to discuss it – at least with vision we know about colour spectrums which allow us to differentiate, and indeed we have a whole vocabulary to help us discriminate what we see. But this is not so for smell. Now supposing smell is critical for our sex. Smells emerge as important in early life and play a crucial role in helping our sensuality. Yet we can't articulate this in any way yet. It's a dim thwarted frustration for many. Is this a story which might one day be told, and if it was what kind of difference might this make? (See Diane Ackerman's *A Natural History of the Senses* (1991).)

4 Scott MacDonald, 'Confessions of a feminist porn watcher' *Film Quarterly*, vol. 36, no. 3 (1983); reprinted in Michael Kimmel (ed.), *Men Confront Pornography* (1990) pp. 34–5, 134.

5 For the latest of a long line of exhaustive reviews, see the compendium by Franklin Mark Osanka and Sara Lee Johann, *Sourcebook on Pornography* (1989).

6 The Meese Commission reported in 1986 and was very hostile to all aspects of pornography.

7 See the Carole Vance account of all this in her 'The Pleasures of Looking' (1990).

8 For samples of this discussion see Lynn Segal and Mary McIntosh (eds), *Sex Exposed* (1992), Sara Dunn, 'Voyage of the Valkyries' (1990) and Laura Fraser, 'Nasty Girls' (1990).

9 For a brief account of this, see Jeffrey Weeks, *Coming Out* (1990), p. 161.

10 David Finkelhor, *Child Sexual Abuse* (1984); Glen D. Wilson and David N. Cox, *The Child Lovers* (1983).

11 There are exceptions: see *Lears*, February 1992, Alan Bell and Calvin Hall's *The Personality of a Child Molester* (1971) and *Redbook*, April 1992. But these are tales told by others and do adopt an outsider's stigmatising language. A major exception is the intriguing (but unpublished) Ph.D. thesis of Li Chine-Yeung: *Sexual Experience of Adults with Children*, Cambridge University (1986).

12 For example, see J.Z. Eglinton's *Greek Love* (1971).

13 For a brief history of the US movements, see David Thorstad, 'Man/Boy Love and the American Gay Movement' (1990); on the UK, see my account of the early days of PIE in Ken Plummer, 'The Paedophile's Progress' (1981a), and for the subsequent development and failure of the movement, see Steven A. Smith, 'PIE from 1980 Until its Demise in 1985' (undated). For the Netherlands, see Jan Schuijer, 'Tolerance at Arm's Length' (1990). For valuable personal documents of the history of this movement, see Daniel Tsang (ed.), *The Age Taboo* (1981) and Warren Middleton, *The Betrayal of Youth* (undated). For voices of paedophiles, see Tom O'Carroll, *Paedophilia* (1980), as well as the works of Edward Brongersma, *Loving Boys*, vols 1 and 2 (1986). On the journals, see especially *Paidika*.

14 Compare Parker Rossman, *Sexual Experience Between Men and Boys* (1979) with Tsang, op. cit. Both contain a number of first-hand personal narratives.

15 See O'Carroll, op. cit.

16 This has all been well documented by Joel Best in his extremely valuable *Threatened Children* (1990), p. 80.

17 Ibid., p. 6.

18 I describe some of these in Plummer, op. cit. Note in particular the Childhood Sensuality Circle, the writings of Roger Moody, especially *Indecent Assault* (1980) and the discussions found in Carole Vance (ed.), *Pleasure and Danger* (1984).

19 For an earlier formulation of this question, around 'delinquent stories', see James Bennett, *Oral History and Delinquency* (1981), pp. 240–9. Asking why delinquent stories became pervasive from the late nineteenth century onwards, he outlines four major kinds of conditions – social, rhetorical, personal and technical.

20 See, for instance, Linda Gordon's work, *Heroes of their Own Lives* (1988). In any event, according to many of the 'abused', their abuse often took place many years prior to their talking about it. On a wider historical level, the work of de Mauss suggests significant abuse throughout much of history (including infanticide), an abuse that was clearly not recognised as such.

21 For some discussion of these early tabloids – along with a more sustained analysis of their contemporary counterparts – see S. Elizabeth Bird's *For Inquiring Minds* (1992), Ch. 1; and their workings are revealed in Judith Walkowitz's *City of Dreadful Delight* (1992). John Gagnon in 'The Self, Its Voices and Their Discord' (1992) has eloquently discussed the nineteenth-century shift in reading which gives rise to a more diverse self capable of hearing new voices, 'often alien voices that would not be admitted if their words had to be spoken in the presence of others', p. 230.

22 See Joshua Meyrowitz, *No Sense Of Place: The Impact of Electronic Media on Social Behaviour* (1985). He sees the rise of minorities as a potent force as largely linked to this phenomenon. He writes:

> the rise of minority consciousness actually indicates the demise of aspects of minority status in the traditional sense (as isolated and distinct). The demand for a full equality in role and rights dramatises the development of a mass 'majority', a single large group whose members will not tolerate any great distinctions in roles and privileges.
>
> (p. 132)

I think he overstates this case. Whilst I agree with his general argument, he fails to consider the way in which segregated communities also arise. For an illuminating account of this debate, see W. Russell Neuman, *The Future of the Mass Audience* (1991).

23 For instance, one UK television programme broadcast in early 1993 (18 January), *The Good Sex Guide* (and introduced in a very light-hearted way by Margi Clarke) looked at lots of problems of male sexual inadequacy (including a demonstration of penis size!) and apart from the ubiquitous 'doctor' pronouncing on it, also presented a group of men (playing pool, drinking in a bar) talking to each other about it. This was, however, carefully staged, and in 'real life' such chatting may not be so easy.

24 One way of seeing the new audiences for stories is to see them as markets. People will pay for such stories. Tabloid journalism, docudramas, self help paperbacks, etc. all have their markets.

25 From Jonathan Katz, *Gay American History* (1976), p. 406 and cited in Jeffrey Weeks, *Sexuality and Its Discontents* (1985), p. 188.

26 See Michel Foucault, *The History of Sexuality*, vol. 1 (1979), p. 17, pp. 20 *et seq.*

27 Ibid., p. 23.

28 For discussions of Baudrillard's work, along with comprehensive bibliographies and analyses of his shifting position, see Douglas Kellner's *Jean Baudrillard* (1989) and Mike Gane, *Baudrillard: Critical and Fatal Theory* (1991).

29 See Walkowitz, op. cit. and Elaine Showalter's *Sexual Anarchy* (1991).

30 See David T. Evans, *Sexual Citizenship* (1993), Ch. 3, p. 65. For a pop guide to this whole field of change, and the conflicts within, see Steve Chapple and David Talbot's *Burning Desires: Sex in America* (1990).

31 See Steven Seidman, *Embattled Eros* (1992), p. 5.

32 See Barbara Ehrenreich, Elizabeth Hess and Gloria Jacobs, *Re-making Love: the Feminization of Sex* (1987) for a full documentation of this process.

33 See John D'Emilio and Estelle Freedman, *Intimate Matters* (1988).

34 See Anthony Giddens, *The Transformation of Intimacy* (1992).

35 On the notion of 'plausibility structures', see Peter Berger and Thomas Luckmann's classic formulation in *The Social Construction of Reality* (1966) – an extremely

important and influential book in its own time, heralding the so-called 'constructionist' position, yet now much ignored.

36 See Kenneth Davis, *Two-Bit Culture: The Paperbacking of America* (1984), p. 13.
37 See Alfred Kinsey *et al.*, *Sexual Behaviour in the Human Male* (1948), and *Sexual Behaviour in the Human Female* (1953). The impact these volumes created in academia and popular publishing has been widely discussed, but see Donald Porter Geddes, *An Analysis of the Kinsey Reports* (1954) (especially the celebrated article by Lionel Trilling). On the success of the books, see Davis, op. cit. A more general, but valuable, review is Paul Robinson's *The Modernization of Sex* (1976) which also reviews other influential scientific story tellers!
38 See Davis, op. cit., and W. Simonds, *Women and Self-Help Culture* (1992) for listings of the leading best-sellers.
39 On all this, see Mike Featherstone's helpful guide, *Consumer Culture and Postmodernism* (1991).
40 Here, as elsewhere, the situation in North America is more developed than in the UK – an important point to keep making. The structure of US and UK television, for example, is very different – with a very different funding base. So that consumerism, commercialism and sex are much more intertwined in the USA than the UK. But increasingly there is a convergence, of sorts: whilst SKY is developing in the UK, public service television takes about 20 per cent of the market in the USA.
41 The classic account of the emerging history of youth is contained in Frank Musgrove, *Youth and the Social Order* (1964). See also the recent review of post-war youth as depicted in film narratives: Jon Lewis, *The Road to Romance and Ruin: Teen Films and Youth Culture* (1992). Sensational sex details are documented in Kenneth Anger's *Hollywood Babylon* (1975) and more critically in Michael Medved's *Hollywood vs America* (1992).
42 See Pierre Bourdieu, *Distinction* (1984).
43 See, for example, Morris North, *The Secular Priests* (1972). See also Bernice Martin, *A Sociology of Contemporary Cultural Change* (1981); Jeffrey Weeks, *Sex, Politics and Society*, 2nd edition (1991); and on the US scene, see James Davison Hunter's *Culture Wars: The Struggle to Define America* (1991).
44 On the US situation, see the documentation of Steven Starker in *Evil Influences* (1990), which shows the persistence of media scares around sex.
45 This is the distinction which organises Hunter, op. cit.
46 The distinction which organises the work of Steven Seidman: *Romantic Longings* (1990); *Embattled Eros* (1992) – two very useful accounts of shifts in sexual discourse in the USA over the last century.
47 The distinction made in the earlier UK account of these changes by Christie Davies: see his *Permissive Britain* (1975).
48 As with so much of this book, although I am speaking of sexual stories, much of it is applicable to other kinds of stories; I have used this phrase – generic process – at several points in the book. I take this to be one task of a social scientist – to aid cumulative work. See John Lofland, *Doing Social Life* (1976) and Robert Prus, 'Generic Social Processes' (1987) on all this. The aim is to produce two kinds of sociology: one that is substantive and one that is formal.
49 They have been called by some 'putative' concerns – conditions that may be *alleged* to exist, but about whose actuality we remain unsure for the time being. The 'real' nature of the 'issue' before its recognition – hence construction – remains a source of controversy. For discussions of this important controversy, see Pru Rains 'Imputations of Deviance' (1975), Malcolm Spector and John Kitsuse, *Constructing Social Problems* (1987), p. 76 and the polemics developing around Steve Woolgar and Dorothy Pawluch's 'Ontological Gerrymandering' (1985).
50 See Patricia Hill Collins on all this: *Black Feminist Thought* (1990), but especially Chs

5 and 11 which deal with self-definition, empowerment and consciousness of black women.

51 'Identity formation . . . is not only a matter of ontology but also a matter of *strategy*' says Shane Phelan in *Identity Politics* (1989).

52 On social worlds, see especially the work of Anselm Strauss, 'A Social World Perspective' (1978).

53 Classically, see the work of Paul Willis in *Learning to Labour* (1977) on the stories of young men in factories. Angela McRobbie provides a counterpart on young women: see her *Feminism and Youth Culture* (1991). Both studies deal with the UK.

54 Jeffrey Weeks in *Sexuality and Its Discontents*, op. cit., p. 191 lists five preconditions: (1) large numbers in the same situation; (2) geographical concentration; (3) identifiable targets of opposition; (4) sudden events or changes in social position to act as a catalyst; (5) intellectual leadership with readily understood goals.

55 See Carolyn Wiener, *The Politics of Alcoholism* (1981), p. 14.

56 See Stephen Hilgarten and C. Bosk, 'The Rise and Fall of Social Problems', *American Journal of Sociology*, vol. 94, no. 1, p. 53–78 for a discussion of 'competition' over social problem claims.

57 These three stages can be unpacked as *claims*, *grounds* and *warrants*. 'A *claim* is a demand that one party makes upon another' (Spector and Kitsuse, op. cit., p. 83) There is a distinct parallel between my argument and the statement that social problems are 'the activities or groups making assertions of grievances and claims with respect to some putative conditions' (ibid., p. 75).) The data or *grounds* lay out the facts or the major narrative for claims. It usually includes definitions, typifying examples, statistics, quasi-theories, myth debunking. The *warrant* acts as the bridge which connects them up. This is a pattern in 'rhetorical work' that has been outlined by Joel Best in his discussion of missing children, *Threatened Children: Rhetoric and Concern about Child Victims* (1990). In the earliest days, claims are often couched in extreme form with a vocabulary of moral certainty and rectitude, often righteous indignation. There is little evidence adduced, and the audience is seen as either converted or hostile. But later, the rhetorics become more sophisticated: the claims-makers adopt a 'rhetoric of rationality', make claims from inside, outline reasonable actions, see their audience as persuadable, (p. 42). On all this, see Charles Arthur Willard, *Argumentation and the Social Grounds of Knowledge* (1983). For arguments to be accepted, the audience must be in the same 'paradigm', must accept the broad framework in which the debate is set up.

58 See Joseph Gusfield's brilliant, and too neglected, *The Culture of Public Problems* (1981), p. 3.

59 Randy Shilts, *And the Band Played on* (1988), p. xxi.

60 See James Kinsella, *Covering the Plague: Aids and the American Media* (1989). For an early UK account see Antony Vass, *A Plague in Us* (1986), p. 70.

61 Quoted in Richard Meyer's intriguing account of 'Rock Hudson's Body' (1991), p. 274.

62 Ibid., p. 275.

63 On the important role of the Aids Quilt, see the discussion by Richard Mohr, *Gay Ideas* (1992).

9 THE SHIFTING SEXUAL STORIES OF LATE MODERNITY

1 'Social Change and the New Mentality', address at University of Missouri, December 1960. See Thomas Morrione, (ed.), 'Collected Papers of Herbert Blumer', unpublished. I am grateful to Dwight Fee for bringing this address to my notice.

2 George Herbert Mead, *Movements of Nineteenth-Century Thought*, cited in John Baldwin, *George Herbert Mead* (1986), p. 20.

3 See Arlene Stein's edited collection, *Sisters, Sexperts, Queers* (1993) for a good sampling.

4 See Bonnie Zimmerman, *The Safe Sea of Women* (1990), p. 210.
5 See, for instance, Jane Flax, *Thinking Fragments* (1990); Ken Gergen, *The Saturated Self* (1991); Antony Giddens, *The Consequences of Modernity* (1990) and *Modernity and Self-Identity* (1991) amongst many others, many cited elsewhere. I prefer the term 'late modern' to describe all this, suggesting some kind of continuity with modernist themes, especially those I have called the anti-foundationalist wing. For some the preferred term for all this change is 'postmodern', itself hardly new, and now hopefully peaked in fashionability. Everything, it seems, has had its postmodern expressions: architecture, advertising, art, literature, film and fashion are just the most apparent. Sex has certainly not escaped it: it was the North American sociologist Murray S. Davis who saw in 1983 that 'sexual ideology' was moving into a new phase, 'which I will call postmodern' (see his *Smut* (1983), p. 206). A 'postmodern sexuality', announced alongside the 'death of sexuality' has certainly been signposted in this Age of Aids and Body Panic. Part of postmodernism's mystique lies in its quest for the idiosyncratically incomprehensible, the hyperbolic excess, the breaking beyond of any accepted space, the reworking of everything familiar into surface fragments.

   For me there is something vaguely obscene about much postmodernism when it takes a philosophical turn: it assumes a mind-boggling rejection of everything as utterly known, tired and exhausted whilst some two-thirds of the world still look for a basic meal and a basic shelter. It rejects itself whilst elevating itself. It kills off metanarrative, only to claim a grander metanarrative than before. At the very least it can only be accepted if it is seen as a slender fragment that itself reaches back a long way into history, and which is today still dominated by classical and modernist ideas. For so many people living today have never even heard of the tired old ideas, let alone have the space to become exhausted with them. Postmodernism may thus well only be the cry of an old intellectual elite (often Marxists *manqué*) who have tried everything and gone into depair. And because of this, I have a worry about its use. So wherever possible I will use the term 'late modern society'.
6 On contemporary pragmatism, see: Giles Dunn, *Thinking Across the American Grain* (1992); Hans Joas, *Pragmatism and Social Theory* (1993); James Campbell, *The Community Reconstructs* (1993).
7 Social constructionist theories have a number of sources, but for me the tradition of symbolic interactionism has always been central.
8 See Carole S. Vance, 'Social Construction Theory' (1989), p. 13. Certainly, the earliest of contemporary constructionists – John Gagnon and William Simon – have both written in the postmodern mood. See John Gagnon and Stewart Michaels, 'Answer No Questions' (1989) and William Simon, 'Deviance as History' (1988). And there are some interactionists – most notably Norman Denzin – who clearly take this view. The term possibly entered the interactionist writing in an article by V. Kavolis, 'Postmodern Man' (1970), and has most recently been used by Michael Wood and Louis Zurcher, *The Development of a Postmodern Self* (1988). They use the term to refer to three current concerns: the '"new self" and "new culture" arguments which emphasise the novel and emergent character of these [social] changes', and the '"overdeveloped modernism" arguments which emphasise the continuity of change. The term postmodern self is used . . . to refer collectively to all three', p. 18.
9 Christopher Jencks, *What is Postmodernism?* (1987), p. 7.
10 For an important and classic statement of the history and power of autobiography, see Karl Weintraub, *The Value of the Individual: Self and Circumstance in Autobiography* (1978). A general sense of the 'changes in the making' are found in the discussions edited by James Olney: *Autobiography: Essays Theoretical and Critical* (1980). Feminism has played a major part in the revision of this so-called 'male form of writing': see, for instance, the critique by Mary Jo Maynes in *Interpreting Women's Lives* (1989), edited by the Personal Narratives Group, in which she ponders why

autobiography takes on a male form and the history of it always seeks as key examplars Augustine, Rousseau or Goethe. I am not happy with the potential gender essentialism of such comments, but they are helpful if taken as a way of fracturing the monolith of autobiographical style, cf. Rita Felski, *Beyond Feminist Aesthetics* (1989).

11 See David Jackson, *Unmasking Masculinity: A Critical Autobiography* (1990). A less explicit attempt would be John Stoltenberg's *Refusing to be a Man: Essays on Sex and Justice* (1989) which speaks personally of academic and political concerns. A review of many 'men's studies' books by Jeff Hearn, 'Reviewing Men and Masculinities' (1989), reveals a strong sensitivity to such issues. Of course, most male writing continues in the bold, brash and biographical model of the past.

12 This is abridged from Jackson's summary discussion. See Jackson, op. cit., Ch. 1 esp. pp. 5–12. The quote within a quote, on narrative time, is drawn from Paul Ricoeur, 'Narrative Time' (1981).

13 See Kenneth Clatterbaugh, *Contemporary Perspectives on Masculinity* (1990), who discusses all these types. There are, of course, many examples including the popular discussion of *Iron John* by Robert Bly (1990).

14 Nicholson Baker, Vox (1992).

15 For a discussion of sexual imagery on MTV see E. Ann Kaplan, *Rocking Around the Clock: Music Televison, the Consumer Culture and Postmodernism* (1987), esp. Ch. 5 which reviews a number of gender issues around MTV videos.

16 On visual literacy, see Gregory Ulmer, *Teletheory* (1989).

17 On the evolution of video and film as self-reflexive ethnography, see Gary J. Krug, 'Visual Ethnographies and the Postmodern Self' (1992).

18 See esp. Carolyn Ellis and Michael G. Flaherty (ed.), *Investigating Subjectivity: Research on Lived Experience* (1992); and the work of Laurel Richardson, Patricia Clough and many contemporary interactionists who are exploring ways of writing social science first-person narratives without resorting to the standard practices of such writing.

19 On virtual reality, and its much-discussed development, virtual sex, see Howard Rheingold, *Virtual Reality* (1991) and Barrie Sherman and Phil Judkins, *Glimpses of Heaven, Visions of Hell* (1992), esp. pp. 190 *et seq.*

20 The term originally derives from Herbert Gans and signifies cultural strata of tastes for all members of a society – from lower to upper.

21 See Ralph Lowenstein and John Merrill, *MacroMedia* (1990), Ch. 3.

22 See Arnie Kantrowitz, 'Friends Gone With the Wind', in John Preston, *Personal Dispatches* (1989), pp. 13–26.

23 On Nancy Ziegenmeyer, see Ziegenmeyer, *Taking Back My Life* (1993).

24 See the (in)famous biography which traces Foucault's intellectual life side by side with his personal life by James Miller: *The Passion of Michel Foucault* (1993).

25 Both in the film *In Bed With Madonna* and the book *Sex* (1992).

26 For disussion of some of these films, see Norman Denzin's *Images of Postmodern Society* (1991).

27 See Todd Gittlin, 'Postmodernism Defined at Last!' (1989). He outlines no less than six versions including 'the global shopping center', 'Marxist mass consumerism', 'science corrodes', 'couch potato and video fiction', 'the American grab bag'; 'the post-60s syndrome' and 'the yuppie factor'.

28 See Carol Rambo Ronai, 'The Reflexive Self Through Narrative', in Ellis and Flagherty, op. cit., pp. 104–5.

29 See Arnie Kantrowitz, op. cit. pp. 21–2. This is a most moving illustration of 'intertextuality' – especially given the heightened importance that the film *Gone With The Wind* has in many gay men's lives.

30 For Ihab Hassan, there are two main themes: indeterminancy – 'openess, pluralism, eclecticism, randomness, revolt, defamation ... deconstruction, disappearance,

discontinuity, detotalization, delegitmation etc.'; and immanences – 'the capacity of the mind to generalize itself in the world, to act upon both self and world, and so become more and more immediately, its own environment.' Hassan, 'The Culture of Post Modernism' (1985), p. 126.

31 This literature is now enormous, and enormously recursive: it often features amongst the best-selling non-fiction. See for example Christopher Lasch, *The Culture of Narcisissm* (1979) and *The Minimal Self* (1985), Robert Bellah *et al.*, *Habits of the Heart* (1985) and Gergen, op. cit.

32 See Douglas Kellner, 'Popular Culture and the Construction of Postmodern Identities' (1992), p. 173.

33 See Jean-François Lyotard, *The Postmodern Condition: A Report on Knowledge* (1979/86), introduction.

34 See Jencks, op. cit., p. 30, a phrase he uses after Lyotard.

35 'Panic Penis', in Arthur and Marilouise Kroker (eds), *Body Invaders* (1987), p. 181.

36 Ibid, p. 203.

37 See also Planet HOMO, and Queer LA leaflets in wide circulation in Los Angeles during 1992.

38 See Donna Haraway, *Simians, Cyborgs and Women* (1991).

39 E.g. Teresa de Lauretis (ed.), *Queer Theory* (1991); Eve Kasofsky Sedgwick, *Epistemology of the Closet* (1991) and Diane Fuss (ed.), *Inside/Out* (1991).

40 Cf. Karla Jay and Joanne Glasgow (eds), *Lesbian Texts and Contexts* (1990), p. 1. These stories have been taken furthest in the work of Eve Kasofsky Sedgwick. In *The Epistemology of the Closet*, op. cit., she has developed an account of feminist gay male theory, or anti-homophobic inquiry, in the most dazzling fashion. Seeing the homo/hetero distinction as a key classifier emerging in the late nineteenth century, she challenges all reading to become inscribed with an awareness of this distinction which can ultimately rupture it and move beyond it.

> What was new from the turn of the century was the world mapping by which every given person, just as he or she was necessarily assignable to a male or a female gender, was now considered necessarily assignable to homo- or a hetero-sexuality . . . [these] relations of the closet . . . have the potential for being peculiarly revealing, in fact, about speech acts more generally.
>
> (Sedgwick (1991), p. 2, p. 3)

10 INTIMATE CITIZENSHIP: THE POLITICS OF SEXUAL STORY TELLING

1 Jeffrey Weeks, *Sexuality and Its Discontents* (1985), p. 251.

2 Audre Lorde, 'Who Said It Was Simple?', (1970) reprinted in her *Chosen Poems: Old and New* (1982), p. 49

3 Norman K. Denzin, *Images of Postmodern Society* (1991), p. 5.

4 See, for example, Alasdair MacIntyre, *After Virtue* (1981).

5 See, for example, William E. Connolly, *Identity/Difference* (1991); Benjamin Barber, *An Aristocracy of Everyone* (1992).

6 See, for example, Anthony Giddens, *Modernity and Self-Identity* (1991) and Kenneth Gergen, *The Saturated Self* (1991).

7 Seyla Benhabib, *Situating The Self* (1992), p. 198.

8 From Robert Jay Lifton to Mick Mann, from Angela Davis to Donna Haraway there are accounts of this shift in power. Not all, however, are as optimistic as Giddens seems in his account.

9 See Iris Young, *Justice and the Politics of Difference* (1990), Ch. 2. As I am writing

this, in Spring 1992, the conflicts in Los Angeles over the police brutality towards Rodney King, the video-tape which clearly revealed this, and the 'not guilty' verdict of a jury of all-white members are all to the forefont, and make the above cautions even more important.

10 In the USA see James Davison Hunter, *Culture Wars* (1991).

11 Giddens, op. cit., p. 210–12, italics in original.

12 See Peter Clecak's *America's Quest for the Ideal Self* (1983), Ch. 11. Like me, Clecak is cautious in his assessment of progress, but for him it is never the less unmistakable – even 'remarkable'(cf. p. 181). His thesis has however been heavily attacked – notably by Christopher Lasch in *The Minimal Self* (1984), pp. 45 *et seq.*

13 See Gergen, op. cit., Ch. 9.

14 As I am finally finishing this book in November 1993, the trial concerning Jamie Bulger – murdered by two 10-year-olds – has precipitated the latest round of attacks on this falling morality. But I am struck that this cry has been around for a long time, and even whilst writing this book, the 'panic' of declining values has been raised publicly on a number of occasions.

15 There is a feminist postmodernism, of course (e.g. Flax, Harding, Haraway) and indeed a gay/lesbian postmodernism (e.g. Fuss, Butler, Sedgwick). But I am saying that the main strands of postmodern thought – Lyotard, Baudrillard, Jameson, many contributors to *Theory, Culture and Society* (TCS) – have been curiously silent on feminist and lesbian/gay concerns. All the more so for so-called 'radical' thinkers. Indeed, in the writings of some like Baudrillard there is more than a hint of anti-feminism, making them strange partners in radical thought.

16 Amongst these many developments are:

i   Iris Young on 'The politics of difference' (not assimilation);
ii   Laclau and Mouffe on a new politics of 'radical and plural democracy';
iii A new moral, romantic and/or humanist liberalism championed by some feminists such as Nancy Rosenblum, *Liberalism and the Moral Life* (1989) and Susan Moller Okin, *Justice, Gender and the Family* (1989);
iv   a new politics of 'communitarianism', of traditions and shared understandings in the work of Alasdair MacIntyre, Michael Waltzer and Charles Taylor;
v   a new politics of participation in the *Strong Democracy* of Benjamin Barber (1984);
vi   a new 'cultural politics', more concerned with deconstructing signs and fostering resistance, especially in the work of Stuart Hall, Cornell West, bell hooks and others;
vii a new 'life politics' found in the work of Anthony Giddens dealing with the problem of 'Who do I want to be?' in Giddens, op. cit., p. 216;
viii a new politics of citizenship being developed by Bryan Turner and others;
ix   a new politics of transgression found in the lineage from Nietzsche to Michel Foucault;
x   a new politics of social movements, based especially on identities in the work of Jeffrey Weeks, Diane Fuss, Alan Tourraine and others;
xi   a new politics of marginalisation (e.g. Cornell West);
xii a new politics of communications based on 'ideal speech situations' (Habermas, Benhabib, Fraser).

This listing is far from complete, and many of the proposals are contradictory. Yet whilst there are major disagreements, there is also a curious sense of a wider common project emerging. A reading of much of this literature helped me work out this schematic summary here.

17 See Cornell West, 'The New Cultural Politics of Difference' (1990).

18 On all this, see Benjamin Barber's idea of *Strong Democracy*, op. cit., and Alan Tourraine's *Return of the Actor* (1988).

19 Connolly, op. cit., p. 25.
20 It might be added that for symbolic interactionists there is little that is new in such themes.
21 See for instance Susan Faludi, *Backlash* (1991).
22 Michael Sandel, *Liberalism and the Limits of Justice* (1984), p. 6.
23 See T.H. Marshall, 'Citizenship and Social Class', in his *Sociology at the Crossroads* (1963).
24 For some key reviews of this field, see Geoff Andrews (ed.), *Citizenship* (1991); David Held, 'Citizenship and Autonomy' (1989); Michael Mann's 'Ruling Class Strategies and Citizenship' (1987); and Bryan S. Turner's 'Outline of a Theory of Citizenship' (1990).
25 I have found the work of Barber, op. cit., most illuminating on all this. As he writes:

> the two terms *participation* and *community* are aspects of one single mode of social being: citizenship. Community without participation first breeds unreflected consensus and uniformity, then nourishes coercive conformity, and finally engenders unitary collectivism of a kind that stifles citizenship and the autonomy on which political activity depends. Participation without community breeds mindless enterprise and undirected, competitive interest-mongering. Community without participation merely rationalizes collectivism, giving it an aura of legitimacy. Participation without community merely rationalizes individualism, giving it an aura of democracy.
>
> (p. 155)

26 Like, I suspect, many books, as I bring this one to a close I sense another in the making. This next listing opens up whole fields for analysis. A caution should also be made here. Sociology is not in itself a prescription, but it is an analysis with recursive consequences. In writing of intimate citizenship here I am being both sociological and recursive. By the former I mean that I am describing and analysing a new social form – a dialogue around sexuality that has been emerging in the past two decades. But in the act of labelling it as a new social form and identifying some of its features, however, I also bring it into the public sphere as a phenomenon perhaps not quite so clearly recognised and articulated previously. Hence, the very idea feeds back into a culture, and may itself become part of the process of political change.
27 See Stephanie Coontz, *The Way We Never Were* (1992), p. 73
28 Ibid., p. 2.
29 Ibid., p. 6
30 There is a fear over the male becoming superfluous. See David Popenhoe, co-chair of the Council of Families in America, *Disturbing the Nest* (1989).
31 The suggested 7 per cent figure is quoted from Judith Stacey, 'Backward Toward the Postmodern Family' (1991), p. 19. Adding a life-cycle perspective to her statement would increase this number, but as an image for society's households at any one point of time, it is a useful corrective to the ideology of 'familism'. In the USA the number of single women giving birth in 1989 was 1.1 million. Single Mothers by Choice has over 1,600 members in a dozen chapters. Twenty-four per cent of children lived with only one parent. Nearly 90 per cent of black children will spend part of their childhood with a single parent. Some 50 per cent of all new marriages end in divorce. In the UK in 1990, 28 per cent of all births were outside marriage. And so the details could be multiplied of non-traditional family forms everywhere.
32 Stacey, op. cit., p. 33.
33 On all this, see the section on families in Ken Plummer (ed.), *Modern Homosexualities* (1992), Part 4.
34 Weston, *Families We Choose* (1991), esp. p. 28.
35 Robin Warshaw, *I Never Called it Rape* (1988), p. 68. This is what has come to be

recognised as post-traumatic stress disorder or PSTD. See also E. Sue Blume, *Secret Survivors* (1990), p. 78; and Judith Lewis Herman, *Trauma and Recovery* (1992).

36 See, for instance, the TV programme/video by Bill Moyers: *A Gathering of Men*, which dramatically depicts this emotional story telling. It is, of course, based on the best-selling texts of Robert Bly's *Iron John* (1990). For commentary and analysis see 'Pro-feminist men respond to the men's movement', *Masculinities* (1993).

37 On anger, see Larry Kramer, *Reports from the Holocaust* (1990); on fear, see Andrew Holleran's 'The Fear', in John Preston (eds), *Personal Dispatches* (1989), p. 38–46;

38 e.g. Theodore Kemper (ed.), *Research Agendas in the Sociology of Emotions* (1990).

39 Carole S. Vance, 'The Pleasures of Looking' (1990).

40 See Linda Williams, *Hard Core* (1989).

41 See Andrea Dworkin, *Pornography* (1981).

42 George Gilder, *Sexual Suicide* (1973), p. 27.

43 See especially the writings of the spiritual wings of feminism (Mary Daly *et al.*), some of the eco-feminists, and much 'cultural feminism', e.g. Janice Raymond's *A Passion for Friends* (1986).

44 Judith Butler, *Gender Trouble* (1990): 33.

45 Okin, op. cit., p. 171.

46 See Barbara Ehrenreich *et al.*, *Re-Making Love* (1986).

47 There is a substantial literature on all this, and the shifts in sexuality in the wake of Aids. See, for example, Peter Davis *et al.*, *Gay Men, Safe Sex and Aids* (1993).

48 For a sampling see Gerald Greene and Caroline Greene, *S-M: The Last Taboo* (1974); Michael Grumley, *Hard Corps* (1977); Bert Herrman, *TRUST/The Handbook* (1991); Geoff Mains, *Urban Aboriginals* (1984); SAMOIS, *Coming to Power* (1981); Mark Thompson (ed.), *Leatherfolk* (1991); Larry Townsend, *The Leatherman's Handbook II* (1989).

49 Thompson, op. cit., p. xvii.

50 See especially Susie Bright, *Susie Sexpert's Lesbian Sex World* (1990) and *Susie Bright's Sexual Reality* (1992), as well as Pat Califia's *Macho Sluts* (1988) and Joan Nestle's *A Restricted Country* (1988).

51 See Ann Ferguson, *Blood at the Root* (1989).

52 Richard Mohr, *Gays/Justice* (1988).

53 See Peter Tatchell, in Plummer, op. cit. (1992).

54 Giddens, op. cit., p. 70.

55 See the best-seller *Backlash*, op. cit. by Susan Faludi on this.

56 See Hunter, op. cit., p. 44, 45.

57 Secularists are more likely to be part of the latter group, but not exclusively so (witness some of the new conservatives and neo-conservatives, who are not religious *per se* but who hold to other traditions of authority). For Hunter it is a cultural war, not a straightforward political one. What is important for him is that new alliances are being made across former loyalties.

58 Giddens, op. cit. p. 231.

59 Bruce Ackerman, 'Why Dialogue?' (1989), pp. 16–17.

60 Quoted from the novel *The Lost Language of Cranes* by David Leavitt (1986), p. 173. Here a gay son is revealing his homosexuality to his mother who does not wish to hear in front of a closeted gay father!

61 See Benhabib (1986), p. 298, cited in Dryzack *Discursive Democracy* (1990). See also Benhabib *Situating the Self* (1992).

62 Ferguson, op. cit. is another major attempt to build a new ethics/morality/politics for the future. Providing one of the most sustained analyses, she makes many important distinctions – for example, between short-term, transitional strategies and goals, and longer-term ones; and she finds a place for both separatist and assimilationist politics though her own position clearly favours a coalition. Her clear commitment to socialism

means that her blueprint takes in a much wider range of issues than some other similar blueprints. She wants to champion a feminist morality of 'restricted diversity', and suggests that a key question for framing such a morality is: 'How can we both support a consensual sexual ethics that promotes sexual experimentation for pleasure, and yet take account of the social domination structured into certain sorts of sexual practices in capitalist patriarchy?' For her, a threefold distinction needs to be made between forbidden, basic and risky sex. Some sexual practices are simply to be seen as beyond the pale: they are forbidden and nearly all feminists would agree that they should be outlawed by law (1989; p. 210). For another feminist view of the future see Carol Anne Douglas, *Love and Politics: Radical Feminist and Lesbian Theories* (1990) which provides a wide listing of the possible goals of a radical feminist world. She writes that it will involve:

> the abolition of distinctions between men and women, the end of characterization of people by gender; the end of all forms of male supremacy, class oppression and race oppression; complete integration of women and men; economic and/or political autonomy for women; the establishment of separate nations or nations-within-nations for women; mixed societies ruled by women; and no doubt others.
>
> (p. 211)

63 See Faye Ginsburg, *Contested Lives* (1989b), p. 114.
64 See Ginsburg, op. cit., p. 126.
65 But see especially Kristin Luker, *Abortion and the Politics of Motherhood* (1984); Rosalind Petchesky, *Abortion and Woman's Choice* (1984).
66 See Ginsburg, op. cit. (1989), p. 193.
67 See Jane Flax, *Thinking Fragments* (1990), p. 28.
68 See Richard Rorty, *Contingency, Irony and Solidarity* (1989), p. xvi.
69 See Steven Seidman, *Embattled Eros* (1992), p. 191, Ch. 5.
70 See Weeks, op. cit. But see also *Against Nature* (1991).
71 William James, *'The Will to Believe' and Other Popular Essays* (1956), p. 30.

11 EPILOGUE: BEYOND STORIES? THE PRAGMATICS OF STORY TELLING

1 Cited in Bonnie Zimmerman's *The Safe Sea of Women* (1990), p. 26.
2 Personal Narratives Group, *Interpreting Women's Lives* (1989), p. 261.
3 Delany, pp. 196–7, quoted in Bergman, *Gaiety Transfigured* (1991), p. 7. Bergman himself has a very interesting discussion of this process and his own reactions to *Psychopathia Sexualis* – which he found muddled but helpful. These great volumes have had such an impact on so many twentieth-century lives – in mixed ways. But by the end of the twentieth century, they had largely been replaced with more upbeat stories, as much of this book has suggested.
4 Andrew Ross, 'The Private Parts of Justice' (1992), p. 47.
5 For the original transcript, see *Black Scholar*, vol. 22, nos 1 and 2 (1991/2).
6 For a general account, see Timothy Phelps and Helen Winternitz, *Capitol Games: The Inside Story of Clarence Thomas, Anita Hill and a Supreme Court Nomination* (1992).
7 David Brock, *The Real Anita Hill: The Untold Story* (1993). This was published in the UK a little later, and partially serialised in the Sunday Times.
8 See their article in the New Yorker, 'The Surreal Anita Hill', 17 May 17 1993 (and their forthcoming book, *Strange Justices: the Selling of Clarence Thomas*).
9 See *New Yorker*, 14 June 1993 for the *New Yorker* defence, and the *American Spectator*, August 1993, for Brock's rebuttal.
10 See his article in Robert Chrisman and Robert L. Allen, *Court of Appeal: The Black*

Community Speaks out on the Racial and Sexual Politics of Thomas vs Hill (1992).

11 For a valuable selection of essays which analyse the metaphorical impact of the Hill–Thomas affair, see Toni Morrison (ed.), *Race-ing Justice, En-gendering Power* (1992).

12 For an excellent analysis of the rhetoric of science, see J. Gusfield, 'The Literary Rhetoric of Science' (1976). See also the very valuable discussions on the writing of social science by Paul Atkinson, *The Ethnographic Imagination* (1990) and Laurel Richardson, *Writing Strategies* (1990a).

13 Donald P. Spence, *Narrative Truth and Historical Truth* (1982).

14 See Dan McAdams, *Power, Intimacy and the Life Story* (1985), pp. 18, 29.

15 See Hall Carpenter Archives, *Inventing Ourselves: Lesbian Life Stories* (1989b), pp. 1, 2.

16 See Robin Norwood, *Robin Norwood Answers Letters from Women Who Love Too Much* (1988), pp. 284, 286, 287.

17 For a valuable discussion which amplifies these points on identity formation, see Roy Baumeister, *Identity: Cultural Change and the Struggle for Self* (1986); and for a discussion on the constructions of the past, see Fred Davis: *Yearning for Yesterday* (1979).

18 Roy Schafer also remarks, though from an analytic perspective, on the importance of stories in self-construction: 'We are', he says,

> forever telling stories about ourselves. In telling these self-stories to others we may . . . be said to be performing straightforward narrative actions. In saying that we also tell them to ourselves, however, we are enclosing one story within another. This is the story that there is a self to tell something to, a someone else serving as audience who is oneself or one's self.
>
> (p. 31 in W. Mitchell (ed.), *On Narrative* (1980)

19 This idea has been discussed by Anthony Giddens in his *Modernity and Self-Identity* (1990), but he is only the most recent in a long line of social commentators to sense this shift in identity work.

20 See Arthur Kleinman's wonderful account of these questions and the process of narrative in illness in his *The Illness Narratives: Suffering, Healing and the Human Condition* (1988), p. 29.

21 David Payne's book *Coping With Failure* (1990) is a powerful account of narrative in therapy. Although Payne is concerned with wider issues of rhetoric, he suggests a series of recurrent underlying strategies or *topois* ('the place one goes to discover the available ideas that are likely to be persuasive on a given topic', p. 44) concerned with consolation and compensation.

22 See Judith Lewis Herman's important statement on *Trauma and Recovery* (1992). Story and community play very central roles in her account.

23 See Wendy Kaminer, *I'm Dysfunctional, You're Dysfunctional* (1992), pp. 164–5. She comments

> Self-help literature tends to ensure that the selves readers find or make are standardized and socially congenial. The potentially disruptive quest for individual identity is collectivized. . . . What I miss most in the self-help tradition is a spirit of improvization. For all their talk about intuition, 'feeling realities', experts rely on readers' willingness to surrender not just rationality but intuition, by which they might lead themselves to unexpected places.

24 See James Bennett, *Oral History and Delinquency* (1981), pp. 256–60, for a brief discussion of the 'functions' of stories in attracting audiences.

25 See Gabrielle Brown, *The New Celibacy: A Journey to Love, Intimacy, and Good Health in a New Age* (1989).

26 Robert Davidoff, 'Memorial Day 1988', in John Preston (ed.), *Personal Dispatches* (1989), pp. 176–8.

27 Robert Park's fine phrase.
28 Christine Jorgensen, *A Personal Autobiography* (1967), p. xvi.
29 Patricia Ruppelt, 'From the Outside In', in Ines Rieder and Patricia Ruppelt, *Matters of Life and Death: Women Speak About AIDS* (1989), pp. v, vii.
30 Marc E. Burke, *Coming Out of the Blue* (1993). p. x.
31 Frédérique Delacoste and Priscilla Alexander (eds), *Sex Work* (1987), pp. 16, 18.
32 Gayle Rubin – a major feminist libertarian – has commented that 'since sexuality in Western cultures is so mystified, the wars over it are often fought at oblique angles, aimed at phony targets, conducted with misplaced passions, and are highly intensely symbolic' ('Thinking Sex' (1984), p. 297). There is nothing new about this. Many different societies have written sexual stories, made sex a powerful symbol, in order to wage moral wars.
33 See Randolph Trombach, *Journal of Social History*, vol. II, pp. 1–33.
34 See J. Hillis Miller, *On Narrative* (1990), p. 70.
35 Ibid., p. 71. See Charlene Haddock Seigfried's *William James's Radical Reconstruction of Philosophy* (1990).
36 On all this, the literature is vast. But see Nachman Ben-Yehuda, *Deviance and Moral Boundaries* (1985), Mary Douglas, *Purity and Danger* (1966) and Robert Scott, 'A Proposal Framework for Analysing Deviance as a Property of Social Order'(1972).
37 See Ken Plummer, 'Organizing AIDS' (1988), p. 45. There is a very substantial amount of writing around this theme, but perhaps most notable examples are: Antony A. Vass, *AIDS: A Plague in Us* (1986); Douglas Crimp (ed.) *AIDS: Cultural Analysis/Cultural Activism* (1987); Erica Carter and Simon Watney (eds) *Taking Liberties* (1989); Douglas Crimp (ed.), *Aids Demo Graphics* (1990); and Cindy Patton, *Inventing AIDS* (1990).
38 Faye Ginsberg, *Contested Lives* (1989b), p. 143.

Bibliography

Abbott, Phillip (1987) *Seeking Many Inventions*, Knoxville: University of Tennessee Press.
Abelove, Henry, Barale, Michèle Aina and Halperin, David M. (eds) (1993) *Lesbian and Gay Studies Reader*, London: Routledge.
Abrams, Phillip (1982) *Historical Sociology*, London: Open Books.
Ackerman, Bruce (1989) 'Why Dialogue?', *Journal of Philosophy*, 86, pp. 5–22.
Ackerman, Diane (1990) *A Natural History of the Senses*, New York: Random House.
Adam, Barry (1987) *The Rise of a Lesbian and Gay Movement*, Boston: Twayne Publishers.
Allen, Robert C. (ed.) (1987) *Channels of Discourse*, Chapel Hill: University of North Carolina Press.
Allport, Gordon (1942) *The Use of Personal Documents in Psychological Science*, New York: Social Science Research Council.
Allport, Gordon (1961) *Pattern and Growth in Personality*, New York: Holt, Rhinehart & Winston.
Altman, Dennis (1971) *Homosexual: Oppression and Liberation*, New York: Outerbridge & Dienstfrey (reprinted in 1993).
Altman, Dennis (1982) *The Homosexualization of America and the Americanization of the Homosexual*, Boston: Beacon Press.
Altman, Dennis (1986) *Aids and the New Puritanism*, London: Pluto.
Anderson, Benedict (1983) *Imagined Communities*, London: Verso.
Andrews, Geoff (ed.) (1991) *Citizenship*, London: Lawrence & Wishart.
Ang, I. (1991) *Desperately Seeking the Audience*, London: Routledge.
Anger, Kenneth (1975) *Hollywood Babylon*, New York: Dell.
Armstrong, Louise (1976) *Kiss Daddy Goodnight*, New York: Pocket Books.
Armstrong, Louise (1990) 'Making an Issue out of Incest', in Dorchen Leidholdt and Janice Raymond (eds), *The Sexual Liberals and the Attack on Feminism*, Oxford: Pergamon Press, pp. 43–55.
Arnold, June (1970) 'Consciousness Raising', in *Women's Liberation: Blueprints for the Future*, compiled by Sookie Stambler, New York: Ace Books.
Atkinson, Paul (1990) *The Ethnographic Imagination: Textual Constructions of Reality*, London: Routledge.
Baker, Nicholson (1992) *Vox*, London: Granta Books.
Baldwin, John (1986) *George Herbert Mead*, London: Sage.
Banks, Olive (1981) *Faces of Feminism*, Oxford: Martin Robertson.
Barbach, Lonnie (1984) *Pleasures: Women Write Erotica*, New York: Doubleday.
Barber, Benjamin R. (1984) *Strong Democracy: Participatory Politics for a New Age*, Berkeley: University of California Press.
Barber, Benjamin (1992) *An Aristocracy of Everyone*, New York: Oxford University Press.
Barry, Kathleen (1979) *Female Sexual Slavery*, New York: Avon Books.

Bart, Pauline (1979) 'Rape as a Paradigm of Sexism in Society', *Women's Studies International Quarterly*, vol. 2, no. 3, pp. 347–57.

Barthes, Roland (1977) 'The Death of the Author', in *Image-music-text*, Glasgow: Fontana/Collins.

Bass, Ellen and Thornton, Louise (eds) (1983) *I Never Told Anyone: Writings by Women Survivors of Child Sexual Abuse*, New York: Harper & Row.

Baudrillard, Jean (1983) *In the Shadows of the Silent Majorities*, New York: Semiotext(e).

Baudrillard, Jean (1987a) *Forget Foucault*, New York: Semiotext(e).

Baudrillard, Jean (1987b) 'The Year 2000 has Already Happened', in A. and M. Kroker (eds), *Body Invaders*, Montreal: New World Perspectives.

Baumeister, Roy F. (1986) *Identity: Cultural Change and the Struggle for Self*, New York: Oxford University Press.

Bayer, Ronald (1981) *Homosexuality and American Psychiatry: The Politics of Diagnosis*, New York: Basic Books.

Beam, Joseph (ed.) (1986) *In The Life: A Black Gay Anthology*, Boston: Alyson.

Beam, Joseph (ed.) (1991) *Brother to Brother: New Writings by Black Gay Men*, Essex Hemphill, Boston: Alyson.

Beattie, Melody (1987) *Codependent No More: How to Stop Controlling Others and Start Caring for Yourself*, New York: Harper Hazelden.

Beck, Evelyn (ed.) (1989) *Nice Jewish Girls: A Lesbian Anthology*, New York: Beacon Press.

Beck, Ulrich (1992) *Risk Society: Towards a New Modernity*, London: Sage.

Becker, Howards S. (1967) 'Whose Side Are We On?', *Social Problems*, 14 (Winter), pp. 239–47.

Becker, Howard S. (1986) *Doing Things Together*, Chicago: Aldine.

Belenky, Mary Field, *et al.* (1986) *Women's Ways of Knowing: The Development of Self, Voice and Mind*, New York: Basic Books/HarperCollins.

Bell, Alan P. and Hall, Calvin S. (1971) *The Personality of a Child Molester: An Analysis of Dreams*, Chicago: Aldine.

Bellah, Robert N., Madsen, Richard, Sullivan, William M., Swidler, Ann and Tipton, Steven M. (1985) *Habits of the Heart: Individualism and Commitment in American Life*, New York: Harper & Row.

Benedict, Helen (1992) *Virgin or Vamp: How the Press Covers Sex Crimes*, Oxford: Oxford University Press.

Beneke, Timothy (1982) *Men on Rape: What They Have to Say About Sexual Violence*, New York: St Martin's Press.

Benhabib, Seyla (1992) *Situating the Self: Gender, Community and Postmodernism in Contemporary Ethics*, Oxford: Polity Press.

Benjamin, Walter (1970) 'The Storyteller', in Hannah Arendt (ed.) *Illuminations*, London: Jonathan Cape.

Bennett, James (1981) *Oral History and Delinquency: The Rhetoric of Criminology*, London: University of Chicago Press.

Benstock, Sarah (1988) *The Private Self: Theory and Practice of Women's Autobiographical Writings*, London: Routledge.

Ben-Yehuda, Nachman (1985) *Deviance and Moral Boundaries*, Chicago: University of Chicago Press.

Berger, Peter and Berger, Brigitte (1984) *The War over the Family: Capturing the Middle Ground*, New York: Anchor Books.

Berger, Peter and Luckmann, Thomas (1966) *The Social Construction of Reality*, Middlesex: Allen Lane.

Bergman, David (1991) *Gaiety Transfigured: Gay Self-Representation in American Literature*, London: University of Wisconsin Press.

Bertaux, Daniel (ed.) (1981) *Biography and Society*, London: Sage.

Bertaux, Daniel, and Kohli, M. (1984) 'The Life Story Approach: A Continental View', *Annual Review of Sociology*, 10, pp. 215–37.

Bérube, Alan (1991) *Coming Out Under Fire: The History of Gay Men and Women in World War Two*, New York: Plume.

Best, Joel (ed.) (1989) *Images of Issues*, New York: Aldine de Gruyter.

Best, Joel (1990) *Threatened Children: Rhetoric and Concern about Child Victims*, Chicago: University of Chicago Press.

Bhavani, Kum Kum (1992) 'Talking Racism and the Editing of Women's Studies', in Diane Richardson (ed.) *Introducing Women's Studies*, London: Macmillan.

Billig, Michael (1987) *Arguing and Thinking: A Rhetorical Approach to Social Psychology*, Cambridge: Cambridge University Press.

Billings, David. B. and Urban, T. (1982) 'The Socio-Medical Construction of Transexualism: An Interpretation and Critique', *Social Problems*, vol. 29, no. 3 (February), pp. 266–82.

Bird, S. Elizabeth (1992) *For Enquiring Minds: A Cultural Study of Supermarket Tabloids*, Knoxville: University of Tennessee Press.

Blachford, Gregg (1981) 'Male Dominance and the Gay World', in Ken Plummer (ed.), *The Making of the Modern Homosexual*, London: Hutchinson.

Blume, E. Sue (1990) *Secret Survivors: Uncovering Incest and its Aftereffects in Women*, New York: Ballantine.

Blumer, Herbert (1960) 'Social Change and the New Mentality', unpublished manuscript, University of Minnesota, December.

Blumer, Herbert (1969) *Symbolic Interactionism: Perspective and Method*, London: University of California Press.

Blumer, Herbert (1981) 'George Herbert Mead', in B. Rhea (ed.), *The Future of the Sociological Classics*, London: Allen & Unwin, pp. 136–69.

Bly, Robert (1990) *Iron John: A Book About Men*, New York: Addison Wesley.

Bobo, J. (1988) 'The Color Purple: Black Women as Cultural Readers', in E. Pribram (ed.), *Female Spectators*, London: Verso.

Bogdan, Robert (ed.) (1974) *Being Different: The Autobiography of Jane Fry*, London: Wiley.

Bok, Sissela (1983) *Secrets: On the Ethics of Concealment and Revelation*, New York: Random House.

Bouchier, David (1983) *The Feminist Challenge*, London: Macmillan.

Bourdieu, Pierre (1984) *Distinction: A Social Critique of the Judgement of Taste*, London: Routledge.

Bradbury, Malcolm (1988) *The Modern World*, London: Secker & Warburg/Channel 4.

Bradshaw, John (1988) *Bradshaw on The Family*, Deerfield Beach, Florida: Health Communications, Inc.

Bray, Alan (1982) *Homosexuality in Renaissance England*, London: Gay Men's Press.

Bright, Susie (1990) *Susie Sexpert's Lesbian Sex World*, San Francisco: Cleis Press.

Bright, Susie (1992) *Susie Bright's Sexual Reality: A Virtual Sex World Reader*, San Francisco: Cleis Press.

Brisset, Dennis and Edgley, Charles (eds) (1990) *Life as Theatre: A Dramaturgical Sourcebook*, New York: Aldine De Gruyter.

Brock, David (1993) *The Real Anita Hill: The Untold Story*, New York: Free Press.

Brongersma, Edward (1986) *Loving Boys*, vols 1 and 2, Elmhurst, New York: Global Academic Publishing.

Bronski, Michael (1984) *Culture Clash: The Making of Gay Sensibility*, Boston: South End Press.

Brown, Gabrielle (1989) *The New Celibacy: A Journey to Love, Intimacy and Good Health in the New Age*, New York: McGraw Hill

Brown, Joe (ed.) (1992) *A Promise to Remember: Names Project Book of Letters*, New York: Avon.

Brown, Richard (1987) *Society as Text: Essays on Rhetoric, Reason and Reality*, London: University of Chicago Press.

Brown, Rita Mae (1973) *Rubyfruit Jungle*, Plainfield, Vt: Daughters, Inc. (reprinted in 1977 and published by Bantam Books).

Brownmiller, Susan (1975) *Against Our Will: Men, Women and Rape*, New York: Simon & Schuster.

Bruner, Jerome (1986) *Actual Minds, Possible Worlds*, London: Harvard University Press.

Bruner, Jerome (1987) 'Life as Narrative', *Social Research*, vol. 54, no. 1, pp. 11–32.

Bullough, Vern (1976) *Sexual Variance in Society and History*, Chicago: University of Chicago Press.

Burger, John R. (1993) *One-Handed Histories: Popular Memory and the Eroto-Politics of Gay Male Video Pornography*, New York: Haworth Press.

Burgess, Ann Wolbert (1984) *Child Pornography and Sex Rings*, Lexington, Mass.: DC Heath/Lexington Books.

Burgess, Ann Wolbert and Holmstrom, Lynda Lyle (1979) *Rape: Crisis and Recovery*, Bowie, Maryland: Prentice-Hall.

Burke, Marc. E. (1993) *Coming Out of the Blue*, London: Cassell.

Burt, Martha R. (1991) 'Rape Myths and Acquaintance Rape', in Andrew Parrott and Laurie Bechofer (eds), *Acquaintance Rape: The Hidden Crime*, London: Wiley, pp. 26–40.

Butler, Judith (1990) *Gender Trouble*, London: Routledge.

Cain, Roy (1991) 'Disclosure and Secrecy Among Gay Men in the United States and Canada: A Shift in Views', *Journal of the History of Sexuality*, vol. 2, no. 1 (1991), pp. 25–45.

Califia, Pat (1988) *Macho Sluts*, Boston: Alyson.

Campbell, James (1992) *The Community Reconstructs*, Urbana: University of Illinois Press.

Caputi, Jane (1988) *The Age of Sex Crime*, London: Women's Press.

Carbaugh, Donal (1988) *Talking American: Cultural Discourses on Donahue*, New Jersey: Ablex Publishing.

Carnes, Patrick (1983) *The Sexual Addiction*, Minneapolis: CompCare (revised and reprinted in 1983 as *Out of the Shadows*, Minneapolis: CompCare).

Carnes, Patrick (1989) *Contrary to Love: Helping the Sexual Addict*, Minneapolis: CompCare.

Carter, Erica and Watney, Simon (eds) (1989) *Taking Liberties: Aids and Cultural Politics*, London: Serpent's Tail.

Chapple, Steve and Talbot, D. (1990) *Burning Desires: Sex In America*, New York: Signet.

Cherry, Kittredge (1991) *Hide and Speak: How to Free Ourselves from our Secrets*, San Francisco: Harper.

Chin-Yeung, Li (1986) *Sexual Experience of Adults with Children: An Analysis of Personal Accounts*, Ph.D. thesis, Institute of Criminology, University of Cambridge.

Clarke, Anna (1987) *Women's Silence, Men's Violence: Sexual Assault in England 1770–1845*, London: Pandora.

Classen, Constance (1993) *Worlds of Sense: Exploring the Senses in History and Across Culture*, London: Routledge.

Clatterbaugh, Kenneth (1990) *Contemporary Perspectives on Masculinity: Men, Women and Politics in Modern Society*, Oxford: Westview Press.

Clatterbaugh, Kenneth (1993) 'Mythopoetic Foundations of New Age Patriarchy', *Maculinities*, vol. 1, nos 3 and 4, pp. 2–12.

Clecak, Peter (1983) *America's Quest for the Ideal Self: Dissent and Fulfillment in the 60's and 70's*, Oxford: Oxford University Press.

Clifford, J. and Marcus, G. (eds) (1986) *Writing Culture*, Berkeley: University of California Press.

Clough, Patricia Ticineto (1992) *The End (s) of Ethnography*, London: Sage.

Collins, Patricia Hill (1990) *Black Feminist Thought: Knowledge, Consciousness and the*

Politics of Empowerment, London: Unwin Hyman.

Collins, Randall (1983), 'Micromethods as a Basis for Macrosociology', *Urban Life*, vol. 12, no. 2 (July), pp. 184–202, reprinted in Ken Plummer (ed.) (1991) *Symbolic Interactionism*, vol. 2, Aldershot: Edward Elgar Reference, p. 431.

Comolli, Jean-Louis (1980) 'Machines of the Visible', in T. de Lauretis and S. Heath (eds), *The Cinematic Apparatus*, New York: St Martin's Press.

Comstock, Gary David (1992) *Violence Against Lesbians and Gay Men*, New York: Columbia University Press.

Connell, R.W. (1987) *Gender and Power*, Oxford: Polity Press.

Connerton, Paul (1989) *How Societies Remember*, Cambridge: Cambridge University Press.

Connolly, William E. (1984) 'The Politics of Discourse', in Michael Shapiro (ed.), *Language and Politics*, New York: New York University Press.

Connolly, William E. (1991) *Identity/Difference: Democratic Negotiations of Political Paradox*, Ithaca: Cornell University Press.

Connor, Steven (1989) *Postmodernist Culture*, Oxford: Blackwell.

Conrad, Peter and Schneider, Joseph, W. (1980) *Deviance and Medicalization: From Badness to Sickness*, London: C.V. Mosby.

Coontz, Stephanie (1992) *The Way We Never Were: American Families and the Nostalgia Trip*, New York: Basic Books.

Cornwall, Anita (1983) *Black Lesbian in White American*, Talahasee: Naiad.

Cory, Donald Webster (1951) *The Homosexual in America*, New York: Greenberg.

Couch, Carl and Chen, Shing-Ling (1988) 'Orality, Literacy and Social Structure', in David Maines and Carl Couch (eds), *Communication and Social Structure*, Springfield, Illinois: Charles C. Thomas.

Coveney, Lal, Jackson, Margaret, Jeffreys, Sheila, Kay, Leslie and Mahony, Pat (1984) *The Sexuality Papers: Male Sexuality and the Social Control of Women*, London: Hutchinson.

Cox, M. and Theilgaard, A. (1987) *Mutative Metaphors in Psychotherapy*, London: Tavistock.

Craib, Ian (1994) *The Importance of Disappointment*, London: Routledge.

Crawford, David (1991) *Easing the Ache: Gay Men Recovering from Compulsive Behaviour*, New York: Dutton.

Crimp, Douglas (ed.) (1987) 'Aids: Cultural Analysis/Cultural Activism', *October*, 43, (Winter).

Crimp, Douglas and Rolston, Adam (1990) *Aids Demo Graphics*, Seattle: Bay Press.

Cruikshank, Margaret (ed.) (1982) *Lesbian Studies*, Old Westbury, NY: Feminist Press.

Cruikshank, Margaret (1992) *The Gay and Lesbian Liberation Movement*, London: Routledge.

Curtis, Wayne (ed.) (1988) *Revelations: A Collection of Gay Male Coming Out Stories*, Boston: Alyson.

Daniell, Rosemary (1984) *Sleeping with Soldiers: In Search of the Macho Man*, New York: Warner Books.

Davidoff, Leonore (1979), 'Class and Gender in Victorian England: The Diaries of Arthur J. Munby and Hannah Cullwick', *Feminist Studies*, 5 (Spring).

Davidson, Joy (1988) *The Soap Opera Syndrome*, New York: Berkeley Books.

Davies, Christie (1975) *Permissive Britain: Social Change in the Sixties and Seventies*, London: Pitman.

Davis, Fred (1973) 'The Martian and the Convert: Ontological Polarities in Social Research', *Urban Life and Culture*, vol. 2, no. 3 (October), pp. 333–43.

Davis, Fred (1979) *Yearning for Yesterday: A Sociology of Nostalgia*, New York: Macmillan.

Davis, Kenneth C. (1984) *Two-Bit Culture: The Paperbacking of America*, Boston: Houghton Mifflin.

Davis, Murray S. (1983) *Smut: Erotic Reality, Obscene Ideology*, Chicago: University of Chicago Press.

Davis, Peter, Hickson, Ford, Weatherburn, Peter and Hunt, Andrew J. (1993) *Sex, Gay Men and AIDS*, London: Falmer Press.

de Beauvoir, Simone (1972) *The Second Sex*, Harmondsworth, Penguin. Originally published in 1949.

De Certeau, Michel (1984) *The Practice of Everyday Life*, Berkeley, University of California Press.

Delacoste, Frederique and Alexander, Priscilla (eds) (1987) *Sex Work: Writings by Women in the Sex Industry*, San Francisco: Cleis Press.

Delaney, Samuel R. and Beam, Joseph (1986) 'Samuel R. Delany: The Possibility of Possibilities', in Joseph Beam (ed.) *In the Life: A Black Gay Anthology*, Boston: Alyson.

De Lauretis, Terresa (ed.) (1991) 'Queer Theory', *Differences*, vol. 3, no. 2.

D'Emilio, John (1983) *Sexual Politics, Sexual Communities: The Making of a Homosexual Minority in the United States 1940–1970*, Chicago: University of Chicago Press.

D'Emilio, John (1984) 'Capitalism and Gay Identity', in Anne Snitow, Christine Stansell and Sharon Thompson, *Powers of Desire*, London: Virago.

D'Emilio, John (1992) *Making Trouble: Essays on Gay History, Politics and the University*, London: Routledge.

D'Emilio, John and Freedman, Estelle (1988) *Intimate Matters*, New York: Harper & Row.

Denzin, Norman K. (1988) 'Blue Velvet: Postmodern Contradictions', *Theory, Culture and Society*, vol. 5, pp. 461–73.

Denzin, Norman K. (1989a) *The Research Act*, 3rd edition, New Jersey: Prentice-Hall.

Denzin, Norman K. (ed.) (1989b) *Studies in Symbolic Interaction*, volume 10 'Critique and Renewal in Symbolic Interaction' Connecticut: JAI Press.

Denzin, Norman K. (1989c) *Interpretive Biography*, London: Sage.

Denzin, Norman K. (1990a) 'Harold and Agnes: A Feminist Narrative Undoing', *Sociological Theory*, vol. 8, no. 2, pp. 198–216.

Denzin, Norman K. (1990b) 'The Spaces of Postmodernism: Reading Plummer on Blumer', *Symbolic Interaction*, vol. 13 (Fall).

Denzin, Norman K. (1991) *Images of Postmodern Society: Social Theory and Contemporary Cinema*, London: Sage.

Denzin, Norman K. (1992) *Symbolic Interactionism and Cultural Studies*, Oxford: Blackwell.

Doty, Alexander (1993) *Making Things Perfectly Queer: Interpreting Mass Culture*, Minneapolis: University of Minnesota Press.

Douglas, Carol Anne (1990) *Love and Politics: Radical Feminist and Lesbian Theories*, San Francisco: Ism Press.

Douglas, Mary (1966) *Purity and Danger: An Analysis of Concepts of Pollution and Taboo*, London: Routledge.

Dowling, Colette (1981) *The Cinderella Complex*, New York: Pocket Books.

Dryzek, John S. (1990) *Discursive Democracy*, Cambridge: Cambridge University Press.

Duberman, Martin (1993) *Stonewall*, New York: Dutton.

Duberman, Martin, Vicinus, Martha and Chauncey, George Jr (1989) *Hidden From History: Reclaiming the Gay and Lesbian Past*, New York: Meridian.

Dubois, Ellen Carol and Gordon, Linda (1984) 'Seeking Ecstasy on the Battlefield: Danger and Pleasure in Nineteenth-Century Feminist Thought', in Carol Vance (ed.), *Pleasure and Danger*, London: Routledge, pp. 31–49.

Dunn, Giles (1992) *Thinking Across the American Grain: Ideology, Intellect and the New Pragmatism*, Chicago: University of Chicago Press.

Dunn, Sara (1990) 'Voyages of the Valkyries: Recent Lesbian Pornographic Writing', *Feminist Review*, no. 34 (Spring), pp. 161–70.

Dworkin, Andrea (1981) *Pornography: Men Possessing Women*, New York: Perigee.

Dworkin, Andrea (1987) *Intercourse*, New York: Free Press.

Dyer, Richard (1991) *Now You See It*, London: Routledge.

Eagleton, Terry (l983) *Literary Theory: An Introduction*, Oxford: Blackwell.

Earle, Ralph and Crow, Gregory (1989) *Lonely all the Time: Recognizing, Understanding, and Overcoming Sex Addiction, For Addicts and Co-Dependents*, New York: Pocket Books.

Echols, Alice (1989) *Daring to be Bad: Radical Feminism in America 1967–1975*, Minneapolis: University of Minnesota: .

Edelman, Murray (1988) *Constructing the Political Spectacle*, Chicago: University of Chicago Press.

Edwards, Susan (1981) *Female Sexuality and the Law*, Oxford: Martin Robertson.

Eglington, J.Z. (1971) *Greek Love*, London: Spearman.

Ehrenreich, Barbara, Hess, Elizabeth and Jacobs, Gloria (1987) *Re-Making Love: The Feminization of Sex*, New York: Anchor.

Eichberg, Rob (1990) *Coming Out: An Act of Love*, New York: Plume.

Ekins, Richard (1983) 'The Assignment of Motives as a Problem in the Double Hermeneutic: The Case of Transvestism and Transexualism', paper presented at the 1983 Conference of the Sociological Association of Ireland.

Ekins, Richard (1993) 'On Male Femaling', *Sociological Review*, vol. 41, no. 1, pp. 1–30.

Ellis, Bret Easton (1991) *American Psycho*, London: Pan.

Ellis, Carolyn and Flaherty, Michael G. (eds) (1992) *Investigating Subjectivity: Research on Lived Experience*, London: Sage.

Elsbree, Lawrence (1982) *The Rituals of Life: Patterns in Narratives*, London: Kennikat Press.

Evans, David, T. (1993) *Sexual Citizenship: The Material Construction of Sexualities*, London: Routledge.

Evans, Sara (1980) *Personal Politics: The Roots of Women's Liberation in the Civil Rights Movement and the New Left*, New York: Vintage.

Everman, Welch, D. (1988) *Who Says This? The Authority of the Author, the Discourse, and the Reader*, Carbondale: Southern Illinois University Press.

Faderman, Lillian (1981) *Surpassing the Love of Men: Romantic Friendships Between Women from the Renaissance to the Present*, London: Junction Books.

Faderman, Lillian (1984) 'The "New Gay" Lesbians', *Journal of Homosexuality*, vol. 10, nos 3/4 (Winter), pp. 85–96.

Faderman, Lillian (1991) *Odd Girls and Twilight Lovers: A History of Lesbian Life in Twentieth Century America*, New York: University of Columbia Press.

Faludi, Susan (1991) *Backlash: The Undeclared War Against American Women*, New York: Crown.

Farley, Lin (1978) *Sexual Shakedown: The Sexual Harassment od Women in the Working World*, London: Melbourne House.

Farrell, Warren (1986) *Why Men Are the Way They Are*, New York: McGraw Hill.

Fausto-Stirling, Anne (1985) *Myths of Gender*, New York: Basic Books.

Featherstone, Mike (ed.) (1988) *Postmodernism*, London: Sage.

Featherstone, Mike (1991) *Consumer Culture and Postmodernism*, London: Sage.

Feinbloom, Deborah Heller (1976) *Transvestites and Transexuals*, New York: Delta Books.

Felski, Rita (1989) *Beyond Feminist Aesthetics: Feminist Literature and Social Change*, Cambridge, Mass.: Harvard University Press.

Fentress, James and Wickham, Chris (1992) *Social Memory*, Oxford: Blackwell.

Ferguson, Ann (1989) *Blood at the Root: Motherhood, Sexuality and Male Dominance*, London: Pandora.

Ferguson, Ann (1991) *Sexual Democracy*, Oxford: Westview Press.

Fine, Gary Alan (1990) 'Symbolic Interactionism in the Post-Blumerian Age', in G. Ritzer, *Frontiers of Social Theory*, New York: Columbia University Press.

Fine, Gary Alan (1993) 'The Sad Demise, Mysterious Disappearance, and Glorious Triumph of Symbolic Interactionism', *Annual Review of Sociology*, vol. 19, pp. 61–87.

Finkelhor, David (1984) *Child Sexual Abuse*, New York: Free Press.

Fish, Stanley (1980) *Is there a Text in this Class?* Cambridge, Mass.: Harvard University Press.

Flax, Jane (1987) ' Postmodernism and Gender Relations in Feminist Theory', *Signs*, vol. 12, no. 4, pp. 621–43.

Flax, Jane (1990) *Thinking Fragments: Psychoanalysis, Feminism and Postmodernism in the Contemporary West*, Berkeley: University of California Press.

Foote, Nelson (1954) 'Sex as Play', *Social Problems*, vol. 1, pp. 159–63.

Foucault, Michel (1976) *Discipline and Punish*, Harmondsworth: Penguin.

Foucault, Michel (1977) *Language, Counter-Memory, Practice: Selected Essays and Interviews*, New York: Cornell.

Foucault, Michel (1979) *The History of Sexuality: Vol. 1*, Harmondsworth: Penguin.

Foucault, Michel (1980) *Herculine Barbine: Being the Recently Discovered Memoirs of an Nineteenth-Century Hermaphrodite*, Hassocks, Sussex: Harvester.

Fraser, Laura (1990) 'Nasty Girls', *Mother Jones*, (February–March), pp. 32–5.

Fraser, Nancy (1986) 'Toward a Discourse Ethic of Solidarity', *Praxis International*, 5, pp. 425–9.

Fraser, Nancy (1989) *Unruly Practices: Power, Discourse and Gender in Contemporary Social Theory*, Minneapolis: University of Minnesota Press.

Fraser, Nancy (1990) 'Talking About Needs: Interpretive Contests as Political Conflicts in Welfare State Societies', in C.R. Sunstein (ed.), *Feminism and Political Theory*, Chicago: University of Chicago Press, pp. 159–84.

Freedman, Estell, Gelpi, Barbara C., Johnson, Susan L. and Weston, Kathleen M. (1985) *The Lesbian Issue*, Chicago: University of Chicago Press.

Freud, Sigmund (1977) *Case Histories*, The Pelican Freud Library, vol. 8, Harmondsworth: Penguin.

Fricke, Aaron (1981) *Reflections of a Rock Lobster: A Story about Growing Up Gay*, Boston: Alyson.

Fricke, Aaron and Fricke, Walter (1991) *Sudden Strangers: The Story of a Gay Son and his Father*, New York: St Martin's Press.

Friday, Nancy (1974) *My Secret Garden: Women's Sexual Fantasies*, New York: Pocket Books.

Friday, Nancy (1975) *Forbidden Flowers: More Women's Sexual Fantasies*, New York: Simon & Schuster/Pocket Books.

Friday, Nancy (1991) *Women on Top: How Real Life has Changed Women's Sexual Fantasies*, New York: Simon & Schuster.

Fuss, Diane (1990) *Essentially Speaking*, London: Routledge.

Fuss, Diane (ed.) (1991) *Inside/Out*, London: Routledge.

Gagnon, John (1992) 'The Self, Its Voices, and Their Discord', in Carolyn Ellis and Michael Flaherty (eds), *Investigating Subjectivity*, London: Sage, pp. 221–43.

Gagnon, John and Michaels, Stewart (1989) 'Answer No Questions: The Theory and Practice of Resistance to Deviant Categorization', paper presented at ASA meeting, San Francisco, August.

Gane, Mike (1991) *Baudrillard: Critical and Fatal Theory*, London: Routledge.

Geddes, Donald Porter (ed.) (1954) *An Analysis of the Kinsey Report*, New York: Mentor Books.

Geertz, Clifford (1975) *The Interpretation of Cultures*, London: Hutchinson.

Geraghty, Christine (1991) *Women and Soap Operas: A Study of Prime Time Soaps*, Oxford: Polity Press.

Gergen, Kenneth (1991) *The Saturated Self*, New York: Basic Books.

Giddens, Anthony (1990) *The Consequences of Modernity*, Oxford: Polity Press.

Giddens, Anthony (1991) *Modernity and Self-Identity*, Oxford: Polity Press.

Giddens, Anthony (1992) *The Transformation of Intimacy*, Oxford: Polity Press.

Gilder, George (1973) *Sexual Suicide*, New York: Quadrangle.

Gilligan, Carol (1982) *In A Different Voice*, Cambridge, Mass.: Harvard University Press.

Ginsburg, Faye (1989a) 'Dissonance and Harmony: The Symbolic Function of Abortion in Activists' Life Stories', in Personal Narratives Group, *Interpreting Women's Lives*, Bloomington: Indiana University Press, pp. 59–84.

Ginsburg, Faye (1989b) *Contested Lives: The Abortion Debate in an American Community*, Berkeley: University of California Press.

Giroux, Henry (1992) *Border Crossings: Cultural Workers and the Politics of Education*, London: Routledge.

Gittlin, Todd (1989) 'Postmodernism Defined At Last!', *Utne Reader*, no. 34 (Summer), pp. 52–61.

Goff, Tom W. (1980) *Marx and Mead*, London: Routledge.

Goffman, Erving (1963) *Stigma: Notes on the Management of Spoiled Identity*, New York: Simon & Schuster.

Goodman, Nelson (1978) *Ways of Worldmaking*, Hassocks, Sussex: Harvester.

Gordon, Linda (1988) *Heroes of their own Lives: The Politics and History of Family Violence: Boston 1880–1960*, New York: Viking.

Gordon, Margaret T. and Riger, Stephanie (1989) *The Female Fear*, London: Collier Macmillan.

Grahn, Judy (1984) *Another Mother Tongue: Gay Words, Gay Worlds*, Boston: Beacon Press.

Grant, Julia (1980) *George and Julia*, London: New English Books.

Grateful Members (1975) *The Twelve Steps for Everyone . . . Who Really Wants Them*, Minneapolis: CompCare.

Greenberg, David F. (1988) *The Construction of Homosexuality*, Chicago: University of Chicago Press.

Greene, Gerald and Greene, Caroline (1974) *S-M: The Last Taboo*, New York: Grove Press.

Greer, Germaine (1971) *The Female Eunuch*, London: Paladin.

Griffin, Susan (1979) *Rape: The Power of Consciousness*, New York: Harper & Row.

Gronbeck, Bruce and Farrell, Thomas J. (eds) (1991) *Media, Consciousness and Culture: Explorations in Walter Ong's Thought*, London: Sage.

Gross, Larry (1993) *Contested Closets: The Politics and Ethics of Outing*, Minneapolis: University of Minnesota Press.

Grossberg, Lawrence, Nelson, Cary and Treichler, Paula (eds) (1991) *Cultural Studies*, London: Routledge.

Grumley, Michael (1977) *Hard Corps: Studies in Leather and Sadomasochism*, New York: Dutton.

Gubrium, Jaber F. and Silverman, David (eds) (1989) *The Politics of Field Research*, London: Sage.

Gusfield, Joseph (1976) 'The Literary Rhetoric of Science: Comedy and Pathos in Drinking Driver Research', *American Sociological Review*, vol. 41, no. 1, pp. 16–34.

Gusfield, Joseph (1981) *The Culture of Public Problems: Drinking-Driving and the Symbolic Order*, Chicago: University of Chicago Press.

Hagan, Kay Leigh (1992) *Women Respond to the Men's Movement*, San Francisco: Harper.

Hall Carpenter Archives (1989a) *Walking After Midnight: Gay Men's Life Stories*, London: Routledge.

Hall Carpenter Archives (1989b) *Inventing Ourselves: Lesbian Life Stories*, London: Routledge.

Hall, Peter M. (1987) 'Interactionism and the Study of Social Organisation', *Sociological Quarterly*, 28, pp. 1–22.

Hall, Radclyffe (1950) *The Well of Loneliness*, New York: Pocket Books. Originally published in 1928.

Hall, Stuart (1981) 'Encoding/Decoding', in S. Hall, D. Hobson, A. Lowe and P. Willis (eds), *Culture, Media, Language*, London: Hutchinson. Halperin, David (1990) *One Hundred Years of Homosexuality*, London: Routledge.

Hanmer, Jalna and Saunders, S. (1984) *Well-Founded Fear: A Community Study of Violence to Women*, London: Hutchinson.

Haraway, Donna J. (1991) *Simians, Cyborgs, and Women: The Reinvention of Nature*, London: Free Association Press.

Hardy, Barbara (1975) *Tellers and Listeners: The Narrative Imagination*, London: Athlone.

Harvey, David (1989) *The Condition of Postmodernity*, Oxford: Blackwell.

Haskell, Molly (1987) *From Reverence to Rape: The Treatment of Women in the Movies*, Chicago: University of Chicago Press.

Hassan, Ihab (1985) 'The Culture of Post Modernism', *Theory, Culture and Society*, vol. 2, no. 3, pp. 119–31.

Hassan, Ihab (1987) *The Postmodern Turn*, Ohio: Ohio State University Press.

Hearn, Jeff (1987) *The Gender of Oppression: Men, Masculinity and the Critique of Marxism*, Brighton: Wheatsheaf.

Hearn, Jeff (1989) 'Reviewing Men and Masculinities – or Mostly Boys' Own Papers', *Theory, Culture and Society*, vol. 6, pp. 665–89.

Hearn, Jeff and Morgan, David (eds) (1990) *Men, Masculinities and Social Theory*, London: Unwin Hyman.

Heath, Stephen (1982) *The Sexual Fix*, London: Macmillan.

Held, David (1989), 'Citizenship and Autonomy', in D. Held and J. Thompson (eds), *Social Theory of Modern Society*, Cambridge: Cambridge University Press.

Hepworth, Mike and Turner, Bryan S. (1982) *Confessions: Studies in Deviance and Religion*, London: Routledge.

Herdt, Gilbert (ed.) (1992) *Gay Culture in America*, Boston: Beacon.

Herdt, Gilbert and Boxer, Andrew (1993) *Children of Horizons: How Gay and Lesbian Teens are Leading a New Way Out of the Closet*, Boston: Beacon Press.

Herman, Judith Lewis (1992) *Trauma and Recovery*, New York: Basic Books.

Herrman, Bert (1991) *TRUST/The handbook: A Guide to the Sensual and Spiritual Art of Handballing*, San Francisco: Alamos Square Press.

Herschberger, Ruth (1970) *Adam's Rib*, New York: Pellegrini & Cudahy.

Hilgarten, Stephen and Bosk, C. (1989) 'The Rise and Fall of Social Problems', *American Journal of Sociology*, vol. 94, no. 1, pp. 53–78.

Hillis Miller, J. (1990) 'Narrative', in F. Lentricchia and T. McLaughlin (eds), *Critical Terms for Literary Study*, Chicago: University of Chicago Press.

Hite, Shere (1976) *The Hite Report: A Nationwide Study of Female Sexuality*, New York: Dell.

Hite, Shere (1978) *The Hite Report on Male Sexuality*, London: MacDonald.

Holleran, Andrew (1988) *Ground Zero*, New York: New American Library.

Holmes, Sarah (ed.) (1988) *Testimonies: A Collection of Lesbian Coming Out Stories*, Boston: Alyson.

hooks, bell (1989) *Talking Back: Thinking Feminist, Thinking Black*, Boston: South End Press.

hooks, bell (1993) *Sisters of the Yam: Black Women and Self Recovery*, Boston: South End Press.

Humphreys, Laud (1979) 'Exodus and Identity: The Emerging Gay Culture', in M. Levine (ed.), *Gay Men*, New York: Harper & Row.

Humphreys, Steve (1988) *A Secret World of Sex, Forbidden Fruit: The British Experience 1900–1950*, London: Sidgwick and Jackson.

Hunter, B. Michael (ed.) (1993) *Sojourner: Black Voices in the Age of AIDS*, Other Countries Press.

Hunter, James Davison (1991) *Culture Wars: The Struggle to Define America*, New York: Basic Books.

Innis, Harold (1972) *Empire and Communication*, Toronto: University of Toronto Press.

Irvine, Janice (1990) *Disorders of Desire*, Philadelphia: Temple University Press.

Irwin, John (1977) *Scenes*, London: Sage.

Jackson, David (1990) *Unmasking Masculinity: A Critical Autobiography*, London: Unwin Hyman.

Jaget, Claude (1980) *Prostitutes: Our Life*, Bristol: Falling Wall Press.

James, William (1952) *The Varieties of Religious Experience*, London: Longman, Green & Co. (originally delivered as the Gifford Lectures in 1901–2).

James, William (1956) *'The Will to Believe' and Other Essays in Popular Philosophy*, New York: Dover Publications.

James, William (1978) *Pragmatism and the Meaning of Truth*, ed. A.J. Ayer, Cambridge, Mass.: Harvard University Press.

Jameson, Fredric (1984) 'Postmodernism, or the Cultural Logic of Late Capitalism', *New Left Review*, 146, pp. 53–92.

Janeway, Elizabeth (1981) *Powers of the Weak*, New York: Morrow Quill.

Jardine, Alice (1985) *Gynesis: Configurations of Women and Modernity*, Ithaca: Cornell University Press.

Jay, Karla and Glasgow, Joanne (eds) (1990) *Lesbian Texts and Contexts: Radical Revisions*, New York: New York University Press.

Jeffreys, Sheila (ed.) (1987) *The Sexuality Debates*, London: Routledge.

Jeffreys, Sheila (1990) *Anticlimax: A Feminist Perspective on the Sexual Revolution*, London: Women's Press.

Jencks, Christopher (1987) *What is Postmodernism?* New York: St Martin's Press.

Jenkins, Philip (1992) *Initimate Enemies: Moral Panics in Contemporary Great Britain*, New York: Aldine de Gruyter.

Joas, Hans (1993) *Pragmatism and Social Theory*, Chicago: University of Chicago Press.

Johnson, John (1987) 'The Third Generation of Field Research Conduct', *Journal of Contemporary Ethnography*, vol. 16, no. 1, pp. 94–110.

Johnson, John M. and Altheide, David (1990) 'Reflexive Accountability', in *Studies in Symbolic Interactionism*, vol. 11, pp. 25–34.

Jorgensen, Christine (1967) *A Personal Autobiography*, New York: Bantam.

Kaminer, Wendy (1992) *I'm Dysfunctional, You're Dysfunctional*, New York: Random House (paperback edition 1993, New York: Vintage, with a new preface).

Kantrowitz, Arnie (1989) 'Friends Gone With the Wind', in John Preston (ed.), *Personal Dispaches*, New York: St Martin's Press.

Kaplan, E. Ann (1987) *Rocking Around the Clock: Music Television, Consumer Culture and Postmodernism*, London: Methuen.

Kaplan, E. Ann (ed.) (1988) *Postmodernism and its Discontents*, London: Verso.

Kaplan, Helen Singer (1978) *The New Sex Therapy*, Harmondsworth: Penguin.

Katz, Jack (1988) *Seductions of Crime: Moral and Sensual Attractions in Doing Evil*, New York: Basic Books.

Katz, Jonathan (1976) *Gay American History*, New York: Avon.

Katz, Jonathan (1990) 'The Invention of Heterosexuality', *Socialist Review*, vol. 20, no. 1, pp. 7–34.

Kavolis, V. (1970) 'Postmodern Man: Psychocultural Responses to Social Trends', *Social Problems*, 17, pp. 435–48.

Kayal, Philip M. (1993) *Bearing Witness: Gay Men's Health Crisis and the Politics of AIDS*, New York: Westview.

Kearney, Richard (1988) *The Wake of Imagination*, London: Hutchinson.

Keen, Sam (1991) *Fire in the Belly: On Being a Man*, New York: Bantam.

Kehoe, M. (1988) 'Lesbians Over 60 Speak for Themselves', *Journal of Homosexuality*, vol. 16, nos 3/4.

Kellner, Douglas (1989) *Jean Baudrillard: From Marxism to Postmodernism and Beyond*, Oxford: Polity Press.

Kellner, Douglas (1990) 'The Postmodern Turn: Positions, Problems and Prospects', in George Ritzer (ed.), *Frontiers of Social Theory*, New York: Columbia University Press.

Kellner, Douglas (1992) 'Popular Culture and the Construction of Postmodern Identities', in Scott Lash and Jonathan Friedman (eds), *Modernity and Identity*, Oxford: Blackwell.

Kelly, Liz (1988) *Surviving Sexual Violence*, Oxford: Polity Press.

Kemper, Theodore D. (ed.) (1990), *Research Agendas in the Sociology of Emotions*, New York: State University of New York Press.

Kimmel, Michael S. (ed.) (1990) *Men Confront Pornography*, New York: Crown Publishers.

King, Dave (1986) 'The Transvestite and the Transexual: A Case Study of Public Categories and Private Identities', unpublished Ph.D. thesis, University of Essex.

King, Dave (1993) *The Transvestite and the Transexual*, Aldershot: Avebury.

Kinsella, James (1989) *Covering the Plague: AIDS and the American Media*, New Brunswick: Rutgers University Press.

Kinsey, Alfred, Pomeroy, Wardell B. and Martin, Clyde E. (1948) *Sexual Behaviour in the Human Male*, Philadelphia: W.B. Saunders.

Kinsey, Alfred, Pomeroy, Wardell B., Martin, Clyde E. and Gebbard, Paul H. (1948) *Sexual Behaviour in the Human Female*, Philadelphia: W.B. Saunders.

Kirk, Marshall and Madsen, Hunter (1990) *After the Ball*, New York: Plume.

Kitsuse, John I. (1980) 'Coming Out All Over: Deviants and the Politics of Social Problems', *Social Problems*, vol. 28, no. 1, pp. 1–13.

Klapp, Orrin (1991) *Inflation of Symbols*, New Brunswick: Transaction.

Klein, Marty (1988) *Your Sexual Secrets: When to Keep Them, When and How to Tell*, New York: Dutton.

Kleinman, Arthur (1988) *The Illness Narratives: Suffering, Healing and the Human Condition*, New York: Basic Books.

Kohli, Martin (1981) 'Biography: Account, Text, Method', in D. Bertaux (ed.), *Biography and Society*, London: Sage, pp. 61–75.

Koss, Mary and Harvey, Mary (1987) *The Rape Victim*, Lexington: Stephen Greene Press.

Kotre, J. (1984) *Outliving the Self: Generativity and the Interpretation of Lives*, Baltimore: Johns Hopkins University Press.

Krafft-Ebing, Richard von (1931) *Psychopathia Sexualis*, New York: Physicians and Surgeons. Translation of 12th edition.

Kramer, Larry (1990) *Reports from the Holocaust: The Making of an AIDS Activist*, Harmondsworth: Penguin.

Kroker, Arthur and Kroker, Marilouise (eds) (1987) *Body Invaders: Panic Sex in America*, Montreal: New World Perspectives.

Kroker, Arthur, Kroker, Marilouise and Cook, David (1989) *Panic Encyclopedia: The Definitive Guide to the Postmodern Scene*, London: Macmillan.

Kronhausen, Eberhard and Kronhausen, Phyllis (1967) *Walter: My Secret Life – The Unique Memoirs of England's most Uninhibited Lover*, London: Polybooks.

Krug, Gary J. (1992) 'Visual Ethnographics and the Postmodern Self', *Studies in Symbolic Interaction*, vol. 13, pp. 59–76.

LaFountain, Marc J. (1989) 'Foucault and Dr Ruth', *Critical Studies in Mass Communication*, vol. 6, pp 123–37.

Lakoff, George (1987) *Women, Fire and Dangerous Things: What Categories Reveal About the Mind*, Chicago: University of Chicago Press.

Lakoff, George. and Johnson, M. (1980) *Metaphors We Live By*, Chicago: University of Chicago Press.

Langer, Suzanne K. (1942) *Philosophy in a New Key*, Cambridge, Mass.: Harvard University Press.

Langness, L. and Frank, G. (1981) *Lives*, Chandler & Sharp.

Laqueur, Thomas (1990) *Making Sex: Body and Gender from the Greeks to Freud*, London: Harvard University Press.

Lasch, Christopher (1979) *The Culture of Narcissism: American Life in an Age of Diminishing Expectations*, New York: Warner Books.

Lasch, Christopher (1984) *The Minimal Self: Psychic Survival in Troubled Times*, London: Pan.

Laswell, Harold (1960), 'The Structure and Function of Communication in Society', in W. Schramm (ed.), *Mass Communications*, Illinois: University of Illinois Press.

Lather, Patti (1991) *Getting Smart*, London: Routledge.

Leavitt, David (1986) *The Lost Language of Cranes*, London: Penguin.

Lederer, Laura (ed.) (1980) *Take Back the Night: Women on Pornography*, New York: William Morrow.

Lee, John Alan (1978) *Getting Sex*, Toronto: General.

Leidholt, Dorchen and Raymond, Janice G. (eds) (1990) *The Sexual Liberals and the Attack on Feminism*, Oxford: Pergamon Press.

Lemke, Jürgen (ed.) (1991) *Gay Voices from East Germany*, Bloomington: Indiana University Press.

Lentricchia, Frank and McLaughlin, Thomas (eds) (1990) *Critical Terms for Literary Study*, Chicago: University of Chicago Press.

Lesbian History Group (1989) *Not a Passing Phase: Reclaiming Lesbians in History 1840–1985*, London: Women's Press.

LeVay, Simon (1993) *The Sexual Brain*, Cambridge, Mass.: MIT Press.

Levine, Martin P. (ed.) (1979) *Gay Men: The Sociology of Male Homosexuality*, New York: Harper & Row.

Levine, Martin P. (1992) 'The Life and Death of Gay Clones', in G. Herdt (eds), *Gay Culture in America*, Boston: Beacon Press.

Lewis, Jon (1992) *The Road to Romance and Ruin: Teen Films and Youth Culture*, London: Routledge.

Li, Chin-Keung (1986) *Sexual Experiences of Adults with Children*, unpublished Ph.D., University of Cambridge.

Lichterman, Paul (1992) 'Self-Help Reading as a Thin Culture', *Media, Culture and Society*, vol. 14, pp. 421–47.

Lips, Hilary M. (1992) *Women, Men and Power*, London: Mayfield.

Lipstadt, Deborah E. (1993) *Denying the Holocaust: Growing Assault on Truth and Meaning*, New York: Free Press.

Livingstone, Sonia and Lunt, Peter (1993) *Talk on Television: Audience Participation and Public Debate*, London: Routledge.

Lofland, John (1976) *Doing Social Life*, New York: Wiley.

London Rape Crisis Centre (1984) *Sexual Violence: The Reality for Women*, London: Women's Press.

Lorde, Audre (1982) 'Who Said It Was Simple?', in *Chosen Poems: Old and New*, New York: Norton.

Lowenstein, Ralph L. and Merrill, John C. (1990) *Macromedia: Mission, Message and Morality*, London: Longman.

Luczak, Raymond (ed.) (1993) *Eyes of Desire: A Deaf Gay and Lesbian Reader*, Boston: Alyson.

Luker, Kristin (1984) *Abortion and the Politics of Motherhood*, Berkeley: University of California Press.

Lyotard, Jean-François (1979) *The Postmodern Condition: A Report on Knowledge*, Manchester: Manchester University Press.

McAdams, Dan (1985) *Power, Intimacy and the Life Story*, New York: Guildford Press.

McCall, Michael M. (1990) 'The Significance of Story Telling', *Studies in Symbolic Interaction*, vol. 11, London: JAI Press, pp. 145–61.

McCloskey, D.N. (1985) *The Rhetoric of Economics*, Madison: University of Wisconsin Press.

MacDonald, Scott (1990) 'Confessions of a Feminist Pornwatcher', in M.S. Kimmel (ed.) (1990) *Men Confront Pornography*, New York: Crown Publishers, pp. 34–42.

MacIntyre, Alasdair (1981) *After Virtue*, London: Duckworth.

MacKinnon, Catherine A. (1979) *Sexual Harassment of Working Women: A Case of Sex Discrimination*, London: Yale University Press.

MacKinnon, Catherine A. (1987) *Feminism Unmodified: Discourses on Life and Law*, Cambridge, Mass.: Harvard University Press.

McLuhan, Marshall (1962) *The Gutenberg Galaxy: The Making of Typographic Man*, Toronto: University of Toronto Press.

McMullen, Richie (1990) *Male Rape*, London: Gay Men's Press.

McNamee Sheila and Gergen, Kenneth J. (eds) (1992) *Therapy as Social Construction*, London: Sage.

McNaran, Toni, and Morgan, Yarrow (eds) (1982) *Voices in the Night: Women Speaking About Incest*, Pittsburgh, Cleis Press.

MacPherson, C.B (1962) *The Political Theory of Possessive Individualism*, Oxford: Oxford University Press.

MacPike, Loralee (ed.) (1989) *There's Something I've Been Meaning to Tell You*, Florida: Naiad Press.

McRobbie, Angela (1991) *Feminism and Youth Culture: From Jackie to Just Seventeen*, London: Macmillan.

Madonna (with Steven Meisel and Glenn O'Brien) (1992) *Sex*, New York: Warner Books.

Maines, David R. (1993) 'Narrative's Moment and Sociology's Phenomena: Toward a Narrative Sociology', *Sociological Quarterly*, vol. 34, no. 1, p. 17–38.

Maines, Geoff (1984) *Urban Aboriginals: A Celebration of Leather-Sexuality*, San Francisco: Gay Sunshine Press.

Mair, Miller (1986) 'Toward a Reconstruction of Psychology', Memorial Symposium for Don Bannister, 28 November, University of Leeds.

Mair, Miller (1989) *Between Psychology and Psychotherapy: A Poetics of Experience*, London: Routledge.

Malinowski, Robert (1987) *International Directory of Gay and Lesbian Periodicals*, Phoenix, Arizona: Oryx Press.

Mann, Michael (1987) 'Ruling Class Strategies and Citizenship', *Sociology*, 21, pp. 339–54.

Marcus, Maria (1981) *A Taste For Pain: On Masochism and Female Sexuality*, London: Souvenir Press.

Marcus, Steven (1966) *The Other Victorians*, London: Weidenfeld & Nicolson.

Marshall, John (1981) 'Pansies, Perverts and Macho Men: Changing Conceptions of Male Homosexuality', in Ken Plummer (ed.), *The Making of the Modern Homosexual*, London: Hutchinson, pp. 133–54.

Marshall, T.H. (1963) *Sociology at the Crossroads*, London: Heinemann.

Martin, Bernice (1981) *A Sociology of Contemporary Cultural Change*, Oxford: Blackwell.

Masciarotte, Gloria-Jean (1991) 'C'mon, Girl: Oprah Winfrey and the Discourse of Feminine Talk', *Genders*, no. 11 (Fall), pp. 81–110.

Matza, David (1969) *Becoming Deviant*, Englewood Cliffs, NJ: Prentice-Hall.

Maupin, Armistead (1987) *Significant Others*, New York: Harper & Row.

Mead, George Herbert (1933) *Mind, Self and Society*, Chicago: University of Chicago Press.

Mead, George Herbert (1938) *The Philosophy of the Act*, Chicago: University of Chicago Press.

Medea, Andrea and Thompson, Kathleen (1974) *Against Rape*, New York: Farrar, Straus & Giroux.

Medved, Michael (1993) *Hollywood vs America*, London: HarperCollins.

Meyer, Richard (1991) 'Rock Hudson's Body', in D. Fuss (ed.), *Inside/Out*, London: Routledge.

Meyrowitz, Joshua (1985) *No Sense of Place: The Impact of Electronic Media on Social Behaviour*, Oxford: Oxford University Press.

Middleton, David and Edwards, Derek (eds) (1990) *Collective Remembering*, London: Sage.

Middleton, Warren (ed.) (undated) *The Betrayal of Youth: Radical Perspectives on Childhood Sexuality, Intergenerational Sex, and the Social Oppression of Children and Young People*, London: C.L. Publications.

Miller, James (1993) *The Passion of Michel Foucault*, New York: Simon & Schuster.

Miller, Neil (1988) *In Search of Gay America: Women and Men in a Time of Change*, New York: Harper Perennial.

Miller, Neil (1992) *Out in the World: Gay and Lesbian Life from Buenos Aires to Bangkok*, New York: Random House.

Mills, Charles Wright (1959) *The Sociological Imagination*, Oxford: Oxford University Press.

Mills, Trudy (1985) 'The Assault on Self: Stages in Coping with Battering Husbands', *Qualitative Sociology*, vol. 8, no. 2, pp. 103–23.

Mitchell, W.J.T. (ed.) (1980) *On Narrative*, Chicago: University of Chicago Press (originally published in *Critical Inquiry*, vol. 7, no. 1 (1980)).

Modleski, Tania (1982) *Loving with a Vengeance: Mass-Produced Fantasies for Women*, Connecticut, Archon Books.

Mohr, Richard (1988) *Gays/Justice: A Study of Ethics, Society and Law*, New York: Columbia University Press.

Mohr, Richard D. (1992) *Gay Ideas: Outing and Other Controversies*, Boston: Beacon Press.

Monette, Paul (1988) *Borrowed Time*, Orlando, Florida: Harcourt, Brace.

Monette, Paul (1992) *Becoming a Man: Half a Life Story*, San Francisco: Harper.

Moody, Roger (1980) *Indecent Assault*, London: Word is Out/Peace News.

Moore, Robert and Gillette, Douglas (1990) *King, Warrior, Magician, Lover: Rediscovering the Archetype of the Mature Masculine*, San Francisco: Harper.

Moores, Shaun (1993) *Interpreting Audiences*, London: Sage.

Moraga, Cherrie and Anzaldúa, Gloria (eds) (1981) *This Bridge Called My Back: Writings by Radical Women of Colour*, Watertown, Mass.: Persephone Press.

Morley, David (1986) *Family Television: Cultural Power and Domestic Leisure*, London: Comedia.

Morley, David (1992) *Television, Audiences and Cultural Studies*, London: Routledge.

Morris, Jan (1974) *Conundrum*, London: Faber and Faber.

Morrison, Toni (ed.) (1992) *Race-ing Justice, En-gendering Power: Essays on Anita Hill, Clarence Thomas and the Construction of Social Reality*, New York: Pantheon Books.

Mulvey, Laura (1975) 'Visual Pleasure and Narrative', *Screen*, vol. 16, no. 3 (Autumn), pp. 6–18.

Murphy, J.W. (1989) 'Making Sense of Postmodernism', *British Journal of Sociology*, vol. 39, no. 4, pp. 600–14.

Musgrove, Frank (1964) *Youth and the Social Order*, London: Routledge.

Myerhoff, Barbara (1978) *Number Our Days*, New York: Simon & Schuster.

Nardi, Peter M. (ed.) (1992) *Men's Friendships*, London: Sage.

Nash, Christopher (ed.) (1990) *Narrative in Culture: The Uses of Storytelling in the Sciences, Philosophy and Literature*, London: Routledge.

Nestle, Joan (1988) *A Restricted Country*, London: Sheba.

Neuman, Russell (1991) *The Future of the Mass Audience*, Cambridge: Cambridge University Press.

North, Maurice (1972) *Secular Priests*, London: Allen & Unwin.

Norwood, Robin (1985) *Women Who Love Too Much*, New York: Simon & Schuster.

Norwood, Robin (1988) *Robin Norwood Answers Letters from Women Who Love Too Much*, New York: Pocket Books.

O'Carroll, Tom (1980) *Paedophilia: The Radical Case*, London: Peter Owen.

Okely, Judith (1986) *Simone de Beauvoir: A Re-reading*, London: Virago.

Okin, Susan Moller (1989) *Justice, Gender and the Family*, New York: Basic Books.

Olney, James (ed.) (1980) *Autobiography: Essays Theoretical and Critical*, Princeton: Princeton University Press.

O'Reilly, Harry J. (1984) 'Crisis Intervention with Victims of Forcible Rape: A Police Perspective', in June Hopkins (ed.), *Perspectives on Rape and Sexual Assault*, London: Harper, Ch. 7, pp. 89–103.

Osanka, M. and Johnson, S.L. (1989) *Sourcebook on Pornography*, Lexington, Mass.: Lexington Books.

Parrot, Andrea and Bechofer, Laurie (eds) (1991) *Acquaintance Rape: The Hidden Crime*, London: Wiley.

Pastore, Judith L. (eds) (1993) *Confronting Aids through Literature*, Chicago: University of Illinois Press.

Patton, Cindy (1990) *Inventing Aids*, London: Routledge.

Payne, David (1990) *Coping with Failure: The Therapeutic Uses of Rhetoric*, Chapel Hill: University of South Carolina Press.

Peabody, Barbara (1986) *The Screaming Room*, New York: Avon Books.

Penelope, Julia and Valentine, Sarah (eds) (1992) *Finding the Lesbians: Personal Accounts from Around the World*, Freedom, California: Crossing Press.

Penelope, Julia and Wolfe, Susan J. (eds) (1989) *The Original Coming Out Stories*, 2nd edn, Freedom, California: Crossing Press. Originally published in 1980.

Penley, Constance (1991) 'Brownian Motion: Women, Tactics and Technology', in Constance Penley and Andrew Ross (eds), *Technoculture*, Minneapolis: University of Minnesota Press, pp. 135–61.

Penley, Constance (1992) 'Feminism, Psychoanalysis, and the Study of Popular Culture', in L. Grossberg, Cary Nelson and Paula Treichler (eds), *Cultural Studies*, London: Routledge, pp. 479–94.

Perinbanayagam, Robert. S. (1985) *Signifying Acts: Structure and Meaning in Everyday Life*, Carbordale: Southern Illinois University Press.

Perinbanayagam, Robert S. (1991) *Discursive Acts: Communication and Social Order*, New Yorker: Aldine de Gruyter.

Personal Narratives Group (1989) *Interpreting Women's Lives*, Bloomington: Indiana University Press.

Petchesky, Rosalind Pollack (1986) *Abortion and Woman's Choice*, London: Verso.

Phelan, Shane (1989) *Identity Politics: Lesbian Feminism and the Limits of Community*, Philadelphia: Temple University Press.

Phelps, Timothy and Winternitz, Helen (1992) *Capitol Games: The Inside Story of Clarence Thomas, Anita Hill and a Supreme Court Nomination*, New York: Hyperion.

Plant, Richard (1987) *The Pink Triangle: the Nazi War Against Homosexuals*, Edinburgh: Mainstream Publishing.

Plummer, Ken (1975) *Sexual Stigma*, London: Routledge.

Plummer, Ken (1981a) 'The Paedophile's Progress: A View from Below', in B. Taylor (ed.), *Perspectives on Paedophilia*, London: Batsford.

Plummer, Ken (ed.) (1981b) *The Making of the Modern Homosexual*, London: Hutchinson.

Plummer, Ken (1982) 'Symbolic Interactionism and Sexual Conduct: An Emergent Perspective', in M. Brake (ed.), *Human Sexual Relations: A Reader*, Harmondsworth, Penguin.

Plummer, Ken (1983) *Documents of Life: An Introduction to the Literature of a Humanistic Method*, London: Allen & Unwin.

Plummer, Ken (1984) 'Social Uses of Sexuality: Symbolic Interaction, Power and Rape', in June Hopkins, ed, *Perspectives on Rape and Sexual Assault*, London: Harper & Row, Ch. 4, pp. 37–56.

Plummer, Ken (1987) 'Beyond Childhood: Organising "Gayness" in Adult Life', Paper presented at 'Homosexuality: Beyond Disease' conference, Amsterdam, 1987.

Plummer, Ken (1988) 'Organising Aids', in Peter Aggleton and Hilary Homans, *Social Aspects of Aids*, London: Falmer.

Plummer, Ken (1990a) 'Herbert Blumer and the Life History Tradition', *Symbolic Interaction*, vol. 11, no. 2 (Fall), pp. 125–44.

Plummer, Ken (1990b) 'Staying in the Empirical World: A Response To Denzin', *Symbolic Interaction*, vol. 11, no. 2 (Fall), pp.155–60.

Plummer, Ken (ed.) (1991) *Symbolic Interactionism: Volumes 1 and 2*, Aldershot: Edward Elgar Reference.

Plummer, Ken (ed.) (1992) *Modern Homosexualities: Fragments of Lesbian and Gay Experience*, London: Routledge.

Polkinghorne, Donald E. (1988) *Narrative Knowing and the Human Sciences*, Albany, NY: State University of New York Press.

Popenhoe, David (1988) *Disturbing the Nest*, New York: Aldine de Gruyter.

Porter, Roy (1986) 'Rape – Does it Have a Historical Meaning?', in Sylvanna Tomaselli and Roy Porter (eds), *Rape*, Oxford: Blackwell.

Potter, Jonathan and Wetherell, M. (1987) *Discourse and Social Psychology*, London: Sage.

Preston, John (ed.) (1989) *Personal Dispatches: Writers Confront Aids*, New York: St Martin's Press.

Preston, John (ed.) (1991) *HomeTowns: Gay Men Write About Where they Belong*, New York: Dutton.

Preston, John (ed.) (1992) *A Member of the Family: Gay Men Write About their Families*, New York: Dutton.

Propp, Vladimir (1968) *Morphology of the Folktale*, Austin: University of Texas Press.

Prus, Robert (1987) 'Generic Social Processes: Maximizing Conceptual Development in Ethnographic Research', *Journal of Contemporary Ethnography*, 16 (3 October), pp. 250–93, and reprinted in Ken Plummer (ed.) (1991) *Symbolic Interactionism*, vol. 2, Aldershot: Edward Elgar Reference.

Rabkin, E.S. (1973) *Narrative Suspense*, Ann Arbor: University of Michigan Press.

Radway, Janice (1987) *Reading the Romance: Women, Patriarchy and Popular Literature*, London: Verso.

Rafkin, Louise (ed.) (1990) *Different Mothers: Sons and Daughters of Lesbians Talk About Their Lives*, Cleis Press.

Rains, Pru (1975) 'Imputations of Deviance: A Retrospective Essay on the Labelling Perspective', *Social Problems*, 30, pp. 410–24.

Rapping, Elayne (1992) *The Movie of the Week: Private Stories, Public Events*, Minneapolis: University of Minnesota Press.

Ratti, Rakesh (ed.) (1993) *A Lotus of Another Color: An Unfolding of the South Asian Lesbian and Gay Experience*, New York: Alyson.

Raval, S. (1987) 'Recent Books on Narrative Theory: An Essay Review', *Modern Fiction Studies*, vol. 33, no. 3, pp. 559–70.

Raymond, Janice (1986) *A Passion for Friends*, Boston: Beacon Press.

Reinarman, Craig and Phillips, Mary Dana (1991) 'The Politics of Self-Control in Postmodernity: An Interpretation of the Twelve-Step Movement', presented at the 'Contemporary Social Movements and Cultural Politics' conference, 22–4 March, University of California, Santa Cruz.

Renzetti, Claire M. (1992) *Violent Betrayal: Partner Abuse in Lesbian Relationships*, London: Sage.

Reynolds, Janice (1974) 'Rape as Social Control', *Catalyst*, vol. 8, pp. 62–8.

Rheingold, Howard (1991) *Virtual Reality*, New York: Summit Books.

Rich, Adrienne (1979) *On Lies, Secrets and Silence: Selected Prose 1966–78*, New York: Norton.

Rich, Adrienne (1980) 'Compulsory Heterosexuality and Lesbian Existence', *Signs*, 5, pp. 631–60.

Richardson, Laurel (1990a) *Writing Strategies: Reaching Diverse Audiences*, London: Sage.

Richardson, Laurel (1990b) 'Narrative and Sociology', *Journal of Contemporary Ethnography* (April), vol. 9, no. 1, pp. 116–35.

Richardson, Laurel (1992) 'Resisting Resistance Narratives: A Representation for Communication', *Studies in Symbolic Interaction*, vol. 13, pp. 77–82.

Ricoeur, Paul (1981) 'Narrative Time', in W. Mitchell (ed.), *On Narrative*, Chicago: University of Chicago Press.

Rieder, Ines and Ruppelt, Patricia (eds) (1989) *Matters of Life and Death: Women Speak Out About Aids*, London: Virago.

Riessman, Catherine Kohler (1993) *Narrative Analysis*, London: Sage.

Rist, Darrell Yates (1992) *Heartlands: A Gay Man's Odyssey Across America*, New York: Dutton.

Ritzer, George (ed.) (1990) *Frontiers of Social Theory: The New Syntheses*, New York: Columbia University Press.

Ritzer, George (1992) *The McDonaldization of Society*, Newbury Park, California: Pine Forge Press.

Robinson, Paul (1976) *The Modernization of Sex*, London: Paul Elels.

Roberts, Ken (1978) *Contemporary Society and the Growth Of Leisure*, London: Longman.

Roiphe, Katie (1994) *The Morning After: Sex, Fear and Feminism*, London: Hamish Hamilton.

Rojek, Chris (1985) *Capitalism and Leisure Theory*, London: Tavistock.

Romanyshyn, R.D. (1982) *Psychological Life: From Science to Metaphor*, Milton Keynes: Open University Press.

Ronai, Carol Rambo (1992) 'The Reflexive Self Through Narrative: A Night in the Life of an Erotic Dancer/Researcher', in C. Ellis and M. Flaherty, *Investigating Subjectivity*, London: Sage, pp. 102–25.

Roof, Judith (1992) *A Lure of Knowledge: Lesbian Sexuality and Theory*, New York: Columbia University Press.

Rorty, Richard (1989) *Contingency, Irony, and Solidarity*, Cambridge: Cambridge University Press.

Roscoe, Will (1988) 'Making History: The Challenge of Gay and Lesbian Studies', *Journal of Homosexuality*, vol. 15, nos 3/4, pp. 1–40.

Rose, Vicki McNickle (1981) 'Rape as a Social Problem: A Byproduct of the Feminist Movement', *Social Problems*, vol. 25, no. 1, pp. 75–89.

Rosenblum, Nancy L. (1987) *Another Liberalism*, Cambridge, Mass.: Harvard University Press.

Rosenblum, Nancy (ed.) (1989) *Liberalism and the Moral Life*, Cambridge, Mass.: Harvard University Press.

Ross, Andrew (ed.) (1988) *Universal Abandon*, Minneapolis: University of Minnesota.

Ross, Andrew (1992) 'The Private Parts of Justice', in Toni Morrison (ed.), *Race-ing Justice, En-gendering Power: Essays on Anita Hill, Clarence Thomas and the Construction of Social Reality*, New York: Pantheon Books.

Rossman, Parker (1979) *Sexual Experience Between Men and Boys*, London: Temple Smith.

Rousseau, Jean-Jacques (1782: 1931 edn) *Confessions*, London: Everyman Library.

Rubin, Gayle (1984) 'Thinking Sex: Notes for a Radical Theory of the Politics of Sexuality', in Vance, Carole (ed.), *Pleasure and Danger*, London: Routledge, pp. 267–319.

Rubin, Lilian (1990) *Erotic Wars: What Happened to the Sexual Revolution?*, New York: Harper.

Ruitenbeck, Hendrik M. (1970) *The New Group Therapies*, New York: Avon Books.

Runyan, W.M. (1982) *Life Histories and Psychobiography: Explorations in Theory and Method*, Oxford: Oxford University Press.

Russell, Diana (1982) *Rape in Marriage*, New York: Macmillan.

Russell, Diana (1984) *Sexual Exploitation: Rape, Child Sexual Abuse and Workplace Harassment*, London: Sage.

Russell, Diana (1986) *The Secret Trauma: Incest in the Lives of Girls and Women*, New York: Basic Books.

Salvatore, Diane (1993) 'What's so Bad About Being in Love? In Defence of the Coming Out Novel', *Lamda Book Report*, vol. 4, no. 1, pp. 6–7.

Samois (1981) *Coming To Power: Writings and Graphics on Lesbian S/M*, Boston: Alyson.

Sanday, Peggy Reeves (1990) *Fraternity Gang Rape: Sex, Brotherhood and Privilege on Campus*, New York: New York University Press.

Sandel, Michael J. (1982) *Liberalism and the limits of Justice*, Cambridge: Cambridge University Press.

Sandfort, Theo (1982) *The Sexual Aspect of Paedophile Relations*, Amsterdam: Pan/Spartacus.

Sandfort, Theo (1987) *Boys on their contacts with Men*, New York: Global Academic Press.

Sandfort, Theo, Brongerma, E. and Van Naerssen, A. (eds) (1990) *Male Intergenerational Intimacy*, New York: Harrington Park Press.

Sarbin, Theodore R. (1986) *Narrative Psychology: The Storied Nature of Human Conduct*, New York: Praeger.

Savin-Williams, Ritch C. (1990) *Gay and Lesbian Youth: Expressions of Identity*, New York: Hemisphere Publications.

Saward, Jill (with Green, Wendy) (1991) *Rape: My Story*, London: Pan.

Schaef, Anne Wilson (1987) *When Society Becomes an Addict*, San Francisco: Harper & Row.

Scheff, Thomas J. and Retzinger, Suzanne (1991) *Emotion and Violence: Shame and Rage in Destructive Conflicts*, Lexington, Mass.: Lexington Books.

Schlesinger, Philip, R., Dobash, Emerson, Dobash, Russell P. and Weaver, C. Kay (1992) *Women Viewing Violence*, London: British Film Institute.

Schneider, Beth (1992) 'Lesbian Politics and Aids Work', in Ken Plummer (ed.), *Modern Homosexualities*, London: Routledge, Ch. 13.

Schneider, Jennifer P. and Schneider, Burt (1990) *Sex, Lies and Forgiveness: Couples Speaking Out on Healing from Sex Addiction*, New York: Hazeldine, Harper Collins.

Schuijer, Jan (1990) 'Tolerance at Arm's Length: The Dutch Experience', *Journal of Homosexuality*, vol. 20, nos 1/2, pp. 199–230.

Schulman, Sarah (1984) *The Sophie Horowitz Story*, Tallahasee: Naiad Press.

Schur, Edwin M. (1976) *The Awareness Trap: Self-Absorption Instead of Social Change*, New York: McGraw Hill.

Schur, Edwin M. (1988) *The Americanization of Sex*, Philadelphia: Temple Press.

Schwendinger, Julia and Schwendinger, Herman (1974), 'Rape Myths in Legal, Theoretical and Everyday Practice', *Crime and Social Justice*, 13, pp. 18–26.

Schwendinger, Julia and Schwendinger, Herman (1983) *Rape and Inequality*, Beverley Hills: Sage.

Scott, Robert A. (1972) 'A Proposed Framework for Analysing Deviance as a Property of Social Order', in Robert A. Scott and Jack D. Douglas (eds), *Theoretical Perspectives on Deviance*, London: Basic Books.

Scully, Diana (1990) *Understanding Sexual Violence: A Study of Convicted Rapists*, London: Unwin Hyman.

Sedgwick, Eve Kasofsky (1991) *Epistemology of the Closet*, London: Harvester.

Segal, Lynn and McIntosh, Mary (eds) (1992) *Sex Exposed: The Sexuality and Pornography Debate*, London: Virago.

Seidman, Steven (1990) *Romantic Longings*, London: Routledge.

Seidman, Steven (1992) *Embattled Eros: Sexual Politics and Ethics in Contemporary America*, London: Routledge.

Seigfried, Charlene (1990) *William James's Radical Reconstruction of Philosophy*, Albany, New York: State University of New York.

Selden, R. (1985) *A Reader's Guide to Contemporary Literary Theory*, Hassocks, Sussex: Harvester.

Sheffield, Carole J. (1987) 'Sexual Terrorism: The Social Control of Women', in B.B Hess and M.M. Ferree (eds), *Analyzing Gender: A Handbook of Social Science Research*, London: Sage, pp. 171–89.

Sherman, Barrie and Judkins, Phil (1992) *Glimpses of Heaven, Visions of Hell: Virtual Reality and Its Implications*, London: Hodder & Stoughton.

Shilts, Randy (1988) *And the Band Played On*, New York: St Martin's Press.

Shotter, John (1984) *Social Accountability and Selfhood*, Oxford: Blackwell.

Showalter, Elaine (1991) *Sexual Anarchy: Gender and Culture at the Fin de Siècle*, London: Bloomsbury.

Shuman, A. (1986) *Storytelling Rights: The Uses of Oral and Written Texts by Urban Adolescents*, London: Cambridge University Press.

Signorile, Michelangelo (1993) *Queer In America: Sex, The Media and the Closets of Power*, New York: Random House.

Simon, William (1988) 'Deviance as History: The Future of Perversion', paper presented at ASA meetings, Atlanta, August.

Simonds, Wendy (1992) *Women and Self-Help Culture: Reading Between the Lines*, New Brunswick: Rutgers University Press.

Smith, Steven A. (undated) 'PIE from 1980 Until its Demise in 1985', in W. Middleton, *The Betrayal of Youth*, London: C.L. Publications, pp. 215–44.

Snitow, Ann Barr (1984) 'Mass Market Romance: Pornography for Women is Different', in Ann Barr Snitow *et al.* (eds), *Desire: The Politics of Sexuality*, London: Virago.

Soothill, Keith and Walby, Sylvia (1991) *Sex Crime in the News*, London: Routledge.

Sorokin, Pitrim A. (1956) *Fads and Foibles in Modern Sociology and Related Sciences*, Chicago: Henry Regnery Co.

Sparks, Richard (1992) *Television and the Drama of Crime: Moral Tales and the Place of Crime in Public Life*, Buckingham: Open University Press.

Spector, Malcolm and Kitsuse, John I. (1987) *Constructing Social Problems*, New York: Aldine de Gruyter. Originally published in 1977.

Spence, Donald P. (1982) *Narrative Truth and Historical Truth: Naming and Interpretation in Psychoanalysis*, New York: Norton.

Spence, Donald P. (1987) 'Turning Happenings into Meanings: The Central Role of the Self', in P. Young-Eisendrath and J. Hall (eds), *The Book of the Self*, New York: New York University Press, pp. 132–50.

Spender, Dale (1982) *Women of Ideas and What Men Have Done to Them*, London: Routledge.

Stacey, Judith (1990) *Brave New Families: Stories of Domestic Upheaval in Late Twentieth-Century America*, New York: Basic Books.

SSRC (1980) *Report on Symbolic Interactionism and Sexual Differentiation: A Study*, London: SSRC.

Stacey, Judith (1991) 'Backward Toward the Postmodern Family', in Alan Wolfe (ed.) (1991) *America at Century's End*, Berkeley: University of California Press.

Stahl, Sandra K.D. (1977) 'The Personal Experience Narrative as Folklore', *Journal of the Folklore Institute*, vol. 44, pp. 9–30.

Stanley, Liz (ed.) (1984) *The Diaries of Hannah Cullwick*, London: Virago.

Stanley, Liz and Morgan, David (1993) *Biography and Autobiography in Sociology*, special issue of *Sociology*, vol. 27, no. 1.

Starker, Steven (1989) *Oracle at the Supermarket: The American Preoccupation With Self-Help Books*, New Brunswick: Transaction.

Starker, Steven (1990) *Evil Influences: Crusades Against the Mass Media*, New Brunswick: Transaction.

Stein, Arlene (ed.) (1993) *Sisters, Sexperts, Queers: Beyond the Lesbian Nation*, New York: Plume.

Stein, Edward (ed.) (1991) *Forms of Desire*, London: Routledge.

Stoltenberg, John (1989) *Refusing to Be a Man: Essays on Sex and Justice*, New York: Penguin/Meridian.

Strauss, Anselm (1978) 'A Social World Perspective', in Norman K. Denzin (ed.), *Studies in Symbolic Interaction*, London: JAI Press, vol. 1, pp. 119–28.

Strauss, Anselm (1991) *Creating Sociological Awareness: Collective Images and Symbolic Representations*, New Brunswick: Transaction.

Summer, Bob (1992) 'A Niche Market Comes of Age', *Publishers Weekly*, (29 June), pp. 36–40.

Sumrall, Amber Coverdale and Taylor, D. (1992) *Sexual Harassment: Women Speak Out*, Freedom, California: Crossing Press.

Sunstein, Cass. R. (ed.) (1990) *Feminism and Political Theory*, Chicago: University of Chicago Press.

Swidler, Ann (1986) 'Culture in Action: Symbols and Strategies', *American Sociological Review*, vol. 51, pp. 273–86.

Swindells, Julia (1989) 'Liberating the Subject? Autobiography and Women's History: A Reading of the Dairies of Hannah Cullwick', in *Personal Narratives Group, Interpreting Women's Lives*, Bloomington: Indiana University Press, pp. 24–37.

Szasz, Thomas (1980) *Sex: Facts, Frauds and Follies*, Oxford: Blackwell.

Tambling, Jeremy (1991) *Narrative and Ideology*, Milton Keynes: Open University Press.

Tanner, Leslie B. (ed.) (1970) *Voices from Women's Liberation*, New York: New American Library.

Taylor, Bryan (1976) 'Guilt-free Motives for Pederasty', *Sociological Review*, 24, pp. 97–114.

Taylor, Charles (1989) *Sources of the Self: The Making of the Modern Identity*, Cambridge, Mass.: Harvard University Press.

Taylor, Laurie (1972) 'The Significance of Replies to Motivational Questions: The Case of Sex Offenders', *Sociology*, 6, pp. 23–39.

Thompson, John (1990) *Ideology and modern Culture*, Oxford, Polity.

Thompson, Mark (ed.) (1991) *Leatherfolk: Radical Sex, People, Politics and Practice*, Boston: Alyson.

Thompson, Paul (1978) *The Voice of the Past: Oral History*, Oxford: Opus.

Thorstad, David (1990) 'Man/Boy Love and the American Gay Movement', *Journal of Homosexuality*, vol. 20, nos 1/2, pp. 251–74.

Tielman, Rob (19??) *Homosexualitiest in Nederland*, Amsterdam: Meppel.

Timmons, Stuart (1990) *The Trouble with Harry Hay*, Boston: Alyson Publications.

Tong, Rosemarie (1989) *Feminist Thought: A Comprehensive Introduction*, London: Unwin Hyman.

Tonkin, Elizabeth (1992) *Narrating Our Pasts: The Social Construction of Oral History*, Cambridge: Cambridge University Press.

Townsend, Larry (1989) *The Leatherman's Handbook II*, New York: Caryle Communications.

Trachtenberg, Peter (1988) *The Casanova Complex: Compulsive Lovers and Their Women*, New York: Pocket Books.

Troiden, Richard. R. (1988) *Gay and Lesbian Identity: A Sociological Analysis*, New York: General Hall.

Trumbach, Randolph (1977) 'London's Sodomites: Homosexual Behaviour and Western Culture in the Eighteenth Century', *Journal of Social History*, vol. 11, pp. 1–33.

Tsang, Daniel (ed.) (1981) *The Age Taboo: Gay Male Sexuality, Power and Consent*, London: Gay Men's Press.

Turner, Bryan S. (1990) 'Outline of a Theory of Citizenship', *Sociology*, vol. 24, no. 2 (May), pp. 189–217.

Ulmer, Gregory (1989) *Teletheory: Grammatology in the Age of Video*, London: Routledge.

Umans, Meg (ed.) (1988) *Like Coming Home: Coming Out Letters*, Austin: Banned Books.

Unger, Arthur (1991) 'Phil Donahue: "I cannot be the BBC in an MTV world" ', *Television Quarterly*, vol. 30, no. 2, pp. 31–43.

Van der Veen, Evert (1988) 'A Global View of the Gay and Lesbian Press', in *Second ILGA Pink Book*, Utrecht: ILGA, pp. 13–32.

Van Gelder, Lindsy (1992) 'Lipstick Liberation', *Los Angeles Times Magazine*, 15 March.

Van Lieshout, M. (1989) ''The Context of Gay Writing and Reading', in D. Altman *et al.*, *Which Homosexuality?*, op cit, pp. 113–26.

Van Maanen, J. (1988) *Tales from the Field*, London: Sage.

Vance, Carole S. (ed.) (1984) *Pleasure and Danger*, London: Routledge.

Vance, Carole S. (1989) 'Social Construction Theory: Problems in the History of Sexuality', in D. Altman *et al. Which Homosexuality??*, London: Gay Men's Press, pp. 13–34.

Vance, Carole S. (1990) 'The Pleasures of Looking: The Attorney-General's Commission on Pornography vs. Visual Images', in Carol Squiers (ed.), *The Critical Image*, Seattle: Bay Press.

Vansina, Jan (1985) *Oral Tradition as History*, Madison, Wisconsin: University of Wisconsin Press.

Vascha, Keith (1985) *Quiet Fire: Memoirs of Older Gay Men*, New York: Crossing Press.

Vass, Antony A. (1986) *Aids: A Plague in Us*, St Ives. Cambs.: Venus Academia.

Walby, Sylvia (1990) *Theorising Patriarchy*, Oxford: Blackwell.

Walkowitz, Judith (1992) *City of Dreadful Delight: Narratives of Sexual Danger in Late-Victorian London*, London: Virago.

Wall, Cheryl A. (1989) *Changing Our Own Words: Essays on Criticism, Theory and Writing by Black Women*, New Brunswick: Rutgers University Press.

Ward, Elizabeth (ed.) (1984) *Father-Daughter Rape*, London: Women's Press.

Warner, Michael (1992) 'From Queer to Eternity', *Village Voice Literary Supplement*, 106 (June), p. 19.

Warshaw, Robin (1988) *I Never Called it Rape: The Ms Report on Recognizing, Fighting, and Surviving Date and Acquaintance Rape*, New York: Harper & Row.

Watney, Simon (1987) *Policing Desire: Pornography, Aids and the Media*, Minneapolis: University of Minnesota Press.

Webster, Paula (1984) 'The Forbidden: Eroticism and Taboo', in Carole Vance (ed.), *Pleasure and Danger*, London: Routledge, pp. 385–96.

Weeks, Jeffrey (1985) *Sexuality and Its Discontents*, London: Routledge.

Weeks, Jeffrey (1986) *Sexuality*, London: Tavistock/Routledge.

Weeks, Jeffrey (1989) *Sex, Politics and Society*, London: Longman. Originally published in 1981.

Weeks, Jeffrey (1990) *Coming Out: Homosexual Politics in Britain from the Nineteenth Century to the Present*, London: Quartet. Originally published in 1977.

Weeks, Jeffrey (1991) *Against Nature: Essays on History, Sexuality and Identity*, London: Rivers Oram Press.

Weinberg, Thomas. S. (1984/5) 'Biology, Ideology, and the Reification of Developmental Stages in the Study of Homosexual Identity', *Journal of Homosexuality*, vol. 10, nos 3/4, pp. 77–84.

Weintraub, Karl, J. (1978) *The Value of the Individual: Self and Circumstance in Autobiography*, Chicago: University of Chicago Press.

West, Cornell (1990) 'The New Cultural Politics of Difference', in R. Ferguson , M. Gever, T.T. Minhaha and C. West, *Out There: Marginalization and Contemporary Cultures*, Cambridge, Mass.: MIT Press, pp. 18–38.

Westheimer, Ruth (1983) *Dr Ruth's Guide to Good Sex*, New York: Warner Books.

Weston, Kath (1991) *Families We Choose: Lesbians, Gays, Kinship*, New York: Columbia University Press.

White, Edmund (1980) *States of Desire: Travels in Gay America*, London: André Deutsch.

White, Hayden (1973) *Metahistory: The Historical Imagination in Nineteenth-Century Europe*, London: Johns Hopkins University Press.

White, Hayden (1987) *The Content of the Form: Narrative Discourse and Historical Representation*, Baltimore: Johns Hopkins University Press.

White, Mimi (1992) *Tele-Advising: Therapeutic Discourse in American Television*, London: University of North Carolina Press.

White, Ryan and Cunningham, Ann Marie (1992) *Ryan White: My Own Story*, New York: Signet.

Wiener, Carolyn (1981) *The Politics of Alcoholism*, New Brunswick: Transaction.

Willard, Charles Arthur (1983) *Argumentation and the Social Grounds of Knowledge*, Tuscaloosa, Alabama: University of Alabama Press.

Williams, Linda (1989) *Hard Core: Power, Pleasure and the Frenzy of the Visible*, Berkeley: University of California Press.

Williamson, Judith (1989) 'Every Virus Tells a Story: The Meanings of HIV and Aids', in Erica Carter and Simon Watney (eds), *Taking Liberties*, London: Serpent's Tail, pp. 69–80.

Willis, Paul (1977) *Learning to Labour*, Aldershot: Saxon House.

Wilson, Glenn D. and Cox, David N. (1983) *The Child Lovers: A Study of Paedophilia in Society*, London: Peter Owen.

Wolfe, Alan (1992) *America at Century's End*, Berkeley: University of California Press.

Wolfe, Tom (1977) 'The Me Decade' in *Mauve Gloves and Madmen, Clutter and Vine*, New York: Bantam.

Wolfenden Report (1957) *The Report of the Committee on Homosexual Offences and Prostitution*, Command Paper 247, London: HMSO.

Wolff, Kurt H. (ed.) (1950) *The Sociology of Georg Simmel*, New York: Free Press.

Wood, Michael. and Zurcher, Louis. A. (1988) *The Development of a Postmodern Self: A Computer-Assisted Comparative Analysis of Personal Documents*, New York: Greenwood Press.

Woolgar, Steve and Pawluch, D. (1985) 'Ontological Gerrymandering: The Anatomy of Social Problems Explanations', *Social Problems*, vol. 32, no. 3, pp. 214–37.

Yoder, Barbara (1990) *The Recovery Resource Book*, New York: Simon & Schuster.

Young, Iris Marion (1990) *Justice and the Politics of Difference*, Princeton: Princeton University Press.

Zerubavel, Eviatar (1981) *Hidden Rhythms: Schedules and Calendars in Social Life*, Berkeley: University of California Press.

Ziegenmeyer, Nancy with Larkin Warren (1993) *Taking Back My Life*, New York: Avon Books.

Zimmerman, Bonnie (1985) 'The Politics of Transliteration: Lesbian Personal Narratives', in E. Freedman, Barbara C. Gelpi, Susan L. Johnson and Kathleen M. Weston, *The Lesbian Issue*, Chicago: University of Cicago Press.

Zimmerman, Bonnie (1990) *The Safe Sea of Women*, Boston: Beacon Press.

Zimmerman, Don H. and Pollner, Melvin (1971) 'The Everyday World as Phenomenon', in J. Douglas (ed.), *Understanding Everyday Life*, London: Routledge & Kegan Paul.

Index